INVENTIONS OF NEMESIS

D1714469

Inventions of Nemesis

UTOPIA, INDIGNATION, AND JUSTICE

DOUGLAS MAO

PRINCETON UNIVERSITY PRESS
PRINCETON & OXFORD

Published by Princeton University Press
41 William Street, Princeton, New Jersey 08540
6 Oxford Street, Woodstock, Oxfordshire OX20 1TR

press.princeton.edu

Library of Congress Cataloging-in-Publication Data

Names: Mao, Douglas, 1966– author.
Title: Inventions of nemesis : utopia, indignation, and justice / Douglas Mao.
Description: Princeton : Princeton University Press, [2020] | Includes bibliographical
    references and index.
Identifiers: LCCN 2020025506 (print) | LCCN 2020025507 (ebook) |
    ISBN 9780691199252 (paperback) | ISBN 9780691212302 (hardback) |
    ISBN 9780691211640 (ebook)
Subjects: LCSH: Utopias. | Utopias—Social aspects. | Utopias—Political aspects.
    Classification: LCC HX806 .M36 2020 (print) | LCC HX806 (ebook) |
    DDC 335/.02–dc23
LC record available at https://lccn.loc.gov/2020025506
LC ebook record available at https://lccn.loc.gov/2020025507

British Library Cataloging-in-Publication Data is available

Editorial: Anne Savarese and Jenny Tan
Production Editorial: Kathleen Cioffi
Production: Brigid Ackerman
Publicity: Alyssa Sanford and Katie Lewis
Copyeditor: Plaegian Alexander

Cover art: Albrecht Dürer (1471–1528), *Nemesis*, c. 1501. Engraving.

This book has been composed in Arno

Printed on acid-free paper. ∞

Printed in the United States of America

10 9 8 7 6 5 4 3 2 1

To Chip

CONTENTS

ACKNOWLEDGMENTS

THIS IS A BOOK about what people are due, and thanks on its behalf are due many people. I must acknowledge first my faculty colleagues and students at Johns Hopkins, who have led me to consider utopia and its mysteries from scores of angles I could never have come to on my own. I'm especially grateful to Robert Carson, whose research at a crucial point opened up new vistas on the question of the worker; to Matt Roller for his clarifications on Greek and Latin; to Wilda Anderson and Derek Schilling for their notes on French; to Leonardo Proietti and Stephen Campbell for their assistance with Italian; and to Jeanne-Marie Jackson and Anne Eakin Moss for their insights on Russia. (And with Russia in mind, let me thank also Karen Petrone of the University of Kentucky—extraordinary historian, adored friend, unfailing inspiration.) I'm grateful, too, to Johns Hopkins's Krieger School of Arts and Sciences for research funds, leave, and general encouragement without which this work would have had no chance of seeing completion.

I owe a great debt as well to my former colleagues and students at Cornell, Harvard, and Princeton who helped nurture the first shoots of this project and to those at Columbia (especially Sarah Cole, Mia Florin-Sefton, Naomi Michalowicz, and Diana Newby) who brought such keen eyes to its latest growths. The last phase of revision also benefited enormously from the kindness of the Zukunftskolleg of the University of Konstanz, which provided space in which—and interlocutors with whom—to see this manuscript and see it whole. To that most charming of hosts and most perceptive of scholars, Udith Dematagoda, I'm grateful beyond measure.

Surely no exchanges have done more, collectively, to improve this book than those I've enjoyed at talks and workshops over the past twenty years—at Wake Forest, Concordia, Montclair State, the University of Virginia, Reed College, Johns Hopkins, Stanford, Berkeley, Sussex, Uppsala, Brown, Yale, Cornell, and the University of Pennsylvania; at the Modernist Studies Association conferences in Houston, Tulsa, Nashville, Sussex, Boston, Pasadena, and Amsterdam; at the Narrative Conference at Northwestern; at the James Joyce conferences at Goldsmiths, the University of London, and the University of Maryland; at utopia conferences at Oxford and Birmingham; at the Modern

Language Association in Los Angeles; at the European Network for Avant-Garde and Modernism Studies in Helsinki; at the New York–New Jersey Modernism Seminar; and at the Northeast Modern Language Association in Baltimore. The participants in these forums who have helped me think about the large themes and small details of this work are too many to mention—though I do want to acknowledge one: Robert Appelbaum, for his kindness in handing me a book that taught me a great deal.

Although at most a few sentences in the pages that follow have been published in precisely the same form elsewhere, I'm much indebted to the editors of three collections who offered me the chance to get into print thoughts on utopia that shaped this study: Maurizia Boscagli and Enda Duffy; Rosalyn Gregory and Benjamin Kohlmann; and Alice Reeve-Tucker and Nathan Waddell. Not one sentence in this book, meanwhile, could have seen the light of day without the extraordinary offices of the folks at Princeton University Press. Here I thank for their lucid guidance Jenny Tan, Laurie Schlesinger, Kathleen Cioffi, and, above all, Anne Savarese, whose shepherding of this book and clarity about its meanings have been the greatest of gifts. My infinite thanks as well to those who evaluated this study in manuscript with such acuity and rigor, and to Plaegian Alexander and Steven Moore, whose suavity of copyediting and indexing has made me feel the most fortunate of authors.

Those to whom most is due, as always, are the friends and family who have rendered the years of this book's progress so much lovelier, whether by being willing to toss around thoughts about ideal societies or by affirming that it's worthwhile to press forward with a project such as this one or just by being their elegant selves. Special thanks here to Molly Meloy, Jeff Fitts, Kirsten Johnson, Nan Zhang, and Donald Wilmes; and a long overdue word in memory of Jeanne K. Burchell, who would have turned ninety on the day this manuscript went into final form. My longest-accruing debt remains to Evelyn Schwarz, who has given so much that this book could come to be and who has shown what it means to treat people justly for as long as I can remember. My profoundest and most ecstatic thanks, finally, to Chip Wass, for his care—and for his genius. This book is filled with responses to thoughts that could have come from no one else. And it tells, all through, how he brings to every day in this our sublunary world a thousand twinkles of a perfect one.

INVENTIONS OF NEMESIS

Introduction

NOT FAR into Thomas Hardy's *Tess of the d'Urbervilles,* Tess and her younger brother Abraham drive together toward Casterbridge, by night, to deliver beehives. To keep their spirits up, they make "an artificial morning" with a "lantern, some bread and butter, and their own conversation," amid which the following exchange takes place:

> "Did you say the stars were worlds, Tess?"
> "Yes."
> "All like ours?"
> "I don't know; but I think so. They sometimes seem to be like the apples on our stubbard-tree. Most of them splendid and sound—a few blighted."
> "Which do we live on—a splendid one or a blighted one?"
> "A blighted one."[1]

So astounding a verdict might bring many narratives to a halt, but Hardy seems bent on making this one as little a set piece as possible. For one thing, Abraham's response suggests that he's unfazed by any emotion Tess might have betrayed: "'Tis very unlucky that we didn't pitch on a sound one," he reflects, "when there were so many more of 'em!"[2] A few paragraphs later, the Durbeyfields' horse, Prince, is killed on collision with a mail-cart, which means that the reader has little time to ruminate on the blighting of the world in general—exemplified for Tess by their father's impairments and their mother's endless toil—before a still more acute case of misfortune intrudes. Nor is this all. Prince's death will inaugurate a chain of disasters for Tess, further heightening the likelihood that as the narrative continues, her assessment of the world in general will be eclipsed, even as it may also be illustrated, by her sad particular fate.

Yet Tess's extraordinary opinion lingers in the mind. Shocking and poignant in its sheer hardness, it's also remarkable for what it opens and forecloses, gives and retracts, in a single stroke. With her three brutal words, Tess at once affirms that existence could be far better than it is here and denies that

1

possibility for here, categorically. In this sense, it would be fair to describe her verdict as half-utopian, or as halfway to utopian thinking. On the one hand, it gestures to utopia by imagining planets that differ from our own in being splendid and sound; on the other, it declares that the star we're doomed to will suffer no amelioration, even using the finality of the organic to clinch its case. The world we've unluckily pitched on can no more be mended than a bad apple on a stubbard-tree.

The dates of Hardy's novel—1891 (serial) and 1892 (single volume)—place it at a moment that saw an explosion in the publication of utopian fiction in English. Already before the 1880s, some works such as Edward Bulwer-Lytton's *The Coming Race* (1871) had enjoyed enormous sales; the tremendous success of Edward Bellamy's *Looking Backward: 2000–1887*, published in 1888, led to a vast outpouring of utopian visions around the world, among which the most celebrated by an English writer was William Morris's deliberate riposte to Bellamy, *News from Nowhere* (1890).[3] Though dates of composition seem to preclude Hardyan intention,[4] Tess's simultaneous evocation and withholding of utopian possibility might almost be read as a rejoinder to Morris—to whom Hardy sent a presentation copy of *Tess*,[5] and whose utopia is the opposite of blighted, a future England regreened by wise stewardship of land, an elevation of artisanal practices, and a near erasure of heavy industry. Or Tess might be imagined—though dates again make conscious intention impossible—as commenting on Oscar Wilde's "Soul of Man under Socialism," published in *The Fortnightly Review* in February 1891, or five months before *Tess* commenced in *The Graphic*. In addition to delivering one of the most ubiquitously rehearsed epigrams on utopia—"A map of the world that does not include Utopia is not worth even glancing at, for it leaves out the one country at which Humanity is always landing"—Wilde there announces that under socialism, "the true personality of man," a "marvellous thing" never yet seen in history, will "grow naturally and simply, flowerlike, or as a tree grows."[6] For Wilde, efflorescence. For Tess, blight.[7]

Obviously, one feeling debarred from Tess's verdict is hopefulness. But Hardy refrains from telling us all we might want to know about her state of mind when she delivers it, and we may wonder, in particular, whether she does so with bitterness. Given Abraham's apparently undevastated reply, we might guess her tone to be flat or wistful, but she could very well render her opinion in accents of anger and scorn. And precisely by leaving that tone unmarked, Hardy recalls that if resignation tends to imply hopelessness, it may be more subtly colored by indignation. To be indignant is to be less likely to be resigned, but to be resigned isn't necessarily to be free of rancor. If Tess's stunning credo is halfway to utopia on the side of content, it's also halfway there on the side of affect, so to speak, neither clearly accepting nor clearly aggrieved.

But what would we do with—how would we make sense of—thorough indignation at a world badly formed?

One answer is that we would recognize it as a driving force of utopianism itself. And the simple observation at the heart of the present study is indeed that utopian speculation, at least since its key crystallization in Thomas More's *Utopia* of 1516, has been crucially animated by just such indignation. This may not strike many readers as a controversial claim. Yet the vast critical and theoretical literature on utopia has devoted curiously little attention to this point and, in so doing, has left certain features of utopianism looking not only more perplexing or contradictory than they really are but also more damagingly trivial. We can get some purchase on this matter with the help of another halfway-to-utopia declaration, this one from a text by the writer who, perhaps more disarmingly than any other in the twentieth century, insisted on conveying fundamental philosophy through old-fashioned gags.

In Samuel Beckett's *Endgame* (1957), the dustbin-inhabiting Nagg tells a story that makes him happy "every time" he recites it. In brief: "an Englishman" requires a pair of trousers on a fast schedule, but each time he returns to the tailor engaged to make them, the latter puts him off, explaining that he has made "a mess of the seat," or "a hash of the crotch." Finally, after three months, the exasperated customer explodes: "In six days, do you hear me, six days, God made the world," he thunders; "Yes Sir, no less Sir, the WORLD!" To which the tailor, "But my dear Sir, my dear Sir, look . . . at the world . . . and look . . . at my TROUSERS!"[8]

Taking the joke without the philosophy or the philosophy without the joke would, of course, divest the moment of much of its significance. To dismiss the tailor's assessment of the world because it arrives as a punch line would be to ignore how the assessment may be fair. On the other hand, to assume that the trousers are just a disposable vehicle for the philosophical observation would be to miss how the world really *can* be judged by contrast to other things that, if not as immense and important, appear much better made. Like Tess's verdict, the tailor's utterance may or may not be accompanied by full-blown indignation at the world's poor quality; Beckett's stage direction reads, "disdainful gesture, disgustedly." Here again, however, the very possibility of outrage reminds us that one can be righteously indignant at poor craftsmanship—and that such indignation may be the more truly righteous, though it may initially look the more absurd, when applied to the totality we all inhabit.

In the first of the three long chapters that make up this study, I argue that just such a recognition is important for our understanding of utopian thinking, not least because the latter has long been assailed for its putatively demented fussiness, its insistence on holding the order of things to a standard that should only be adopted for items less vast and complex. Antiutopians have often staked their claims on the assumption that utopianism is untenable because it demands absolute perfection in human affairs, to which defenders of utopia have answered that this simply isn't true, that perfection isn't demanded. Even many partisans of the utopian imagination, however, admit embarrassment at its devotees' obsession with minutiae of design. Fredric Jameson does so especially memorably in *Archaeologies of the Future* (2005), when he observes that writers of utopian fictions are "not exclusively driven by indignation at social injustice or compassion for the poor and the oppressed" but have also been "intellectuals, with a supplementary taste for systems . . . , for maps . . . , and for schemes of all kinds . . . , know-it-alls willing tirelessly to explain to anyone who would listen the solution to all those problems; tinkerers, blackening reams of paper writing and rewriting their projects and their propaganda pamphlets, drawing up endless seating charts and plans and urban reconstructions: in short, obsessives and maniacs." There is no way, he claims, to reconcile these two images of the utopian projector—those of the laudably impassioned crusader and the pitiably obsessive engineer. The "only way of dealing with this contradiction is to think both perspectives together simultaneously."[9]

Is Jameson right about this? With Tess's and the tailor's appraisals of the order of things in mind, we can see immediately how the conundrum to which he bows may not be so very confounding after all. For what Tess and the tailor illuminate is that "indignation at social injustice" can read, very precisely, as rage against bad design in a capacious sense—against a totality that may seem the more cruelly defective because so many of the things within it are elegantly fashioned and demonstrably functional. To apologize for the obsession with design is therefore to miss something important about the coherence of utopian thinking. Certainly, one link between utopian imagining and rearrangement lies in the affinity of both with daydreaming, that exercise of mind in which one can order the world as one pleases and whose centrality to utopianism Ernst Bloch magisterially renders in *The Principle of Hope* (1954–59). But utopianism is also linked to rearrangement, I would argue, by the kind of indignation that lends it urgency.

Moreover, as I also show in chapter 1, it has been possible to dignify outrage at wrongness in human arrangements with a particular name, *nemesis*. *Nemesis* is an ancient Greek word whose meanings evolved in complicated ways over hundreds of years, but in most of its acceptations it suggests, directly or indirectly, umbrage taken at a state of affairs or an action that in some basic or absolute sense is not right. It marks, that is, anger at some violation of *nomos*, where the latter—a noun with an even more diverse array of significations— betokens an apposite arrangement of things, the order that should prevail. (As we'll see, *nomos* can also name the system, as of laws or customs, that actually prevails in our world even if it shouldn't, which is why it's possible to feel *nemesis* against an extant *nomos* on behalf of an ideal one.) *Nemesis* is salient for our concerns in part because utopian literature has owed so much to the fountainheads of Plato's *Republic* and the *Utopia* of More, who was crucially steeped in Greek and Latin views on human needs and the proper ordering of society. But *nemesis* matters also because in Greek and Latin writings it was closely, if again ambiguously, bound up with an ideal still widely cherished, and on behalf of which countless people struggle, at the present time. That ideal is *justice.*

As I show in chapter 1, there's ample warrant for understanding justice as, fundamentally, a condition of right arrangement. And once we have this point before us, it becomes still clearer that discontent with inadequate arrangement is not merely some embarrassing compulsion that attached itself contingently to serious utopian speculation. Rather, this discontent proves a propelling source of that speculation—one that, once recognized, illuminates how the achievement of justice is utopia's essential project.

If my earlier assertion of indignation's importance seemed self-evident, this last claim may appear implausible. Over its long life, utopia has most usually been understood as devoted to the provision of universal happiness; other principal aims with which it has been credited include comprehensive material well-being, full employment, absolute equality, unbroken public order, and unimpeded freedom of lifestyle. Why has justice, in spite of its prominence in both the *Republic* and More's *Utopia,* far more rarely been identified as utopia's consistent concern? There are, I think, at least two reasons. First, justice as a state of things is a kind of metagood, a good of goods, that might be said to lie concealed beneath the more particular desiderata through which it would be realized. It has always been obvious that views on what an ideal society must be like will differ; what has been harder to see is that these various formulations have in common an impulse to bring rightness to the arrangement of things. Yet the salience of justice is easy to confirm. We need only notice, really, that if someone proposes a utopia in which people aren't particularly happy or secure, we might grant that it *could* be a utopia for that person, whereas if someone were to propose a utopia in which things were wrong, out of joint, unfair, misaligned, we would have trouble understanding in what sense it could be utopian.

Second, rightness as such has rarely been a virtue that holds great visceral appeal or inspires intense devotion. And it has perhaps been particularly out of favor in the last hundred and fifty years or so, thanks to its evocation of sanctimoniousness, uptight moralizing, unimaginative obedience, and—once again—pathological or otherwise off-putting devotion to the tidy and well kept. As we'll see in chapter 1, justice has suffered from some of the same stigma, since one of its sturdiest definitions—the receiving by all and each of what is due them—can read as a narrow-minded privileging of the quantitative over the qualitative, a balancing of accounts that cannot but look shabby next to openhearted liberality. To say that utopian imagining pitches itself against bad conditions seems quite acceptable, and it seems fine, too, to say that its bête noire is a state of wrongness in the world: these constructions align it with the impulses of reformers and revolutionaries in general. But to add that what it seeks is right arrangement may be to kill the buzz, to reveal it as passionless just where passion is most needed.

It's partly for this reason, I think, that many utopians since the later twentieth century have favored what Russell Jacoby calls "iconoclastic" utopias over what he calls "blue print" utopias—that is, have cast their lot with the view that true utopianism is a desire or hope for a better society that betrays its best intentions as soon as it starts to propagate specific plans and designs. In one sense, there can be no arguing with this idea. If iconoclastic utopias (those that mainly negate what is, without proposing replacements) are by definition really utopian, while blueprint utopias (where some plan for the ideal society is laid out) are by definition fallings away, then the discussion has to end there. Further, the privileging of iconoclastic utopias is arguably backed by the authority of Bloch, whose 1918 *Spirit of Utopia* Jacoby names "the classic work in this genre" and whose *Principle of Hope* remains the longest, and one of the most influential, studies of utopian imagination ever published.[10]

Yet if we accept the antiblueprint view that genuine utopian imagining resists the temptation to develop concrete schemes, we clearly bracket much of the history of utopian thinking before (and after) Bloch. And this history is of moment not only because history is always of moment but also because it continues to inform our conceptions of what utopia is. However pragmatically, theoretically, or ethically valuable it might be for utopian vision to purge itself of afterimages of More's or Tommaso Campanella's cities, of Bellamy's or H. G. Wells's organized work forces, of Morris's or Marge Piercy's bucolic and affectionate anarchist communities, utopianism is surely distinguished from a less specific yearning for a better order of things precisely by the presence—dimly remembered, spectral, far in the periphery of vision though it may be—of such concretely imagined designs.

It may be, then, that the antiblueprint view partakes of roughly the same logic that has obscured utopia's deep connection with justice as rightness. To say that things are imperfectly ordered can sound like the sheerest common sense, whereas to declare oneself possessed of a scheme for fixing something as big as society or the world is to invite incredulity and derision. Chapter 1's exploration of utopian *nemesis*, accordingly, includes a look at how it prompts a species of reaction that I call, not too imaginatively, *counterindignation.* Culminating in an extended reading of Nathaniel Hawthorne's 1852 fiction *The Blithedale Romance,* this line of inquiry takes up not only utopian indignation's layered relation to satire but also its capacity to be construed as hostile to humanity, humanness, or natural human relations. And it examines ongoing negotiations of a dilemma that we might call utopia's people problem: a tension arising from persons' dual role as beneficiaries of utopian arrangements and material means of those arrangements—that is, as both the ends and the instruments of utopia.

These last matters take us to the concerns of chapter 2, which begins by examining an aspect of utopia that has provided especially ample fodder for counterindignation. Analysts of utopian writing have long noted that some utopias promise to realize their goals by means of rules and institutions that work with people as they inevitably are, while other utopias propose to arrange conditions that will reshape human character (or release a finer human nature buried under the accretions of wayward custom). In 1952, J. K. Fuz proposed a distinction between "Utopias of measures" and "Utopias of men"; seeking a less confusing and less sexist terminology, I distinguish between *managerial* utopias, which operate mainly through wittily engineered incentives and disincentives, and *transformative* utopias, which arrange conditions (especially for the young and unformed) in ways that help determine what utopian people will be like (and implicitly how they will differ from people in the here and now).[11] Both kinds of utopias have inspired vehement counterindignation because they can be seen as assaulting, if in somewhat different ways, human freedom. But the transformative utopia has proven especially inflammatory because it seems to imply a forcing of the soul by the powers that be—and because, as Jameson and others have discerned, it seems at its furthest to threaten the replacement of humanity as we know it with something else. Thus it is that after tracing the history of these two utopian modes in the first section and a half of chapter 2, I turn to the acme of the transformative mode as it emerges, in the middle of the twentieth century, in antiutopian alarms about behavioral conditioning as well as a radical defense of conditioning mounted by B. F. Skinner.

Skinner's claims, and those of his detractors, are of particular relevance to this study because they illustrate how utopia's concern with arrangement becomes particularly visible when it seems most threatening to freedom. Any student of utopia will recognize that utopia's imagined *nomos* engenders especially powerful anxiety, and invites especially serious scrutiny, where its mechanisms for controlling human behavior seem signally overt or tuned to the molding of intimate aspects of personality such as desire. And as chapter 2 shows, mid-twentieth-century antiutopianism was especially strongly marked by anxieties about how the administered society (in both its first-world and second-world styles) might imperil authenticity. While utopias on a small scale—intentional communities, for example—could seem a path away from what Herbert Marcuse dubbed "one-dimensional man," utopia as a total project could inspire a counterindignation appropriate, in its intensity, to the singularly dramatic transformations of the human soul, and hence the dissolutions of freedom, that seemed to arrive with more powerful and pervasive forms of conditioning.

As I observe in the final section and a half of chapter 2, however, the criterion of authenticity itself points to the possibility that transformative utopias are unnerving less because they threaten freedom than because they give rise to a dilemma of value, a perplexity pertaining to human worth. Turning here to several texts, mostly recent, that extend the preprogramming of people's lives to schemes in which part or all of human experience is virtual or false, I try to show that long-running debates about the possibility of freedom under utopian regimes have tended to obscure a more fundamental problem relating to utopian subjects' capacity to be recipients of justice. The question posed at the end of chapter 2, and to which the preceding historical reconstruction in fact tends, is that of whether radically transformative designs cease to be utopian— both intuitively and in fact—because they fail to solve the problem of injustice that impels utopian *nemesis* in the first place.

The third chapter of this study, like the second, begins by tracking a question pertaining to the right ordering of things through a few centuries of utopian writing. But where the work of chapter 2's first sections is in a way to flesh out the textual history of a phenomenon well noted by other commentators (the tension between managerial and transformative utopian methods), the first sections of chapter 3 excavate a theme that has attracted little sustained discussion. Many analyses of utopian writing have dwelt on matters of arrangement, but their focus has usually been on orchestrations of the physical terrain, as in urban planning, or on organizational innovations that can be figured in architectonic terms—on designs for living that literally or metaphorically distribute functions across what Gilles Deleuze and Félix Guattari would call "striated space."[12] This with good reason, of course: dispositions of buildings, roads, and the like tend to be especially memorable elements of fictional as of real-world utopias, and many utopian writers have affirmed that the literal or figurative division of space is key to the utopian project. Yet a careful examination of utopian writing over the centuries reveals that ordering associated with the grid or the master plan has often been accompanied by a multifaceted concern with a different kind of arrangement—with provisions for people, and particularly for people qua workers, conceived of as being in motion.[13]

As Jacques Rancière has forcefully argued, Plato's *Republic* is much occupied with the question of where the worker may or may not be at a given time. More's *Utopia* positions itself as an answer to the real-world problem of the displacement of masses of people from their former employments thanks to the enclosure of common lands. Most crucially for our purposes here, many utopias from the turn of the nineteenth century through the middle of the twentieth posit satisfaction with the when and where of work—often understood to comprehend a liberty of physical movement on the part of the worker—as a value any ideal social arrangement would have to secure. From this point of view, to conceive of the utopian *nomos* in essentially static terms would be to fall prey to what the anthropologist Liisa Malkki has named, in a phrase much taken up by mobility studies, "sedentarist metaphysics."[14] I begin chapter 3, then, by tracing how the where of work and workers appears as a problem and a value in utopian writing, arguing that we misunderstand the justice utopia strives for if we think of it as a right allocation only of benefits resulting from (or emerging apart from) labor rather than, also, of benefits that can inhere in labor. I also note how utopian contrivances for the distribution of work bespeak a hope deriving from the people problem described above: that the utopian system might transcend the fallibility of its individual human agents.

The first two sections of chapter 3 having followed the tracks of utopian workers through the middle of the twentieth century, the last two then remark a key change in utopian imagining in the years since: the abandoning, as a major constituent of utopian aspiration, of the dream of people working where and how they like. We can posit many reasons for this shift, including a general drift away from vocabularies of social amelioration that center on the worker, but the chapter concentrates on two significant developments. The first is an increasing concern with freedom to live as one chooses—that is, with liberty of lifestyle—that in the ambit of utopian writing seems increasingly to subsume specifically work-related prerogatives under a larger figure of mobility and whose arrival front and center in utopian thinking is registered by Robert Nozick's metautopia, or what Jameson has dubbed "the utopian archipelago." The second is the ever increasing visibility of labor-driven migration as a fraught feature of life in the contemporary world. As the where of work has increasingly come to be associated with survival rather than preference, utopian imagining (and dystopian imagining, too) seems to have adjusted by turning away from the dream of freedom of choice in labor. And it turns out that one of the things that has come to occupy this vacant space is a desideratum of less restricted migration in which justice would materialize not as a desirable distribution of work specifically but in some other form—a point that emerges in the final section's explorations of theories of global justice.

The foregoing summary may elicit questions about how exactly I propose to use the word *utopia* itself in this book. In the preceding pages, I've deployed a fairly shamelessly reifying rhetoric, asserting that utopia is this or that, that the utopian imagination has this or that quality, that utopianism proves essentially driven by this or that impulse. I do so a great deal in the chapters that follow as well, and so it behooves me to explain what justifies such language.

Perhaps the most straightforward way to begin is to make clear that this book's work is essentially descriptive, its effort to examine a wide range of utopian writings (nearly all of them produced in "the West," about which more in a moment) and, as suggested, to illuminate aspects of them that have not so far received the attention they deserve. As it happens, the actual researching of this book was inductive along just these lines. I began my exploration with some thoughts about what I might find in utopian writing, but almost none of those expected foci have made it into the study at hand. In other words, the matters of indignation, of justice, and of mobility in work, along with the umbrella matter of utopian arrangement, emerged as central without my consciously seeking them out. More important than this genetic detail, however, is that this book is not intended as a polemic about what utopian thinking ought to look like, a forecast of what it might become, an exposé of what it has darkly encrypted, or a critique of its premises or realizations. Again, *Inventions of Nemesis* is rather an examination of some through lines in the literature of utopia that have been little treated, even in the vast and often brilliant body of scholarship on utopia that has emerged in the last half century.

As indicated earlier in this introduction, *Inventions* turns to classical and especially Greek nomenclature to develop some of its governing concepts. And while it brings into the discussion many less widely read utopias and numerous nonliterary texts, it does devote a fair measure of attention to some works that seem firmly in the canon (if there is such a thing) of utopian texts produced by writers ordinarily identified as Western, or as inhabiting what would become the global North. My intention in giving these works the time I do is not to endorse the position, articulated some years ago by Krishan Kumar but subject to important critique since, that there "is no tradition of utopia and utopian thought outside the Western world."[15] Nor is it to attribute some aesthetic or political superiority, or some greater interestingness, to the canonical as against the less well known, or to Western utopian texts and speculations as against non-Western ones. On the contrary, I would hazard that much of the most interesting scholarly work on utopia in the years to come will be concerned with less studied texts; with texts whose origins are in salient ways non-Western or that challenge the very notion of "the West" by highlighting the porousness of the construct; or with texts that aren't written but oral, filmic, musical, or otherwise associated with media not dominated by verbal inscription. (*Inventions* wholly concerns written texts, save for a few exceptions at the end of this introduction and late in chapter 2.)

The main reason this study devotes itself to the corpus just described is, like the main reason its takes up the topics it does, not axiological but a kind of artifact of process. In setting out to learn a lot about utopian speculation across the centuries, I thought it important not only to look at a diverse array of materials but also to get well grounded in a set of texts (many originally written in English) that had apparently exerted a wide influence on utopian thinking. I soon discovered in those works, along with the less famous ones I had come to, not just a few matters that seemed worth writing about but enough to fill a good-sized book—and one that might obtain a certain coherence precisely from limiting its (still very expansive) field of view. Whether or not my arguments generalize to texts, movements, visions, and theories not examined in this study will, I very much hope, be a question other scholars take up. And this particularly because this study touches only scantly on utopian treatments of race, gender, sexuality, species dominance, environmentalism, and other matters that bear crucially on utopian justice—treatments whose exploration might dramatically revise the arguments I put forward here.

This doesn't yet fully explain, however, why I presume to venture broad pronouncements about utopia on the basis of a less than global sampling of texts. And here I have to plead that canonicity, or rather scope of influence, does matter some. In making my descriptive claims about utopian speculation in general, I recur to documents such as Plato's *Republic*, More's *Utopia*, and Bellamy's *Looking Backward* in part because they've so powerfully affected later creators of utopias—and, partly for this reason, seem to embody many of our ordinary intuitions about what utopia is. Pressed to state how I use *utopia* in this book, I might say—with due respect to the many other compelling definitions brought to the fore by utopian studies—that it names a much better society that might (vaguely or meticulously) be limned in a prose narrative, poem, screed, theoretical foray, dialogue, daydream, or other form. But in truth my practice here does not even hew to this characterization. It would be more accurate to say that in this book, *utopia* operates as a fuzzy-edged domain of significations having the foregoing definition at its center.

Obviously, this less than hard-and-fast delimitation, along with the fact that the texts considered here have not been selected according to some one rigorous principle, may invite the suspicion that my claims will on inspection prove circular. If I say that utopia generally shows quality X or that the utopian imagination is fundamentally concerned with Y, this could be because I've decided that the texts, ideas, and historical enterprises that count are the ones that exhibit X and Y. I hope that even were this so, readers might find this book interesting, if only for its entertaining or appalling errors. But in fact I expect that readers will agree that most of the texts, perspectives, and enterprises I call utopian really are utopian and will find most of my claims here portable to other utopian configurations. I trust that wherever I make a claim about utopia on the basis of something the reader wouldn't think utopian, or on a sampling whose meaningfulness would be controverted by other examples, the reader will question or reject that claim.

A few more clarifications seem required. First, as will probably be clear by this point, one of my recurrent endeavors in *Inventions* is to push back against certain critiques of utopianism. This does not mean, however, that I'm a fervent partisan of utopian projects. I believe that utopian imagining is important to political life, but I'm extremely wary of attempts to establish utopia at the scale of a whole state or society (smaller-scale intentional communities being quite a different matter) for most of the reasons others have been wary of them. The violent imposition of a particular vision of the good life on people who don't share that vision can hardly be considered progressive or ethically sound, and the historical record suggests that—almost always, if not always— things go poorly when those in power try to usher in utopia over the short haul. Like a number of other studies of utopia and its enemies, however, this book does set out to counter a range of antiutopian arguments and positions that seem perniciously misguided. In *Archaeologies of the Future*, Jameson makes the case for a "slogan of anti-anti-Utopianism," and that is precisely the position this study adopts.[16]

Second, there's no denying that my references to justice in this book operate at a high level of abstraction. Encountering the subtitle *Utopia, Indignation, and Justice*, a prospective reader might well expect to find here a survey of real-world social justice struggles fueled by outrage at particular cases of gender-related oppression, racism, worker exploitation, or other forms of domination and abuse. And the very contrast between such an indication and the actual focus of this book might suggest that I've mistaken Olympian philosophizing or parlor-game literary criticism for active work on the ground or that I mean to make a strong claim for the value of the former while looking on the latter with tacit disdain. But this would be completely untrue. It's by no means my intention to slight practical endeavors in the cause of justice in favor of theoretical reflection. I know very well that the kind of work I do in this book is, on the whole, much less important. Nonetheless, I see some value in pursuing basic questions about justice—what we're really thinking about when we talk about justice, for example, and how justice relates to utopia— because these could have some practical ramifications in addition to what seems to me their clear intellectual interest. In other words, I don't regard the questions about justice considered here as operating on some plane high above real-world action. I rather see them as *beneath* such action, in the sense of underlying it, grounding it, giving it a foundation that may be unconscious but whose character can, perhaps beneficially, be brought to conscious attention.

These points—about fundamental aspects of justice and about what matters—lead to another clarification, which is also a contention. As I noted a moment ago, utopian desires, schemes, and perspectives seem to me perennially important, and this for a reason that will be very familiar to any of those who have concerned themselves with utopia. Quite simply, it's hard to see how conditions in the world could be improved if human beings were to cease imagining better alternatives to what is. But a more particular rationale for this study is that it invites us to reconsider one further assumption about utopia that has surely had some consequence in the real world. This invitation isn't elaborated explicitly in the chapters to come, but portions of those chapters do support it. And it seems worthwhile to lay it out here.

Earlier in this introduction, I acknowledged that the definition of justice as a condition in which all and each receive what's due them will have disheartening associations for some readers. Yet this is, again, the acceptation of justice that mainly operates in this book. The desire for justice (and the indignation against failures of justice) that has often propelled utopian speculation is, to my understanding, a desire that people have what they ought to have, that they be treated as they should be treated, that they be able to live as they ought to be able to live. This book is in a basic sense *descriptive* of utopian writings, but those writings themselves lead me to conclude that utopia is essentially *normative*.

As parts of each chapter should make clear, "what's due" in this sense isn't a matter of minutely calibrated entitlements or rewards. It doesn't depend on (though it has often been confused with) the view that people should have only what they merit through their labor or intelligence or place in a social hierarchy, let alone that some should have more while others have less. Justice as the arrangement that ought to prevail, the condition of rightness for each and all, is much more capacious than that. But justice as what's due *does* mean that the presence or absence of justice is determined by how individuals or other components of the larger utopian whole are treated, by what they receive and perhaps by what they give—not by how the whole utopian entity might be faring according to other measures. It may be claimed that only a just society can be a healthy society, but a society deemed healthy by reason of its large population, its affluence, or its likelihood of survival couldn't on any of these counts be considered just. As several moments in this book make clear, then, I join with many theorists of justice in finding it impossible to understand justice as something that could prevail absent individual recipients of justice—people, groups of people, animals, or other entities—that would be part of the larger totality that might be adjudged as just or as failing of justice.

Of course, invocation of the individual in a context such as this one might carry a lot of baggage even more disaffecting for some readers than a conception of justice as what's due. It might intimate, for example, a hallowing of the atomized subject of an imperializing Enlightenment; a more general disdain for philosophies and belief systems, especially non-Western ones, that don't privilege what has come to be called liberal individualism; a secret or unconscious deference to the hegemony of neoliberalism; or a tendentially conservative insistence that the power of social circumstances is as nothing to the force of personal will and personal responsibility. But such surmises would be incorrect. My point here is not that the individual is to be set against, let alone privileged over, the collective in some thoroughgoing sense. It's perfectly possible to hold that individuals are the structurally meaningful recipients of justice *and* that, in practice, they best receive justice under some arrangement where what are ordinarily thought of as individual interests are subordinated to collective ones—where, say, private property doesn't exist or everyone has to be ready to die for the sake of the nation or people are understood as fundamentally embedded in larger ecosystems that include the nonhuman. To say that rightness for components of the larger whole is the test of whether an envisioned order is utopia isn't to assume that people are best conceived of as free-floating monads ideally divested of bonds to kin, tribe, party, and religious community, nor is it to assert that society is best conceived of as an aggregate of rational adults whose individual satisfactions can be tallied to determine that aggregate's success.

What I do assert here is that justice is something enjoyed by or withheld from components of the totality—persons, in many renderings, but again animals or things or groups of people, as may be—and thus not something that the totality itself can enjoy or be deprived of. Justice is a condition that may *obtain in* or *characterize* the totality, but it is not something the totality can receive. Utopian *nemesis* is directed against a state of affairs in which components making up the whole aren't treated as they ought to be treated. It looks toward a condition in which this wrong arrangement of things for those components, for beings or elements structurally speaking subordinate to the whole, is rectified.

What this means in turn—and here we come at last to the contention I promised—is that it's actually not possible, at least not in any way I can see, to urge a properly *utopian* alternative to the present order where one takes as one's principal value the well-being (by whatever measure) of the order itself rather than the well-being of those who exist within it. If we imagine a society that's perfect in one or another sense but whose perfection excludes concern with what's right or wrong for those it contains, we'll usually find ourselves confronting not a utopia but rather an antiutopia or a dystopia—the most nightmarish rather than the most desirable of social arrangements, as in the infinitely repressive One State in Yevgeny Zamyatin's *We*.

Of course, the thought that in this important, if limited, sense utopia isn't about the totality flies in the face of widely held assumptions about utopia. And it would seem to have some significant implications for the past and future of utopian thinking. For one thing, it suggests that certain forms of antiutopian hostility from the political Right are grounded in a simple mistake about utopia's character. The memory (however attenuated by this time) of Soviet exhortations to sacrifice for the sake of the collective, coupled with a tendency for left rhetoric to prioritize community interests and for right rhetoric to stoke mistrust of government in the name of personal liberty, has led many on the Right to assume that utopia is fundamentally at odds with the interests of the human individual. Yet for reasons just described, this proves not actually to be the case. And once we recognize this misprision, we can not only understand better the self-blinding of free marketeers, who reject the label "utopian" for their in fact quite utopian belief in an endless prosperity to be engendered by the advent of true laissez-faire but also see how it is that, as a number of commentators have noted over the years, there's nothing inherently paradoxical about the idea of a rightist or conservative utopia.[17]

Further, the perspective I advance here helps us to recognize that what makes utopia fit uneasily with recent incarnations of right populism is not that it privileges the totality too highly but something like the reverse. The populist far Right certainly doesn't eschew visions of an ideal future society, of course: its thinking can be quite utopian insofar as it's premised on a belief that an ideal order of things will be ushered in once the favored nation or group achieves immitigable precedence over others. This defining conviction implies a certain friction between nationalism and utopia, however, inasmuch as the idea of justice it implies strains against more general intuitions about what justice is—inasmuch as, that is, its chauvinism asserts that some members of the totality must not enjoy, or must not enjoy with the same freedom, what others enjoy. Right-wing nationalism will read as violently antithetical to utopia for anyone who believes that true justice must extend to all persons or beings, not just those deemed authentic or legitimately favored members of this or that national community.

Understanding utopia as a corrective to inadequate arrangements for members of the totality also, I think, helps us to get a handle on the Left's often uneasy relation to utopia and utopianism. In the ideological configuration of the present, the Left's more or less definitional opposition to unfettered capitalism means that there can be an ultrastatism of the Left but also an ultra-anarchism, depending on whether the state is considered the adversary or the bedfellow of corporations, markets, commodification, concentrations of inherited wealth over generations, worker-disenfranchising practices and technologies, or anything else capitalism may be understood to entail. This means that utopia appears a friend to the Left in general as long as it promises an alternative to the what-is of present economic configurations but morphs into the enemy of the more anarchist Left when it looks like the triumph of the state and into the enemy of the more statist Left when it portends the end of the state as we know it. If I'm right that utopian *nemesis* is fundamentally concerned not with the fortunes of the collective as such but with injustice suffered under the extant order of things by components of the collective, however, it becomes obvious that utopia is not by necessity either anarchist or statist in character—though it *is* profoundly linked to what we've come to think of as social justice. This is a point well borne out by the vast corpus of utopian literature, which gives us both utopias of top-down bureaucracies micromanaging human affairs and utopias where there are no laws to enforce and formal hierarchies have been eliminated.

Having thus cast on an eye on contemporary polarities in the vicinity of thinking about ideal social orders, I should perhaps say something about utopia and the present more generally. It has become de rigueur for writers of books on utopia to reflect on the vitality or decline of utopianism at the moment of writing and on utopia's prospects for the years to come. Given the vast array of metrics and anecdotes that might bear on such a judgment, I can't imagine venturing such a general assessment here. But I can express my agreement with what seem to me some widely held views on the fortunes of utopia over the past century-plus. Like many commentators, I believe that an upwelling of utopian imagining crested in the years just before and after 1900; that at least in Europe and North America utopia lost some of its luster around the middle of the twentieth century; and that recent decades have seen a resurgence of sophisticated inquiries into utopia coupled with an increase in the ratio of dystopian narratives to utopian ones in print and on screen. I would also agree that globalization has had important effects on utopian thinking, not least in raising questions about whether capitalism's geocultural penetration leaves any remainder for alternative enclaves and whether once vast utopian dreams must now be rescaled to local opportunities.

I would also like to offer a thought that pertains less to the present condition of utopian imagining than to this imagining's general resilience. Variations of Jameson's remark, in *The Seeds of Time* (1994), that "it seems to be easier for us today to imagine the thoroughgoing deterioration of the earth and of nature than the breakdown of late capitalism" have been cited frequently, even ritually, in the literature on utopia.[18] But it seems to me easier even to imagine the end of capitalism than to imagine the disappearance of utopian imagining (provided there are still human beings to do the imagining). That ancient texts represent justice—in the person of Astraea—as having fled the earth at the end of a long-ago golden age crystallizes, for me, how difficult it in fact is for people to cease dreaming of justice as an ideal, even if they find it equally difficult to imagine a condition of justice actually arriving. Utopia, as a realization of justice, seems to me to partake of this same persistence. One doesn't need to credit the idea of a fundamental human essence or of universal values to conclude that utopia abides as a kind of logical possibility—that the idea of a world better than this one will simply be out there for anyone, at any time, dissatisfied with the present order of things.

But the reference to Astraea leads to a final question: whether, in asserting a deep connection between utopia and justice, I'm promoting a version of utopia finally powered more by nostalgia than by hope, one in which the golden age or the prelapsarian masquerades as what Bloch called the Not-Yet (*das Noch-Nicht*). To this I would answer, first, that to assume that utopian vision's significance must be undercut where that vision is revealed to be deeply engaged with the past would be to ignore the power of utopias that are interested as much in reparative forms of justice as in other kinds. As we'll consider at the close of the first section of chapter 1, indignation about historical dispossession has been a crucial aspect of the *nemesis* driving antiracist, anti-imperialist, and antipatriarchal utopian writing—writing that indeed highlights utopia's connection to justice particularly strongly. But I would answer, second, that I have no problem with the view—though I don't quite hold it myself—that the desire for justice is in some fundamental sense always a longing for a past perfection that never was. And I would happily call attention to three works that seem, with illuminating dividends, to point in just this direction.

Among literary texts in English, perhaps none does so more famously, or with more concentrated political purpose, than Langston Hughes's 1936 poem "Let America Be America Again," which contrasts the ideals of "America" with the historical realities of the United States (for the fooled "poor White," the "Negro bearing slavery's scars," the "red man driven from the land," and the immigrant "clutching . . . hope") and then entreats, "O, let America be America again—/ The land that never has been yet—/ And yet must be—the land where *every* man is free." One of Hughes's points here is that a kind of idealism, however insulated from reality, has had real effects in the world ("made America the land it has become").[19] But a no less important one is that there's value in maintaining, in productive tension, a kind of affective belief in what never was together with a firmly grounded, rigorously skeptical understanding *that* it never was.

To take another example: from around 1980 until the years before his death in 2015, the Congolese artist Bodys Isek Kingelez produced a collection of what he called *extrêmes maquettes*, small-scale constructions of imaginary buildings and cities that combined extraordinary craftsmanship with a scintillating exuberance of invention. Describing his general intentions in producing this work, Kingelez wrote of wanting to "façonner un habitat modèle et moderne en pensant à une autre façon de vivre" (make a model and modern habitat with another way of living in mind), of how he "pense à une monde meilleur, plus pacifiste" (thinks of a better world, more pacifist).[20] In comments on specific maquettes, he also underlined the utopian aspirations of his project, which have been much highlighted by curators and critics.[21] Writing about a 1997 piece, for example, he describes "une ville libre, paisible . . . où les délinquants, la police et les prisons n'existent pas" (a free and peaceful city . . . where delinquents, police, and prisons don't exist).[22] That work's title—*Projet pour le Kinshasa du troisième millénaire* (1997)—points directly to the future, as do others such as *Ville de Sète 3009*. Other titles, however, suggest shadow cities that might haunt this world as unrealized utopian alternatives or even dystopian incursions. Kingelez associates the dizzying *Ville Fantôme* (1996) with an imagined "paix durable" (lasting peace) and "l'équilibre de justice de Liberté mondiale" (the balance of justice of worldwide Freedom), but Okwui Enwezor, a curator who did much to bring Kingelez's work to public attention, writes of how *Ville Fantôme* "communicates the unease we feel in dreams gone awry. . . . It is a space of anomie, temporally in the past, the bad dream of modernist planning schemes."[23] Erica Perlmutter Jones similarly argues that in "semiotic and formal elements in his work, Kingelez emphasizes how external forces such as structural adjustment, neo-colonialism and war contribute to the problems of Kinshasa today."[24]

Perhaps most instructive for us here, however, is *Kimbembele Ihunga* (1994). In the exhibition catalogue for MoMA's 2018 Kingelez retrospective, Chika Okeke-Agulu calls this maquette at once "a futuristic fantasy" and "a meditation on a past that never was or on a reality the artist has placed in perpetual doubt."[25] Kingelez's own longest commentary on the work, "The Essential Framework of the Structures Making Up the Town of Kimbembele-Ihunga (Kimbéville)," indeed collapses times and referents in an elusive and fascinating way. The reader may conclude that although Kingelez largely uses the present tense, he's mainly describing the town of the future that the maquette previews—a Kimbembele-Ihunga-to-come that will attract tourists thanks to its beautiful vistas and provision of "an environment where everyone can feel at home." Yet having described the town as "the very image of [his] ability to create a new world," Kingelez only two sentences later calls it "a town where Kingelez, the enlightened artist was born on 27 August 1948." And further on, he writes that it would take him "a lifetime to relate even half its history."[26] Quite in line with Okeke-Agulu's take, then, Kingelez seems partly to be introducing his real-world birthplace as it might have been under different circumstances, not only a future Kimbembele-Ihunga but also an alternative Kimbembele-Ihunga of the present. In other words, part of the effect of his commentary, and of the maquette itself, arises from something like what Hughes captures in "Let America": an intimation of the power of what never was but ought to have been and in some manner might be yet. The call of the "paix durable" and of "justice de Liberté mondiale" is the more urgent precisely because it seems to issue not only from the Not-Yet but also from an unlived past.

The same summer (2018) that saw the opening of the MoMA Kingelez retrospective saw a performance, at the Ojai Music Festival in California, of *La Lontananza nostalgica utopica futura,* one of the last works of the Italian composer Luigi Nono, who died in 1990. Nono was a committed avant-gardist who arguably outdid his fellow New Music pioneers Pierre Boulez and Karlheinz Stockhausen in escaping the trammels of tonality; he was also a committed communist and antifascist whose early and mid-career works honored Resistance fighters, victims of the Holocaust, detained migrant workers, champions of African decolonization, and Vietnam's National Liberation Front. *La Lontananza* is a work for solo violin and eight-track tape played (nowadays digitally, usually) over eight loudspeakers in the performance space. What this tape contains is a selection from hours of recordings, made in 1988, of the violinist Gidon Kremer, including not only playing by Kremer based on a score from Nono but also background noises that filtered into the taping sessions, such as those of a falling pencil and a passing train.[27] In a given performance of the piece, the sound technician is, in the words of Tim Rutherford-Johnson, "free to fade each channel" of the Kremer recordings "up or down, or into complete silence."[28] Meanwhile, the live violinist plays from a score, but the sheet music is placed on six music stands on stage or in the audience, "irregularly and asymmetrically," in Nono's instructions, "*never near each other*, but in such a way as to permit free although *never direct* passage between them." This placement can also be "complicated" with "2 or 4 empty music stands in order to make the passage way more varied and imaginative."[29]

The piece's title—which might be translated *The Future Utopian Nostalgic Distance*—clearly evokes the recession of communist hopes in 1989, even as the encounter between recording and soloist suggests the haunting of the present by what was once a dream of the future and might now be seen as relegated to the past. Viewing the piece as primarily an inscription of loss and doubt, we might see the path of the performer not only as an iteration of Nono's long-standing concern with wandering and migrancy but also as a figure for a temporarily lost sense of direction in utopian imagining.[30]

Yet the actual sound of the work is not, for the most part, nearly as melancholic as one might expect from a duet with a *temps perdu*. On the contrary, its jolting and jagged quality, both on the tape and in the live violin part, suggests less a mournful haunting than an unpredictable breaking into the present by the past and perhaps by the future. Taking its title, construction, and sound together, we might say that like "Let America" and *Kimbembele Ihunga*, the piece evokes not some sentimental nostalgia but the never quite eradicable force, in utopian imagining, of a past that never was but should have been. As Seth Brodsky puts it, "Nono, knowing that the socialist horizon is closing, wants to open it back up in a nonexistent future, one potentially derivable from a never entirely accessible or exhausted past" (192).

And there's something more here. Inserting *utopica* between *nostalgica* and *futura* in his title, Nono wittily places the "nowhere" of utopia in the position usually reserved for the present. One could interpret this as simply a further enhancement of the work's jumbling of temporalities, but I think it points to a specific way in which the piece places its audience in a kind of temporary utopian scene even as it thematizes utopia's distance.[31] In joining strictures from the past—the musical score itself and the tape—with improvisations and wanderings in the present of performance, *La Lontananza*, of course, highlights a feature of any performance of anything: the combination of the planned with the aleatory, the way infinite possibilities are grounded in a pregiven substrate. But it also suggests, it seems to me, how this kind of convergence will be the condition of any true utopia. Whether a given utopia be anarchistic or centralized, plentiful in regulations or disdainful of rules, life within in it at any given moment will be governed by the past not only in the sense that it may be suffused by some dream of a golden age but also, more straightforwardly, because such present life will be lived in relation to arrangements developed at an earlier point. At the same time, a society or a world cannot be utopia, as we'll see again in chapter 2, if it's so thoroughly engineered that the unexpected is impossible. Nono gives a score and instructions and even an old tape to play, and these parameters set the terms of what can happen. Yet anything can happen.

1

Utopian *Nemesis*

Savage Indignation

The anonymously authored 1755 fiction *A Voyage to the World in the Centre of the Earth*, abridged in 1802 as *Bruce's Voyage to Naples*, has a somewhat curious ending.[1] Bruce, the tale's narrator, is propelled on his adventures by a want of money and friends: the younger brother in a family of unspecified size and rank, he receives but a small inheritance, after quickly running through which he's disowned by his relations. Worse than the penury itself, however, is his discovery that the very people who had helped him exhaust his fortune are those who had slandered him to his kin. Indeed, he tells the reader, "One in particular, whom I had entirely supported while my money lasted . . . was at the head of those that railed the most against me; and I verily believe that he was the chief cause of my disgrace." Obtaining employment at last as clerk to a sea captain, Bruce travels to Italy, where he soon tumbles into the opening of Mount Vesuvius. He then falls for about three thousand miles, until he finds himself at last in a subterranean utopia, notable for its illumination by jewels, for its use of birds instead of horses for transport, and, above all, for the generosity and goodness of its inhabitants. All of the citizens of this society being equal in fortune, "nothing but friendship, hospitality, and a brotherly affection to all their fellow-creatures, reigns in this happy world."[2]

One day, when strolling through the underground empire, Bruce sees another person falling from the sky. It happens to be the very Mr. Worldly who had earlier repaid Bruce's kindness by doing him "all the injury that lay in his power" (288). Telling Bruce feelingly of the guilt that overcame him and Bruce's family in the wake of Bruce's apparent demise, he begs forgiveness, which Bruce bestows; shortly after this reconciliation, Worldly dies of his injuries. Bruce eventually returns to England, where he's welcomed by his relations—but only to be betrayed again. This time, the ingrate is Bruce's professed friend Mr. Silvertongue, who "owes all he [has] in the world to [Bruce's] family" but alerts a tailor to whom Bruce has an unpaid debt that Bruce has returned. The account fills Bruce with "rage and indignation" (295) and seems to confirm the advice of his friend from the subterranean world: "Look henceforward on all mankind as your enemies, and guard against them as such" (295). The narrative ends with Bruce "keep[ing] little company" and hoping for a return to the center of the earth, where people treat each other well and honestly and where—as a trial scene in the middle of the tale attests—no crime is held more reprehensible than that of ingratitude, which though almost unheard of in practice is punishable by death when it does occur (281).

What may seem odd about the episode of Mr. Silvertongue is that it so pointedly undercuts the prior reconciliation with Mr. Worldly. Either the reconciliation makes the closing betrayal seem gratuitous or the closing betrayal makes the reconciliation seem aberrant. Why undo the comedy of redemption with the machinations of another wretched ingrate? Or why, alternatively, complicate the picture of human turpitude with Mr. Worldly's sincere repentance? One part of the answer, of course, is that with the Mr. Worldly episode, the author lays a kind of trap, lulling the reader into a confidence in human beings' fundamental goodness that only makes the betrayal by Mr. Silvertongue more devastating. The fiction, in other words, betrays the reader just as Bruce's world betrays Bruce, heightening indignation at the untrustworthiness of human beings in its final moments. Indeed its operation evokes the Roman rhetorical form of the *indignatio*, which penultimate section of the final part (*peroratio*) of a judicial oration was designed to arouse righteous anger (also called *indignatio*) against the speaker's target.[3]

The reader's sense of indignation at the close of *Bruce's Voyage* may be particularly acute because Worldly, Silvertongue, and the defendant on trial in the utopian empire are not just any kinds of betrayers but ingrates specifically. Perhaps no intersubjective relation more reliably generates indignation than ingratitude, which seems doubly to wrong its victim because the latter seems to be owed a positive rather than a negative recompense or at least to enjoy a particularly strong claim to be spared ill treatment. In his role of trial judge, the emperor of the world at the center of Earth declares ingratitude "a crime so detestable in itself, that it ought above all others to be punished with the utmost severity"; it makes his "blood run cold to repeat the word" (281). The episode thus echoes a moment in the first part of Jonathan Swift's *Gulliver's Travels* at which the reader learns that among the Lilliputians, ingratitude is "a capital crime, as we read it to have been in some other countries; for they reason thus, that whoever makes ill returns to his benefactor must needs be a common enemy to the rest of mankind, from whom he hath received no obligation, and therefore such a man is not fit to live."[4]

The proximity between this remark and the representation of ingratitude in *Bruce's Voyage* is no accident, of course. *Gulliver's Travels* is clearly the great precedent for the later text, which in its 1755 version marks it debt by venturing that the practice of giving foreigners' comments both in the original and in English translation has been used "by many of our Historians, not even the famous *Gulliver* himself excepted," with "no other View than to fill up a Page."[5] Like Bruce, Gulliver is happy to place his tale within the lineage of utopian travelogue, if only negatively, noting in his prefatory letter that some "have gone so far as to drop hints that the Houyhnhnms and yahoos have no more existence than the inhabitants of Utopia" (5). And Gulliver partakes, too, of the later narrator's encompassing indignation at human behavior. A few sentences further on in his preface, for example, he reports that after two years of following the example of the Houyhnhnm he calls his master, he was able to divest himself of "that infernal habit of lying, shuffling, deceiving, and equivocating, so deeply rooted in the very souls of all my species, especially the Europeans" (5). This kind of catalogue of human offenses notably makes its appearance more than once in *Bruce's Voyage* (as it does in *Gulliver's Travels*), as when one of Bruce's interlocutors observes that "treachery, deceit, fraud, ingratitude, slander, and backbiting are unknown among what you are pleased to call the brute part of creation. Strange they should be so universal among the rational part!" (265–66).

In *Bruce's Voyage*, indignation enters the scene almost as soon as the narrator-hero arrives at the center of Earth. Upon his postdescent rescue by a member of that happy society, he tries to thank his benefactor by falling on his knees and kissing his hand, but the man snatches that hand away and "with a most angry countenance" raises him from the ground. The mysterious behavior is explained when, shortly after, the rescuer prays for God's blessing: Bruce again falling prostrate and "embrac[ing] his feet," the man flies from him "with the utmost indignation" and reminds him that "none but God is to be worshiped" (256). In Swift's narrative, indignation first appears by name in part 4, where it's twice attributed to Gulliver's Houyhnhnm master—first on his hearing that yahoos presume to ride horses (194) and again when Gulliver tries "to give him some ideas of the desire of power and riches, of the terrible effects of lust, intemperance, malice and envy" that prevail among human beings. At this, his master becomes "like one whose imagination was struck with something never seen or heard of before," lifting "up his eyes with amazement and indignation" (197). Working up to its climactic condemnation of humanity, in other words, Swift's fiction, too, summons a breath of rhetorical *indignatio*, the master Houyhnhnm modeling the indignation that will become Gulliver's dominant passion, as it will become Bruce's, once the traveler returns to the society he had left.[6]

If in his moment of indignation the Houyhnhnm master anticipates Gulliver and perhaps the imagined reader of *Gulliver's Travels*, however, he also stands in for Jonathan Swift, whose memorial in Saint Patrick's Cathedral Dublin famously announces that the body of the Dean lies there, "*Ubi saeva Indignatio Ulterius Cor lacerare nequit*"—"where savage indignation can no longer lacerate his heart." Given that indignation evidently powers so much of Swift's writing, it seems apposite that this is the only emotion mentioned in the epitaph, which Swift himself composed; as Claude Rawson notes, *saeva indignatio* has been used by many to "define the character of Swift's satire." Yet in Rawson's view, the epitaph also marks a departure for Swift, the "pervasive, and indeed defining, feature" of whose style is an "interplay between what are sometimes called [his] 'intensities' and the edgily playful guardedness which undercuts without neutralising them." According to Rawson, Swift understood that "displaying rage would make him vulnerable" and thus eschewed "Juvenalian majesties of satiric indignation" in favor of "a more intimately needling" manner: Swift preferred to make his victims, as well as his readers, "'wriggle, howl, and skip,' . . . rather than pounding them with indignant tirades which might only expose his own lack of composure." In the epitaph, however, Swift "for once adopts . . . a note of Juvenalian grandeur, not only proclaiming the trademark *indignatio* of Juvenal's first satire (*facit indignatio versum*, 1. 79) but accentuating it beyond the Roman original by adding the adjective *saeva*." Rawson wonders whether the epitaph doesn't give vent to a declaration that "seemed to Swift unthinkable in his lifetime writings."[7]

Careful as Rawson's reading is, it gives perhaps too little weight to the point that even Juvenalian tirades could be joined to claims to reasonableness. When one sees dreadful wrongs everywhere, Juvenal asserts in his first satire, "*difficile est saturam non scribere*," "it is difficult not to write satire."[8] In other words, there would be something aberrant in *not* decrying such tendencies.[9] And thus if "*facit indignatio versum*"—if indignation makes satiric verse in the sense of impelling it—then indignation serves not madness but sanity. As Andrew Stauffer has shown in *Anger, Revolution, and Romanticism*, indignation indeed became particularly prominent in the British print culture of the eighteenth century's last decade, amid the bitter partisanship succeeding the French Revolution, because it could be adopted as a posture of impassioned rationality maintained against the irrational emotion to which one's opponent had succumbed. "Like Juvenal," Stauffer writes, the Edmund Burke of the 1796 *Letters on a Regicide Peace* "turns to *indignatio* as the only rational option for the *bonus vir*, the good man surveying a world gone wrong." And though conservatives at first sought alone to seize "the elevated ground of noble indignation," both reactionaries and reformers were soon "claiming righteous indignation as their weapon" as debates over the meanings of the French Revolution ground on. Mary Wollstonecraft, for example, presented "her anger as a rational, even requisite, response to falsehood, performed for the public good," while Thomas Paine understood that indignation could serve revolution inasmuch as it was "an emotion predicated on the essential dignity of those who feel it." To "claim indignation," Stauffer observes, "is to appropriate a three-fold bonus for one's anger: it is justified . . . , it is righteous . . . , and it is dignified."[10]

Whatever attractions or dangers Swift discerned in the Juvenalian mode, his Gulliver, like the Bruce of *Bruce's Voyage*, shares Juvenal's self-positioning as a "good man surveying a world gone wrong," in Stauffer's formulation. With "surveying," Stauffer elegantly evokes the "equal, wide survey" described by John Barrell—the idea that the landed gentleman of the British eighteenth century could have a meaningfully "panoramic" perspective on society by virtue of a "two-fold qualification to be regarded as disinterested: his permanent stake in the stability of the nation, and his freedom from engaging in any specific profession, trade, or occupation which might occlude his view of society as a whole."[11] But the word from Stauffer's epitome that really requires our attention is "world." For Juvenal's sixteen satires present a catalogue of evils— many of them involving women usurping male authority, men lapsing into effeminacy, upstarts gaining power over their betters, criminal behavior proving profitable, inheritances being squandered, and infidelity or other sexual improprieties growing commonplace—that together add up to a totality of derangement, a world unhinged to the last degree. The astonishing spectacle of a man marrying another man, which comes at the culmination of Satire 2, serves as a voluble synecdoche for the state of things in a time that is, for Juvenal, radically out of joint.

Indeed so topsy-turvy is the world that, as the satirist says in 13, "if I discover an upright and blameless man, I liken him to a boy born half beast, or to fishes found by a marveling rustic under the plough, or to a pregnant mule." The natural has become unnatural, and we "are living in a ninth age; an age more evil than that of iron—one for whose wickedness Nature herself can find no name, no metal from which to call it." Things have thus reached their moral nadir relatively recently; and yet Juvenal also makes clear that there has for some time been no shortage of goads to indignation in the world, it being long since that Astraea (Justice) "withdrew by degrees to heaven, with Chastity as her comrade, the two sisters taking flight together." Thus, as the satirist tells us right after his *facit indignatio versum*, "all the doings of mankind, their vows, their fears, their angers and their pleasures, their joys and goings to and fro"— back to the postdiluvian emergence of Deucalion and Pyrrha—"shall form the motley subject of my page."[12]

In thus expressing his intention, Juvenal highlights a crucial affinity between satire and comprehensiveness. Not every satirist explicitly takes the position that the world in general is in catastrophic condition, but a satire may strive to enhance its hold on the reader by some appeal to the sense that wrong is pervasive rather than localized, and lengthy narrative satires tend toward the encyclopedic in their presentation of ills. In François Rabelais's *Gargantua and Pantagruel* and in *Gulliver's Travels*, this plenitude is facilitated by characters who travel widely, a device taken to yet more exotic lengths in the section of the 1755 *Voyage to the World in the Centre of the Earth* that was excised to make the more compact *Bruce's Voyage*. This lengthy tract consists mainly of "The History of an Inhabitant of the Air," a fantastical and at times bawdy inset testimony by a four-thousand-year-old being from the planet Jupiter who passes successive lives on a comet, Saturn, Earth, Mars, and Earth again. Through these phases, the inhabitant witnesses earthly folly and evil in numerous guises (from tyrants' lust for power to lawyers' prevarication, from social climbing to sexual incontinence) as well as several varieties of celestial *contrapasso*, including evildoers' transformation into "horrid and loathsome Beasts," whose characteristics recall their vices pretransformation.[13]

Lacking "The History of an Inhabitant of the Air," *Bruce's Voyage* is mainly taken up with the wonders of that subterranean society where there are no distinctions of rank, where greed is unheard of, where animals never suffer human cruelty, and where the first trial for a public misdeed to take place in at least sixty years (perhaps many more) is the aforementioned arraignment for ingratitude. Thus although the 1802 version retains a strongly satirical element (especially in the finale, where detestation of his fellow surface-dwellers leaves the protagonist dreaming of returning to the better place below), it reads more securely as a utopia, while the 1755 seems a generic hybrid, closer in many ways to *Gulliver's Travels* than to the line of celebrated utopias that commences with Thomas More's *Utopia* of 1516. Nonetheless, both versions attest (as do Juvenal, Rabelais, and Swift) that if satire and utopia are closely related, this is not just because the two genres critique things. It's also because both spring from indignation against a world gone wrong, an ardent sense that a totality is in need of righting.

This crucial combination of elements—outrage and a quality of totality in the object of outrage—is nicely concretized in Bruce's tale, where the voicing of indignation at the ways of human beings is supported by an insistent contrast between two worlds qua worlds. When Bruce first falls toward the underground utopia, he discerns "seas, vast continents, mountains, and islands" and perceives that this other place is "neither more nor less than a world like ours" (254). Further on, in lengthily introducing Bruce to the subterranean realm, his utopian host repeatedly contrasts the "world" of the surface with his own and stresses that "the world we are now upon . . . is in the centre of your globe" (258), "the world on which we live . . . the very centre of that globe you call the earth" (259). Reference to worlds even figures prominently in a remark by the narrating Bruce that captures—perhaps as well as any sentence in the immense corpus of utopian fiction—both the overlap and the distinction between utopia and satire. Having vented his indignation concerning the gold for which "we would sell our God, our country, and our very souls," Bruce pauses to collect himself thus: "But I am painting the vices of the inhabitants of our world, when I ought to be acquainting them with the customs of an unknown one" (267).

Critics have, nonetheless, long noted how deeply satire and utopia are connected. The editors of a mid-twentieth-century anthology of utopian writing, for example, describe the utopian genre overall as home to two basic forms, satire and the "speculative or constructive utopia." They also acknowledge, however, that "irony or pathos may tinge [the] speculative construction, and sometimes therefore the clear distinction between constructive and satirical may break down in a single work."[14] In 1979's *Metamorphoses of Science Fiction*, one of the enduringly influential texts of utopian studies, Darko Suvin observes that "the explicit utopian construction is the logical obverse of any satire," utopia "explicat[ing] what satire implicates, and vice versa," but also that there "are strong indications that the two are . . . connected in the folk-inversions and 'saturas' of the Saturnalias" and that the most significant utopias are those exhibiting the strongest interaction between "constructive-utopian and satiric aspects."[15] Krishan Kumar, meanwhile, notes that where for "a considerable time after More," satire in utopian texts "presented the writer's world negatively, as anti-utopia, to which utopia was the constructive, positive, response," the genres bifurcated in the later nineteenth century. According to Kumar, utopia "could incorporate anti-utopia only so long as its own utopian scheme seemed simply a moral, heuristic device, or a remote fantasy. . . . Once, however, utopia appeared as a real possibility," a "detailed picture of present ills seemed irrelevant and out of place," and "the negative and positive poles of the old satirical utopia were pulled apart and assigned to separate genres or sub-genres."[16]

Not quite articulated in these formulations is that if indignation propels satire, it no less fundamentally, if more quietly and indirectly, subtends utopian construction. An especially vivid illustration of this point is provided by More's *Utopia*, where the traveler Raphael Hythlodaeus's impassioned dissection of injustices in sixteenth-century England in part 1 is answered by his own report of Utopia's innovations in part 2 (as well as briefer references to well-run societies in part 1 itself). Quite in line with Kumar's formulation, the initial satire presents "the writer's world negatively, as anti-utopia, to which utopia [is] the constructive, positive, response." In the first part, to take one example, Hythlodaeus decries the harsh punishments visited on those poor who have been driven to steal by the fecklessness of the rich; he

then answers this with a description of the excellent society of the Polylerites, where thievery is punished not with death but with socially productive
labor, and answers it again in part 2 with his report of Utopia, where all have
work and none are idle.[17] What makes More's text particularly instructive,
with respect to utopian indignation, is that part 1 doesn't merely imply outrage on the part of the author-satirist but exhibits a sincere performance of
that emotion. For the setting in which the social critique in part 1 is delivered
is a dinner, hosted by the benevolent Cardinal Morton and recalled by Hythlodaeus, at which fools and parasites attack Hythlodaeus's arguments while
that wise traveler rebukes those worthies and the failures of justice they excuse. In other words, part 2 may be a report of a happy society, but it's delivered by someone whose fervent sense of wrong has been shown in action.
The inaugural narrative of the utopian genre is explicitly the tale of an indignant man.

Against what, however, is utopian indignation directed? Can we say anything more than what we said above, which is that it seems addressed to some
form of totality? One common assumption about utopian imagining is that
it's keyed, above all, to the promotion of happiness. In *Utopia*, Hythlodaeus
repeatedly describes the Utopians' social arrangements as conducive to this
end and reports that the chief matter of debate among Utopia's philosophers,
who hold the immortal soul to be "by the goodness of God ordained to felicity," is "in what thing . . . the felicity of man consisteth."[18] Almost all subsequent utopias describe the relative happiness of their citizens, so it seems with
good reason that Ernst Bloch, the grandest of theorists of utopia, writes in
volume 2 of *The Principle of Hope*, "The social utopia predominantly aims at
human happiness and considers, in more or less *novelistic form*, its economic-
social form"—this as against natural-right theory, which "aims predominantly
at *human dignity.*"[19] If happiness is the desideratum of utopia, it should follow
that the target of utopian indignation is unhappiness.

Directly we try this formulation out, however, we recognize that something
is amiss. Unhappiness, even in the form of immiseration on a large scale, may
be something to lament, but people will rarely describe themselves as indignant *at* unhappiness itself, which is, after all, the condition of unhappy people.
Rather, the indignation at play here must be directed against whoever or whatever is responsible for the unhappiness (or other evils) that render the totality
in need of righting. In satire, the stress is arguably on the *whoever*, in the sense
that indignation's target is human vice and folly. Utopias, by contrast, tend to
train their attention at least as strongly on the *whatever*—on the systems, institutions, customs, and practices that seem most implicated in the going-awry
of the world. This, too, is well illustrated by More's *Utopia*, where Hythlodaeus
evinces no shortage of anger at selfish and foolish people, but where what most

grounds the utopian vision of part 2 is his indignation at social arrangements whose greatest affront is not even their failure to produce felicity. What most provokes Hythlodaeus's ire is their injustice and inefficiency—qualities that are, for him, tightly linked.

Hythlodaeus indeed highlights this link at the start of his discourse before Morton in part 1, when he observes that capital punishment for thievery "passeth the limits of justice, and is also very hurtful to the weal-public" (18). Mentioned first, the code's failure of justness arguably enjoys a faint priority, but Hythlodaeus signals that the more practical harms such retribution engenders are no less worthy of concern. From here, he'll unfold his argument that rather than "horrible punishments be[ing] appointed for thieves," it would be better that "provision should have been made, that there were some means whereby they might get their living, so that no man should be driven to this extreme necessity, first to steal and then to die" (19). In taking this line, Hythlodaeus clearly shifts the ethical burden from the poor who steal (and even from the magistrates who condemn) to the system that does or does not provide a living (and to those responsible for that system). But he also suggests a deep connection between the "limits of justice" and the injury "to the weal-public." The system's failure to treat justly those enmeshed in it may be of a piece with its failure to be just in the sense of well calibrated, well designed.

Something similar obtains in Hythlodaeus's subsequent observation that instating the death penalty for robbery gives the robber an incentive to murder the robbed. The thief knows that if conviction for theft means execution, homicide won't incur a worse punishment than will thieving, so that "while we go about with such cruelty to make thieves afraid, we provoke them to kill good men" (27). Again, what arouses Hythlodaeus's scorn is the failure of the present system on the scores both of justice as a moral matter and of effective design: the punishment is wrong in the sense that sin is wrong, but it's also wrong in the sense that a tool unfitted to a given task is wrong. Taken together, Hythlodaeus's expostulations in part 1 suggest how reflection on the wellsprings of human depravity can lead to exasperation at badly constructed mechanisms. And in this, they set the pattern for subsequent utopias, whose characteristic work will be to explore the relationship between dual objects of indignation: faulty people and faulty arrangements.

A look at eruptions of utopian indignation in some post-eighteenth-century texts—at additions to the catalogue of incredulity and disgust we've begun with Hythlodaeus, the Houyhnhnm master, Gulliver, Bruce's subterranean benefactor, and Bruce—will give a sense of the variety of forms this exploration can take. We can start with the allegory that launches the most influential of all utopian novels, Edward Bellamy's *Looking Backward: 2000–1887*, first published in 1888. The narrator here is Julian West, who falls asleep in Boston toward the end of the nineteenth century and wakes up in the year 2000 to find that class division in the United States has nominally been eliminated by a straightforward system of equal income for all. The conceit of *Looking Backward* is that the intended audience for West's memoir (his account of how he became acquainted with utopian ways) is not the reader of 1887 but the reader of 2000; one of its initial tasks is therefore to give the citizen of the twenty-first century a sense of nineteenth-century conditions.[20]

To do so, West makes use of an extended parable in which society circa 1887 is likened to "a prodigious coach which the masses of humanity were harnessed to and [which they] dragged toilsomely along a very hilly and sandy road," while "the top was covered with passengers who never got down, even at the steepest ascents" (26–27). Having described how those above counseled patience to those toiling below but did not assist them, for fear of losing their own seats, West acknowledges that "this will appear . . . an incredible inhumanity" (28)—a spur to indignation on the part of the reader. But he goes on to observe, in putative mitigation, that "it was firmly and sincerely believed that there was no other way in which Society could get along" and that those on top genuinely thought themselves "of finer clay, in some way belonging to a higher order of beings who might justly expect to be drawn" (28).

West's figure of the arduously hauled coach does several things at once. Literalizing the "high" and "low" ordinarily used to describe the economic tiers of a class-based society, it also makes the poor the wellspring of all meaningful labor and mocks nineteenth-century complacency about the meaning and momentum of social progress. No less significant, however, is that it fully embeds all the people of the nineteenth century within the social organization of the time. In the parable as West unfolds it, there is no possibility of simply walking away from the coach or arranging other transportation, which means that although the rich have one or two more options than the poor have, all parties are consigned to a gallingly ineffective apparatus. This representation of constraint by no means exempts the wealthy from moral scorn, which in fact Bellamy is pleased to stoke.[21] But it does require that a substantial fund of indignation also be directed at the hideous arrangement in which all are trapped—which steering of censure toward structure or system then serves the larger project of *Looking Backward*. For Bellamy's aim throughout is to persuade readers that utopia can be realized by changes in social arrangements only, without modification of the fundamentals of human character. The newly awakened West responds to nearly every improved aspect of life in 2000 with a version of the remark "Human nature itself must have changed very much" (56), to which his utopian guide, Dr. Leete, responds with some variant of "Not at all" (56) .

For our second study in indignation, we can turn to the most celebrated of rejoinders to Bellamy, William Morris's *News from Nowhere* of 1890. At one point in that narrative, the focalizer William Guest—a nineteenth-century Englishman who visits a far better England of the future—engages his utopian interlocutors on the subject of prisons, a topic familiar in utopian writing by Morris's time. In the course of this conversation, the younger of Guest's hosts, one Dick, reflects ruefully on the moral predicament of people in ages past, remarking how strange it is to "to think that there have been men like ourselves . . . who . . . had feelings and affections like ourselves" and yet could "do such dreadful things" as permit their fellow citizens to languish in jail.[22] When Guest goes on to ask, a little obtusely, if prisons are still to be found in the happier age he has entered, Dick answers with some heat: "Man alive! how can you ask such a question? Have I not told you that we know what a prison means by the undoubted evidence of really trustworthy books, helped out by our own imaginations? . . . Prisons, indeed! O no, no, no!" (80).

Appalled by the suggestion that people in his time could perpetrate wrongs like those committed in the nineteenth century, Dick at the same time evinces no doubt that those who tolerated the existence of prisons "had feelings and affections like" his own. By implication, then, what must have changed from the earlier age to the later is the way society is organized: if utopians treat each other far better than people treated each other in Morris's day, and yet human nature has not itself altered, then amended arrangements must be at the root of the transformed conduct. Like Bellamy, Morris is committed to the principle that the way society is organized will determine whether the basically invariant human material issues in good or evil, although his utopia runs on a minimum of overt governance where Bellamy's is predicated on powerful central institutions. More to the point, however, the two texts exhibit similar structurings of utopian outrage. In both, indignation against morally compromised people carries the greater affective weight, but something like a greater logical force is borne by indignation against the systems that make people what they are. Indeed in being torn between anger at the iniquities of people of the past and sympathy for those people's condemnation to lives of moral wrong, Dick presents a figure for the utopian text itself, energized by indignation at human fallibility even as it (more soberly, so to speak) marks bad social design as the proper object of rage.

A somewhat different version of this productive tension can be found in *A Modern Utopia*, published by H. G. Wells a decade and a half after *News from Nowhere*. In this strange fiction, Utopia is a planet like our own Earth in that each person in our world has a double there, yet unlike our Earth in that its (global) society is very differently organized. The tale is told by "the Owner of the Voice," as we're advised to think of him, a man who, along with a companion known as "the botanist," is one day transported to utopia in a flash. The pair learn a great deal about the organization of this utopia as they make their way through alternative-reality Switzerland (and eventually alternative-reality London), but while our narrator is captivated by utopia's superior arrangements, the botanist remains preoccupied, much to the narrator's irritation, with a failed love affair back on Earth.

In the closing movement of the story, the botanist asserts that human beings are no more than the sum of their emotional woundings—"the scars of the past"—whereupon the two are returned to the grim world of England around 1905. Indignation predictably follows. The narrator "becomes quarrelsome," berating his companion for his attachment to the unparadise they've regained, and after a few more exchanges, he finds himself "furiously seeking in [his] mind for a word, for a term of abuse, for one compendious verbal missile that shall smash this man for ever," a word "to express total inadequacy of imagination and will, spiritual anæmia, dull respectability, gross sentimentality, a cultivated pettiness of heart."[23]

In giving us a utopia whose people are doubles of those in the nonutopian world, and thus made of precisely the same clay as nonutopians, Wells crystallizes in a particularly schematic way the confidence just noted in Bellamy and Morris: that better social arrangements can transform human conduct without necessarily altering human nature. The botanist's function (as representative of antiutopian views) is therefore not to state the pragmatic argument that utopia *cannot* be realized through changes in institutions, codes, norms, and so on, but rather to vent the moral or affective argument that utopia *should not* be realized because it misses or perverts the essence of humanity. We therefore encounter here a notable torquing of the dual indignation against faulty people and faulty mechanisms that we've been considering thus far. In Bellamy and Morris, and even to a certain extent in More, indignation against bad social design trumps indignation at human depravity in the sense that the former promises do away with the latter: indignation directed at design suggests that such depravity is no necessary thing and indeed casts a kind of retrospective mantle of forgiveness over the depraved, who did not, after all, enjoy the advantage of being born into a better-arranged world. In insisting that human beings *are* the sum of their wounds, however, the botanist pits utopian rearrangement against humanity, making such reconfiguration the enemy, even the would-be extinguisher, of people in their existential truth.

We'll return to this kind of antiutopian argument in the third section of this chapter and in chapter 2, and we'll consider the particular assessment of people propounded by *A Modern Utopia* in chapter 3. Here, however, it seems important to acknowledge a political kinship of utopian indignation as it has just

been characterized. If it's true that utopia's action involves admitting indignation against human depravity while insisting on the comparative productivity
of indignation against social arrangements that are unjust in the double sense
of unfair and badly designed, utopia must at a deep level be aligned with progressive political orientations—orientations that dwell not on failures of individual
responsibility but on the potential of reforms that would permit individuals'
characters to be improved or their lives otherwise enriched. In so observing,
however, we need to be careful about how we understand progress and systems. Utopia's affiliation with satire bids us remember that forms of conservatism, too, put their faith in the shaping power of supraindividual forces—
traditions, institutions, customs that have been valuable not only in themselves
but also because they have shaped people's values and behaviors.[24] As was
noted in the introduction to this study, there is nothing intrinsically paradoxical about a conservative utopia.

Moreover, a significant group of utopian fictions concerns itself explicitly
with the recovery of societies, civilizations, and communities that have in one
or another sense been lost. In these works, utopia stands not merely as a
rectification-by-example of inadequate systems in the present but also as a
remediation of injustice in the past—as an ideal arrangement that not only
contrasts with flawed forms of social organization but also resists, though it
can never in any full sense make up for, historical dispossession. A model here
is the land of Telassar in Pauline Hopkins's *Of One Blood*, which appeared in
The Colored American Magazine in 1902 and 1903 and was published as a stand-
alone volume in 2004. In Hopkins's narrative, Reuel Briggs, an American
mixed-race medical student passing for white, joins an English expedition to
"the site of ancient Ethiopian cities; its object to unearth buried cities and
treasure which the shifting sands of Sahara have buried for centuries."[25] During
one of the caravan's night halts, the expedition's leader, Professor Stone, explains to Briggs and his friend Charlie that "it is a *fact* that Egypt drew from
Ethiopia all the arts, sciences and knowledge of which she was mistress" (87)
and hence that in Ethiopia lay the fountainhead of European civilization. A
couple of weeks later, the party arrives at the necropolis of Meroe, capital of
ancient Ethiopia, of which Hopkins's narrator observes that anyone

who had visited the chief galleries of Europe holding the treasures accumulated from every land, could not be unmoved at finding himself on the site
of the very metropolis where science and art had their origin. . . . And then
it [would be] borne in upon him that where the taste for the arts had
reached such perfection, one might rest assured that other intellectual pursuits were not neglected nor the sciences unknown. Now, however, her
schools are closed forever; not a vestige remaining. Of the houses of her

philosophers, not a stone rests upon another; and where civilization and learning once reigned, ignorance and barbarism have reassumed their sway. (105)

Briggs soon discovers, however, that the civilization of Meroe has not ended but rather contracted and concealed itself. Knocked unconscious one night while exploring Meroe's Great Pyramid, he awakes days later in Telassar, which is—as his guide, Ai (who is also Telassar's prime minister), explains— the hidden city wherein live "the direct descendants of the inhabitants of Meroe" (114). Telassar is paradisal in every detail, its buildings magnificent and beautiful, its land fertile and pleasing to the eye, its people handsome, graceful, and wise. When, looking out over the city, Ai asks Briggs, "Do you find the prospect fair?", the visitor replies, "Fairer than I can find words to express; and yet I am surprised to find that it all seems familiar to me, as if somewhere in the past I had known just such a city as this" (119). The significance of this feeling is soon revealed: Briggs learns that he's the long-awaited king of this people, representative of a lineage lost to Telassar for centuries but identifiable by a lotus-shaped birthmark appearing on the breast of "every descendant of the royal line" (102). He also learns that with his ascension, the hidden civiliza- tion will regain its global prominence: "Ethiopia, too, is stretching forth her hand unto God, and He will fulfill her destiny. The tide of immigration shall set in the early days of the twentieth century, toward Afric's shores, so long bound in the chains of barbarism and idolatry" (142–43).

Hopkins is careful to make clear that Meroe's loss of preeminence was di- vinely ordained. According to Ai, the ancestors of those who live in Telassar committed grave sins, "and the white stranger was to Ethiopia but a scourge in the hands of an offended God" (123). Yet if *Of One Blood* thus subsumes his- torical racial injustice within a larger providential framework, it by no means discourages readerly outrage at the particular injustices it depicts. The novel's passing characters are subject to blackmail that serves as a synecdoche for permeating structural and affective racism; "the horror, the degradation" of slavery are recalled in song (15) and eventually by the appearance of Reuel's grandmother, a former slave; injustice emerges as well, needless to say, in white civilization's effort to erase the historical fact of its debt to Ethiopia. In *Of One Blood*, then, the characteristic utopian tension between indignation at system and indignation at people materializes in part as a tension between, on the one hand, a divine plan that makes use of white dominance and, on the other, beneficiaries of that plan who perpetuate injustice by their methods for main- taining white rule and their insistence on transhistorical white superiority.

This last point emerges starkly when Briggs's white friend Charlie, brought to Telassar two months later, praises the people of his own "race" as "bold and venturesome, who know not fear if we can get a few more dollars and fresh information" (153). In response, Ai asks, "They are the people who count it a disgrace to bear my color; is it not so?" (153). In the wake of Hopkins's extensive rendering of Telassar's aesthetic, moral, spiritual, and social superiority to the rest of the world, the question strikes particularly keenly at the irony of white presumption. And while Ai may loftily rise above indignation in his phrasing, Hopkins's reader will feel triply indignant at this presumption: to count it a disgrace to be Black is to be unjust to the talents of living Black people, to the achievements of their ancestors, and to the future whose path is opened by Reuel's claiming of his birthright. Again, if Telassar resembles most utopias in presenting a society whose excellent arrangement stands as an alternative to badly arranged societies everywhere, its very existence counters the ongoing injustice of white-supremacist thinking and the historical injustice (God's wrath notwithstanding) of the loss of a Black homeland.

Africa as a whole plays a similar role in "The Black Internationale: Story of Black Genius against the World" and its sequel, "Black Empire: An Imaginative Story of a Great New Civilization in Modern Africa," two fictions by George Schuyler published serially in the *Pittsburgh Courier* from 1936 to 1938 and reprinted in a single volume in 1991. Recounting a reconquest of Africa by a cadre of Black Americans possessing astonishing strategic gifts and technological know-how, *Black Empire* at once parodies the Afro-utopian vision Hopkins puts forward in *Of One Blood* and extends it. By his own admission, Schuyler plays with "race chauvinism" in order to hold it up to scorn.[26] But he also includes in *Black Empire* passages of soaring rhetoric that cannot be read as purely tongue-in-cheek—and this precisely, we might say, because they bring utopia's justice of effective arrangement together with forms of justice that answer ideologies of white superiority and histories of imperial theft. Midway through the second tale, for example, the narrator, Carl Slater, sums up the achievement of the Black Internationale as follows:

> We had seen the white men run off the continent and black men triumphant from Cairo to the Cape. We had hope for peace, for time to build here on the bosom of Mother Africa a great united land—one people, one soul, one destiny. We had hoped to build here a haven for all those wearing the burnished livery of the sun, who wearied of battling discrimination and segregation, disenfranchisement and perpetual insult in alien lands and yearned for a place of rest. We had hoped, now that we were able to hold up our heads with the free people of the earth, to be able to demonstrate here the genius of the black people in the pursuits of peace.[27]

Like Utopia in More's *Utopia*, the utopia of *Black Empire* is founded upon land seized. But where in More the claiming of utopia is simply imperial—Utopus conquers a land previously called Abraxa (50)—in Schuyler it's at once imperial and counterimperial, conquest as reclamation, a righting of injustice whose meaning is inescapably bound up with real-world history. To be sure, More's text is unimaginable apart from the political, social, and economic problems of the European sixteenth century. Yet his Utopia's significance, qua achievement of justice, doesn't depend in any explicit way on the course of European events. We might even say that it depends on Utopia's relative freedom, within its own diegetic world, from enmeshment with Europe. By contrast, Schuyler's Black Empire (and, mutatis mutandis, Hopkins's Telassar) comes into its full significance within a global configuration whose wrongness is, again, diachronic as well as synchronic, consisting not only in white domination in the world of the present but also in the history (and the prehistory and posthistory) of the European conquest of Africa.

This kind of double rectification also figures centrally in a novel published in the same year that saw Schuyler's stories reprinted as *Black Empire*, 1991. In *The Heirs of Columbus*, which for some might evoke Schuyler in its combination of freewheeling technological fantasy and rhetorical roguishness, Gerald Vizenor tells the tale of the Heirs of Christopher Columbus, a group of Native Americans who claim—and prove via genetic analysis—descent from Columbus (himself, it turns out, a descendant of the Mayas and also the lover of Samana, a New World "natural healer, a tribal hand talker" [5] who "touched his soul and set the wounded adventurer free" in 1492 [10]). In 1992, the Heirs establish their own state at Point Assinika, on the location of Point Roberts in the State of Washington. Having purchased land on the south shore, and helped by the assumption of most people that the tribal insurrection is simply "part of the quincentenary for Christopher Columbus, . . . one of many counterevents of the day" (123), the Heirs fashion

> a free state with no prisons, no passports, no public schools, no missionaries, no television, and no public taxation; genetic therapies, natural medicine, bingo cards, and entertainment were free to those who came to be healed and those who lived on the point. The residents who owned land on the point were overcome with the humor of the moment; there was no resistance, because there was nothing to lose. Bingo would pay for local services, and games of chance would heal the wounded and the lonesome. (124)

"Several government agencies" have "the heirs, the scientists, and their research under surveillance," but "state and federal officials" refrain from "mov[ing] against the insurrection," national polls having indicated that the public supports the "new nation," which "honor[s] humor and common sense" (124).

Point Assinika's status as a truly sovereign independent territory is especially significant, needless to say, given the centrality of land claims to Native
Americans' contention for justice. The righting of injustice is here consubstan-
tial in the highest degree with genuine autonomy, which point Vizenor sharply
reinforces by siting the new nation at Point Roberts—not only a "place 'of
special cultural and spiritual significance' in the tribal history of the Coastal
Salish" group of peoples, as Stuart Christie notes,[28] but also an exclave of the
United States. The tip of a peninsula otherwise belonging to Canada, the Point
is reachable directly from the United States only by travel across water (the
Strait of Georgia or Boundary Bay) or by air. The new country more firmly
purges itself of the trammels of the reservation by being not just unencircled
by the United States but also free of shared land boundaries.

Further, its geographical configuration makes Vizenor's Point Assinika a
kind of revision of More's Utopia. Hythlodaeus reports that the latter was
transformed into an island by the digging of a canal: Utopus, who eventually
"brought the rude and wild people to that excellent perfection in all good
fashions, humanity, and civil gentleness, wherein they now go beyond all the
people of the world," at the time of his conquest "caused fifteen miles space of
uplandish ground, where the sea had no passage, to be cut and digged up. And
so brought the sea round about the land. He set to this work not only the inhabitants of the island (because they should not think it done in contumely
and despite) but also his own soldiers" (50). Where More's ideal nation is
physically severed from its peninsula by the labor of conscripted indigenous
people (who become some of Utopia's future inhabitants), Vizenor's new nation severs itself from its settler-colonial former ruler by legal means, even as
it enjoys a greater geographical distance from that nation. Moreover, the Heirs
dispense with this legal framework as far as they can, transforming the official
border with Canada into a nonboundary by abjuring passports and, within
Point Assinika itself, instituting practices that contrast with its former ruler's:
"Point Assinika is a natural nation. . . . Humor rules and tricksters heal in our
state, and we have no checkpoints or passports, no parking meters to ruin the
liberty of the day" (126).

This divergence in government points to an aspect of just rearrangement in
the restorative utopia that, though bound up with territorial sovereignty, is
distinguishable from historical redress as such. In Mat Johnson's 2010 novel
Pym, the narrator, Chris Jaynes, is propelled on a quest for the island of
Tsalal—described in Edgar Allan Poe's 1828 *Narrative of Arthur Gordon Pym
of Nantucket* as inhabited by people of "complexion a jet black, with thick and
long woolly hair"—by the discovery that Dirk Peters, a character in the *Narrative* (a "half Indian," in Jaynes's words, with "Negroid traits") was a real person who left behind his own manuscript account of the journey recounted in

Poe's tale.[29] In contemplating the allure of Tsalal, Jaynes reflects, "This is an American thing: to wish longingly for a romanticized ancestral home. This is a black American thing: to wish to be in the majority within a nation you could call your own, to wish for the complete power of that state behind you. It was the story of the maroons and black towns on the frontier, it was the dream of every Harlem pan-Africanist" (30). For many Native Americans, of course, the longing for an ancestral home can hardly be described as romanticizing, and, of course, there are nations in the world where the Black majority holds power. What Jaynes's remark points to, however, is that if maroon communities, Black frontier towns, Telassar, the Black Empire, Point Assinika, and Tsalal read more pointedly as refuges than do most utopias, this is because their sovereignty *in itself* provides their inhabitants a form of justice that they would not, as members of dominated groups, enjoy outside the utopia's boundaries.

This aspect of utopian justice also crucially obtains in utopias that don't take the form of a historically reclaimed homeland. In Sutton Griggs's *Imperium in Imperio* (1899), the capitol of the eponymous secret Black society offers a respite from exposure to anti-Black violence outside its walls; in Charlotte Perkins Gilman's *Herland* (1915), the utopian enclave efficiently undoes the subordination of women, within its borders, by including no male inhabitants.[30] Perhaps not surprisingly, *Imperium* and *Herland* depict yet more frequently and intensely than do Hopkins's, Schuyler's, and Vizenor's fictions the experience of white-supremacist or patriarchal injustice in the nonutopian world. Griggs's characters endure discrimination, segregation, arrest for vagrancy, illegal subordination of Black laborers by white, and attempted lynching, while in Herland, the subjugation of women is represented both in the male explorers' accounts of gender hierarchy in their world (which the Herlanders greet with indignant incredulity) and by inversion, in the form of the humiliations and deprivations to which the explorers are subjected by the Herlanders. In these utopias, the attainment of territorial sovereignty is linked especially strongly to freedom from domination in daily life.

If Herland most closely resembles the Imperium in the sense just mentioned, however, it also shares something important with Telassar and Tsalal as against the other utopias just named—namely, that it is not established by recent revolt against identity-based forms of domination but rather has existed for many years apart from the hierarchies that prevail elsewhere. For two thousand years, Herland has been without men; in Telassar and Tsalal, Black people have lived for centuries or millennia sequestered from the white-controlled world. These utopias thus subsist both within and apart from history, what happens in them perforce counting among the accumulated events of humankind but also standing at a remove from all the transactions and entangled stories by which the rest of the globe has been connected. Jaynes, of *Pym*, notably foregrounds this inside-outside dimension when he muses on the implications of his discovery that Dirk Peters really lived: it means that "Tsalal, the great undiscovered African Diasporan homeland, might still be out there, uncorrupted by Whiteness. That there was a group of our people who did achieve victory over slavery in all its forms, escaping completely from the progression of Westernization and colonization to form a society outside of time and history" (39).

Unlike postcolonial nations in the real world or newly established states such as the Black Empire, then, Tsalal presents justice in the form of a historical as well as a structural alternative to arrangements prevailing elsewhere. To a much higher degree than utopias such as More's, but with some resemblance to Wells's utopian double of our own Earth, Tsalal concretizes a path not taken in the blighted world outside, a counterfactual or optative history. In this, Johnson's unconquered island imparts—as, with various modifications, do the utopias of Hopkins, Griggs, Gilman, Schuyler, and Vizenor—a sense of the world as out of joint that evokes that same spur to indignation in Juvenal and other satirists and utopian writers. In the fictions just considered, however, this sense is immensely sharpened by characters' lived experience of racist, patriarchal, and imperial domination—by a suffusion of the narrative with immediate injustices whose sting may be felt even before the mind casts itself toward larger systems such as those, say, of enclosure in More's moment or of class exploitation in Bellamy's.

This indignation may then be further intensified by a sense that the real-world order of things is yet more manifestly askew, metaphysically speaking, than the economic systems against which Hythlodaeus and Bellamy rail—systems that, however grotesque their deformations of the common good, do not seem to have malice baked in as a premise. "'Tis very unlucky that we didn't pitch on a sound one, when there were so many more of 'em!": Abraham Durbeyfield seems to respond to the news of our blight philosophically, but his words, like his sister's, point to the possibility of an indignation all the more furious because the world on which we've landed seems to have been made miserable against the odds, with a certain ingenuity. Or as Jaynes puts it in the breathtaking final sentences of *Pym*, when he and his shipmate alight at what may or may not be the longed-for homeland: "Whether this was Tsalal or not . . . Garth and I could make no judgments. On the shore all I could discern was a collection of brown people, and this, of course, is a planet on which such are the majority" (322).

Nemesis, Nomos, and Justice

Indignation derives from the Latin *indignārī*, meaning "to regard as unworthy, to be indignant at,"[31] which is in turn affiliated to *dignus*, "appropriate, suitable, worthy," "deserving, worthy, meriting."[32] *Dignus* appears in turn to be related to *decet*, "whose basic transitive meaning," in one scholar's words, "is 'it is due,'" and which "later com[es] to mean 'it is proper.'"[33] Etymologically, then, indignation is rooted in a sense that something is not right, and more narrowly in an intuition of some failure of fairness or reciprocity. Of course, we hardly need etymology to understand that indignation is predicated on a sense of things not standing as they ought to, since where anger, rage, or fury can be imagined absent a feeling of essential wrongness, indignation cannot. That matters aren't as they should be—that benefits and pains aren't going to the proper recipients—is, succinctly, the preoccupation of Juvenal. And it's vividly illustrated, again, in *Bruce's Voyage*, where the narrator's fondness for the world at the earth's center owes much not only to its high civility and equality of condition but also to its devotion to appropriate recompense, as foregrounded by the ingrate's trial.

An etymology no longer credited but that nonetheless remains suggestive connects *dignus* with the ancient Greek *dike* (δίκη), commonly translated into English as "justice."[34] Though philologically insupportable, the link is intuitively plausible because *dike* or *dikaiosune* (δικαιοσύνη) could mean "broadly what is right, as well as more specifically what is justly owed or justly expected."[35] In other words, justice in the sense of *dikaiosune* is itself a giving-due, a point especially brought out in book 5 of the *Nicomachean Ethics*, where Aristotle famously considers *dikaiosune* in two related senses. There is, first, fairness in a contractual sense, the giving of what's due among individuals; there is also a wider distributive justice that speaks to social organization. In Bloch's handy summary:

> Aristotle is the first (and here he is followed by Thomas) to distinguish between communicative and distributive justice. The first . . . is related to contracts . . . the latter form is concerned with the apportionment of social advantages and honors as a function of the worthiness of the recipient. Indeed because (since Pythagoras) justice has been thought without hesitation as proportionality par excellence . . . it is no surprise that we find that *dikaiosyne* in Aristotle is further mathematized in its dual form: Communicative justice works arithmetically, distributive justice works according to a geometrical proportion.[36]

In marking the continuity between contractual fairness and distributive fairness, Aristotle illuminates the close relationship between indignation roused by failures of just relation between individuals (as in the ingratitude to which Bruce is subject in *Bruce's Voyage*) and indignation roused by broader social injustice. In both cases, the problem is a wrongness that takes the form of an imbalance or a disproportion. As Bloch notes, however, the geometrical trumps the arithmetical in Aristotle inasmuch as that antidemocratic philosopher favors a social distribution in which people are given to not equally but in proportion to merit. In book 6 of the *Politics*, Aristotle writes that the (disfavored) "democratic conception of justice is the enjoyment of arithmetical equality, and not the enjoyment of proportionate equality on the basis of desert," while in book 5 of the *Nicomachean Ethics*, he insists that reciprocity in an eye-for-an-eye sense (*antipeponthos*, ἀντιπεπονθός) should not be identified with "the just unqualifiedly, as the Pythagoreans asserted." Rather, "the city stays together by means of proportional reciprocity" because it must be based on "mutual exchange" of unlike things: the house builder must be able to exchange with the shoemaker, the doctor with the farmer.[37]

This effort to legitimate social hierarchy harks back, in turn, to Plato's *Republic*, where *dikaiosune* is a desideratum both for the state and for the individual qua analogue of the state, and where it's shown (upon philosophical investigation) to inhere in a proper distribution of roles and tasks. In book 4, Socrates concludes that justice will prevail in the state where "one man [does] one job, the job he [is] naturally suited for," that "justice is keeping what is properly one's own and doing one's own job." Concomitantly, justice in the individual is a condition in which "the three elements which make up [a person's] inward self"—reason, appetite, and "spirit" or *thumos*—are in tune with each other, "a disciplined and harmonious whole."[38] As Bloch puts it, statecraft is for Plato "the fusing of basic characterological-social circumstances into . . . the harmony of 'justice,'" which is to say that "long before freedom found its novel of an ideal state, Plato's 'Republic' utopianized order. A perfect Spartan order, with people as pedestals, walls, and windows."[39]

We'll return to the matter of utopian structure further on. Here, however, it will be worthwhile for us to probe a little more fully why justice seems to hold a special priority in thinking about ideal social relations—to consider what licenses Aristotle's declaration, at the beginning of the *Politics*, that "justice belongs to the polis; for justice, which is the determination of what is just, is an ordering of the political association."[40] We can do so with the help of three twentieth-century commentators and one eighteenth-century one.

At the beginning of *A Theory of Justice* (1971), John Rawls asserts, with an echo of Aristotle, that "justice is the first virtue of social institutions, as truth is of systems of thought."[41] This may sound categorical in a bad sense, and indeed on quoting this formulation in her own *Residues of Justice* (1996), Wai Chee Dimock argues that for Rawls, justice

is analogous to truth not only because it presides as an absolute ideal but also because it exists as an ontological given. Whether or not it is actually achieved, it will always be imagined as having an objective reality, a reality coincidental with the immanent relations among things and discoverable through a rational process of deliberation. Indeed Rawls sees justice as nothing less than the axiomatic expression of human reason itself.[42]

Dimock positions her own study against this kind of understanding, explaining that her project is to contest "the self-image of justice as a supreme instance of adequation, a 'fitness' at once immanent and without residue, one that perfectly matches burdens and benefits, action and reaction, resolving all conflicting terms into a weighable equivalence" (2). In other words, her effort is to interrogate justice understood as "the reification of commensurability itself," to critique a "dream of objective adequation" that "makes the concept of justice intelligible" not just in the case of retributive and compensatory justice but also "in distributive justice, where we yearn for a benefit equal to the desert" (6). And this "on behalf of the incommensurate . . . what remains unredressed, unrecovered, noncorresponding" (6), the "losses as well as the residues occasioned by the exercise of justice" (7).

One of Dimock's most vivid examples of what exceeds or undoes justice's "dream of objective adequation" appears in her discussion of a passage from Jonathan Edwards. In *The Nature of True Virtue* (1756), Edwards observes that

> there is a beauty in the virtue called *justice*, which consists in the agreement of different things, that have relation to one another, in nature, manner and measure: and therefore is the very same sort of beauty with that uniformity and proportion, which is observable in those external and material things that are esteemed beautiful. There is a natural agreement and adaptedness of things that have relation one to another, and a harmonious corresponding of one thing to another: that he which from his will *does* evil to others, should *receive* evil from the will of others . . . in *proportion* to the evil of his doings. (quoted in Dimock 138)

As Dimock lucidly notes, justice here seems for Edwards "an *aesthetic* phenomenon." And it is

> this formal aesthetics that underlies our language of desert, our insistence on retribution and recompense. . . . Our attraction to justice, from this perspective, is no different from our attraction to the "beauty of squares, and cubes, and regular polygons in the regularity of buildings, and the beautiful figures in a piece of embroidery." It is also no different from those attractions in having no ultimate claim to ethical primacy.

Dimock goes on to note, with admiration, Edwards's subsequent insistence on justice's limitations. Justice, she writes, "is considerably less than a cornerstone" in his ethics, which rather "gestures toward a world in which the language of justice must always contend with the unceasing, ungrammatical language of love" (139). In representing love as a divine excess over justice's mensurations, Edwards thus offers an exceptionally clear instance of how an earlier writer articulates, as Dimock also wishes to, a conception of justice that would be "less immanent, less exhaustive, less evident both in its ethical primacy and its jurisdictional scope" (5) than would be the justice delineated by Rawls and others working within a Kantian tradition.

Three years later, Elaine Scarry would advance a view of justice similar to Edwards's and Dimock's, though she would draw from it a rather different lesson about justice's virtues. In *On Beauty and Being Just* (1999), which was both an intervention of sorts in turn-of-the-century culture wars and a key contribution to what came to be known as "the aesthetic turn" in humanities scholarship, Scarry defends the appreciation of beauty against charges that it interferes with the pursuit of social justice, asserting contrarily, if not always persuasively, that "beauty prepares us for justice" in several interrelated ways.[43] Among these, the way that seems most specific to aesthetic experience pertains to symmetry: "it is the very symmetry of beauty," according to Scarry, "which leads us to, or somehow assists us in discovering, the symmetry that eventually comes into place in the realm of justice" (97). In support of this contention, she turns to Augustine's "conviction that equality is the heart of beauty, that equality is pleasure-bearing, and that . . . equality is the morally highest and best feature of the world" (98, Scarry's phrasing).[44]

Dimock and Scarry appear to agree, then, that aesthetic feeling and the feeling for justice are psychologically entangled or phenomenologically continuous and that what links the two is a basic human affinity for equality, proportion, and symmetry. In Scarry, recognition of this deep connection helps to legitimate the aesthetic as a field of human activity; in Dimock, it supports justice's deserved demotion or circumscription as a social ideal. Both of these analyses, however, have the effect of opening the desire for justice to dismissal as the product of a *merely* aesthetic inclination, even perhaps the emanation of a personal rigidity or the expression of a constitutional finickiness. If an inclination toward symmetry or a liking for commensurability is a preference without any higher or profounder rationale, and if such a preference proves the basis of the impulse toward justice, then it might be that justice not only lacks an "ultimate claim to ethical primacy" but lays no truly ethical claim at all.

Yet we may come to a different view if we take note of a certain key slippage in Edwards's representation of justice. Edwards relates justice's beauty to "the agreement of different things, that have relation to one another, in nature, manner and measure"; asserts that "uniformity and proportion" make this beauty of "the very same sort" visible in beautiful material things; and likens "a natural agreement and adaptedness of things that have relation one to another, and a harmonious corresponding of one thing to another" to what we can recognize as *antipeponthos*, "that he which from his will *does* evil to others, should *receive* evil from the will of others . . . in *proportion* to the evil of his doings." The problem with these assertions is that the "harmonious corresponding" associated with the beautiful is not a matter of quantitative equality only. As Edwards's own phrasing acknowledges, "nature" and "manner" contribute a qualitative dimension to agreement or adaptedness, and as many commentators on beauty over the centuries have observed, it will ordinarily be very hard to specify by means of mathematical relations alone why a certain thing is beautiful. In other words, the aesthetic itself includes an element of mystery, of irreducible excess, that arguably places it in opposition to, not in alignment with, the rigid adequation of *antipeponthos*. Even if we grant (as not every theorist of the aesthetic would) that the sense of beauty always in some way depends on an apprehension of equivalence, proportion, or symmetry, most would agree that it's not subsumable by these kinds of relations.

In truth, if the feeling for beauty bears a likeness to the feeling for justice, this is finally not because both depend on an attachment to symmetry but rather because both are versions of a feeling for *rightness*. A moment's reflection makes clear that when we speak of rightness and wrongness, we take up a vocabulary at which the ethical, the mathematical, the practical, and the aesthetic all converge. A deed can be wrong because it subjects another person to poor treatment; a calculation can be wrong because it yields an incorrect result; a decision can be wrong because it leads to an undesired outcome; a stylistic choice or layout can be wrong because it falls inadequately on the ear or the eye. Yet it might be objected that even this recognition hardly frees justice from the charge of being merely aesthetic. On the contrary, if one holds that conceptual abstractions are always beholden to modes of physical perception for their comprehensibility, then one might go on to assert that our sense of right and wrong in general is but an elaboration of a more basic feeling for equality, proportion, and symmetry as against inequality, disproportion, and asymmetry. From this point of view, moral feeling could be vulnerable to the same charge of lack of "ethical primacy" as justice. Ethics itself would be deprived of the claim to be truly ethical.

What keeps ethics ethical, however, is that it concerns what's right or wrong for and between people. Even if the feelings of rightness or wrongness that subtend an ethical judgment aren't altogether different in quality from feelings of rightness and wrongness pertaining to mathematical calculations, aesthetic success, and practical results, their consequentiality for persons would meaningfully distinguish them. And the same holds for feelings of justice or injustice. Although justice may not be thinkable absent an apprehension of adequation and proportion, its essence lies not in a quantitative relation as such but rather, as already noted, in the giving of people what they're due.

This understanding does, to be sure, lead Aristotle to the necessity of the money form (which, as Dimock aptly notes, even he regards as imperfect[45]) and to a social hierarchy in which the amplest benefits are disbursed to the most deserving. Yet giving people what they're due need not be construed only in terms of merit. Rawls's invention of the "original position" and "veil of ignorance," for example, is predicated on a fundamentally anti-Aristotelian, and really a startlingly radical, conviction that the distribution of native talents is itself unjust. If one imagines persons before they enter existence as equally entitled to the goods of existence, then one would, according to Rawls, discern a fundamental injustice even in the liberal principle of "fair equality of opportunity," which asserts "that those with similar abilities and skills should have similar life chances." A system organized in accordance with this principle would still permit "the distribution of wealth and income to be determined by the natural distribution of abilities and talents," an outcome that "is arbitrary from a moral perspective. There is no more reason to permit the distribution of income and wealth to be settled by the distribution of natural assets than by historical and social fortune" (Rawls 73–74). Rawls works, in other words, with a sense of what's due that seeks to cut through merit, a matter of contingency, to a morally fundamental and thoroughly egalitarian rightness.

Indeed Rawls immediately unpacks his "justice is the first virtue of social institutions, as truth is of systems of thought" as follows:

> A theory however elegant and economical must be rejected or revised if it is untrue; likewise laws and institutions no matter how efficient and well-arranged must be reformed or abolished if they are unjust. Each person possesses an inviolability founded on justice that even the welfare of society as a whole cannot override. For this reason justice denies that the loss of freedom for some is made right by a greater good shared by others. (3–4)

Under this view, a specious commensurability—as, for example, in Plato's and Aristotle's swift passage from adequation to the balancing of differing parts and from the balancing of parts to the functioning of the whole as measure of justice—must be resisted precisely out of care for what each person is due ("possesses an inviolability") in a yet more fundamental sense. Commensurability is certainly essential to Rawls inasmuch as equality, including the radical form of moral equality he proposes, cannot do without equivalence as a basic structure of thought; no more, perhaps, can the idea of what's due purge itself wholly of the quantitative (though further on, we'll encounter briefly another theorist's effort to imagine something like this very divestiture). Nonetheless, Rawls's "inviolability" presses against the reduction of social relations to versions of adequation precisely insofar as it introduces the person-who-must-receive-what-is-due as a kind of ultimacy, a term whose status can't be bargained over and whose rights can't be negotiated away in the name of any formula of proportion.

In her own treatment of the "veil of ignorance," Dimock observes astutely that the problem Rawls tries to solve with it is nothing less than that of the ultimate unfairness we call luck. For Rawls, she remarks, "the ubiquity of luck . . . is a grievous wrong, one that carries with it a silent directive, a demand for rectification. . . . As Rawls himself admits, his theory of justice is very much a theory to combat luck, a theory to 'nullify the accidents of natural endowment and the contingencies of social circumstance'" (106). And this imagined nullification perforce ends up leaving him, as many critics have noted, with "what he himself acknowledges to be a 'thin' theory of the person, one that bears . . . a suspended relation to people as they ordinarily appear and as they are ordinarily perceived, thick with particular traits" (105). Dimock thus elucidates with great clarity the indignation that seems most to propel *A Theory of Justice*. Yet in her reading as a whole, she emphasizes the quixoticness and abstraction of Rawls's position at the expense of the reason why his indignation is so passionate—which is that the arrangement of things by luck is profoundly bad for people. Rawls's theory of the person is certainly "thin" in the sense Dimock describes, but we might say that his commitment to the cause of persons is extremely robust. What stirs his outrage is not luck's offensive contingency per se; such a reaction might indeed invite dismissal as a merely aesthetic irritation. Rather, Rawls is indignant that the poor arrangement of the world hurts those who have been subsumed by it—meaning, of course, every person who has ever lived.

The assumption governing the rest of *A Theory of Justice*, further, is that if there's to be any rectifying of the wrongs that follow from the contingency of talent, this must occur not through acts of a divinity, individual moral conduct, or mere chance but through intelligently designed social institutions. Rawls's inaugural "Justice is the first virtue of social institutions" is thus less an ontological claim than a logical one, almost a tautology. Social institutions are the arrangements that most help determine whether people do or don't receive what's due them, and justice is the perfection of that receiving-due. Similarly, when Aristotle asserts that "justice belongs to the polis; for justice, which is the determination of what is just, is an ordering of the political association," what he captures is a sense that a good society is one in which people receive what they ought to receive (however one construes the particulars of this rightness) thanks to one or another form of arrangement.

What all of this helps us to see is that utopian indignation may hardly be distinguishable from the kind of passion for justice in an expansive sense that animates *A Theory of Justice*. This is so not only because Rawls's proposals can sound extravagantly utopian, in the sense of sweeping and difficult to realize, but also because they point to a correction of wrong arrangement by means of a redesign of the social mechanism. Like the kind of passion for rectification at work in Rawls, utopian indignation holds that arrangements that are bad for people on the largest scale need to be set right, and while it draws some of its specific character from antagonism to bad design as such, it draws much of its affective intensity from the conviction that this design failure is enormously consequential for human beings.[46] We might say that what differentiates utopian indignation from more general rage against unjust social systems is less its nature than where it issues—in certain genres of writing rather than others, in the imagining not just of new institutions and procedures but of life as actually lived in a better world.

Something like the passage from a more basic concern with justice to the plenitude of utopian imagining can, not surprisingly, be discerned in More's *Utopia* itself. At the end of part 1, to take one illustration, Hythlodaeus offers this summary of the superiority of the propertyless society: "Thus I do fully persuade myself that no equal and just distribution of things can be made, nor that perfect wealth shall ever be among men, unless this property be exiled and banished" (45). Hythlodaeus's language here reaffirms how justice requires some apprehension of equivalence yet resists reduction to mere equalizations; for him, the claim of distributive equality as well as the greater interest of the whole ("perfect wealth") demands not the continued use of money and property but their abolition, the happy consequences of which will then be depicted in the description of Utopia in part 2. *Utopia* is much less interested in the inviolability of persons than is *A Theory of Justice*, but as in Rawls, a care for what's proper for each person to have is precisely what annuls the claim of a narrower kind of propriety oriented toward the actually calculable (in this case, the claim of the property relation itself). In More as in Rawls, in other words, justice understood as giving people what's due them is in a sense as antimathematical as it is mathematical. Right distribution may depend on measure but it also stands in tension with mensuration.

The salience for *Utopia* of the classical sense of justice as right allocation is confirmed by a letter added to the second edition of the book in 1517 and still often published alongside More's text.[47] In an invective against lawyers—another eventual staple of the utopian genre—the renowned classicist (and More's fellow humanist) Guillaume Budé remarks that "if you chose to define Justice nowadays, in the way that early writers liked to do, as the power who assigns to each his due, you would . . . find her non-existent in public." [48] A couple of pages later, however, Budé observes that in the excellent state of Utopia, "one might verily suppose that there is a risk of Aratus and the early poets having been mistaken in their opinion, when they made Justice depart from earth. . . . For, if we are to believe Hythloday, she must needs have stayed behind in that island, and not yet made her way to heaven."[49] In naming Utopia the land where Justice abides, Budé captures nicely how the "no-place" of More's imagining responds, with a sort of brilliant literalization, to ancient and contemporary laments about the absence of justice in the world. But Budé also underscores how Utopia emerges from a vision of justice as a righting of the wrongs that fire Hythlodaeus's (and his own) indignation, wrongs that may be succinctly described as failures to realize the principle that people should receive what they're due.

We might pause here to observe that if the work of *Utopia*, and the genre of imaginative writing to which it would give its name, is to conjure a place where Astraea still dwells, this means that utopia concerns itself with social arrangements in two slightly different senses at once. In referring to arrangements, we may be pointing to some state of things, but we may alternatively be pointing to something more instrumental, a means to achieving some state of things. Like some forms of satiric indignation, utopian indignation protests against a condition (arrangements) in which people don't receive what they should; but like many forms of work on behalf of social justice, concrete as well as theoretical, utopian indignation takes issue with institutions, norms, and so on (arrangements) that lead to this unjust condition. Utopian representation, we might say, concerns itself both with allocation and with allocating, though it often blurs the distinction between the two. And if we ask why utopia tends to do so, we can answer that the principal reason is that in its representations, the recipients of allocation—people—and the means by which allocating happens tend to be one and the same.

Something like a parable of this double role of persons—as ends and as means—emerges in the very exchange that begins with Hythlodaeus's just-quoted assertion that "no equal and just distribution of things can be made" where there's still property. To this, More-the-narrator objects that without property there would be no incentive to labor. But Hythlodaeus replies in turn, "if you had been with me in Utopia and had presently seen their fashions and laws . . . you would grant that you never saw people well ordered but only there" (46). In utopias, the equal and just distribution of things to people can't always be differentiated from the way people are ordered, in part because the latter may causally determine the former and in part because the way people are ordered is itself a distribution—a distribution of roles, tasks, and positions. This last point, to which we'll return in chapter 3, is particularly foregrounded by Plato and Aristotle, whose plans for society devote less attention to the way material goods are distributed than to the allocation of places and jobs.

Hythlodaeus's reference to "people well ordered" can certainly read as an ominous anticipation of the surveillance and strict control under which, as it turns out in part 2 of *Utopia*, the Utopians actually live. But it's important to see that the right ordering required by justice and sought out by utopian indignation need not be characterized by hierarchy, structure, or even orderliness. Utopian indignation asserts only, as it were, that whatever arrangements prevail at present are not the ones that must prevail if people are to be given their due. In the propertyless utopia of *News from Nowhere*, people do more or less as they like, in stark contrast to the restrictions that prevail in More's Utopia; in the propertyless utopia of Ursula Le Guin's *Dispossessed* (1974), much in life is highly organized, yet the form of (non)government is explicitly an anarchy. It's even possible to reject all plans for utopian ordering in the name of utopia, as when Fredric Jameson, in *The Seeds of Time* (1994), notes that

> the ideals of Utopian living involve the imagination in a contradictory project, since they all presumably aim at illustrating and exercizing that much-abused concept of freedom that, virtually by definition and in its very structure, cannot be defined in advance, let alone exemplified: if you know already what your longed-for exercise in a not-yet-existent freedom looks like, then the suspicion arises that it may not really express freedom after all but only repetition; while the fear of projection, of sullying an open future with our own deformed and repressed social habit in the present, is a perpetual threat to the indulgence of fantasies of the future collectivity.[50]

Jameson will then variously develop this point in his later *Archaeologies of the Future* (2005). If "our imaginations are hostages to our own mode of production," then "at best Utopia can serve the negative purpose of making us more aware of our mental and ideological imprisonment," meaning in turn that "the best Utopias are those that fail the most comprehensively."[51] And indeed one of the forms of negation played out within utopian texts themselves is the "'unknowability thesis' . . . whereby so radically different a society cannot even be imagined" (142). The "Utopian form itself," Jameson argues, "is the answer to the universal ideological conviction that no alternative is possible, that there is no alternative to the system. But it asserts this by forcing us to think the break itself, and not by offering a more traditional picture of what things would be like after the break" (232). Strangely enough, then, our "increasing inability to imagine a different future enhances rather than diminishes the appeal and also the function of Utopia" (232).

In *Picture Imperfect: Utopian Thought for an Anti-utopian Age*, published the same year as *Archaeologies*, Russell Jacoby similarly declares that at the present time, in "an image-obsessed society such as our own," what he calls "blue print" utopias may have exhausted their relevance, which is to say that "iconoclastic" utopias are to be preferred. Creators of the blueprint kind "map out the future in inches and minutes. From the eating arrangements to the subjects of conversation the blueprinters . . . give precise instructions." But "the day for those overplanned castles may be over," and so Jacoby turns "instead to the

iconoclastic utopians, those who dreamt of a superior society but who de-
clined to give its precise measurements. In the original sense and for the original reasons, they were iconoclasts; they were protesters and breakers of images." For Jacoby, as we noted in the introduction to this study, the "classic
work in this genre" is *The Spirit of Utopia* (1918), wherein Bloch "offers no concrete details about the future. He invokes a utopian spirit purely by his reflections on music, poetry, and literature."[52] Although we may wonder, as we did
in the introduction, whether the imagining of alternatives wouldn't cease to be
meaningfully utopian without at least the shadow of the blueprint, Jameson's
and Jacoby's preference for the iconoclastic does highlight an important point:
that yet more fundamental to utopian thinking than an idea of how things
might be better arranged is a sense that wrongness characterizes the ordering
of the world as it is. We might say that what differentiates iconoclastic utopianism from satire is not that the former has a better design in mind (for it
doesn't), but rather its conviction that human beings have the *capacity* to organize themselves in a way that would be superior to the way of here and now.

Ancient Greek does not have a standard term to express indignation at injustice for which *dike* serves as a root. But it does possess a word that fulfills
something like this function, a word that over the centuries developed a complex relation with *dike*. This word is *nemesis* (νέμεσις), often assumed to be
related to *nomos* (νόμος). In book 1 of the *Politics*, immediately after he makes
his well-known claim that the person "who is isolated—who is unable to share
in the benefits of political association, or has no need to share because he is
already self-sufficient—is no part of the polis, and must therefore be either a
beast or a god," Aristotle adds that "man, when perfected, is the best of animals; but if he be isolated from law [*nomos*] and justice [*dike*] he is the worst
of all."[53] For Aristotle, humans' lack of self-sufficiency underwrites community, which elevates the human being—but only where the person is in communion with *dike* and *nomos*.[54]

The much-studied word *nomos* does not only mean law, however. Ernest
Barker, whose mid-twentieth-century translation of the *Politics* has just been
quoted, describes *nomos* as "close to *dike*, which . . . is a showing or indication
of the right and straight thing to do; and conversely *dike* (defined by Aristotle
as 'an ordering of the political association') is close to the *nomos* which assigns
and apportions places and bounds."[55] In Helmuth Berking's summary:

> The Greeks used the concept *nomos* to characterize the internal structure
> and legal order of the polis. *Nomos* refers to *nemein* ("to distribute"), an
> activity originally related to the cutting up and apportionment of roast meat
> which was later extended to other spheres of distribution. *Nomos*, accord-
> ing to [Gerhard] Baudy's etymological analysis, initially meant nothing
> more than distribution of meat, a ritual codification of a first form of

distributive justice. The main authority here is Hesiod. In the *Theogony*, a just distributive order takes shape in the goddess Eunomia, daughter of Themis and sister of Dike, Eirene and the Moirai. Dys[n]o[m]ia—who stands for unjust distribution—is the daughter of Eris, the goddess of discord and sister of the goddess of retribution, Nemesis.[56]

Citing the same view that *nomos* derives from *nemein* and is associated with the dividing of meat, Richard Seaford proposes that the "beginning of civilisation is associated with the ordered distribution of food. . . . Full citizenship and entitlement to participation in the sacrificial meal seem to be one and the same. Even the division of urban space may use the terminology of dividing up the animal."[57] Meanwhile, summarizing parts of Emmanuel Laroche's magisterial 1949 *Histoire de la Racine "nem-" en Grec Ancien*, Ronald Bogue focuses on another aspect of *nomos*, an "archaic sense . . . coming from the usages associated with pasturage and nomads." In this early usage, according to Laroche, the term "in no way indicates a partitioning of land," though "after the reforms of Solon, *nomos* comes to mean 'assigned plot of land.'"[58]

The most exhaustive study of the term, however, is a 1969 analysis of all occurrences of *nomos* "from the beginning of Greek writing to the end of the fifth century," in which Martin Ostwald elucidates thirteen distinct, though overlapping, senses it can carry. To take a few examples: *nomos* may refer to a way of life or a given set of mores; to norms having universal rather than local validity; to a widespread belief about what's proper; to rules pertaining to religious observance; to political principles underlying a way of governing; or to something approaching positive law. (A major argument of Ostwald's study is that by the end of the fifth century BCE, the term was "firmly entrenched as the authoritative term for 'statute' in Athens.") There's a common thread through all these meanings, however: *nomos* always "signifies an 'order' and implies that this order is, or ought to be, generally regarded as valid and binding by the members of the group in which it prevails."[59]

Ostwald examines as well the trajectory of a word closely related to *nomos* that's also clearly relevant to the imagining of utopia: *eunomia* (εὐνομία), which either describes "a quality of personal behaviour, in which sense it reflects the νόμος which connotes the normal and proper conduct of an individual, or . . . refers to the condition of a well-ordered society, a condition which implies not only the prevalence of good laws and good government within the state, but also the good functioning of the social organism as a whole." Of particular note here is Solon's use of *eunomia* to refer to "the condition of the society which he hopes to create by his reforms" in the poem "Our City," sometimes called "Eunomiē" by later scholars. Here, Solon tells of Dike "bid[ing] her time as she silently watches the citizens' actions past and present" and noting "how their depravity results in faction, war, and slavery"; he then goes on to describe "his impending reforms, by which he hopes to aid Dike to restore to Athens that εὐνομίη which will guarantee for the city permanence and the continued protection of Zeus and Athene."[60]

Though the meanings of *nomos* and *eunomia* are various, then, the terms consistently suggest both an ordering principle and a state of what is apposite. Associated with the idea of appropriate distribution, they're clearly connected to *dike* in both its communicative and its distributive senses. And although the rightness to which they point is often a rightness or norm existing in the present, they may also gesture to a future condition, a return to rightness after a period in which bad arrangements prevail.[61]

Since the middle of the twentieth century, *nomos* has been adapted to various purposes by historians, scholars of literature, and theorists of law and politics, including Martin Heidegger ("Letter on Humanism," 1947); Carl Schmitt (*The Nomos of the Earth*, 1950); Peter Berger (*The Sacred Canopy*, 1963); Gilles Deleuze (*Difference and Repetition*, 1968 and, with Félix Guattari, *Rhizome*, revised as *A Thousand Plateaus*, 1976); Michael Oakeshott (*On Human Conduct*, 1975); Robert Cover ("Nomos and Narrative," 1983); Jacques Derrida (*Given Time*, 1991); and Giorgio Agamben (*Homo Sacer*, 1995).[62] Deployments of *nomos* in all of these texts bear in one way or another on our concerns in this chapter, but to do justice to their resonances we would need the space of another book entirely. Two more recent episodes in the adventures of *nomos*, however, do warrant brief exposition here, for their way of speaking to the matter of utopian indignation. One comes from the work of Jacques Rancière, the other from a meditation by Jean-Luc Nancy.

Though Rancière doesn't always invoke the term explicitly, *nomos* is central to his body of thought, his pivotal concepts of the *partage du sensible* ("partition of the sensible" or "distribution of the sensible") and of politics as democratic disruption being unthinkable without the springboard of *nomos* as a feature of Greek political thought. For Rancière, the

> partition of the sensible is the dividing-up of the world [*de monde*] and of people [*du monde*], the *nemeïn* upon which the *nomoi* of the community are founded. This partition should be understood in the double sense of the word: on the one hand, as that which separates and excludes; on the other, as that which allows participation. . . . Politics . . . is the instituting of a dispute over the distribution of the sensible, over the *nemeïn* that founds every *nomos* of the community.[63]

We'll return to Rancière's ideas at length in chapter 3. Here, we need only note that inasmuch as the distribution of roles and rewards promoted by Plato and Aristotle is the implicit backdrop for his explorations in political philosophy, Rancière more than any of the other theorists just listed trains attention on the idea of *nomos* as the framework or condition that, in determining how things are allocated to people, also determines how people are positioned.

Given this focus, it's not surprising that for Rancière, utopia is to be understood both as an idea that destabilizes current configurations and arrangements (therein aligning with the "dispute" engendered by politics) *and* as a name for an achieved state that would be beyond disruption, a kind of terminal condition of repression. Utopia is "the unacceptable, a no-place, the extreme point of a polemical reconfiguration of the sensible, which breaks down the categories that define what is considered to be obvious." But it is also "the configuration of a proper place, a non-polemical distribution of the sensible universe where what one sees, what one says, and what one makes or does are rigorously adapted to one another."[64]

Nomos isn't nearly as prominent a term in Nancy. But it does receive a noteworthy mention in "Cosmos Basileus," which was first published in English as a part of *Being Singular Plural* in 1996 and republished in 2002's *The Creation of the World; or, Globalization*. For Nancy in this text, *nomos* means "the distribution, the repartition, and the attribution of the parts. Territorial place, nourishment, a delimitation of right and duties: to each and each time as appropriate." Yet Nancy goes on to remark that if *nomos* is thus tightly associated with justice, the "determination of appropriateness—the law of the law, absolute justice—is nowhere but in the sharing itself in the exceptional singularity of each, of each case, according to this sharing," which is to say that absolute justice would be "the return to each existent its due according to its unique creation, singular in its coexistence with all other creations."[65]

In so writing, we might say, Nancy moves the idea of justice in general toward the classical (indeed Aristotelian) notion of *epieikeia*, or equity—justice applied to the particular case even in contravention of some general rule. More to the point, however, Nancy here adumbrates a version of justice that reads as something like the antithesis of the view of justice as adequation that Dimock critiques. As Nancy paints it, justice would be a giving of what's due to every particular; but since no two particulars are due the same thing, justice would be a distribution in which what's given in one case is never precisely equal to what's given in any other case. For this reason, justice is a kind of impossible entreaty, "always also—and perhaps first—the demand for justice: the complaint and protestation against injustice, the call that cries out for justice, and the breath that exhausts itself for it."[66] In positing a radical incommensurability at the heart of true justice, Nancy offers a version of justice that would stand as a "'fitness' at once immanent and without residue," in Dimock's terms, and yet would not be "a supreme instance of adequation" that resolves "all conflicting terms into a weighable equivalence"—even as he suggests that indignation against injustice may be justice itself.[67]

Which brings us to *nemesis*, a term whose long career has been no less strange than that of *nomos*. *Nemesis* is itself often assigned an early meaning of "allotment" or "apportionment" and is, as Michael Hornum notes at the outset of a book-length study of *nemesis* and the Roman state, "related to the Greek root νέμω [*nemo*], meaning to allot or distribute."[68] Many commentators (including Rancière, as we saw above) have exploited the possibility, advocated by Laroche, that *nemo* is related to *nomos*. In Homer, as Hornum notes, *nemesis* conveys "the idea of moral blame or indignation" and "is used variously as an attribute of gods with regard to the divine/human relationship, and of men with regard to interhuman affairs" (6). Or as Bernard Williams has it, "The reaction in Homer to someone who has done something that shame should have prevented is *nemesis*, a reaction that can be understood, according to the context, as ranging from shock, contempt, and malice to righteous rage and indignation."[69] Thus, to take three Homeric examples: in the *Iliad*, the Trojan elders, contemplating Helen, murmur, "Surely there is no blame [νέμεσις] on Trojans and strong-greaved Achaians / if for long time they suffer hardship for a woman like this one," while in *The Odyssey*, Telemachus declares that if he should send Penelope away, "There'll be righteous anger [νέμεσις] / for me from men" and Zeus is described as "the god of strangers, who is the one most outraged [νεμεσσᾶται] at evil deeds."[70] Meanwhile, Homer contains ten uses of the verb *nemein*, "to distribute," most of which refer to food and drink[71] and one of which notes that "Olympian Zeus himself allots [νέμει] to men good fortune / to good and bad, to each as he wishes."[72] In fifth-century Greek tragedy (Aeschylus, Sophocles, Euripides), Nemesis personified has "the task of punishing human hubris and improper actions toward the dead" (Hornum 9); in Plato, "Nemesis, messenger of Dike, punishes frivolous words directed towards one's parents, and in Aristotle . . . Righteous Indignation is specifically identified as a virtue and contrasted with its 'counterfeit,' Envy" (Hornum 9).

Many concepts were venerated as deities in Greek antiquity—especially in local cults of the fourth century and the Hellenistic period—but Nemesis enjoyed a particularly strong tradition of worship, perhaps because as a deity she was associated with potential ill fortune, with forces in need of propitiation. In "the most prosperous period of the Athenian empire" (late fifth century BCE), as Jennifer Larson notes, "Nemesis was one of the Attic deities selected to receive a lavish new peripteral temple." But there were also cults of Nemesis in the Archaic period (ending 480 BCE), the "Attic cult of Nemesis" furnishing, according to Larson, "a rare early example of full-blown worship paid to a personification."[73] Hornum observes that one can detect in Nemesis "traces of a less rational, and probably older, concept of deity and its relationship with man. Nemesis recurs in the literary sources . . . as an expression of divine envy at any good received by man," although Plato and Aristotle make "a conscious attempt to rid Greek religious thought of such a conception of the divine" (9).

While Hornum notes that "no personification appears to be involved" (6) in references to *nemesis* in Homer, Nemesis is distinctly personified in Homer's rough coeval Hesiod. We've already seen that in the *Theogony*, Nemesis is the aunt of Dysnomia, the negative counterpart to Eunomia; in the *Works and Days*—whose fantasia of the prior conditions of the world, beginning with the more perfect ages of silver and gold, serves as an important intertext for later utopias—Nemesis is the divinity who, along with Aidos (Shame) leaves the earth in the iron age: "Self-respect and upright Indignation [*Aidos* and *Nemesis*, Αἰδὼς καὶ Νέμεσις] will go on their way to Olympus, / Quitting the wide-pathed earth and concealing their beautiful forms in / Mantles of white, preferring the company of the immortals, / Wholly abandoning mankind, leaving them sorrow and grievous / Pain for the human condition, till there's no ward against evil."[74] Hornum adds that Nemesis is "explicitly connected with Dike for the first time" in Plato; that this connection is "found again in the Hellenistic . . . and early Roman Imperial periods"; and that in the later Imperial period, where this association of Nemesis with justice persists, "her punishment of those who exceed the proper is seen as extending specifically into the realm of the law" (87–88).

References to Nemesis in English-language writing have tended to favor the personification, and especially the figure of retribution or divine envy, over the abstraction. The first use of Nemesis cited in the *Oxford English Dictionary* (*OED*) comes from a translation of Erasmus's *Apothegms*, where Nicholas Udall gives "Nemesis (ye Goddesse of takyng vengeaunce on suche as are proude & disdeignefull in tyme of their prosperite)"—thus very distantly connecting this figure of requital to the crimes of the rich that concern More's Hythlodaeus. In a later *OED* citation, from Henry Fielding's *Tom Jones*, Nemesis appears more simply as a deity who "was thought" by the ancients "to look with an invidious Eye on human Felicity." By the twentieth century, "nemesis" could come to serve, especially in North American English, as (in the *OED*'s words) "a persistent tormentor; a long-standing rival, an arch-enemy." The tenacity indicated here carries a whiff of the old notion of appropriateness inasmuch as one's nemesis is an enemy specially fitted or attuned to one, an opponent not wholly contingent or arbitrary. This meaning therefore abuts on one more listed in the *OED*, the "unavoidable consequence *of* . . . a specified activity or behaviour; an inevitable penalty or price."[75] And thus although most English speakers today would be surprised to learn that *nemesis* was for the Greeks a feeling or expression of indignation at what's not right or proper,[76] even contemporary usage associates it with the restoration of what ought to be, a settling of unfinished business that amounts to a setting to rights.

We need to be careful, of course, about what these ancient and modern significations can actually mean for our analysis. Whatever the mystique imparted to scholarship by etymologies and observations of continuity in usage, these may in many applications be of limited factual or interpretive value, especially where they're alleged to extend across millennia. It may not be the case that *nemein* as allocation, let alone as distribution of meat, was tied as a matter of actual speech forms to the developed concept of *nomos* in ancient Greek,[77] and even if it was, it would be impossible, in many cases, to establish this relation's bearing on recent writing around ideas of apportionment, retribution, justice, and so on. The claim here is not, then, that a primal sense of *nemesis* as related to *nomos* is embedded in every utopian vision, let alone that there resides deep in the human brain or in some phantasmatic Mind of Literature a feeling for *nemesis and nomos* as the ancient Greeks understood those terms. The claim is rather that attunement to *nomos, nemesis,* and *dike* enriches our examination of utopian indignation for at least three interrelated reasons.

First, it's clear that Thomas More was indebted to classical theories of justice in the well-ordered state, including those of Plato and Aristotle, and was well aware, too, of the myth of Astraea and Nemesis departing the earth. Given the exceptional power of *Utopia* as a founding text of utopian writing—the visibility of its effects on later works, the durability of its influence—this means that the relevance of *dike, nomos,* and *nemesis* to the genre is discernible in intertextual relations, without need of appeal to persistent, deep-buried structures of thought. Second, the range of thinkers in the past three quarters of a century or so who have been taken either by the specific proposition that *nomos* relates to *nemein* or by the capacity of *nomos* to point to distribution across some total field affirms that there is, in the speculative intellectual life of our own time, a continuing interest in the relation between (on the one hand) a set of concepts that includes law, order, what's proper, what prevails, and what ought to be and (on the other) a set of ideas pertaining to the arrangement of persons and the allocation of things. Eschewing *nomos, nemesis,* and *dike* would mean counterproductively severing our examination of utopia from important ways these terms have been used to address questions of existential being (Heidegger), the geopolitical order (Schmitt), socialization and secularism (Berger), the configurations of capitalism (Deleuze and Guattari), the rule of law (Oakeshott), communal norms (Cover), the work of the gift (Derrida), biopolitics (Agamben), the nature of the political (Rancière), and world-making (Nancy).

The most important reason why *nemesis* assists us in our consideration of utopian indignation, however, is simply that it affirms that it was possible for at least *one* culture—or, less pompously and problematically, one group of ancient writers—to give a name to the feeling of indignation not at one's own mistreatment but at something wrong in the order of things. *Nemesis* gets at the heart of such indignation better than the word *indignation* itself does, we might say, both because it foregrounds antipathy to what's not fitting or apposite (which for speakers of English is buried in the *dignus* in the middle of *indignation*) and because it foregrounds how a conviction of wrongness in a particular case will have reference to some pattern, context, totality, or system. When we add to this the explicit linking of *nemesis* and *nomos* with *dike* and the legend of Astraea in Greek texts, we can recognize how *nemesis* stands at the convergence of quite a number of features of utopian thinking and writing. We can see, that is, how the vocation of utopian indignation is the vocation of *nemesis*, where *nemesis* decries the absence of the *nomos* that would be *dike*—a calling to set things right where they've been wrong.[78]

Invention and Counterindignation

These considerations invite us to reexamine Jameson's elucidation of a peculiar tension or incongruity in utopian writing. In chapter 4 of *Archaeologies of the Future*, he notes that when we read the likes of More, Rousseau, Fourier, Owen, and Chernyshevsky, "we confront a truly ferocious indictment of contemporary society, violent and oppressive, riddled with corruption and injustice, hierarchical as well in its reproduction of class privilege and inequality," but that we may also find these writers' "'savage indignation' . . . trivialized by our simultaneous insistence on the eccentricities of the Utopian inventors, and their delight in the cloud-cuckoo-lands in which they indulge themselves" (42). Wondering whether we can "reconcile these seemingly incompatible perspectives," Jameson proposes (in a passage quoted in the introduction to this study) that we need to acknowledge that "not only political passion . . . is involved here"—that authors of utopian fictions are "not exclusively driven by indignation at social injustice or compassion for the poor and the oppressed" (42) but have also been

> intellectuals, with a supplementary taste for systems . . . , for maps . . . , and for schemes of all kinds . . . , know-it-alls willing tirelessly to explain to anyone who would listen the solution to all those problems; tinkerers, blackening reams of paper writing and rewriting their projects and their propaganda pamphlets, drawing up endless seating charts and plans and urban reconstructions: in short, obsessives and maniacs, even where they seemed to be no more than public figures with a literary hobby (like More) or men-about-town with a wide curiosity (like the young Saint-Simon) or indeed Science Fiction writers with a sideline. (43)

Jameson then concludes that "it is impossible to reconcile our two initial antithetical characterizations," that the "only way of dealing with this contradiction is to think both perspectives together simultaneously" (43).

But are the indignation and the obsessive tinkering in fact impossible to reconcile? Is Jameson too hasty in accepting a separation between utopian visionaries' outrage at injustice and their urge to rectify what we might call design problems? Our explorations in this chapter suggest, of course, that he is. For they indicate that both impulses derive from a conviction of inappositeness in social arrangements, of an unrightness whose correction would permit members of society to receive justice in the sense of what's due them. Further on, Jameson will suggest that, in contrast to the grand schemes that form the backbone and main interest of utopian writing, the eccentric minor inventions with which utopia is littered may be worthy of the kind of "aesthetic admiration" (53) Proust's Marcel feels for the ultrafine work on the inside of some of Madame Swann's garments—"a thousand details of execution," in Proust's words, "which had had every chance of remaining unobserved" (quoted at 54). As we've just seen, however, aesthetic admiration is pertinent to the grand schemes themselves inasmuch as these are motivated by a concern with right distribution and with rightness and wrongness more generally. Adopting a somewhat different vocabulary, we might say that the eccentric elements Jameson spotlights, far from standing irremediably in tension with righteous anger at injustice, bring out especially clearly how utopian indignation is a designer's or an engineer's, if not a indeed a tinkerer's, fury.

Jameson does suggest that the pleasure of the designer may be at the heart of the utopian enterprise. "The Utopian calling," he observes in an earlier chapter of *Archaeologies*,

> seems to have some kinship with that of the inventor in modern times, and to bring to bear some necessary combination of the identification of a problem to be solved and the inventive ingenuity with which a series of solutions are proposed and tested. There is here some affinity with children's games. . . . There is also the delight in construction to be taken into account. (11)

A little further on, Jameson reiterates that "the Utopian operation" must be grasped "in terms of home mechanics, inventions and hobbies" and avers that Utopia is "by definition an amateur activity in which personal opinions take the place of mechanical contraptions and the mind takes its satisfaction in the sheer operation of putting together new models of this or that perfect society" (35).

From a certain point of view, this depiction is hard to quarrel with. Joy in clever contrivances is obviously integral to utopian writing from Plato onward, and we can agree that Jameson gets at something important in characterizing utopian discourse as non- or antiprofessional. It must be added, however, that in so doing he temporarily brackets all those utopias conceived by active political agents—the Bolsheviks, for example—with an eye to near-term implementation in the real world. And it's clear, too, that in so vividly calling up the image of the hobbyist at home, he suppresses an element of grandeur in utopias' self-positioning that forms a crucial link between individual devices and the vastness of total social reorganization, between leisure-time puzzle-solving and the gravity of *nomos*.

Both Jameson's unimpeachable arguments and his more doubtful ones, then, illuminate the utopian passion for rearrangement. And to get a still better sense of this passion's implications, it will be helpful for us to examine a few more of the claims he makes as he develops the theme of invention and eccentricity over the course of his chapter. We can begin with the proposal, which follows his conclusion that it will be "impossible to reconcile our two initial antithetical characterizations," that we take a fresh tack "by recalling Coleridge's distinction between Imagination and Fancy" (44). In the *Biographia Literaria*, Coleridge had famously described Imagination as "the prime agent of all human perception" (primary Imagination) as well as a vital power that "dissolves, diffuses, dissipates, in order to re-create; or . . . struggles to idealize and to unify" (secondary Imagination), while construing Fancy as a "a mode of memory" that "has no other counters to play with, but fixities and definites" and "must receive all its materials ready made from the law of association" (quoted in Jameson 44). Imagination, in other words, is originary and synthetic, whereas Fancy at best rearranges elements that come to it preformed; as Jameson says, Imagination appears as "the noble term" while "Fancy or secondary elaboration" seems "a mere decorative afterthought" (45). Linking Coleridge to Freud on dreams, Jameson further affiliates Imagination with a wish fulfillment that "has somehow been universalized and made interesting, indeed often gripping and insistent, for other people" and with what the Greeks called knowledge, while associating Fancy with an "individual 'egoistic' type" of wish fulfillment and with "sheer opinion," or what Plato called *doxa* (46).

Jameson then maps this set of binaries onto the aforementioned division between utopian elements. He aligns imagination, knowledge, and objective significance with the large schemes and principles that maintain readerly interest in a given utopia, while Fancy, *doxa*, and subjective self-indulgence are placed on the side of those eccentric inventions that seem tossed into a utopian text merely because the author couldn't resist an additional display of ingenuity. Finally, Jameson proposes that we might be able

to register Utopian opinion or doxa by our own readerly reactions, by the barely perceptible movements of irritation or annoyance that are aroused by this or that detail of the Utopian scheme, by momentary withdrawals of credibility and trust, by punctual exasperation that can only too easily be turned against the writer in the form of contempt or amusement. Paradoxically, these are not the reactions one brings to the principal proposals and as it were the very scaffolding of the Utopian plan itself. . . . It is rather in the detail, the implementation and decoration or embellishment, of the scheme that we are sometimes drawn up short. (49)

As one example of such an eccentric detail, Jameson calls up the liturgical lighting scheme described by Hythlodaeus in More's *Utopia*:

> The temples are all rather dark. This feature is due not to an ignorance of architecture but to the deliberate intention of the priests. They think that excessive light makes the thoughts wander, whereas scantier and uncertain light concentrates the mind and conduces to devotion. (quoted at 49)

This detail "may startle us," Jameson writes, "owing to the seemingly gratuitous character of the choice of feature and the explanation given it" (49). He then draws a second example from *Walden Two*, the 1948 novel in which B. F. Skinner imagines a community perfected through the techniques of behavioral psychology. At the moment in question, Frazier—the creator of Walden Two, here giving some visitors a guided tour—speaks of one of its handy inventions, much to the irritation of the skeptic in the visiting party, a philosophy professor named Augustine Castle:

> In spite of Castle's obvious impatience with the details of a domestic technology, Frazier talked at length about the trays. One of their innumerable advantages was the transparency, which saved two operations in the kitchen because the tray could be seen to be clean on both sides at once. . . . "The main advantage of the tray," [Frazier] went on, "is the enormous saving in labor." (quoted in Jameson 50–51)

Jameson speculates that the inefficiency of opaque trays "must have caught Skinner's attention . . . during luncheon lines and stray moments of attention to the dining-room staff." But where Skinner was evidently proud enough of his solution to insert it into his utopia, his readers may "feel some annoyance with this self-indulgent intrusion of Skinner-Frazier's pride into more serious matters"— an annoyance then inscribed in the text via Castle, against whom Skinner-Frazier may "assert the full Utopian appropriateness of just such details" (51).

To Jameson's two examples, we can add any of countless other local inventions popping up in utopias over the centuries, from the "sound-houses," "perfume-houses," and "engine-houses" in Francis Bacon's *New Atlantis* to the compostable party clothes in Marge Piercy's *Woman on the Edge of Time*; from the boat-propelling wind engines in Margaret Cavendish's *Blazing World* to the rain-free passageways or coverable sidewalks proposed by Fourier, Bellamy, and others; from the automatic floor-scrubbers and elastic glass of Mary E. Bradley Lane's *Mizora* to the termite-proofing resins and hand-cranked fans in Norman Rush's *Mating*.[79] From Skinner alone, we might adduce the "portable electric fence" for sheep, the spill-preventing jacket for carrying glasses of tea, and the shared buildings in which the members of Walden Two reside, which offer "a great saving of time and money" over individual structures as well as that protection from inclement weather so dear to Fourier and company.[80] Yet contra Jameson's assessment of such inventions, we can notice that these have effects beyond exhibiting the writer's low-level ingenuity and arousing readerly impatience.

For one thing, they reinforce, as metaphor or synecdoche, the basic point that the nonutopian world is badly designed. For some readers in some contexts, certainly, these gadgets may undermine the credibility of the utopian visionary, but in others they seem positioned to sell utopia by exploiting readerly irritation with inefficiencies in the world at hand. This certainly seems to be a hope of Bellamy, whose Boston of the year 2000 is, among other things, a consumer's dream, and of Skinner, whose Walden Two promises a sort of cross between bright college years' dorm-life bonhomie and the higher material comforts of what we would now call a gated community. Further, and perhaps more crucially, such small improvements tend to fortify the premise that their utopian creators are intelligent and happy in a well-grounded way— not idle dreamers but possessors of practical good sense who are able to invent (and then to employ as a matter of course) devices that make daily life function more smoothly and palatably.

This second virtue of clever inventions will be especially significant where the depicted utopians fall into a category of persons that popular opinion of the age might be slow to credit with technical or pragmatic shrewdness. In early utopias, this would mean inhabitants of places remote from enlightened Europe, which is to say that while More's ideal society gains much from being placed far over the seas, it would also court dismissal as backward and irredeemably other if its inhabitants seemed uninterested in everything Europeans would consider of practical importance. Even if a given reader finds the dark temples silly, in other words, the Utopians' attention to environmental spurs to devotion shows them to be attentive to material reality, *not* off in cloud-cuckoo-land, just as their famous use of gold for chamber pots shows them to be ingeniously ahead of their European counterparts in figuring out how greed might be eradicated. We may locate an extreme, or perhaps an allegory, of invention's diminution of alienness in Bacon's *New Atlantis*, where strangeness in the Bensalemites' rituals and apparel is more than balanced by their moral wisdom and the modernness of their scientific academy. We might similarly locate the parodic antithesis to utopian mundane pragmatism in book 3 of *Gulliver's Travels*, where the cloud-inhabiting Laputans' obsession with music and mathematics leaves them painfully ill equipped for the tasks of daily life.

In later utopias, the inhabitants' practical savvy can make the case for the intelligence and wisdom of categories of people less remote from the presumptive nonutopian reader but subjected to forms of domination and dismissal at home, as it were. This point is illustrated nowhere more resplendently than in

Gilman's *Herland* and nowhere more archly than in Schuyler's *Black Empire*. In Gilman's rendering of an ideal society populated entirely by women, the excellence not only of the Herlanders' social arrangements but also of their more mundane contrivances is clearly designed to substantiate the intellectual power and practical creativity of women in general (as are the similar achievements found in Lane's earlier all-female utopia of Mizora). Terry, the skeptic who plays in *Herland* a role similar to that of Castle in *Walden Two*, is "incredulous, even contemptuous" when told that women have managed to build a brilliant society in the absence of men, insisting that we "all know women can't organize—that they scrap like anything—are frightfully jealous," that they "cannot cooperate—it's against nature."[81] But the other male visitors, Van and Jeff, repeatedly remark the justness of the Herlanders' social arrangements as well as the "action of practical intelligence" (74) that leads to numerous enhancements of material existence.

Indeed we learn that having observed, over the centuries, "the value of certain improvements," the Herlanders "took the greatest pains to develop two kinds of minds—the critic and the inventor" (77). The results are everywhere to behold. Their clothing, described on several occasions, is "mighty sensible" compared to American garments for either sex (28); their furniture is "solid, strong, simple in structure, and comfortable in use—also, incidentally, beautiful" (29); their language is "as scientific as Esparanto [*sic*] yet [bears] all the marks of an old and rich civilization (33); their roads, "sloped slightly to shed rain, with every curve and grade as perfect as if it were Europe's best" (20), are "perfect . . . , as dustless as a swept floor" (44). And the country as a whole is "as neat as a Dutch kitchen" (55).

In discussing Skinner's tray, Jameson notes the centrality of kitchens and dining rooms in utopias "from More to Bellamy and down to our own time" and observes that in utopia, the idea of communal cooking and dining allegorizes, even as it helps to bring about, gender equality (52–53). We might say, then, that in having her narrator Van compare Herland to a Dutch kitchen (or its civilization to "a pleasant family in an old established, perfectly run country place" [100]), Gilman is not only touting the pragmatic efficacy of the Herlanders' imagination but also deploying, in an unprecedented way, the allegory Jameson brings into view. In Herland, gender equality (or female superiority) is coextensive with the nation, is indeed the very core of the utopian *nomos*.

Gilman's depiction of right social arrangement as skillful domestic management—of perfect *oikonomia* as the means to perfected *nomos*—also highlights, once again, the connection between indignation against injustice and the goal of right ordering. *Herland* as a whole clearly emerged from concrete outrage, on Gilman's part, at bad arrangements—at the disenfranchisement of half of humankind and, more particularly, at a socioeconomic configuration conducive neither to justice nor to the advancement of civilization. In *Women and*

Economics (1898), she wields the clear-eyed perspective of the (feminist) sociologist against artists' and naturalists' sentimental extolling of the "lovely relation" under which women are dependent upon (and thus enslaved by) men[82]; in *Herland*, she opposes this relation with an imagined place whose quite different norms are no less fervently praised by those who live them. The women of Herland, that is, seem consciously devoted to their *nomos* to a degree beyond that of most utopians in other fictions. Although they have no direct experience of inferior systems, they take exceptional pride in their efficiency, their fellow feeling, and their privileging of motherhood.

This permeating sense of rightness is notably reinforced by two key encounters of the contact zone. Van, Jeff, and Terry first meet the Herlanders in numbers in what appears to be the principal square of their town, when in well-ordered ranks they surround the male adventurers. Looking at their "calm, grave, wise, wholly unafraid, evidently assured and determined" faces, Van recalls, "I had . . . that sense of being hopelessly in the wrong that I had so often felt in early youth when my short legs' utmost effort failed to overcome the fact that I was late to school" (21). Shortly after, the ways of Van and company are again associated with wrongness, in the first words spoken by a Herlander that Gilman actually inscribes in the text. The male visitors and their eventual Herlandian love interests are at this point playing a game where the object is to use a thrown stone to dislodge a nut placed atop a tripod of sticks without knocking down the whole construction (43). Of the men's inadequate technique, the Herlandian Celis exclaims, "No . . . Bad—wrong!"

Van and his friends' ineptitude at the game clearly figures the inability of men in general to maintain a good society, and it pointedly associates that inability with destructive violence, a poor feeling for how to resolve delicate situations delicately. But the exclamation of "wrong!", like Van's earlier feeling of wrongness, also underscores the point that in *Herland*, the fruit of feminist *nemesis* is a *nomos* very firmly presented as an immersive and right system of norms. Against a world badly arranged, Gilman quite visibly sets a beneficent order that is (to use Ostwald's phrasing) "generally regarded as valid and binding by the members of the group in which it prevails."

In the first of the two stories comprising Schuyler's *Black Empire*, as noted earlier, a group of African Americans known as the Black Internationale reconquers Africa; in the second, the Internationale secures its hold over the retaken continent even as it begins to build "a cooperative civilization unexcelled in this world" (142). In both, the group is led by Dr. Henry Belsidus, a ruthless genius whose path to victory is partly enabled by what he calls "a new philosophy . . . a philosophy of courage, singleness of purpose, of loyalty, of intelligence" (257) in combination with an extraordinary strategic brilliance (particularly at fomenting intrawhite hostilities that lead to full-scale war in Europe). Belsidus's success is grounded most strongly, however, in technical achievements exceeding any known to the world before. As he explains to the tale's narrator, Slater, "It is the skilled technician, the scientist, who wins modern wars, and we are mobilizing the black scientists of the world. Our professors, our orators, our politicians have failed us. Our technicians will not" (46). In subsequent pages, Slater is introduced to all manner of extraordinary inventions: chemically infused pools that produce vegetables at the rate of "200 tons an acre" (49); a "sun engine," which captures solar energy by means of a system of mirrors, boilers, and tubes (53); a radio and television station powered by the sun engine that "can send and receive to and from the ends of the earth by short wave" (158); "stratosphere planes" that dump cages full of disease-carrying rats on the major cities of Europe (173–77); and, at the climax of the tale, a machine capable of incapacitating any other machine (including enemy aircraft) by generating "an atomic or proton beam which can disintegrate any metal" as well as a "radio beam which possesses the faculty of stopping the propellers of machines and rendering batteries and connections useless" (245).

Over the course of *Black Empire*, Belsidus and his followers repeatedly affirm the superiority of Black knowledge and brainpower to white. Noting Slater's awe on his visit to the vegetable farms, one of his guides, Pat, remarks, "We're using the weapons and knowledge of the white man against him," to which another, Sam, offers the corrective, "Shucks. . . . We are way past white science already" (50). After the Internationale's conquest of Africa, Slater worries that the continent can't possibly be defended from white attempts to retake it, at which the physicist Vincente Portabla assures him that the whites can be stopped "by the same means" that the Internationale deployed for the initial conquest: "by using our brains. No matter what the white man's got, black men have the brains to duplicate it, improve upon it or originate something entirely different" (171). Belsidus himself echoes the point a few chapters later, just before he unveils the machine that "will change the history of warfare and of mankind" (241); Pat reiterates it after the machine has secured its first victory (246); and Belsidus states it one more time, after the rout of the European forces, to a gathering of dignitaries "from outlying districts of the Black Empire, from America, from Malaysia, and from India" (256–57).

In a letter of April 1937, as the editors of the 1991 single-volume issue of *Black Empire* note, Schuyler told P. L. Prattis, the city editor of the *Pittsburgh Courier*, "I have been greatly amused by the public enthusiasm for 'The Black Internationale,' which is hokum and hack work of the purest vein. I deliberately set out to crowd as much race chauvinism and sheer improbability into it as my fertile imagination could conjure. The result vindicates my low opinion of the human race."[83] The rhetorical inflation that parodically serves this chauvinism in *Black Empire* is well exemplified not only by the superlatives already noted but also by some of the headlines Schuyler used for individual installments, among them "Black Empire Has Radio and Television Station Which Is Finest in the World" (157) and "Dr. Belsidus Calls Council of War and Informs Cabinet of Invention of New Device That Will Revolutionize World" (238). In unleashing this over-the-top rhetoric, Schuyler might seem to be issuing an invitation to dismiss utopian fancy in precisely the way Jameson describes—with the consequence, in this case, that far from making a case for the inventive capacity of Black people, the novel would perversely undermine it.

Yet the language in which Schuyler describes the inventions of the Black Empire is not, in the end, so very distant from the modest immodesty with which Gilman presents the innovations of Herland. In both cases, some of the innovations seem either highly plausible in their moment or proleptically inspired (see, for example, Belsidus's reliance on solar power), and even those that seem less practically realizable establish an imaginative scene that makes the blanket reactionary standpoint—women aren't capable of this, people of color aren't capable of that—more evidently absurd than the utopian vision.[84] The reader's temporary inhabitation of the robustly delineated utopian realm where women or Black people have unleashed their powers of invention makes a scandal of real-world restrictions (prescriptive or descriptive) on opportunities to exercise that power. Moreover, the undercutting of the premise that Black technical invention is unthinkable is accompanied, in *Black Empire*, by the hardly missable moral that white historical domination has been secured not by destiny but by what more particularly enables Belsidus to succeed: technological advantage joined to a willingness to lay aside moral scruples when required.

Of course, the utopian passion for apposite rearrangement by no means demands that utopia be as shipshape as Herland or as authoritarian as Belsidus's Black Empire. For some, the best arrangement will be one where everything is as neat as a Dutch kitchen, but as we noted in the previous section, utopian *nomos* needn't be characterized by tidiness, hierarchy, rule-following, or tranquility, let alone by the strong devotion to their *nomos* evinced by the Herlanders or the Black Internationale. The form of "ordering" that answers the call of utopian *nemesis* can be wholly anarchic if the visionary sees anarchy as the best possible condition, but it can also be the reverse of anarchic, or anything in between. What matters, again, is that utopia puts into place the best form of arrangement, which will perforce be a departure from the wrong arrangements prevailing in the world at hand. And this means that any actually depicted utopian social organization can be understood both as a recipe for achieving a particular set of goals and as a synecdoche for the more general reordering that utopia names, the final *nomos* (however egalitarian or hierarchical, chaotic or regimented) toward which utopian *nemesis* urges the imaginer.

In having Van describe Herland as a Dutch kitchen, further, Gilman makes her own version of a characteristic move in which the society's apt arrangement is exemplified by the utopians' skillful superintendence of their terrain. Anyone who has read a few utopian fictions will know that utopias often boast adroit dispositions of streets and quarters, skillful deployments of farms and water resources and administrative boundaries. In some cases, this trope is accompanied by the narrating of an establishing apportionment that further reinforces the link between the engineer's impulse and *nomos* as rightness. At the close of *Black Empire*, for example, we learn that Belsidus has divided Africa into "three thousand districts" (250). But the most famous of these mythic foundings is surely that of More's Utopia.

For Hythlodaeus tells, as we've already seen, of how Utopus, who brought a "rude and wild people to" unrivaled "perfection in all good fashions, humanity, and civil gentleness," on first conquering the territory transformed it into in island, setting to this work "not only the inhabitants of the island . . . but also his own soldiers." Hythlodaeus continues,

> Thus the work, being divided into so great a number of workmen, was with exceeding marvellous speed dispatched. Insomuch that the borderers, which at the first began to mock and to jest at this vain enterprise, then turned their derision to marvel at the success and to fear. (50)

We'll return to the derision in a moment; what solicits our attention for now are the multiple ways in which right division and efficient mechanism come together at this inaugural moment. Not only is the utopian place profitably divided from the mainland; the work is also wisely distributed (by Hythlodaeus's lights), and along surprisingly egalitarian lines. In other words, the division of the labor of dividing the land is also an un-dividing, in which the settler-colonial soldiers are joined to the indigenous inhabitants and, in consequence, the task is quickly and efficiently dispatched.

This passage is immediately followed by Hythlodaeus's note that the fifty-four cities of utopia are "all set and situate alike, and in all points fashioned alike, as far forth as the place or plot suffereth," with no two cities fewer than "twenty-four miles asunder" or "distant from the next above one day's journey afoot" (50).[85] Although editors of *Utopia* have pointed out that the fifty-four cities evoke the fifty-three counties of England plus the city of London, and although some readers may find this careful arrangement admirable, others may feel that with it we already enter the territory Jameson associates with irritatingly subjective wish fulfillment, the "drawing up [of] endless seating charts and plans and urban reconstructions" practiced by the kind of obsessive from whom readers swiftly take their distance. In other words, the disposition of the fifty-four cities may seem to fall at a midway point, along a scale of capriciousness or eccentricity, between the grand gesture of Utopia's dividing from the mainland and the (by Jameson's lights) gratuitous description of lighting in Utopia's temples. But it is not only this disposition that can elicit either admiration or dismissal. Some readers who don't find the great division from the mainland unconscionable will find it risible, while others may consider that partition, the symmetry of the cities, and the temple lighting all admirable inventions.

In other words, the line between the lofty work of utopian Imagination and the embarrassing follies thrown up by utopian Fancy is less easily drawn than Jameson maintains. And if the most sweeping, fundamental, and world-changing utopian proposals can't always be sorted from the most minute, contingent, and silly, this is in part because the specifically utopian urge to set things right has an orientation toward thoroughness that can always veer into laughable micromanagement *or* invite derision for its very ambitiousness. Again, one of the most discussed features of utopian writing has been its foregrounding of physical planning, from the laying out of More's cities to the dedicated public buildings in Robert Owen's communities, from the seven pedagogically instructive (and planetarily dedicated) walls in Campanella's City of the Sun to Charles Fourier's detailed instructions on the layout of his phalansteries. [86] What has not always been emphasized, though, is that this enacting of a topographical rebuke to the *dysnomia* of the world at hand is often a particular point of vulnerability for the Utopian theorist, since there will always be something arbitrary (and hence potentially mockable) in blueprints of this kind, no matter what rational ends may be served by aspects of the design.[87]

Indeed it would seem not just that products of utopian Imagination are subject to the same kinds of dismissal directed at products of utopian Fancy but that they may be even more vulnerable on this front than their more modest counterparts. According to Jameson, as we've seen, the "barely perceptible movements of irritation or annoyance" provoked "by this or that detail of the Utopian scheme . . . are not the reactions one brings to the principal proposals and as it were the very scaffolding of the Utopian plan itself." But we might say: on the contrary. It seems quite possible to bring such reactions to large utopian innovations as to small, and indeed the history of utopian writing suggests that the principal proposals are even more likely to generate derision (and fear) than are contrivances that seem content to ameliorate on a small scale. The skeptical Castle may be fatigued by talk of trays, but he saves his most vehement objections (on all manner of ethical, practical, and emotional grounds) for the larger project of Walden Two. Terry directs most of his acrimony not at Herland's little improvements but at the very possibility of a society that functions without men. No one mocks Dr. Belsidus within *Black Empire* itself, but as depicted by Schuyler, the mastermind seems always but a step or two away from madness, a verdict of insanity on his scheme only forestalled, in the diegetic world of the story, by its indisputable success.[88]

Anticipatory defenses against the laughter, incredulity, or outrage with which they may be greeted are a common feature of utopian texts going back to the *Republic* itself, wherein Socrates ventures "that their novelty would make many of our proposals seem ridiculous if they were put into practice."[89] (The context is a proposal for equality in education, including military training, for men and women.) Clearly, the felt need for this kind of proactive rejoinder may be tied to a given utopian text's self-presentation as an effort to persuade, and in the case of early utopias, it would have been impelled as well by the narrative's framing as a tale of travel whose veracity must be asserted and by the conventional disputatiousness of print culture.[90] The most general reason utopias demand such advance defense, however, is surely that the programs they typically put forward are at once radical and sweeping—schemes that, precisely because so absurd, would be especially dangerous and oppressive (as Utopia's founding by conquest and conscription vividly illustrates) if by some freak they were actually realized.

In England after More, utopias per se were not alone in eliciting this kind of disdain. Beginning in the later sixteenth century, a combination of novelty, dubiousness, and scale evocative of utopian imagining would also attend the work of the projector—which could mean, in Joan Thirsk's words, anyone "with a scheme, whether to make money, to employ the poor, or to explore the far corners of the earth." "Projector" quickly took on unsavory associations, becoming "a dirty word in the early seventeenth century, synonymous with rogue and speculator."[91] Yet the faith of the projector—that, with the help of inventions ranging from the lighting of streets to the redesign of prisons, "social institutions might be improved despite the seeming inertia of society"—remained an important factor in British political life through the eighteenth century.[92] In the most durable commentary on the topic, Daniel Defoe acknowledged that "projector" was a term of abuse, a *"Despicable title,"*[93] yet he also asserted the value of projects that move society forward and, toward the end of his life, "proposed a wide range of reforms for the improvement of London and of the nation."[94] As Kimberly Latta notes, *"projecting . . .* frequently crops up in seventeenth-century texts as a metaphor for the activity of bringing forth the New in property as well as in thought," and this partly in opposition to the belief that any idea claiming novelty will prove on inspection only a reworking of what already exists. Availing ourselves of the Coleridgean terms adopted by Jameson, we might say that projectors were champions of creative Imagination as against the merely rearranging Fancy.[95]

Again, however, it was precisely in promising that society could be improved by new means that projectors and utopians (often one and the same) invited animosity, as many passages in utopian writings attest. In his 1795 *Memoirs of Planetes*, Thomas Northmore—a geologist, chemical experimenter, and (according to the *Oxford Dictionary of National Biography*) author of "short articles claiming improvements on such recent inventions as the semaphore telegraph, the unsinkable lifeboat, and a scheme for renaming the bones in the body"[96]—has his narrator Phileleutherus Devoniensis note that "calumnies and persecutions have ever been accumulated upon the reformers of mankind," whose enemies, "where they are too feeble to punish or imprison, they brand with the titles of visionary and theorist" (139).[97] A few years later, Robert Owen would write characteristically, in his "Further Development of the Plan for the Poor, and the Emancipation of Mankind" (1817), of his awareness that he "must for a time offend all mankind, and create in many feelings of disgust and horror at this apparent temerity of conduct which, without a new understanding, a new heart, and a new mind, they could never comprehend."[98]

Even well into the reforming century that Owen helped initiate, reformers could forecast ridicule proportionate to their plans' audacity. Vera Zarovitch, the narrator of Lane's *Mizora* (first released in serial form in 1880–81), tells her utopian hosts that should she preach the benefits of educating the poor to her own people, "they would call me a maniac," and further on that she would only waste her life and happiness "in trying to persuade them to get out of the ruts they have traveled so long. . . . I should be reviled, and perhaps persecuted. My doctrines would be called visionary and impracticable."[99] In the second (1899) edition of *The Island*, a utopian novel by Richard Whiteing originally published in 1888, the narrator is asked whether in England "a rich man ever buy[s] a slum, and keep[s] on playing with it till he has turned it into a paradise"; he replies, "I know one who has begun; but they have only just left off laughing at him." Later in the same narrative, an American with a sinister plan for reorganizing human (and animal) society passes on the wisdom that "you want to begin somewhere on a small scale—in some place where there's nobody to laugh."[100]

The grand scheme's capacity to elicit derision threads through utopias up to our present moment. In Octavia Butler's *Parable of the Talents* (1998), for example, the protagonist-dreamer and (via her journals) principal narrator, Lauren Oya Olamina, devotes her life to promoting what she calls Earthseed, a belief system centered on a project of sending humans to other worlds. Fiercely committed to her vision as she is, however, Lauren notes at times the inhibiting effect of worry "about seeming ridiculous": "It *is* ridiculous for someone like me to aspire to do the things I aspire to do," she even reflects, two pages before recounting an argument in which she told her husband, "Early on, when I told people about the Destiny, and most of them laughed, I was afraid." Meanwhile, Lauren's daughter Larkin, who in her framing narration offers a sidelong commentary on the journals, nurtures a bitter disapprobation of her mother's dreaming, faulting Lauren for devoting her energies to Earthseed instead of her near relations: "She sacrificed us for an idea"; "she had always been willing to sacrifice others to what she believed was right"; "All Earthseed was her family. We never really were." Certainly, the moral weight of *The Parable of the Talents* is in Lauren's favor, and readers may be drawn to her vision the more strongly as it defends itself against the charges Larkin (another utopian skeptic, in her way, in the line of Skinner's Castle) repeatedly levels. Yet her daughter's unimpressed assessment—after the last quoted comment, she describes Lauren's life as a "long, narrow" one—does linger to disturb any uncomplicated embrace of the projector. By weaving in Larkin's disaffection, Butler seems to go out of her way to suggest that utopian vision will always have its casualties.[101]

Utopia's vulnerability to mockery and other forms of hostility is the subject of some perceptive analysis in Bloch's *Principle of Hope*, which, though not named in the chapter of *Archaeologies* we've been considering, clearly looms in Jameson's discussion. Jameson draws explicitly on Freud's writing on dreams to firm up the distinction between, on the one hand, utopian gadgets that seem mere "egoistic" wish fulfillment and, on the other, those larger scaffoldings that seem wishes "universalized and made interesting, indeed often gripping and insistent, for other people." But if, as Jameson notes, recounting one's night dream can provoke disdain from an unwilling auditor, one opens oneself to even deeper humiliation if one shares one's daydreams. And this is Bloch's subject at some key moments in *Principle*.

In the fourth paragraph of that fifteen-hundred-page, three-volume work, for example, Bloch writes, "How richly people have always dreamed of this, dreamed of the better life that might be possible. . . . Nobody has ever lived without daydreams, but it is a question of knowing them deeper and deeper and in this way keeping them trained unerringly, usefully, on what is right [*es kommt aber darauf an, sie immer weiter zu kennen und dadurch unbetrüglich, hilfreich, aufs Rechte gezielt zu halten*]."[102] Keeping daydreams trained on what is right: even as it pushes against the traditional identification of daydreams with unprofitable idleness, Bloch's phrasing captures how, as has here been argued, utopian imagining is rooted in an impulse toward rightness in the most basic sense. Bloch also attends, however, to daydreams' tendency to invite scorn, especially where they bid most blatantly to expand conceptions of what is possible. At the other end of the first volume of *Principle*, he observes that those who envision a radically different social future will always be at a disadvantage vis-à-vis those who belittle them because the latter appear to have reality on their side: "The New is most easily, even most heartily mocked. Its bringers disturb, because supposedly man gets used to everything, even to what is bad."[103]

This accommodation to what is bad, which for the Marxist Bloch means, above all, accommodation to class inequality, explains why the ruling fraction is particularly able to mobilize mockery, even though "political satire is undoubtedly more natural to the oppressed class than to the owning class." The "first political satire was . . . reactionary, was directed precisely against utopias," its master Aristophanes creating "several of his best comedies at the expense of revolutionary hope."[104] We might add here that although Juvenal, as we've seen, directs his barbs against the regime of what is, his satire is nonetheless emblematically reactionary in that it frames the follies and vices of the present as late developments in a world gone off the rails. We might observe, too, that the positioning of Aristophanes is reproduced in writers such as the author of *A Trip to the Island of Equality* (1792), who savages the egalitarian vision of Thomas Paine by asserting its appropriateness to savages,[105] and the Aldous Huxley of *Brave New World*, whom Bloch excoriates[106] and who, in a letter to his father, describes that book as "a comic, or at least satirical, novel about the Future, showing the appallingness (at any rate by our standards) of Utopia."[107]

Of course, the most famous mocker of the faith that newfangled improvements will lead to a brighter future is the Swift of the third book of *Gulliver's Travels*. For here, Gulliver meets not only the head-in-the-clouds inhabitants of the cloud city of Laputa but also the denizens of the "academy of PROJECTORS in Lagado," down below (143). These industrious optimists are engaged in all manner of endeavors, from (famously) "a project for extracting sunbeams out of cucumbers" (145) to "a new method for building houses, by beginning at the roof and working downwards to the foundation" (146). The "only inconvenience," Gulliver reports, is "that none of these projects are yet brought to perfection, and in the mean time the whole country lies miserably waste, the houses in ruins, and the people without food or clothes" (144).

As has often been pointed out, the ideas of one group of projectors are in fact quite worthy, though Gulliver professes to find them otherwise. The professors in "the school of political projectors" are in his opinion "wholly out of their senses," for they propose

> schemes for persuading monarchs to choose favourites upon the score of their wisdom, capacity, and virtue; of teaching ministers to consult the public good; of rewarding merit, great abilities and eminent services; of instructing princes to know their true interest by placing it on the same foundation with that of their people: of choosing for employments persons qualified to exercise them; with many other wild, impossible chimæras, that never entered before into the heart of man to conceive. (152)

Here borrowing motifs from More's Utopia and subsequent ones, Swift certainly aligns with utopia, rather than with reactionary satire, insofar as he attacks what is rather than what is not. Yet if the political projectors differ from the other members of the fruitless academy in having ideas that would work well if put into practice, they resemble their colleagues in being out of touch with the world around them (since their ideas can't be put into practice). The consistent scandal of the academy of Lagado is not that its innovations are all foolish but that its members all turn away from the real, thus affirming their kinship with the inhabitants of Laputa, sailing overhead.

As Bloch intimates, reactionary zeal on behalf of the extant state of things isn't utterly illogical. Rather, it's grounded in a perception that facticity attests to adequacy or success—a conviction that present arrangements have demonstrated that they work precisely *by* being present. Discussing conservative ideas of the ideal society at one point in *Ideology and Utopia* (1929), Karl Mannheim observes that in the "liberal idea" the "normative, the 'should' is accentuated in experience," but "in conservatism the emphasis shifts to existing reality, the 'is.' The fact of the mere existence of a thing endows it with a higher value." And so "utopia in this case is, from the very beginning, embedded in existing reality." The here and now "is no longer experienced as an 'evil' reality but as the embodiment of the highest values and meanings."[108]

In opposition to outrage against the injustice of the prevailing order of things, then, antiutopian (or as we might call it, conservative-utopian) reaction directs its own outrage at the hubris, lack of common sense, and disconnection from reality exhibited by those utopians, projectors, and reformers who want, against all reason, to reorder things. We might therefore assign this feeling the name of *counterindignation*. Counterindignation, which would be closely associated with counterrevolution and perhaps counterreformation, doesn't demand (though it may encompass) a conviction that present arrangements are conducive to justice or happiness. It only requires a sense that such arrangements possess a higher claim to rightness than any merely imagined alternatives.

Counterindignation's allegiance would thus be to *nomos* where *nomos* means, as it often meant for the Greeks, the system in place, the set of norms upheld by common convention. The *nomos* to which utopian indignation devotes itself may be more absolute (as in Nancy's "law of the law, absolute justice"), but it's also more abstract—its reality, so to speak, the reality of the ideal. Counterindignation is therefore the *nemesis* of the projector's *nemesis*, that which derides the utopian Imagination while presumably caring little about the more contained products of utopian Fancy. And it perhaps finds its most memorable articulation, at least in English, in a work published eight years after *Gulliver's Travels*, by Swift's friend Alexander Pope (who in another poem expressed his pleasure in reading of Gulliver's adventures). Advising his hearers to submit to heaven, Pope's speaker admonishes, "Cease, then, nor order imperfection name," before closing the first epistle of the *Essay on Man* as follows:

All Nature is but Art, unknown to thee;
All Chance, Direction, which thou canst not see;

All Discord, Harmony, not understood;
All partial Evil, universal Good:
And, spite of Pride, in erring Reason's spite,
One truth is clear, "Whatever is, is RIGHT."[109]

Counterindignation has oft been thought, but ne'er so well expressed.

Human Destinies

If Pope here offers one of the pithiest accounts of counterindignation, one of the most prodigious is put forward by Nathaniel Hawthorne in *The Blithedale Romance* (1852). *Blithedale* deserves our extended attention in part because it may be unequaled for sheer volume of references to the perils besetting the utopian projector; indeed so relentless is its recursion to the risibility, shame, and futility invited by projection that these pitfalls can come to seem, once noted, the fiction's preeminent concern. But it's not only the quantity of misgivings voiced in *Blithedale* that lends it a claim on our notice. As will become clear, the play of indignation and counterindignation in this strange nineteenth-century text is accompanied by a quite singular mapping of the relations between arrangement, *nemesis*, and utopia's people problem—one that further illuminates questions we've pursued in this chapter and points the way to some that will occupy us in the next.

The Blithedale Romance is not a utopia in the manner of More's travelogue or Bellamy's *Looking Backward*, in which the action consists mainly of the patient introduction of a nonutopian visitor to utopia's happier ways. It's rather a heavily plotted drama centered on an attempt to build and sustain a utopian community, and thus aligns more closely with later fictions of dogged experiment such as Ursula Le Guin's *Dispossessed* and Lauren Groff's *Arcadia*. In writing it, Hawthorne famously drew upon his experience as part of a real utopian project at Brook Farm, where he lived from April to November 1841. Not unreasonably, many critics have taken the failure of the Blithedale enterprise to indicate a verdict on the validity and politics of that attempt at communal living, an inference bolstered by the brevity of Hawthorne's stay there and the decline of the community beginning in late 1844.

Critics taking this line have always had to contend, however, with Hawthorne's preface to the book, where he asserts that he does not "put forward the slightest pretensions to illustrate a theory, or elicit a conclusion, favorable or otherwise, in respect to Socialism" and that he drew on Brook Farm only because he required a mise-en-scène suitable to the genre of the romance. America, he remarks, has so far furnished no "Faery Land" that is "like the real world, . . . but with an atmosphere of strange enchantment, beheld through which the inhabitants have a propriety of their own," no milieu amid which "the paint and pasteboard" out of which romantic characters are composed would not become "too painfully discernible." Lacking a domestic resource of this kind, "the Author has ventured to make free with his old, and affectionately remembered home, at BROOK FARM, as being, certainly, the most romantic episode of his own life—essentially a daydream, and yet a fact—and thus offering an available foothold between fiction and reality."[110]

Even before the narrative starts, Hawthorne construes the utopian impulse in a way that anticipates Bloch's commendation of keeping daydreams "trained . . . on what is right." Framing the "romantic episode" as he does, Hawthorne invites the reader to infer that if his time at Brook Farm was "fact" by virtue of being lived in actuality, it was "daydream" insofar as it was a sort of inhabitation of what had once been only an idea, or what might in the long run prove no more than an airy hope. In other words, if the experience had one foot in "reality" inasmuch as it unfolded in this world, it may have had its other foot in "fiction" either because the scheme's realization was paradoxically suffused by the not-yet-realized quality it bore when it was *only* a scheme or because Brook Farm's ultimate impermanence could be intuited even when it was still up and running. No less noteworthy, however, is that Hawthorne connects utopian imagining with a kind of romance in which characters have their own "propriety"—a quality of rightness that would hold its own against the impulse to dismiss anything that seems not a part of our reality. In this, Hawthorne gestures toward the *nomos* that utopia sets against the world at hand. He presents a miniature parallel to the proactive defenses we considered in the last section, a momentary parrying of the counterindignation that would condemn what is not on behalf of what is.

Notoriously complicating efforts to determine Hawthorne's true position on utopian experimentation are the opinions delivered by the narrator of *The Blithedale Romance*. One problem is that Miles Coverdale's views align roughly with those of Hawthorne's preface, but only roughly; another is that they're not always consistent among themselves; a third is that Coverdale is riddled with character flaws that diminish readerly trust. Near the start of his recollections, Coverdale asserts that it's wise, if not sagacious, "to follow out one's day-dream to its natural consummation, although, if the vision have been worth the having, it is certain never to be consummated otherwise than by a failure," and that the "airiest fragments . . . will possess a value that lurks not in the most ponderous realities of any practicable scheme" (10–11). Coverdale thus indicates that experiments such as Blithedale are doomed, but also that their very impracticability ennobles those who try them out, which sentiment he reaffirms a few pages later. If the "splendid castles (phalansteries, perhaps, they might be more fitly called)" of his fellow utopians "went to rack," they need take to themselves "no shame"; indeed he rejoices that he "could once think better of the world's improvability than it deserved" and esteems as "the rarer and higher . . . the nature that can thus magnanimously persist in error" (19–20).

By the close of his narrative, however, Coverdale's enthusiasm for youthful folly seems to have curdled somewhat, even as the answer to the question of whether it *was* folly seems to have grown less settled. Summoning up Blithedale's "beautiful scheme of a noble and unselfish life" (245) in the ostentatiously vacillating "confession" that serves as the closing pages' counterpart to Hawthorne's preface, Coverdale remarks that he and the other founders "had struck upon what ought to be a truth" (246) but also that the "experiment, so far as its original projectors were concerned, proved, long ago, a failure; first lapsing into Fourierism, and dying, as it well deserved, for this infidelity to its own higher spirit" (246). The ambiguities here exponentiate each other. It's hard to be sure what something that ought to be a truth (rather than is a truth) would be like; hard to know what aspect of Blithedale theory or practice Coverdale has in mind when he refers to this truth; hard to tell whether he's confident that the experiment would have succeeded if it had remained true to its higher spirit; and so on. (The full passage provokes even more unanswerable questions.) This confusion is then not much diminished by Coverdale's rather sour concluding judgment on "human progress": "Let them believe in it who can, and aid in it who choose. If I could earnestly do either, it might be all the better for my comfort" (246). It seems that where, before, utopian aspiration was the property of a "rarer and higher" nature, it's now merely a delusive comfort—unless Coverdale's point is that he would be easier in mind were his own nature more elevated.

Amid these many uncertainties, one thing that does emerge clearly is Coverdale's preoccupation with the question of whether casting one's lot with utopian projection is wise or foolish. And this fixation makes perfect sense within the larger affective terrain of *Blithedale*, because few if any forms of intersubjective response loom as large, in this story, as ridicule. One of the most remarkable features of Coverdale's narrative, in fact, is the frequency with which mockery, blaming, and shaming erupt within its pages; it seems that almost any occasion will serve. His fellow utopians having failed to answer Hollingsworth's knock on his first arrival at the Blithedale farmhouse, for example, that projector tells them, "It would have served you right if I had lain down and spent the night on the door-step, just for the sake of putting you to shame" (26). Amid a later interview with the unnerving Professor Westervelt, Coverdale reflects that were he to try to protect Zenobia—another of the principals of the Blithedale drama—she would "only make [him] the butt of endless ridicule, should the fact ever come to her knowledge" (94). A page after this, in a remarkable layering of affects, Coverdale professes shame at forfeiting a chance to respond to mockery with indignation: "I take shame to myself, that my folly has lost me the right of resenting your ridicule of a friend" (95).

When, a little further on, Zenobia tells her legend of "The Silvery Veil," Coverdale scarcely knows whether she wishes her audience to "laugh, or be more seriously impressed" (107–8).

And these are only some highlights from the first half. Further on, Coverdale reflects "how very absurd" he has been in tormenting himself "with crazy hypotheses as to what was going on" in the drawing room across from the hotel to which he has repaired (162); he also protests that that are many reasons why he "should have demonstrated [himself] an ass" had he fallen in love with Priscilla, the mysterious young woman who rounds out the narrative's quartet of central characters (170). In subsequently contemplating the fate of a more minor figure, Coverdale thinks how Fauntleroy "had no pride; it was all trodden in the dust. No ostentation; for how could it survive, when there was nothing left . . . save penury and shame! His very gait demonstrated that he would gladly have faded out of view, and have crept about invisibly, for the sake of sheltering himself from the irksomeness of a human glance" (184–85). Zenobia, for her part, imagines how a rejected woman, returning to her former friends, "would be apt to blush . . . under the eyes that knew her secret" (225). And even Priscilla's way of carrying herself occasions mirth: "Everybody laughed at her, to her face," although they also loved her, "and did not laugh, behind her back" (74).[111]

Given this ubiquity of shame and ridicule, actual or anticipated, it's hardly surprising to find Coverdale worrying about the mocking counterindignation that may be directed against visionary schemes. He sets the tone, in this regard, with the sentences that precede his thought about the wisdom of following out one's daydream: "The better life! Possibly, it would hardly look so now; it is enough if it looked so, then. The greatest obstacle to being heroic, is the doubt whether one may not be going to prove one's self a fool; the truest heroism is to resist the doubt—and the profoundest wisdom, to know when it ought to be resisted, and when to be obeyed" (10). The literal sense of this remark is that the truest heroism consists in overcoming worry about proving oneself a fool—which intimates in turn that the very worst that can befall one in life is proactive embarrassment over one's attempts at heroism. Coverdale then modifies this inclination toward noble behavior, however, by suggesting that profound wisdom, a kind of perfect prudence, might trump heroism by being able to discern whether heroism in a given case is right or wrong. Such a snarl of sentiments then proves well suited to the ensuing narrative, where human existence can seem a relentless negotiation of others' opinions and where, therefore, it seems especially unlikely that the projector will fail to be harried by self-doubt.

This self-doubt certainly wastes no time in making its appearance. When, at the start of their experiment, the principals take up the question of what to name their community, Coverdale ventures "Utopia," at which he is "unanimously scouted down, and the proposer very harshly maltreated, as if he had intended a latent satire" (37). From the outset, it appears, Blithedale's founders feel compelled to arm themselves with an irony, or an awareness of irony, that would protect them from imputations of naive optimism. Yet this kind of internalized counterindignation appears to exact a cost, making at least some of them more susceptible to substantive doubt. Exposed to Westervelt's skepticism midway through the narrative, Coverdale indeed finds himself

> possessed by a mood of disbelief in moral beauty or heroism, and a conviction of the folly of attempting to benefit the world. Our especial scheme of reform, which, from my observatory [a little treetop hermitage], I could take in with the bodily eye, looked so ridiculous that it was impossible not to laugh aloud. . . . I recognized, as chiefly due to this man's influence, the sceptical and sneering view which, just now, had filled my mental vision in regard to all life's better purposes. . . . The Professor's tone represented that of worldly society at large, where a cold scepticism smothers what it can of our spiritual aspirations, and makes the rest ridiculous. I detested this kind of man, and all the more, because a part of my own nature showed itself responsive to him. (101–2)

Nor does this "part of [Coverdale's] own nature" manifest itself only with respect to the Blithedale project. Twenty pages later, that narrator will smile at Zenobia's vow to lift up her voice "in behalf of women's wider liberty"—to which she rejoins, "What matter of ridicule do you find in this, Miles Coverdale?" (120).

The project that most attracts Coverdale's derision, however, is neither Blithedale itself nor Zenobia's feminism. It is, rather, the scheme that ultimately diverts Hollingsworth's attention from the Blithedale experiment, a treasured plan for the reformation of prisoners. Immediately before directing an arboreally elevated eyebrow at Blithedale (in the passage just quoted), Coverdale consigns Hollingsworth's venture—of which he has never much approved (36, 56, 70–71)—to the domain of the laughable, wondering why "when there is enough else to do," he and the others should waste their "strength in dragging home the ponderous load of his philanthropic absurdities? At my height above the earth, the whole matter looks ridiculous!" (100). A little further on, Coverdale confronts Zenobia with this same assessment: "Now that I . . . can look at his project from a distance, it requires quite all my real regard for this respectable and well-intentioned man to prevent me laughing at him—as, I find, society at large does!" But if he expects thus to close the question, he's mistaken. Zenobia's retort is itself indignant and calculated to humiliate in turn:

Blind enthusiasm, absorption in one idea, I grant, is generally ridiculous. . . . But a great man . . . attains his normal condition only through the inspiration of one great idea. As a friend of Mr. Hollingsworth, and, at the same time, a calm observer, I must tell you that he seems to me such a man. But you are very pardonable for fancying him ridiculous. Doubtless, he is so— to you! There can be no truer test of the noble and heroic, in any individual, than the degree in which he possesses the faculty of distinguishing heroism from absurdity. (166)

The older, narrating Coverdale will adopt something very like this line, though he rearranges the terms slightly. For him, as we've seen, the truest heroism lies in resisting the worry that one may "prove one's self a fool" and the "profoundest wisdom" in knowing when the doubt "ought to be resisted, and when to be obeyed." It may be that the ground for this introjection of Zenobia's point of view is laid when, sometime after their exchange, he confronts their associate's treatment by the press: "Hollingsworth, too, with his philanthropic project, afforded the penny-a-liners a theme for some savage and bloody-minded jokes; and, considerably to my surprise, they affected me with as much indignation as if we had still been friends" (195). Yet Coverdale doesn't seem, here, to have imbibed either Hollingsworth's indignation at the state of prisons or Zenobia's conviction that Hollingsworth is animated by a "great idea." Rather, his indignation at the journalistic mockery seems to result from personal loyalty—an outrage not at the ridicule of his former friend's ideas but at the attack on the friend himself.

This allegiance to the man rather than the plan is important because it quietly sets the stage for what seems Coverdale's most strongly felt verdict on projects and projectors. In his final encounter with Hollingsworth, now racked with remorse and apparently disburdened of his passion for social reform, Coverdale taunts his once friend by avowing that he has come to see the latter's "grand edifice for the reformation of criminals. Is it finished yet?" Hollingsworth replies, "No—nor begun! . . . A very small one answers all my purposes," at which Priscilla throws Coverdale

> an upbraiding glance. But I spoke again, with a bitter and revengeful emotion, as if flinging a poisoned arrow at Hollingsworth's heart.
>
> "Up to this moment," I inquired, "how many criminals have you reformed?"
>
> "Not one," said Hollingsworth, with his eyes still fixed on the ground. "Ever since we parted, I have been busy with a single murderer!" (242–43)

The murderer to whom Hollingsworth refers is Hollingsworth, and what has replaced his scheme for the improvement of manifold distant others is a program of repentance for that most proximate of beings, himself. The moral Coverdale then draws is that although philanthropy may be useful to society,

> it is perilous to the individual, whose ruling passion, in one exclusive channel, it thus becomes. It ruins, or is fearfully apt to ruin, the heart; the rich juices of which God never meant should be pressed violently out and distilled into alcoholic liquor, by an unnatural process; but should render life sweet, bland, and gently beneficent, and insensibly influence other hearts and other lives to the same blessed end. (243)

This formulation ironically recalls a verdict on Blithedale that *Hollingsworth* had delivered earlier: "I see through the system. It is full of defects—irremediable and damning ones! . . . There is not human nature in it!" (132). It also echoes Coverdale's much earlier representation of Hollingsworth's "philanthropic theory" as "the cold, spectral monster . . . on which he was wasting all the warmth of his heart" (55) and Zenobia's chastisement of Hollingsworth for falling prey to an ambition that is "nothing but self, self, self! . . . You have embodied yourself in a project. . . . You aimed a death-blow, and a treacherous one, at this scheme of a purer and higher life [that is, Blithedale], which so many noble spirits had wrought out" (218). In finally taking up an endless penance, Hollingsworth embodies himself in a different kind of project, one that (whatever Zenobia might think of it) is for Coverdale superior to intentional communities and designs for prison reform because it comports better with what God has ordained for the heart.

Two different, though intimately connected, assertions of the inhumanity of visionary schemes are intertwined within these denunciations of (non–divinely sanctioned) projects. In Hollingsworth's arraignment of Blithedale, and implicitly in Coverdale's appraisal of Hollingsworth's prison initiative, the problem is that the project isn't fitted to the truth of how people are—that it must fail because it relies on a transformation of what can't be transformed. Of course, this kind of move, in which the putative truth about human beings is wielded against utopian imagining, is a familiar form of what we've been calling counterindignation, indeed the one that has arguably been most vital in antiutopian arguments over the centuries. We'll return to it shortly.

The other sense in which projectors' plans constitute a denial of humanity takes center stage in Zenobia's and Coverdale's criticism of Hollingsworth. Here, the complaint is that the scheme in question undoes the humanity of the projector, ruining his heart by inducing him to sacrifice others (and his bonds to them) to insubstantial fantasies. This second avenue of censure has affinities with Swift's representation of the out-of-touch Laputans, whose occupation with math and music leads them to neglect their spouses and other interlocutors; with the botanist's reproach of the narrator in *A Modern Utopia*;

with Larkin's reproach of her mother in *Parable of the Talents*; and with countless biographies (including Lytton Strachey's sketch of Florence Nightingale
in *Eminent Victorians*) in which people of large humanitarian vision are revealed to have had problematic relationships with those close to them. Perhaps
the nearest analogue to this form of indictment, however, comes in a novel
published at almost the same moment as *The Blithedale Romance*: Charles
Dickens's *Bleak House* (1852–53), wherein Mrs. Jellybee's local myopia is a condition of her cross-oceanic philanthropy.

In *Blithedale*, the charge that projection runs against the (best) truth of
human nature is supported by several depictions of projectors turning away
from those around them. An especially striking instance is afforded by an early
passage in which Coverdale recounts how Hollingsworth

> purposed to devote himself and a few disciples to the reform and mental
> culture of our criminal brethren. His visionary edifice was Hollingsworth's
> one castle in the air; . . . and he made the scheme more definite . . . by ren-
> dering it visible to the bodily eye. I have seen him, a hundred times, with a
> pencil and sheet of paper, sketching the façade, the side-view, or the rear of
> the structure, or planning the internal arrangements, as lovingly as another
> man might plan those of the projected home, where he meant to be happy
> with his wife and children. . . . Unlike all other ghosts, his spirit haunted an
> edifice which, instead of being time-worn, and full of storied love, and joy,
> and sorrow, had never yet come into existence. (56)

If in ordinary haunting, the ghost is a less solid being from the past who passes
through the solidity of the present, Coverdale's canny temporal translation asks
us to conceive of the projector as a less solid being from the present passing
through the solidity of the future. Coverdale immediately goes on, however, to
mark this future as itself unreal—it "had never yet come into existence," and
likely never will—which is to say that what really happens is that the future
comes to haunt the present, rendering the projector spectral too. To reinforce
the point, Coverdale contrasts the coldly vaporous castle to the warmer and
much more evidently realizable home, in choosing which the (erstwhile) projector would, very precisely, confirm his devotion to actual human bonds as
against nebulous reveries. In Coverdale's representation, in any case, the two
forms of counterindignation just described notably converge: protest on behalf of the reality of people (the existence of individuals near and dear to one)
and protest on behalf of the reality of people (how human beings actually are)
are leagued together against the inhumanity of projection.

But there's yet one more way in which *Blithedale* presses the conclusion that
utopian experiment comes to blows with human actuality—one that in a sense
further fuses the two just named. Although Coverdale offers no explanation
for the collapse of the Blithedale enterprise, we know that there are a couple

of reasons why the four principals remove themselves. The first is Hollings-worth's competing commitment to his prison scheme; the second is a kind of general explosiveness obtaining in intersubjective relations, the most promi-nent issue of which here is the familiar impasse of the love triangle. In *News from Nowhere*, Morris proposes that romantic conflict (sometimes violent in its results) will persist in utopia without disrupting the otherwise smooth life of society, but in *Blithedale* a suite of romantic resentments proves fatal to the experiment. While many kinds of human limitations have been invoked as obstacles to utopia's realization, therefore, the one apparently certified by Hawthorne's plot is people's inability to live together harmoniously—without jealousy, without rancor, without suspicion and contempt—for very long.

Especially crucial on this front is that Hawthorne doesn't frame the princi-pals' estrangement as unpredictable or contingent. On the contrary, he goes out of his way to prevent us from seeing it this way by repeatedly describing characters as each other's fates. "Fate," or its synonyms, is applied especially frequently to Priscilla, whom Zenobia will call her "evil fate" (220) and whose claim upon the older woman leads the latter to exclaim, much earlier, "With what kind of a being am I linked! . . . If my Creator cares aught for my soul, let him release me from this miserable bond! . . . It will strangle me at last!" (104). Zenobia also theatricalizes the trope of Priscilla as destiny when she tells the story of "The Silvery Veil," recounting how "it was affirmed . . . that whosoever should be bold enough to lift [the veil], would behold the features of that per-son, in all the world, who was destined to be his fate" (110). She reports, too, the Veiled Lady's warning to the woeful Theodore that if he lift the veil without first kissing her, she "is doomed to be [his] evil fate" (113), and a magician's warning to another lady, living "among visionary people, who were seeking for the better life," that the Veiled Lady is her "deadliest enemy . . . doomed to fling a blight over [her] prospects" (114–15). Rewriting herself and Priscilla into a romance only slightly more supernatural than *Blithedale* itself, and offering a sibylline anticipation of her actual future, Zenobia heightens the air of inevita-bility attending the narrative, as if part of her fate is to proclaim her fatedness.

But it's not only Priscilla who's described in this way. When Coverdale in-sists that Hollingsworth reveal his intention to sacrifice Blithedale to his re-form scheme, "Hollingsworth frown[s]; not in passion, but like Fate, inexora-bly" (133). Similarly, when Priscilla later reveals that she has returned to Blithedale at Hollingsworth's behest, she regards Coverdale "with an air of surprise, as if the idea were incomprehensible, that she should have taken this step without his agency" (171). Further on again, when Coverdale infers that he has stumbled upon Zenobia and Hollingsworth in the wake of some crisis in their relations, it strikes him that this turn has left on "Hollingsworth's brow . . . a stamp like that of irrevocable doom, of which his own will was the instrument" (215). Hollingsworth seems, then, to assume the role of fate for

Zenobia, for Priscilla, and even (in the first quotation) for Coverdale—the very three people whom Zenobia will later charge him with sacrificing to a project that is "nothing but self, self, self!" (218).

In addition, Priscilla and Hollingsworth seem each other's fates, or bound up in each other's destinies, beyond the mere fact of their companionship at the story's end. Supporting Hollingsworth in his course of expiation, Priscilla plays a kind of Antigone to his (Colonus-bound) Oedipus, thus adding Greek tragedy to the array of motifs heightening the aura of fatedness about the conclusion of their tale. And as if this were not enough, Zenobia demands to be read as the fate of the other two, particularly at the close of the narrative. Contemplating the final spectacle of Hollingsworth arm in arm with Priscilla, Coverdale imagines Zenobia as she "whose vindictive shadow dogged the side where Priscilla was not" (243)—a vision that captures not only how Zenobia's actions have determined the courses of the other two but also how she has become their destiny in the sense of destination, the center around which their lives now turn.

Even this catalogue, however, fails to exhaust the roster of characters who are identified with fate in these pages. Westervelt, too, carries an air of inescapability, as Coverdale emphasizes when he tells him, near the close, "I have long considered you as Zenobia's evil fate" (240). And earlier, having "a vague idea that some new event would grow out of Westervelt's proposed interview with Zenobia," Coverdale compares his "own part, in these transactions," to "that of the Chorus in a classic play." He indeed muses that "Destiny, it may be—the most skilful of stage-managers—seldom chooses to arrange its scenes, and carry forward its drama, without securing the presence of at least one calm observer" (97). Coverdale may not be anyone's fate in the fullest sense, but given his significant participation in many of the narrative's cruxes, his threading of himself into the web of Blithedale fatedness seems less self-aggrandizing than straightforwardly correct.[112]

Of course, the name for the being who eventually calls one to account—often at the expense of one's happiness and future prospects—is Nemesis. And we can notice at once, in this regard, that by populating *Blithedale* with so many nemeses, so many evil (or at least inescapable) fates, Hawthorne clearly pays homage to a form of inevitability much at home in, and perhaps necessary to, the genre of romance. If realism tends to register the unsatisfying play of contingency in life as it's actually lived, romance can give the gift of appositeness, of resolutions clearly fitted to the characters who suffer them, even if those resolutions are sometimes perplexing in one or another aspect.

A little further reflection suggests, however, that in casting his characters so relentlessly as each other's fates, Hawthorne also exerts himself on behalf of what his preface holds up as romance's opposite number, not realism but reality. And this in a sense highly germane to our concerns here. For to put it in its plainest terms, the takeaway of the narrative is that the true destinies of

Hollingsworth, Zenobia, and Priscilla lie not with the utopian experiment of Blithedale or with Hollingsworth's scheme for the reformation of criminals but with the other members of that triangle (along with, in some ways, Coverdale and Westervelt). The stories of these characters, in other words, embody the inevitable triumph of personal relationships over projects and schemes. And in this, they may seem to substantiate with finality the form of counterindignation we've already seen so heavily at work in the text: the pitting of the truth of humanity against the chimera of utopian daydreaming. Within this oppositional configuration, the *Blithedale* principals emerge as allegories, as well as bearers, of the claims laid on each person by "other hearts and other lives"; one could almost say that these persons personify personhood. And thus what we find in *The Blithedale Romance*—surely the first major work of fiction centered on people attempting to build a utopian society from the ground up—is an ending that exploits with stunning economy the connections between indignation, rightness, faulty arrangements, and faulty humanity that we've been considering here. As manifestations of both *nemesis* (here, a counterindignation that assails the inhumanity of projects) and Nemesis (here, humanity's revenge on projects), the characters appear to uphold doubly the *nomos* of the world as it is against the *nomos* of which utopia dreams.

It would seem, then, that *The Blithedale Romance* has to be accounted a thoroughly antiutopian text. For the reasons just described, it would appear to align neither with the Hawthorne of the preface, who refrains from delivering a verdict "favorable or otherwise, in respect to Socialism," nor with the Coverdale who rejoices that he "could once think better of the world's improvability than it deserved," but rather with the Coverdale who reflects that philanthropy in the Hollingsworthian sense "ruins, or is fearfully apt to ruin, the heart." And yet there's a problem with this interpretation. The ending is, certainly, one in which the principals tidily receive what's due them in a particular sense—and thus one that would seem to legitimate counterindignation's assertion of the rightness of the non-utopian, extant world. Yet this ending also feels, in some ways, quite wrong.

For one thing, the destinies of the characters are by no means alluring. By the end of the tale, Zenobia's singular presence, described earlier by Coverdale as Nature's "fairest handiwork" (244), has been extinguished, and Hollingsworth and Priscilla live enclosed in the gloomy atmosphere of the former's apparently endless self-recrimination. Priscilla's unsettling "veiled happiness" (242) in her last appearance notwithstanding, the characters' ultimate conditions suggest that if other individuals always prove one's fate in life, life is not "sweet, bland, and gently beneficent" but appalling. The reader may readily imagine how much better the characters would have fared if their destiny had proven to be a shared project (such as Blithedale) rather than each other in the sense enforced here; and indeed one effect of their appearance as each other's fates is to make interpersonal relationships look as constricting to Hawthorne's reader as utopian structures have appeared to antiutopians. The world as it is, so frequently represented as more free than utopia because unplanned, here seems stifling, ruled as it is by destinies in the form of those close about us.

But it's not only the denouement of the tale that seems wrong even in its rightness. Equally off-putting is the atmosphere the characters inhabit from the very first, which is not only unhappy much of the time but also what we might call morally ugly. There are, to be sure, moving instances of affection and good will, as in the note that the Blithedaleans universally loved Priscilla and were kind to her. Yet even this tenderness seems to owe something to their cognizance of the general precarity of her existence; and when the emotional note of the text is not ruefulness or benevolent fondness, it's often confusion, outrage, or ridicule. As noted above, the milieu of *Blithedale* can seem one in which thought and action are driven, above all, by fear of others' opinions, by efforts to forestall mockery, by obsessions with humiliation and eruptions of indignation. The overall impression given by the society here described is, we might say, that of an orgy of *nemesis*, in the sense of relentless blaming and shaming, without a compelling *nomos* to which it might be oriented. Hawthorne himself even notes, in the preface, "how few amiable qualities" he has distributed "among his imaginary progeny" (2), and while we might demur so far as to say that the characters aren't always individually disagreeable, we'd be hard pressed to find them very agreeable together.

L'enfer, c'est les autres. Or if other people aren't quite hell here, they're at least purgatory. The irony that attends Coverdale's paean to the sweetness of human ties is that such sweetness isn't, for the most part, vividly present in the world he depicts. Of course, one could insist that interpersonal connections, no matter how oppressive, ought always to be privileged over utopian schemes and projects of speculative reform; one could avow further that it's all to the good if people are purgatorial, since sources of moral challenge conduce to the improvement of the soul. Even were we to accept that this holds in the world to which we ourselves are consigned, however, there would remain the point that *Blithedale* takes as the motor of its plot the dream of a "better life" and in this gestures unignorably toward an order in which things would be less grimly disposed than they prove for its characters—an order arranged not for tribulation but for joy. Regarded from this point of view, *The Blithedale Romance* seems to align itself, after all, with indignation on behalf of a *nomos* truer or higher than the flawed one we experience—to take the part of *nemesis* on behalf of what should be as against what is. Regarded from this point of view, it looks, indeed, like a work of counter-counterindignation, a strike on behalf of the better life against an opponent all the more formidable for being so rarely and riskily dispraised: the mystique of human bonding in the world we know.

2

Shaping Utopians

Managerial and Transformative Utopias

Is there any vicious habit, any practice contrary to good faith, any crime, whose origin and first cause cannot be traced back to the legislation, the institutions, the prejudices of the country wherein this habit, this practice, this crime can be observed? . . . Do not all these observations which I propose to develop further in my book, show that the moral goodness of man, the necessary consequence of his constitution, is capable of indefinite perfection like all his other faculties, and that nature has linked together in an unbreakable chain truth, happiness and virtue?[1]

So demands the Marquis de Condorcet, near the close of his *Sketch for a Historical Picture of the Progress of the Human Mind* (*Esquisse d'un tableau historique des progrès de l'esprit humain*), written in 1793–94 and published posthumously in 1795. A stronger expression of optimism about what social arrangements can do can hardly be imagined. But in asking these rhetorical questions, Condorcet isn't merely affirming his faith that utopia is possible. He's also explaining that something like a utopian condition is the near endpoint of the real history of humankind as that history is irresistibly unfolding. His *Sketch*, which lays out in abbreviated form a vast chronicle of human progress through ten historical stages, concludes with the expectation that the future holds "the abolition of inequality between nations," a "progress of equality within a single people" (inequalities of wealth, status, and education will "constantly diminish without however disappearing altogether" [130]), and "the true perfection of man" (126).

Condorcet's faith in progress includes a conviction that knowledge *about* progress has itself progressed dramatically in recent times; and perhaps accordingly, he exhibits little reverence for older, less enlightened ways of thinking.[2] He notes, for instance, that there's a clear distinction between his own apprehension of circumambient conditions' power over individual morals and assumptions prevailing in Greek antiquity. Discussing the fourth stage in the history of human spirit, earlier in the *Sketch*, he taxes Greek politics with

> the habit of seeing law not so much as an instrument for removing the causes of evil as a means of eradicating its effects by playing those causes off against one another; the practice, in government, of turning prejudices and vices to good account rather than trying to dispel or repress them; a greater interest in depriving man of his true nature, in exalting and inflaming his imagination than in perfecting and purifying those inclinations and predilections which are the necessary product of his moral constitution— all these mistakes arising from the more general mistake of identifying the natural man with the product of the existing state of civilization, with, that is, man corrupted by prejudices, artificial passions and social customs. (36–37)

Suffused with the indignation against extant civilization associated with Jean-Jacques Rousseau, the passage by no means does justice to actual Greek understandings, as we'll have occasion to note below. But it does point to a feature of utopian organization, or utopia as organization, that compels our attention here.

As we've seen, utopia is profoundly a creature of *nomos* in the sense of proper apportionment or allotment, of the provision of what's due and right. Yet utopia must also, clearly, be about arrangement in a more dynamic sense. Being a society, it cannot simply repose in its justness but has also to ensure that its inhabitants live with each other in ways conducive to the general and the individual good. In other words, it has to have a way of maintaining good behavior, whatever exactly may be meant by "good," even as it sustains the best of relations between human capacities and the experience of living. The second quote from Condorcet highlights the point that utopian writers, as well as actual governments, have conceived two broadly different means by which this result can be achieved. One is a social mechanism that works with human character as it's understood to be, more or less inevitably—that orchestrates desires, tendencies, and qualities more or less taken as given. The other is one that in effect creates better persons, however "better" may be defined. In the first case, the accent is on how a system might manage human fallibility; in the second, on how a system might make humans less fallible.

This won't exactly come as news to students of utopia. Already in his 1952 study of welfare economics in English utopias, J. K. Fuz had distinguished "between 'Utopias of men' and 'Utopias of measures,'" the "latter advocating a policy of reform, the former taking as a *conditio sine qua non* a complete change of human nature."[3] Fredric Jameson, for his part, ventures in *Archaeologies of the Future* that "what is perhaps the fundamental Utopian dispute about sub-jectivity" is

> whether the Utopia in question proposes the kind of radical transformation of subjectivity presupposed by most revolutions, a mutation in human na-ture and the emergence of whole new beings; or whether the impulse to Utopia is not already grounded in human nature, its persistence readily explained by deeper needs and desires which the present has merely re-pressed and distorted.[4]

According to Jameson, a resolution of this tension "in either direction would be fatal for the existence of Utopia itself," since if "absolute difference is achieved, . . . we find ourselves in a science-fictional world such as those of Stapledon, in which human beings can scarcely even recognize themselves any longer," whereas if Utopia "is drawn too close to current everyday realities, and its subject begins too closely to approximate our neighbors and our politically misguided fellow citizens, then we slowly find ourselves back in a garden-variety reformist or social-democratic politics . . . which has forfeited its claim to any radical transformation of the system itself" (168).

For utopia, the stakes of the question of what can or can't be done with "human nature" are incalculably high. As we saw in the previous chapter, Dr. Leete in Bellamy's *Looking Backwards* repeatedly counters the utopian visi-tor Julian West's surmise, "Human nature itself must have changed very much," with an insistence that new social arrangements have merely worked with human nature as it is.[5] And it's not hard to see why Leete should respond so defensively. If utopia claims that it can change how humans are, it invites the simple retort that human nature can't be changed, or the complaint that it commits sacrilege against divine creation, or (as Jameson remarks) the charge that its baleful work is ultimately to replace the human race with something else. The first of these objections is a staple of antiprogressivism extending far beyond discussions of utopia per se, while the second (in combination with a version of the first) is aired in G. K. Chesterton's remark that the "weakness of all utopias" is "that they take the greatest difficulty of man," original sin, "and assume it to be overcome."[6] The third worry, meanwhile, finds lavish allegories in twentieth-century science fiction, not only Olaf Stapledon's multibillion-year, multispecies epics but also, for example, Ar-thur C. Clarke's 1953 novel *Childhood's End*.[7] On the other hand, if a particular utopia simply claims to manage humans as they are, it opens itself to the objection that its author's specific view of what humans are like is mistaken, or to the accusation that utopia is cynically resigned rather than ambitious for the highest human good (as in Condorcet's take on Greek politics)—that

it offers nothing in the way of a moral ideal, let alone the revolutionary transformation to which Jameson refers.

Readers familiar with the utopian genre may, certainly, wonder whether the
distinction described here is much more than rhetorical. After all, since no
utopias have yet existed, the appearance of so admirable a society, when it
appears, might equally be said to betoken a fundamental change in human
character or to reveal possibilities always latent but occluded. In the same year
Fuz published his study, Jack Hexter remarked in *More's Utopia: The Biography
of an Idea* that More's

> is the best of commonwealths and Utopians are the best of men; but it is
> not because they are of a better stuff and nature than other men; it is
> because their laws, ordinances, rearing, and rules of living are such as to
> make effective man's natural capacity for good, while suppressing his natu-
> ral propensity for evil. . . . Their institutions are not the creation but the
> creator of their good qualities.[8]

Hexter means to say that human nature hasn't altered in More's Utopia. But
his last sentence might almost be taken to support the view that the Utopians
are of a better stuff, since it credits utopian institutions with the creation of its
inhabitants' good qualities. The ambiguity seems directly inherited from Condorcet and Rousseau, who skirted the charge that wiser government and
proper conditions would inadmissibly change human nature by asserting that
they would instead release a human goodness that had hitherto been
suppressed.

A little reflection reveals, however, that the distinction at issue has more
than rhetorical utility because it can help us refine our sense of a given utopia's
mode of operating. If we divest ourselves for a moment of the urge to classify
each utopia as either wholly managerial (Fuz's "Utopias of measures"; Jameson's subject who approximates our neighbors) or wholly transformative
(Fuz's "Utopias of men"; Jameson's "mutation in human nature"), we may
quickly see that most utopias mix the two styles. Most solicit readers' admiration in part by flourishing a clever system of rules and other structures that
would, in theory, keep more or less anyone in line—so that if, say, a *personne
moyen sensuelle* were suddenly deposited in that society (unaltered in subjec-
tivity but required to live as a utopian), that person would behave acceptably.
At the same time, most utopias also instill in their citizens values, habits, and
feelings sufficiently different from those of our own untransformed world to
warrant the conclusion that human character has in crucial ways been remade.
And they tend to do so by molding the inhabitant of utopia over time, usually
from birth.

Yet different utopias mix these styles in different ways and in differing proportions. The managerial predominates in some; the transformative, in others. Thus we may do well to think of a utopian continuum, to consider that any given utopia roughly inhabits a point on a spectrum ranging from heavy reliance on techniques for dealing with people as it finds them, so to speak, to powerful investments in producing people of a new kind. In this light, Condorcet's *Sketch* becomes noteworthy not least for its claim that the *progrès de l'esprit humain* involves, very precisely, a movement away from the former and toward the latter—away from, again, "the practice, in government, of turning prejudices and vices to good account" and toward "a greater interest in . . . perfecting and purifying those inclinations and predilections which are the necessary product of [man's] moral constitution."

Whether or not Condorcet captures something meaningful about the history of actual governments, he does, as we'll see in the following pages, capture something important about the course of utopian writing and thinking in the centuries after More. As will become evident, a particular utopia's place on this notional spectrum needn't correlate in any strict way with its publication date; and yet something like the trajectory from less managerial to more transformative that Condorcet proposes can be discerned in the most influential utopian fictions from More up to B. F. Skinner's *Walden Two*. To see how this works, we'll need to take a path through the history of key Western utopian writings twice, first examining the managerial line, then examining the transformative—but beginning with More each time.

We can start by turning to a proposition Jameson advances as he launches into his treatment of the tension between admirable indignation and idiosyncratic tinkering—between utopias' "truly ferocious indictment of contemporary society" and "the eccentricities of the Utopian inventors" (42). On the way there, Jameson remarks that More's *Utopia* "seems shadowed by" a "tension between collective evaluation and individual proposal, between a relatively objective inventory of injustices, vices and suffering, and a play of Latin wit and invention that can scarcely be attributed to anyone but the increasingly well-known public figure who is its author" (42). Illuminating as this formulation is, we need to add that the air of witty contrivance in More's *Utopia* extends to elements far more consequential than the gadgets that go on to draw Jameson's scrutiny. For one of the most striking features of More's blueprint is its bid to replace the poorly designed legal and moral codes of the present with rules and practices far better attuned to human desires and fears. *If* the punishment or the practice is constructed in such and such a way, *then* people will behave in such and such a (desirable) fashion, except in rare instances of incorrigibility.

More's Utopia often seems, that is, to operate by means of a carefully crafted system of incentives and disincentives, bringing about a condition of justice less by opening untapped springs of virtue than through shrewd assessment (by a social engineer who's anything but eccentric) of how human beings operate. As the irreplaceable scholar of utopian literature J. C. Davis puts it, "The language of profit, interest, advantage runs, like a *leit-motif*, through More's great work. Men's pursuit of their own interest was a fact of nature which political calculation must recognize."[9] Such language would seem quite obviously associated with the managerial rather than the transformative style of utopia—with the "utopia of measures" rather than the "utopia of men," with the instrumentalization of "prejudices and vices" that Condorcet abominates rather than the perfecting of moral inclinations that Condorcet champions.

And indeed in part 1 of *Utopia*, More-the-character makes this affiliation more or less explicit. Trying to drive new ideas into the heads of the unready is, by his lights, effort expended to no purpose. Rather, in thinking about how to organize a society,

> you must with a crafty wile and subtle train study and endeavour . . . to handle the matter wittily and handsomely for the purpose; and that which you cannot turn to good, so to order it that it be not very bad. For it is not possible for all things to be well unless all men were good. Which I think will not be yet this good many years.[10]

Hythlodaeus responds with indignation. "By this means," he admonishes, "nothing else will be brought to pass, but whiles that I go about to remedy the madness of others I should be even as mad as they" (42). Yet many of Hythlodaeus's own prescriptions for social improvement don't so much replace the bad in human beings with good as wittily and handsomely handle human beings just as they come.

In his discourse before Cardinal Morton, as we saw in chapter 1, Hythlodaeus reasons that it's misguided to make theft a capital offense because this unsurpassable punishment has the effect of encouraging murder. Recognizing that a person "condemned for theft" is "in no less jeopardy" than one "convict of manslaughter," the thief will be "forcibly provoked, and in a manner constrained[,] to kill him"—that is, the person stolen from—"whom else he would have but robbed. For the murder being once done, he is in less fear and more hope that the deed shall not be bewrayed or known" (27). Not long after, Hythlodaeus offers several reasons why the sovereign should work for the practical benefit of his people rather than imagining that they'll be more peaceable if kept poor; among these are that "wrangling, quarrelling, brawling, and chiding" will be found nowhere more prevalent "than among beggars" and that "it is against the dignity of a king to have rule over beggars" rather than "over rich and wealthy men" (39). These incitements to good behavior manage the human material at hand to socially desirable ends; they neither require a moral calculus apart from self-interest nor rely on subjects morally superior to the common run in our world.

In the account of Utopia itself in part 2, Hythlodaeus similarly reports that in time of war, the Utopians conspire to have posted within the enemy's territory proclamations "promis[ing] great rewards to him that will kill their enemy's prince" and similar if lesser gifts for the heads of "their chief adversaries, next unto the prince" (99). By this means, it comes about that their enemies soon "have all other men in suspicion, and be unfaithful and mistrusting among themselves one to another" (100). It may be objected that such a proceeding is but the "cruel act of a base and cowardly mind," but the utopians "count it . . . a deed of pity and mercy," since it permits them to "dispatch great wars without any battle or skirmish," and thus "by the death of a few offenders" to spare "the lives of a great number of innocents as well of their own men as also of their enemies . . . which in fighting should have been slain" (100). This inclination toward a no-nonsense, almost cheerfully amoral deployment of calculation and syllogism extends to other aspects of war: the utopians prefer to "thrust no man forth into war against his will" because such a man will surely be cowardly and infect others with cowardice (102).

On the domestic rather than foreign front, the language of sticks and carrots is less ostentatiously blithe, but the same syllogistic principles apply. Most punishments are decided on a case-by-case basis, but

> most commonly the most heinous faults be punished with the incommodity of bondage. For that they suppose to be to the offenders no less grief, and to the commonwealth more profit, than if they should hastily put them to death, and so make them quite out of the way. . . . But if they, being thus used, do rebel and kick again, then forsooth they be slain as desperate and wild beasts, whom neither prison nor chain could restrain and keep under. But they which take their bondage patiently be not left all hopeless. (92)

In other words, it's not only that people behave well in Utopia out of fear of punishment. It's also that one of the few faults punishable by death—an indication that the malefactor has fallen below the level of the human—is failure to accede to a regime of rewards and punishments. Yet allurements to good conduct aren't only negative. The Utopians "do not only fear their people from doing evil by punishments, but also allure them to virtue with rewards of honour. Therefore they set up in the market-place the images of notable men and of such as have been great and bountiful benefactors to the commonwealth, for the perpetual memory of their good acts, and also that the glory and renown of the ancestors may stir and provoke their posterity to virtue" (93).

These kinds of incitements to good would seem to embody what Albert Hirschman, in *The Passions and the Interests*, calls "the principle of the countervailing passions," wherein "one set of comparatively innocuous passions" is deployed to neutralize, by balancing out, "another more dangerous and destructive set."[11] In the words of Graham Hammill, deploying Hirschman, "early modern literary and political writers became increasingly persuaded that humans were in reality driven by passions and self-interest rather than reason, so government was tasked with using one set of passions to control or countervail others"—precisely the practice that Condorcet disparages.[12] In support of his argument, Hirschman cites a passage from the *Advancement of Learning* (1605) in which Francis Bacon observes the utility "in moral and civil matters" of knowing how "to set affection against affection and to master one by another."[13]And this logic does seem operative at one or two moments in Bacon's own utopia, the *New Atlantis* of 1627. We learn, for example, that on the island of Bensalem, there are "no stews, no dissolute houses, nor courtesans, nor any thing of that kind. . . . For marriage is ordained a remedy for unlawful concupiscence. . . . But when men have at hand a remedy more agreeable to their corrupt will, marriage is almost expulsed."[14]

With respect to sexual conduct and gratification, the most famously scandalous expedient from *Utopia* itself is the custom of presenting courting parties naked to each other before commitment to marriage. Non-Utopians may laugh at this practice, Hythlodaeus acknowledges, but the Utopians "do greatly wonder at the folly of all other nations," wherein people choose spouses without having seen their flesh yet will not buy a colt "unless the saddle and all the harness be taken off, lest under those coverings be hid some gall or sore" (90). Bacon's Bensalemites, for their part, disdain this utopian practice, thinking "it a scorn to give a refusal after so familiar knowledge." But "because of many hidden defects in men and women's bodies, they . . . have near every town a couple of pools . . . where it is permitted to one of the friends of the man, and another of the friends of the woman, to see them severally bathe naked."[15]

Reliance on logic of this kind—on procedures that may in some cases seem counterintuitive but can in short order be shown to be rational, indeed admirably clever in steering rooted human inclinations to good ends—abounds in subsequent utopias. In the anonymously authored *Island of Content; or, A New Paradise Discovered* (1709), for example, the narrating representative of utopia explains that a "Custom of willing Separation" accounts for the

> Vertue of our marry'd Women, and the Continence of their husbands; for knowing, that when they are weary of one another, they may part by Consent, makes the matrimonial Shackles fit the easier without galling, and causes both Sides to consider, if they should bring themselves under

Scandal by any libidinous Practices, during the first Marriage-Contract, that if ever hereafter they should so far disagree, as to be willing to part, no Body would be so mad to trust either Man or Woman a second Time, who had so infamously broken their former Covenant.[16]

The utopian rule here plays not on passion, reason, or self-interest alone but on something like a combination of all three: it permits an exercise of reason that supports self-interest, which may in turn accommodate passion. Again, this engineering doesn't claim to assess human beings' goodness or badness objectively or transcendentally. It only puts in place conditions that conduce to moral behavior.

The acme of witty orchestration of the passions, however, is surely reached a century later, in the writings of Charles Fourier. Published from the first decade of the nineteenth century to the years after his death in 1837, these propound a system in which human beings are organized into self-sustaining agrarian societies of roughly sixteen hundred people (Phalanxes) and governed by rules entirely oriented to the fact of the human passions—of which Fourier distinguished twelve—and their combinations. As Charles Gide summarized the project, Fourier sought an arrangement of society "where the passions of man, all without exception . . . may act normally" and in their free play produce "universal harmony." For Fourier, the history of efforts "to change man so as to adapt him to his environment" had issued in no good result, and so the path forward had to lie in "follow[ing] the opposite scent and chang[ing] the environment so as to adapt it to man."[17]

Fourier's inventions in this area famously extend to the minute as well as the sweeping. Anticipating later emphases on preventive medicine, to take just one example, Fourier writes that in his utopia of Harmony, the physician will not be paid according to "the number of sick he treats," as he is "in civilisation," but rather "by a dividend of the general product of the Phalanx" that "increases by one, two, three, four, six ten-thousandths, or decreases in like proportions, according to the *collective* and *comparative* state of the whole Phalanx. The fewer the cases of sickness and death in the course of a year, the larger will be the dividend allotted to the physicians."[18] Once again, what subtends utopian excellence is no alteration of human character, no production of new kinds of people as such, but rather a mechanism of incentives far cleverer than any to be found in the present world. Offering a capsule statement of his principle of design, Fourier asserts that in Harmony, "where each one is a partner, even if only to the extent of getting a share of the proceeds allotted to labour, each one always desires the prosperity of the whole district [*chacun désire constamment la prosperité du canton entier*]. . . . Thus, already through personal interest, good-will is general among the members."[19]

It should not escape our notice that Fourier here claims to solve at a stroke the most intractable problem of social organization: the structure of common investment he devises will, he insists, render communal interests at one with individual ones. Yet Fourier imagines his design as resulting not in economic parity among Harmony's members but in gradations of wealth: his utopia will be home to both poor and rich, the former never falling below a decent level of well-being, certainly, but the latter enjoying lives of considerable material splendor. At a more micro level, his schemes exploit an innate human drive to competitiveness and even manipulation: among the twelve passions, one especially important to Fourierist social organization is the "Cabalist," an urge to engage in intrigues stimulated by rivalries. Evoking Aristotle on justice, Fourier exemplifies once more how the right allotment utopia pursues needn't take the form of a radical symmetry, even as his confident and endlessly proliferating recipes for orchestrating the passions combine syllogism's gratifications with geometry's.

Yet if Fourier foregrounds dramatically how the managerial strain of utopia is allied to the élan of the witty engineer, the statement just quoted also suggests how difficult it is for the engineer to stick to a purely managerial mode. To say that "each one always desires the prosperity of the whole district" is to say something a little stronger than that Harmony's members accept the district's prosperity as a precondition for the furtherance of their own interests. It's at least to open the possibility that such a feeling for the district's interests has become habitual or internalized.

We've already noted one reason it can be hard to maintain a sharp distinction between managerial and transformative practice in utopia: that what may from one angle look like a working with people as they are may from another appear an attempt to change them. But even if this basic conceptual difficulty did not obtain, it would be inaccurate to say that a text such as More's *Utopia* (to which we must now return, by way of beginning to follow the transformative arc) operates solely by incentives and disincentives calibrated to human beings as they are in the nonutopian world. While Hythlodaeus does indeed describe many mechanisms that assume that the citizen will perform a cost-benefit analysis when tempted to behave badly, he reports numerous other instances in which the Utopians are oriented to good behavior by something more like prejudice or habit founded in custom or by even more deeply buried dispositions.

A case in point appears in the oft-discussed account of how the Utopians come to despise gold and silver. According to Hythlodaeus, they avert the social ills that attend fervor for these metals by using them to make "chamber-pots and other vessels that serve for the most vile uses," as well as "great chains, fetters, and gyves wherein they tie their bondmen," and deck "whosoever for any offence be infamed" with gold about the ears, fingers, neck, and head (71). The insensibility to gold's charms that consequently prevails is then well illustrated by the anecdote of the "ambassadors of the Anemolians" (72), who come to Utopia adorned with these metals in order to dazzle the inhabitants but are met with disdain: "For to the eyes of all the Utopians, except very few which had been in other countries for some reasonable cause, all that gorgeousness of apparel seemed shameful and reproachful" (73). The Utopians are shocked by the ambassadors, in other words, because their customs lead them to see the world in a particular way, which is to say that we seem here to have entered the domain of the transformative.

Or at least to have reached some fuzzy boundary between the transformative and the managerial. For there's a notable peculiarity in the language Hythlodaeus uses to recount this innovation. He doesn't ascribe it to Utopus, who (likely many centuries prior) gave Utopia its first constitution and some of its excellent laws (108–9). Rather, he explains that in deflecting gold's attractions, the Utopians "have found out a means . . . agreeable to all their other laws and customs" (*excogitauere quandam rationem, ut reliquis ipsorum institutis consentaneam*) (71).[20] Taken literally, this would mean that the Utopians have produced an arrangement of whose arbitrariness they're to some extent aware, the better to induce desired behavior in themselves. And the point is made even stranger by Hythlodaeus's subsequent assertion that the Utopians generally "marvel that any men be so foolish as to have delight and pleasure in the doubtful glistering of a little trifling stone" (gems, to which we will return in a moment) (73). Such marveling implies that the utopians should have no need to use the device of the chamber pots to see through gold's or gems' lure, any more than should any person possessed of clarity about the true value of things. Thus even allowing that Hythlodaeus may here be somewhat casual in his use of the third-person-plural indicative perfect (*excogitauere*), it looks as though the Utopians have sought (and found) a way to trick themselves into—or, more accurately, to habituate themselves to—esteeming things according to their real worth. The Utopians seem to understand that some pure appeal to reason in this matter will be insufficient, that common sense won't develop without cultivation.

Of course, there is a process that societies have, immemorially, used to render good behavior a matter more of habit or reflex than of cold cost-benefit analysis. That process is education, and its operation is nicely illustrated by the manner in which the Utopians forestall a love of gems. They "deck their young infants in" in pearls, carbuncles, and diamonds, permitting those of a tender age to "make much and be fond and proud of such ornaments." But when the Utopians "be a little more grown in years and discretion, perceiving that none but children do wear such toys and trifles, they lay them away even of their own shamefastness, without any bidding of their parents" (72–73). Having mentioned this device, Hythlodaeus then proceeds to a broader discussion of Utopian training, and to the explanation that the Utopians hold opinions more sensible than those held elsewhere "partly by education, being brought up in that commonwealth whose laws and customs be far different from these kinds of folly, and partly by good literature and learning" (74).

In this, again, the Utopians aren't notably different from other peoples who mandate education in virtue. Indeed what their treatment of gems highlights is that moral or civic education in effect always attests to a culture's recognition that its preferred ways aren't the only ways possible and that if the child is to be prevented from developing dangerously alternative views, habituation or trickery—including the continuous imputation that no other manner of seeing things will really be valid—will have to be resorted to. Knowing the origins of one's axiology rarely endangers its persistence, yet if guardians and parents are aware that the young must absorb proper ways of thinking as a matter of prejudice, then they must also be aware, at some level, of their own embedding in ideology in the largest sense. The Utopians, like any other people who seek to educate their young in values, seem to incorporate a kind of inverse or sideways version of the "I know, but nevertheless . . ." that Slavoj Žižek finds central to ideology's workings.[21] It's not that they understand that how they proceed is wrong but do it anyway; it's rather that they see their values as at once clearly right and somehow contingent, both absolute and in need of continual reinforcement.

In other words, the deliberate education of the young—in Utopia, or anywhere—attests to a recognition that a given set of mores and norms, however strong its claim to absolute rightness, will emerge under particular conditions. And thus it's not surprising to find Hythlodaeus's praise of Utopian education anchored in a larger understanding that not only educational but also economic and other circumstances will exert a powerful influence on behavior. Railing against the beggaring of the population by enclosure and related practices in part 1, Hythlodaeus observes (as we also saw in chapter 1) that a want of means of honest labor perforce leads to criminality:

> Therefore that one covetous and insatiable cormorant . . . may compass about and enclose many thousand acres of ground together within one pale or hedge, the husbandmen be thrust out of their own . . . : By one means . . . or by other, either by hook or crook, they must needs depart away, poor, silly, wretched souls, men, women, husbands, wives, fatherless children, widows, woeful mothers, with their young babes, and their whole households. . . . And when they have wandered abroad till that [the paltry

sums made from the sale of their possessions] be spent, what can they else do but steal, and then just pardy be hanged, or else go about a-begging? And yet then also they be cast in prison as vagabonds, because they go about and work not, whom no man will set a-work, though they never so willingly offer themselves thereto. (22–23)

This diatribe then links up neatly with the charge, delivered a few paragraphs later, that society as presently organized practices something like the inverse of Utopian conditioning to good outcomes: "By suffering your youth wantonly and viciously to be brought up, and to be infected, even from their tender age, by little and little with vice, then, a God's name, to be punished when they commit the same faults after being come to man's state . . . what other thing do you than make thieves and then punish them?" (24).

It would seem odd, not to say inefficient, for utopian imagination to answer so devastating a failure of education through what we've been calling managerial means alone. Alert to the power of conditions over character, utopia would surely need to work transformatively as well, shaping circumstances—as by education—so that people themselves will in turn be shaped in the right ways. And indeed More's Utopians "use with very great endeavour and diligence to put into the heads of their children, whiles they be yet tender and pliant, good opinions and profitable for the conservation of their weal-public" (114). Witty management thus extends beyond managing people just as they are in the nonutopian world; it extends to altering the conditions that make people what—or at least how—they are. If a given vicious habit, in Condorcet's terms, can "be traced back to the legislation, the institutions, the prejudices of the country wherein" such a habit prevails, then it may be that any ameliorative social vision will have to include legislation, institutions, and prejudices operating more or less subtly to replace bad behavior with good.

Of course, the sixteenth century wasn't the first to notice that behavior can be determined by environmental factors less than fully registered by the human subject. Plato asserts the power of beautiful things over the character when discussing the nurturing of his dream-society's elite in book 3 of the *Republic*: "and then our young men, living as it were in a healthy climate, will benefit because all the works of art they see and hear influence them for good, like the breezes from some healthy country, insensibly leading them from earliest childhood into close sympathy and conformity with beauty and reason."[22] In part 6 of book 2 of the *Politics*, Aristotle remarks just as More does the link between criminality and want: "Poverty begets sedition and villainy," as Robert Burton translates him in *The Anatomy of Melancholy*.[23] And as Rhiannon Evans notes, "Environmental determinism was embraced to a greater or lesser degree by most ancient geographers and ethnographers, apparently stemming from the Hippocratic *Airs, Waters and Places*, particularly Chapter 24, which links character and appearance to both landscape and climate."[24]

Utopian thinkers of the British seventeenth and eighteenth centuries, too, highlighted the shaping power of circumstances. [25] Fuz recalls that Gerrard Winstanley, the leading voice of the Diggers, thought "that material conditions are of very great importance to the moral life of the people, and that one cannot change the mental habits and customs, or crime, without changing the poverty, illiteracy and bad health."[26] Robert Wallace, the author of *Various Prospects of Mankind, Nature, and Providence* (1761) also believed that "the root of human evils would be removed by changed environment."[27] In *An Account of the First Settlement, Laws, Form of Government, and Police, of the Cessares, a People of South America* (1764), the Whig political theorist and educational reformer James Burgh records that the Cessares fund public education because education is but dangerously entrusted to parents, and when bad habits "have taken deep root, in early life, experience shews how very difficult it is to eradicate them. And when these vices become the characteristics of a nation, one may easily prognosticate the approaching dissolution of that state."[28] Thomas Northmore, in the similarly utopian *Memoirs of the Planetes* (1795), lists as the twenty-second article of his constitution of Makar that "primogeniture laws and laws of entail from henceforth cease; for . . . exclusive of the injustice of these systems to the younger branches of the same family, they engender poverty in the lower classes of the people, and poverty is frequently the cause of sedition and crimes."[29]

Of course, the idea of circumstances' formative power finds its great eighteenth-century pivot, at least among philosophers, in Rousseau, whose reframing of basic questions about political legitimacy, the progress of the sciences, and other matters was predicated on a conviction that people's desires and behaviors are shaped by geographical and historical situation. It would be easy to show, he asserts in the *Discourse on Inequality* (1755), "that in all the nations of the world the progress of the mind has been precisely proportioned [*les progrès de l'Esprit se sont précisement proportionnés*] to the needs that peoples received from nature or to those which circumstances subjected them, and consequently to the passions, which prompted them to provide for those needs."[30] Among "the differences that distinguish men," further, "some pass for being natural that are exclusively the work of habit and the various ways of life men adopt in society. . . . Not only does education create the difference between cultivated minds and those which are not, but it increases the differences found among the former in proportion to their cultivation."[31] Part of Rousseau's interest here is to show how "the prodigious diversity of educations and ways of life" in the civilized state, as compared with "animal and savage life," magnifies lived inequality; but he's not only occupied with descriptive critique of modern society.[32] In *Émile* (1762), he presents a training in which the careful arrangement of formative conditions—an extreme of artifice serving the cause of nature, a kind of heterotopia within the fallen civilized world—brings out the best in the individual. ("A good meal ought never to be a reward, but why should it not be the result of the care taken in getting it for oneself? Emile does not regard the cake I put on the stone as the prize for having run well. He knows only that the sole means of having this cake is to get there sooner than somebody else."[33])

Rousseau is mentioned only once in Condorcet's *Sketch*, and not specifically in connection with his pronouncements on circumstances' formative power.[34] Yet one could say that in this area, Condorcet was a kind of Friedrich Schiller to Rousseau's Immanuel Kant. Where Schiller would build on the foundation of Kant's aesthetics a scheme for redeeming society by mobilizing aesthetic feeling, Condorcet would discard Rousseau's pessimism anent human perfectibility while taking up the earlier writer's brief for the force of conditions—which he would then fuse with expectations of progress from other thinkers, especially Anne Robert Jacques Turgot, the second of whose two celebrated Sorbonne lectures of 1750 was titled "Tableau philosophique des progrès successifs de l'ésprit humain." "Finally," writes Condorcet, "we see the rise of a new doctrine which was to deal the final blow to the already tottering structure of prejudice: the doctrine of the indefinite perfectibility of the human race of which Turgot, Price and Priestley were the first and the most brilliant apostles" (102).[35]

Condorcet's optimism has a political component. In his view, the liberation of humanity has been not only delayed by prejudice against certain ideas but also deliberately suppressed by those in power. Yet this suppression can no longer hold. The "principles of the French constitution" are already "too widely propagated, too seriously professed" in Europe "for priests and despots to prevent their gradual penetration even into the hovels of their slaves," and they will inspire those slaves "with that smouldering indignation [*cette sourde indignation*] which not even constant humiliation and fear can smother in the soul of the oppressed" (127). In More, the outrage that fuels utopia is the indignation of the enlightened political thinker whose project is, in imagination, realized over the seas by a philosopher-king who is also a social engineer of egalitarian tendencies. In Condorcet, the ideal society will be brought into being by the power of the masses, or at the very least with their emphatic cooperation, and equality will come into its own against entrenched interests.

Optimism about conditions' capacity to improve character also converges with indignation against political obstruction in the theory and practice of Robert Owen, whose earliest publications followed Condorcet's *Sketch* by only a few years. Owen joins Condorcet in taking as basic assumptions that the upper classes have enjoyed environmental advantages of which the lower have been deprived, that these advantages have produced finer rather than merely different people, and that this monopoly of the privileged needs to be ended. Unconscionable, to Owen, was that the characters of "the poor and working classes of Great Britain and Ireland . . . are now permitted to be very generally formed without proper guidance or direction, and, in many cases, under circumstances which directly impel them to a course of extreme vice and misery."[36] As the director of the mills at New Lanark, accordingly, he went to work on circumstances. As he recounts in the lengthiest and most famous of his early broadsides, *A New View of Society; or, Essays on the Principle of the Formation of the Human Character, and the Application of the Principle to Practice* (1816), the new manager at New Lanark (that is, he himself) "began to bring forward his various expedients to withdraw the unfavourable circumstances by which they [the workers] had hitherto been surrounded, and to replace them by others calculated to produce a more happy result."[37]

With profits from the mills increasing, Owen would eventually found, in Robert P. Sutton's summary, "a new system of education called the Institute for the Formation of Character. It had a nursery school, a day school, an evening school for adults, community rooms, and a public hall."[38] That the centerpiece of Owen's project should be so named accords with his most strenuously repeated assertion: that character is a product of circumstances. In *A New View*, he insists that

> every day will make it more and more evident that the character of man is, without a single exception, always formed for him; that it may be, and is, chiefly created by his predecessors; that they give him, or may give him, his ideas and habits, which are the powers that govern and direct his conduct. Man, therefore, never did, nor is it possible he ever can, form his own character.[39]

The intensity and frequency with which Owen urges this point would by itself make him one of the most determined representatives of the transformative line, as against the managerial, in the history of utopian imagining.

But Owen goes still further, asserting that the erroneous view "that each individual man forms his own character" has been nothing less than the pre-eminent source of human misery.[40] The "fundamental errors now impressed from infancy on the minds of all men, and from whence all their other errors proceed, are, that they form their own individual characters, and possess merit or demerit for the peculiar notions impressed on the mind during early growth, before they have acquired strength and experience to judge of or resist the impression of those notions or opinions, which, on investigation, appear contradictions to facts existing around them, and which are therefore false."[41] The great scourge of human history has been, in other words, an error about error—the view that individuals are to be held responsible for what has affected their character before they're able to distinguish error from truth. This mistake has doubly inhibited the development of proper schemes of social engineering, not only misdirecting the attention of those who would improve the human lot but also sanctifying inaction by naturalizing the disparity between classes.

This last aspect of Owen is well captured by George Bernard Shaw in the preface to his strange utopian cycle of plays, *Back to Methuselah* (1921). In the course of describing Darwinism's meaning for socialism, Shaw recalls that Owen "made desperate efforts to convince England that her criminals, her drunkards, her ignorant and stupid masses, were the victims of circumstance: that if we would only establish his new moral world we should find that the masses born into an educated and moralized community would be themselves educated and moralized." And this, of course, rubbed against the self-congratulation of the affluent. "If you were rich," Shaw writes, "how pleasant it was to feel that you owed your riches to the superiority of your own character!" Darwin's theories then struck a further blow, making

a clean sweep of all such self-righteousness. It more than justified Robert Owen by discovering in the environment of an organism an influence on it more potent than Owen had ever claimed. It implied that street arabs are produced by slums and not by original sin. . . . It shewed that the surprising changes which Robert Owen had produced in factory children . . . were as nothing to the changes—changes not only of habits but of species, not only of species but of orders—which might conceivably be the work of environment acting on individuals without any character or intellectual consciousness whatever. No wonder the Socialists received Darwin with open arms.[42]

We might quibble with one aspect of Shaw's characterization, his claim that environment's influence on the human organism is less potent and subtle in Owen's construction than it is in Darwin's. Contra Shaw, Owen's point is precisely that "street arabs" are produced by "slums," milieu doing its work without always being registered by consciousness. Although Owen doesn't use the terms "environment" and "organism," his claim for the former's power over the latter is hard to exceed. Shaw does, however, well highlight the atmosphere into which Owen and other reformers launched the argument that those born into terrible conditions shouldn't be thought of as meriting such misery. His account evokes in particular the society-coach parable from Bellamy's introduction to *Looking Backward*, where, as we saw in chapter 1, those on top excuse the injustice of the configuration (many haul so that a few may ride) by telling themselves "that there was no other way in which Society could get along" and by thinking themselves "of finer clay, in some way belonging to a higher order of beings who might justly expect to be drawn" (28). Like Bellamy, Shaw highlights the transformative vision's association with a *nemesis* that stands appalled at a condition in which education and other circumstances conducive to Condorcet's "high and delicate feelings" are allocated restrictively, and prior to the formation of the subject who could be said to earn or deserve them.

Yet in indicating the proximity of Bellamy and Owen, Shaw's preface also marks how this style of indignation needn't be aligned with the transformative strain alone. For *Looking Backward* seems to accent the managerial far more heavily. In Bellamy's society of the future, desirable behavior is produced by a system of incentives quite comprehensible to nineteenth-century people, even if monetary compensation as such has been excluded as a motivator. It therefore makes perfect sense for Dr. Leete to insist that human nature in the year 2000 is no different from human nature in 1887. In *Looking Backward*, the new order of things is explicitly an *Aufhebung* of monopoly capitalism in which the central government has become the single (enlightened) employer, and this practical fruit of deft management in production and distribution echoes the novel's moral commitment to managing people as it finds them.

At the same time, however, the incentive system in Bellamy's utopia exerts a continuous pressure on mores. At one point, Julian West asks Dr. Leete's daughter Edith how there can be such "great variety in the size and cost of the houses" in Boston in 2000, given that "all citizens have the same income." Edith explains that

> "although the income is the same, personal taste determines how the individual shall spend it. Some like fine horses; others, like myself, prefer pretty clothes; and still others want an elaborate table. The rents which the nation receives for these houses vary, according to size, elegance, and location, so that everybody can find something to suit. [. . .] It is a matter of taste and convenience wholly. I have read that in old times people often kept up establishments and did other things which they could not afford for ostentation, to make people think them richer than they were. Was it really so, Mr. West?"
>
> "I shall have to admit that it was," I replied.
>
> "Well, you see, it could not be so nowadays; for everybody's income is known, and it is known that what is spent one way must be saved another."
> (84–85)

Competitiveness may still be one of the springs of human conduct, but ostentation has apparently been engineered away. And if Bellamy's society feels like a utopia rather than merely a more pleasant arrangement of things, this will be, for many readers, because a heightened egalitarianism, a juster *nomos*, has made its inhabitants seem better as well as happier than the run of people in nonutopian reality. Leete's full response to West's "Human nature must have changed very much" is, "Not at all . . . but the conditions of human life have changed, and with them the motives of human action" (56). If the motives of human action have changed, hasn't human nature been transformed in some degree?

One of the ways Bellamy tries to forestall this objection is by casting West's progress as a learning what human nature is like—or even a disclosing to himself of what he has always, deep down, known it to be. In reply to West's question about what incentive a man "may have to put forth his best endeavors when, however much or little he accomplishes, his income remains the same," Leete asks, "Does it then really seem to you . . . that human nature is insensible to any motive save fear of want and love of luxury . . . ? Your contemporaries did not really think so, though they might fancy they did" (77). Later in *Looking Backward*, Bellamy intimates that this anamnesis, this unveiling of West's suppressed understanding of human nature, is paralleled by an unveiling of essential human nature in practice that occurred when utopia came into being. In his telephone sermon, the preacher Mr. Barton declares that after the change, "it was for the first time possible see what unperverted human nature really was like" (191). As in Rousseau, the managerial vision evades the charge that it's in truth transformative by asserting that it hasn't really changed human nature, only brought into the light of day what was unconscionably buried before.

Transformation's Apogee

There's a reverse side to this coin, however. If a managerial utopia such as Bellamy's can partake of the *nemesis* associated with more professedly transformative visions, a more or less transformative utopia can, clearly, offer some of the satisfactions of the witty managerial. Owen, who as we've seen is legible as one of the purest proponents of the transformative, often presents his "dream of forming a new humanity,"[43] to borrow Bloch's phrasing, as an engineering problem. In *The New View*, for example, he avows that "the best or the worst" of "the various opinions, manners, vices, and virtues of mankind" may, "with mathematical precision, be taught to the rising generation,"[44] and in the preface to the same work explains that he "viewed the population" of New Lanark, "with mechanism and every other part of the establishment, as a system composed of many parts, and which it was [his] duty and interest so to combine, as that every hand, as well as every spring, lever, and wheel, should effectually co-operate to produce the greatest pecuniary gain to the proprietors."[45] At this moment in his preface, Owen is addressing capitalists and directors who may imagine that the provision of more humane conditions for workers will diminish profits, so the interest here is managerial in a very literal sense. But Owen's language highlights nonetheless how the witty engineer's skill in orchestrating causes and effects can be applied as readily to systems designed to change character as to incentives designed to exploit character as it is.

In nineteenth-century utopian thinking, the interplay between transformative and material approaches was inflected by a high degree of fluidity, amounting sometimes to a near indistinction, between postulates concerning the human organism's response to its environment and postulates concerning the inevitable tendencies of *homo economicus*. Consider, for example, Nikolai Chernyshevsky's incalculably influential *What Is to Be Done?* of 1863. As the editors of the 1989 English translation point out, that novel's radical disposition is against free will as an explanation for human action, in favor of the view that "action, thought, and emotion" are "nothing more than sensual responses to external stimuli and therefore . . . governed by natural laws."[46] It turns out, however, that this socioeconomic and biological determinism by no means precludes a diction that refers to interests. Rather, the pursuit of "advantages" is the law of human nature. At one point, the novel's heroine, Vera Pavlovna, summarizes the doctrines imparted by her love interest, the medical student Lopukhov—essentially the views Chernyshevsky is making a case for—as follows: "We began with the proposition that man acts out of necessity and that his actions are determined by the influences under which these actions occur. . . . When an action has everyday significance, these motives are called 'advantages'. . . . Therefore, a man always acts according to the calculation of his own advantage." Lopukhov then assents to this summary, at which Vera asks whether people never act out of caprice. What about when, in playing the piano, she turns the page of the score with right hand or left, apparently arbitrarily? Lopukhov replies that Vera will "use the hand that's more convenient— there's no question of caprice."[47]

Further on, the narrator addresses in imagination Vera's grasping mother, Marya Aleksevna: "You're now engaged in a bad business because your environment demands it; but if we were to provide you with a different environment, you'd gladly become harmless, even beneficial, . . . and if it were in your own interest, you'd do anything at all, you'd even act decently and nobly if necessary."[48] This adaptability of the language of interests to a paradigm of environmental determination is then supported by the plot of the novel, where the realized utopian scheme begins not with a top-down restructuring of society but with a bottom-up, or rather a grassroots-middle-up, creation of businesses run along cooperative lines. Under this ideal arrangement, the human organism does eschew self-interest in one sense, sharing profits rather than competing. But this sharing conduces to advantage in a more capacious reckoning, since it permits the efflorescence of more morally elevated and culturally richer being. (Vera conspicuously denies pure altruism in explaining, to the laboring women she adopts as partners in a sewing business, her motives for taking what may seem an unfairly low share of the profits: "You know that people have different passions. . . . Some like to go to balls, others like to wear fine clothes or play cards. . . . It happens to be my passion to set up this enterprise with you."[49])

Writing a decade and a half before Chernyshevsky's novel, in what would become a component of *The German Ideology*, Karl Marx and Friedrich Engels suggest a somewhat different interplay of interest and determination. Outlining the principles of their materialist approach to history, they explain that the "social structure and the state are continually evolving out of the life-process of definite individuals . . . not as they may appear in their own or other people's imagination, but as they *actually* are, i.e., as they act, produce materially, and hence as they work under definite material limits, presuppositions and conditions independent of their will." It is "not consciousness that determines life, but life that determines consciousness."[50] This kind of view offers a natural foundation for transformative utopia, of course, and indeed it arguably grounds later Bolshevik annunciations of the Soviet "New Man," as articulated most famously by Leon Trotsky in *Literature and Revolution* of 1924 (though it was only in 1924 that *The German Ideology* itself would begin to be published).[51] Of more immediate moment for Marx and Engels at the time of writing, however, was surely that in so describing the power of material limits, they were able to deploy the kinds of assumptions that ground transformative utopias without endorsing either a naive utopianism or a status quo premised on the motivating power of selfish behavior. If environment is everything in a developmental sense, then identifying it with the conditions of production makes it possible to secure the primacy of the economic without identifying human flourishing with purely economistic measures or values.[52]

On the other side of Chernyshevsky from *The German Ideology*, temporally speaking, Wilde's "Soul of Man under Socialism" confirms in yet a different way that as it grew harder, over the course of the nineteenth century, to dismiss evidence of conditions' immense power to shape human character, the claims of the transformative as against the merely managerial vision perforce became more exalted and more insistent. Though "The Soul of Man" includes much material whose relation to utopia is tangential at best, it does, as noted in the introduction, contain an epigram ritually cited in popular as well as scholarly writing on utopia: "A map of the world that does not include Utopia is not worth even glancing at, for it leaves out the one country at which Humanity

is always landing."[53] More to the point, Wilde places his screed within a familiar genealogy of utopian speculations in taking up matters such as the etiology
of criminality. Like Owen, he raises questions about human responsibility
anticipated in More's "what can they else do but steal . . . ?", but he goes further
by affirming that in the socialist-anarchist future, not only authority but also
"punishment will pass away." And when

> there is no punishment at all, crime will either cease to exist, or, if it occurs,
> will be treated by physicians as a very distressing form of dementia, to be
> cured by care and kindness. For what are called criminals nowadays are not
> criminals at all. Starvation, and not sin, is the parent of modern crime. . . .
> When private property is abolished there will be no necessity for crime, no
> demand for it.[54]

Crediting the new utopian environment with enormous powers as it does,
"The Soul of Man" lies still further toward the transformative end of the
transformative-managerial spectrum even than do Owen's writings. It promises not just that improved conditions will enable the lower orders to be better
and happier but that these conditions will issue in a new humanity. According
to Wilde, the propertyless future of "Socialism, Communism, or whatever one
chooses to call it, by converting private property into public wealth, and sub-
stituting cooperation for competition," will permit a flowering of individualism never yet seen on Earth, and thus a level of human development scarcely
glimpsed before: "It is a question whether we have ever seen the full expression of a personality, except on the imaginative plane of art. . . . It will be a
marvellous thing—the true personality of man—when we see it."[55] Few texts
illustrate more clearly how in the transformative utopia, a conviction of circumstances' power to mold converges with optimism about the emergence of
a new humankind.

Toward the close of "The Soul of Man," Wilde anticipates the charge that
"such a scheme" as he sets forth is "quite unpractical, and goes against human
nature." But his response is to embrace impracticality. He remarks that while
a practical scheme is one "that is already in existence" or one "that could be
carried out according to existing conditions," it "is exactly the existing conditions
that one objects to; and any scheme that could accept these conditions is wrong
and foolish. The conditions will be done away with and human nature will
change. The only thing that one really knows about human nature is that it
changes."[56] Here again, Wilde exceeds Owen in optimism about how far human
beings can be transformed, suggesting indeed that "human nature" is simply
whatever human beings have been and eventually prove capable of being.

But what exactly does Wilde mean by "existing conditions"? Given the last
word of his essay's title, the phrase must be taken to point, in the first instance,

to the regime of private property. Yet it's not long, in this climactic section, before he turns to a yet more encompassing set of conditions in which the human organism finds itself. A few sentences later, he describes individualism as something that "comes naturally and inevitably out of man," as "the point to which all development tends. It is the differentiation to which all organisms grow. . . . Evolution is the law of life, and there is no evolution except towards individualism" (1100–101).[57] Here, we might say, Rousseau's and Condorcet's notion of the stifling antinatural tendencies of society comes together with Herbert Spencer's grand cosmological vision, according to which evolution—the governing principle of the universe from its very inception—"is definable as a change from an incoherent homogeneity to a coherent heterogeneity."[58] The totality of socioeconomic conditions and the totality of the organism's environment here appear as one and the same, or at least as powerfully reinforcing of each other's claims to determine, fundamentally, humanity's qualities.

If the biological organism and the economic animal converge in these ways in Chernyshevsky and Wilde, however, they seem in the main to decouple in the transformative visions of the century that began a month after Wilde's death. Where one prominent line of early twentieth-century utopian faith would emphasize the shaping of the human creature by environment understood as a field of stimuli, another would emphasize the shaping of human outcomes by the conditions of production. We'll have occasion to examine the latter line, with its aspiration to realize something like Trotsky's New Man, in chapter 3. Here we need mainly to pursue the culmination of the former in and around the writings of B. F. Skinner, though this will include a few encounters with socioeconomic determination along the way.

Skinner's works have proven a source of embarrassment for partisans of utopia, a testing of the limits of good will toward utopian thinking, on at least two counts. One is that his utopian novel, *Walden Two* (1948), though widely read and an important inspiration for many real-world intentional communities, is not easily valued for its literary quality or stylistic nuance. Written, by Skinner's own report, in two months in the early summer of 1945, before he assumed a department chairship whose duties might (he worried) leave him no "time for science or scholarship," it presents its solutions with a smugness that would make Bellamy's Dr. Leete blush and, worse, seems incapable of believing that such smugness should diminish readerly enthusiasm.[59] The other problem Skinner poses lies in the extremity of his views—in his willingness to carry his principles through to conclusions that many readers will find repellent or absurd. Skinner's writings merit our sustained attention here, however, precisely because they represent a certain limit case in the transformative utopian strain—and in so doing speak in particularly clarifying ways to questions about freedom and human value that bear heavily on utopian justice.

We can best make our way into these considerations via *Walden Two* itself, which follows the traditional utopian model in which a guide introduces a visitor to the principles and daily activities of the ideal society. In this case, the focal visitor is the narrator, a psychology professor named Burris, and the guide, Frazier, is, as noted in chapter 1, at once Skinner's avatar and the designer of Walden Two. Over the course of the novel, Frazier and his surrogate cicerones lead Burris and a small party of other interested visitors through the facilities of the community, which counts about a thousand members, while discussing its theory and mechanics. The action of the novel is more or less limited to this four-day tour and to debates about Walden Two's plausibility in which the role of blustery skeptic is, as we noted also in chapter 1, played by a philosophy professor named Castle.

With respect to the members who have entered the community as adults, Walden Two seems neither trickily managerial nor strongly transformative. Members' good behavior seems maintained largely by a set of rules that would presumably appeal to most rational, hardworking people and by their own utopian optimism—their will to happiness, and their devotion to a project that will model the good life for humankind and eventually propagate across the world. The more striking innovation of *Walden Two* pertains to its handling not of those who arrive full-grown but of those born into the community, whose fine qualities are ensured by behaviorist techniques that enfold them from their earliest moments. Children learn self-control, for example, through constructed situations in which deferring a lick of a lollipop permits enjoyment of the whole lollipop later, or in which a long, hunger-inducing walk is followed by a requirement that they stand for five minutes in front of steaming bowls of soup.

In 1971's *Beyond Freedom and Dignity*, Skinner quotes G. M. Trevelyan to the effect that it was Owen who first "clearly grasped and taught that environment makes character and that environment is under human control."[60] Owen's legacy is indeed evident in both *Walden Two* and *Beyond Freedom and Dignity*, but Skinner's rhetoric is more aggressively transformative even than anything from the manager of New Lanark. Evoking Wilde more nearly, Frazier insists that the applied behavioral engineering of Walden Two and its offspring will produce a new kind of person: "If we can't solve a problem, we can create men who can! And better artists! And better craftsmen!" (275). Moreover, Skinner addresses head-on a problem that Owen largely skirts: the suspicion that a human being shaped under highly controlled conditions cannot meaningfully possess freedom. At one point in *Walden Two*, Frazier explains that advances in positive reinforcement permit "a sort of control under which the controlled, though they are following a code much more scrupulously than was ever the case under the old system, nevertheless *feel free*. They are doing what they want to do, not what they are forced to do" (246). This feeling of freedom isn't freedom, but in the view of Skinner-Frazier it's legitimately foundational to a better world.[61]

Clearly, the internalization of control through operant conditioning offers Skinner a fresh way of resolving numerous social problems to which utopian thought had long addressed itself, among them the problem of punishment. According to Skinner-Frazier, the operant utopia has no use for punishment because a person rightly conditioned simply won't be inclined to behave badly. Frazier is never asked what happens if a child refuses to wait for the soup or becomes refractory while waiting, but he assures his visitors, "we don't punish. We never administer an unpleasantness in the hope of repressing or eliminating undesirable behavior" (104). For Skinner, punishment has been employed through history both because the world has hitherto known no form of social engineering possessing behaviorism's potency and because punishment's short-term effectiveness is so plainly visible: "the immediate, temporary effect of punishment overshadows the eventual advantage of positive reinforcement" (*Walden Two* 245). In *Beyond Freedom and Dignity*, Skinner insists that "in order to maintain the position that all control is wrong, it has been necessary to disguise or conceal the nature of useful practices, to prefer weak practices just because they can be disguised or concealed, and—a most extraordinary result indeed!—to perpetuate punitive measures" far more openly (41).

Of course, Skinner here gets at precisely the reason why regimes of punishment might be thought to comport better with the dignity of human beings than controlled environments do. Systems of rules with precisely, or even vaguely, stated punishments seem to operate at the level of consciousness, putting a choice of options (to offend or not to offend, at a minimum) before a being at least nominally credited with a meaningful ability to choose. In Hythlodaeus's discourse in part 1 of *Utopia*, the thief is dissuaded from adding murder to his crimes by the recognition that murder would incur a more severe penalty, not by being conditioned to abhor homicide. For Skinner, punishment is inefficient, but both he and his detractors would agree that *if* one believes subjects to possess some real autonomy that must be respected, punishment has, among the various imaginable means of orchestrating conduct, the virtue of a certain transparency. Instead of being manipulated into behaving well by shadowy inducements, the member of society is permitted to exercise volition—which is to say that the managerial utopia, deploying rewards and punishments, would seem to permit real freedom as against the mere feeling of freedom. People subject to the most constraining rules can in theory still elect to disobey, thus enjoying (even if, or especially where, punished) the greater existential liberty that comes with trajectories not wholly set by others' designs. The witty engineer who devises systems of incentives and disincentives that work with human beings untransformed reserves, in this sense, a space for human dignity and autonomy.

As we've seen, however, even More's early utopia acknowledges the power of all manner of conditions to affect a person's willingness to risk being disciplined. If the thief can be dissuaded from murder by a wise gradation of punishments, the ordinary person may, in the best-designed society, be dissuaded from theft by the provision of resources that make theft unnecessary. Even *Utopia*, that is, demonstrates how persuasion to good conduct through well-crafted rules can blend quietly with a devising of conditions that work on the subject in less explicit or foregrounded ways. And this propensity of less transparent prompts to virtue to work in concert with more clearly marked ones has the potential to set up an important moral anxiety for the reader: a worry that if conditions are too propitious for virtue, the inhabitant of utopia will be deprived of the chance to be a genuinely moral being, to achieve the kind of greatness of soul available to those who live in an apparently uncontrolled world. This possibility doesn't seem greatly to have agitated More, but its salience appears to increase as we move further in the direction of transformative systems designed to bring about good behavior without relying on conscious volition. And it would be taken up in the twentieth century in numerous critiques of utopian thinking and rebuttals of these critiques, several of which we'll examine in a moment.

Skinner, for his part, answers the question with remarkable decisiveness. In *Beyond Freedom and Dignity*, he insists that the "problem is to induce people not to be good but to behave well" (67) and holds more generally that what he calls the literatures of freedom and dignity throw up obstacles to the improvement of the human lot. He doesn't name many specific texts in his critique of these literatures,[62] but he does make clear that the literature of dignity affiliates human worth with autonomous (good) action, while the literature of freedom insists on the value of autonomous action itself. Skinner acknowledges that these literatures have accomplished important things historically, but he also asserts that they must be rejected in any serious thinking about future forms of social organization. And this for the immovable reason that there *is* no human autonomy in the sense in which these literatures understand it.

That is to say, because our responses are shaped by all the conditioning factors to which we've been exposed, our behavior in a given instance can't, per Skinner, be said in any meaningful way to originate with ourselves, as if in distinction from all those factors. Owen, again, would insist that "*the character of man is, without a single exception, always formed for him*"; Skinner's Frazier, adapting the classical determinist position that we believe in free will because we can never know the countless factors that lead to a given action, declares,

"I deny that freedom exists at all" (241). In Skinner's view, freedom in the sense of behavior that can be said to originate wholly with an autonomous moral agent is, precisely, an illusion produced by our inability to enumerate all of a behavior's myriad causes.

The idea of dignity, which Skinner associates with a person's being given credit for a good action, founders for similar reasons. In *Beyond,* he observes that we "commend those who behave well without supervision more than those who need to be watched, and those who naturally speak a language more than those who must consult grammatical rules" (49). In general, he maintains, the "amount of credit a person receives is related in a curious way to the visibility of the causes of his behavior" (45): we "withhold credit when the causes are conspicuous" (45). The same is true of good behavior in the sense of avoidance of punishable actions: "When a person derives his own rules from an analysis of punitive contingencies, we are particularly likely to give him credit for the good behavior which follows," but the truth is that in such a case the "visible stages" by which a person learns to avoid punishment "have simply faded farther into history" (69). It's not surprising that "we are likely to admire behavior more as we understand it less" since we "stand in awe of the inexplicable" (53). But the result is that any "evidence that a person's behavior may be attributed to external circumstances seems to threaten his dignity or worth" (44) and that a "scientific conception" of human arrangement such as Skinner propounds "seems demeaning because nothing is eventually left for which autonomous man can take credit" (58).

Skinner does not limit this characterization of dignity to matters we would routinely associate with admiration or the recognition of achievement. On the contrary, in a highly unsettling section of *Beyond,* he indicates that his casting of dignity as the receiving of due credit extends to cases in which "dignity" has a rather different acceptation:

(What is felt when a person protests is usually called resentment, significantly defined as "the expression of indignant displeasure," but we do not protest *because* we feel resentful. We both protest *and* feel resentful because we have been deprived of the chance to be admired or to receive credit.)

A large part of the literature of dignity is concerned with justice, with the appropriateness of rewards and punishment. . . . We are concerned here with that part of the literature of dignity which protests encroachment on personal worth. A person protests (and incidentally feels indignant) when he is unnecessarily jostled, tripped, or pushed around, forced to work with the wrong tools, tricked into behaving foolishly with joke-shop novelties, or forced to behave in demeaning ways, as in a jail or concentration camp. He protests and resents the addition of any unnecessary control. (54–55)

In other words, Skinner sees dignity in the sense of receiving praise for what one has done as continuous with dignity in a sense more usually associated with natural law and human rights. The ill humor that results when one is made to look foolish by a joy buzzer is of a piece with the protest of the concentration-camp detainee, both being species of a bristling against control that also, as he'll go on to explain, encompasses the artist's resentment at "being told that he is painting the kind of picture that sells well" or our irritation at being told that "we are imitating an admired person" (55).

Skinner's elision, here, of exercises of force over human beings might seem to vitiate any prospect of his formulations illuminating problems of social justice, either in utopia or in the world we have. Certainly, Skinner directs no more of his concern to the prospect of justice than he does to that of virtue: the ends his program serves are, rather, enhanced well-being and survival. Having made clear, in *Beyond Freedom and Dignity*, that what's right for the individual is a maximizing of positive reinforcement, Skinner asserts flatly that things "are good (positively reinforcing) or bad (negatively reinforcing) presumably because of the contingencies of survival under which the species evolved" (104). And this point extends to cultures, the only social group in which Skinner seems greatly interested: "Survival is the only value according to which a culture is eventually to be judged, and any practice that furthers survival has survival value by definition" (136).

As we'll see later in this chapter, however, Skinner's construing of the demand for dignity as a demand for proper credit does in a curious way shed light on other understandings of dignity associated with justice and freedom. We'll see, that is, how something like the extremity of his transformative design points to an unexpected link between what we might call worth-based understandings of human dignity and understandings associated with belief in the value of genuine agency, and in this helps us to insights about the relation between meaningful existence and other desiderata such as liberty and material provision. For the moment, however, we need to tarry with a different and more obvious point: that in spite of his denigration of social protest and his rejection of the literatures of freedom and dignity, Skinner is animated by a powerful indignation of his own. That indignation's object, of course, is the present organization of society, and Skinner's anger is very precisely the anger of the engineer confronting poor design. Incomparably frustrating for him is a world that refuses to put into practice the behavioral engineering that will demonstrably make humankind better.

This failure to make use of behaviorist science's capacity to transform the world is bound up with the question of freedom, for Skinner, because it's predicated on the presumption that leaving-alone amounts to bowing to the sanctity of liberty. In *Walden Two*, Frazier insists that refusing to control people according to the principles of behaviorism does not mean freeing them from control but rather leaving control in the hands of the "charlatan, the demagogue, the salesman, the ward heeler, the bully, the cheat, the educator, the priest—all who are now in possession of the techniques of behavioral engineering" (240). "We not only *can* control human behavior, we *must*" (241), in part because others who are not "we," and have something other than society's best interests at heart, are already doing so. Or as Skinner puts it in propria persona in *Beyond Freedom and Dignity*, "Permissiveness is not . . . a policy; it is the abandonment of policy, and its apparent advantages are illusory. To refuse to control is to leave control not to the person himself, but to other parts of the social and non-social environments" (84). The "fundamental mistake made by all those who choose weak methods of control is to assume that the balance of control is left to the individual, when in fact it is left to other conditions" (99), and while those conditions "are often hard to see, . . . to continue to neglect them and to attribute their effects to autonomous man is to court disaster" (99).

Confronting Skinner's incomprehension at those who know how to redeem the world but decline to intervene, we may feel ourselves arriving at the culmination of two histories at once: that of the transformative strain in utopian thinking and that of the indignant engineer. Their convergence makes perfect sense, of course, insofar as Skinner presents his program as a total engineering of development in which the mechanism is to shape every aspect of the human organism. The degree of indignation here seems indeed to match the immensity of opportunity portended by the transformative vision—and thus the immensity of opportunity lost. In *Beyond Freedom and Dignity*, moreover, Skinner's indignation is compounded by a sense that his kind of transformative vision opens the only path out of a worldwide crisis. We might say, then, that at the moment when transformative utopia reaches its apogee in the sense of being most unapologetically transformative, it also confronts a particularly fraught confirmation of its utopianness in the sense of unlikelihood of coming to be. In Skinner's view, a scientifically informed *nomos* is, really for first the time in history, capable of realization. But it remains unrealized thanks to a powerful counterindignation driven by misunderstanding and fear.

Authenticity contra Conditioning

It's hardly surprising, of course, that the counterindignation elicited by Skinner's writings has been intense and widespread. In a moment, we'll turn to one of the richest of philosophical rebuttals to counterindignation in general,

George Kateb's *Utopia and Its Enemies* (1963), whose longest chapter is framed as a metacritique of commentators who "feel that Skinner's program imperils all that is precious in human nature."[63] One of the curiosities of the literary history of utopia, however, is that the most celebrated fictional attack on Skinner's kind of program saw print well before Skinner had begun to publish his more ambitious ideas. Aldous Huxley's *Brave New World* (1932), in which techniques of manipulation that begin at fertilization ensure a docile and contented, if not meaningfully happy, populace, antedated *Walden Two* by sixteen years and *Beyond Freedom and Dignity* by thirty-nine. If with Skinner's postwar proposals we reach a certain culmination of the transformative vision, in other words, we find the counterindignation most suited to this culmination in a text issuing in the interwar years, at a moment when behaviorism had become both a sensation in the United States and the dominant approach to psychological inquiry in the Soviet Union.

Huxley begins his novel with a smiling "Director of Hatcheries and Conditioning" who introduces a flock of students to his world's methods of social control. Taking on the structural role usually filled by a narrating visitor from the nonutopian world, the students trail the Director from the Fertilizing Room (where embryos are made into Alphas, Betas, Gammas, Deltas, and Epsilons) to the Neo-Pavlovian Conditioning Rooms (where administered shocks teach infants to hate books, which are not for their intellects, and flowers, because they'll grow up to consume more if they don't spend time in nature) to the children's dormitories (where ideological training is administered by audio while the children sleep). The Director makes clear that the virtue of the system lies in its closing of the gap between what the person is and what the designers of the society want that person to be; concluding his introduction to hypnopædia, he explains proudly that "at last the child's mind *is* these suggestions, and the sum of the suggestions *is* the child's mind."[64]

Skinner certainly didn't aim to ensure the docility of masses serving an all-powerful state, nor did he recommend Pavlovian techniques as such. As Krishan Kumar has noted, the operant conditioning he promoted favored the replacement of the "two-term, stimulus-response model of Pavlov's by a three-term model: stimulus-behavior-reinforcement," and he and his followers argued that it is "Pavlovian, not Skinnerian, conditioning that is satirized by Huxley in *Brave New World*."[65] At the same time, however, Skinner was essentially in accord with Huxley's future rulers on the importance of total management of the environment in which members of society mature, and there are times when Frazier sounds very much like the Director of Hatcheries and Conditioning. Where the latter eminence declares that "the secret of happiness and virtue" is "liking what you've *got* to do" (26), Frazier, as we've seen, touts the benefits of a system "under which the controlled, though they are following a code much more scrupulously than was ever the case under the old system, nevertheless *feel free*. They are doing what they want to do, not what they are forced to do."

Of course, Huxley's point is that force can have many meanings, as can freedom. And indeed one of the insights afforded by *Brave New World*, as a lens through which to read Skinner, is that the latter defends his program in part by construing freedom in a singularly abstract and existential way. As Skinner deploys the concept, freedom would mean an absence of external factors exercising shaping power over the subject—a manifestly impossible immunity to, or transcendence of, impinging influences. Freedom can, however, be understood in another way, as an exemption from domination by people—an acceptation Skinner attempts to harness to his own ends when he asserts that charlatans, demagogues, and others are all "now in possession of the techniques of behavioral engineering." The problem with this gambit, of course, is that it invites the further observation that if many kinds of people (and institutions) possess techniques of behavioral engineering, they'll compete with each other to apply those techniques, depriving any one person or entity of the capacity to dominate a given subject wholly. People may be subject to various forms of control, but precisely insofar as the real-world chaos deplored by Skinner prevails, people will manifestly not be controlled by one power, as they are in fictions of state-sponsored conditioning such as Huxley's. It's possible to argue that there obtains in the messy world that incites Skinner's indignation a kind of freedom not available in the world described in Huxley's novel.

The climax of *Brave New World* may seem a kind of aberration from the rest of the novel insofar as it introduces a representative of the World State who condescends to debate the ethics of the transformative utopia with the principal rebels against it, Bernard Marx, Helmholtz Watson, and John the Savage. In so bringing this figure of authority, Mustapha Mond, before the reader, Huxley arguably renders the all-powerful State less frighteningly implacable, and its terrors are then further diminished by the relatively mild punishments (as compared to those handed down in dystopias such as George Orwell's *1984*) meted out to the rebelliously minded. (They're simply sent to islands.) Yet in putting forward a human representative of the State, Huxley does make unambiguous the point that domination by other people, however mediated, is a key feature of the radically transformative (anti)utopia he depicts. In Huxley's account, submission to other persons by no means disappears with the ascent of the transformative vision.

The foreword Huxley wrote for the 1946 edition of *Brave New World* confirms this point. Turning to the case of totalitarian regimes, he observes that a

> really efficient totalitarian state would be one in which the all-powerful executive of political bosses and their army of managers control a population of slaves who do not have to be coerced, because they love their servitude. To make them love it is the task assigned, in present-day totalitarian states, to ministries of propaganda, newspaper editors and schoolteachers. But their methods are still unscientific. (11)

A truly scientific ensuring of love of servitude would mean "a deep, personal revolution in human minds and bodies" predicated on four functioning inventions: "a greatly improved technique of suggestion" (partly through "infant conditioning"); a "fully developed science of human differences" conducive to the assignment of every individual to a particular place in the hierarchy; a better "substitute for alcohol and other narcotics"; and finally "a foolproof system of eugenics" (12). For Huxley, in other words, real-world totalitarian governments have fallen short of the most radical transformative program in part because they haven't implemented the conditioning he imagines in his novel—a version of which, benign rather than oppressive, Skinner would soon present in *Walden Two*. What most solicits our notice in the aforementioned remark, however, is that the efficacious totalitarian state Huxley conceives would still be one in which political bosses and managers exercise control over "a population of slaves." Huxley's unfreedom is emphatically a domination of some people by others.

As it happens, the single reference to conditioning in George Schuyler's *Black Empire*, published just a few years after *Brave New World*, tends in a similar direction. In chapter 1, we saw how the Black Internationale pins its hopes for eventual triumph on the abilities of Black scientists; in response to one such expression of this faith, the story's narrator, Carl Slater, asks vis-à-vis the Black masses, "Will they follow you as fanatically as your technicians?" His guide, Pat, replies "airily" that the "masses always believe what they are told often and loud enough. We will recondition the Negro masses in accordance with the most approved behavioristic methods. The church will hold them spiritually. Our economic organization will keep control of those who shape their views. Our secret service will take care of dissenters. Our propaganda bureau will tell them what to think and believe. That's the way to build revolutions, Mr. Slater."[66] Nowhere else in *Black Empire* is enthusiasm for the revolution described as less than genuine, nor is there any suggestion that the work of the Internationale lacks widespread popular support. But it's also true that the masses are absent from the scene of Slater's experiences, and there's no indication that the top-down manipulation Pat describes is other than the order of the day.

As we've seen, *Black Empire* as a whole is characterized by a tension between the use of utopia to assert the positive possibility of an order free from white domination and a deflation of utopian fantasy. Pat's untroubled endorsement of conditioning, of course, aligns with the contempt for popular taste that Schuyler elsewhere expressed, but it also discloses how the tension between inspiration and irony in the text maps onto another, a tension between admiration and repulsion. It's impossible to dismiss the Empire's claim to represent a new day for civilization and justice, but it's nearly as difficult to shed the worry that its authoritarian aspects fatally compromise the freedom of the very people it proposes to liberate.[67] *Black Empire* thus poses in its own fashion a question Huxley seeks to close down but Skinner insists on keeping open: that of whether the radically transformative utopia could, even if an ultimately undemocratic creation of self-appointed paternalistic engineers, nonetheless be emancipatory.

If the story of utopia and antiutopia in the twentieth century is thus bound up with the worry that the freedom of the many might be compromised by the designs of the conditioning-wielding few, however, it also includes another strain of anxiety about unfreedom in which domination is not necessarily, or not in any uncomplicated sense, domination by persons. This strain surfaces in Yevgeny Zamyatin's novel *We*, written in 1921 and first published in 1924 (in an English translation by Gregory Zilboorg). Huxley persistently denied having read *We* when he wrote *Brave New World*, but parallels between the texts have been noted by critics and scholars, beginning with George Orwell in a 1946 review of *We* in French translation.[68] The One State in *We* doesn't appear to rely on Pavlovian conditioning as the World State in *Brave New World* does,[69] but it presents at least as radical a realization of the transformative utopia, its citizens subordinating themselves to a kind of mechanization that they understand to be the path to happiness. As D-503 explains early on,

> Each morning, with six-wheeled precision, at the exact same hour, at the exact same minute, we the millions, rise as one. At the exact same hour, we uni-millionly start work and uni-millionly stop work. And, merged into a single, million-handed body, at the exact same Table-appointed second, we bring spoons to our lips, we go out for our walk and go to the auditorium, to the Taylor Exercise Hall, go off to sleep.[70]

One important point of overlap with *Brave New World* in *We* inheres in its depiction of a direct confrontation with power: like the rebels in Huxley's novel, Zamyatin's ambivalently resistant protagonist, D-503, late in the narrative meets face to face with a representative of the regime that dominates all aspects of life in this grim future. This "Well-Doer," or in the 2006 translation by Natasha Randall quoted here, "Benefactor," is indeed something more than a representative; often described by D-503 as colossal—something between a monument and a person—he seems a dictator to whom all swear fealty, apparently the human incarnation as well as the head of the One State.

It's not entirely clear however, that the person D-503 finally meets is the same as the figure who receives obeisance at grandiose public ceremonies. In the crucial scene of encounter, D-503 is at first too frightened to raise his eyes beyond the Benefactor's "enormous cast-iron hands on His knees"; yet when the Benefactor's admonition provokes D-503 to a spell of laughter and a raising of his eyes, D-503 beholds "a bald, Socratic-bald, person" with "fine droplets of sweat on his baldness," before he somehow flings himself out of the room in which the audience occurs.[71] Zamyatin appears to leave open the possibility that the Benefactor who appears in public is really a projection that more shadowy powers use to inspire the masses—an ambiguity that Orwell would then adapt, for 1984, in the anthropomorphization known as Big Brother. Although the society Zamyatin describes could be one in which slaves are manipulated by a class of bosses, then, it's also possible that what prevails there is something closer to a bossless collectivity. It's possible that the social machine is in some sense running by itself, its precepts enforced by a cadre of police known as the Guardians but with no direction from the kinds of engineers who at some point set the machine going.

Through most of We, devotion to the State appears to be promoted by extremely effective propaganda and ritual, but in the final chapters, it's additionally sustained by a mandatory surgical operation in which the imagination itself is excised from the brain of the subject. Zamyatin thus conjures up, as part of his satire on Soviet authorities' attempts to bring forth the New Man of communism, a hypertrophic transformative mode in which authority remakes its subjects not through conditioning but through a form of physical work upon the organism.[72] Three decades later, Hannah Arendt would offer a similar take on "totalitarian" methods, but with conditioning holding something of the significance it does in Huxley. "Total domination, which strives to reorganize the infinite plurality and differentiation of human beings as if all of humanity were just one individual," she writes in The Origins of Totalitarianism (1951),

> is possible only if each and every person can be reduced to a never-changing identity of reactions, so that each of these bundles of reactions can be exchanged at random for any other. . . .

The camps are meant not only to exterminate people and degrade human beings, but also serve the ghastly experiment of eliminating, under scientifically controlled conditions, spontaneity itself as an expression of human behavior and of transforming the human personality into a mere thing, into something that even animals are not; for Pavlov's dog . . . was a perverted animal.[73]

To achieve really total domination, Arendt argues, it was necessary to seal off the camps, "the true central institution of totalitarian organizational power," because "total power can be achieved and safeguarded only in a world of conditioned reflexes."[74] The camps become the designed heterotopias in which the grimmest of transformative experiments are conducted.

Seven years later, in *The Human Condition*, Arendt would urge that "the all-comprehensive pretension of the social sciences . . . as behavioral sciences," is to "reduce man as a whole . . . to the level of a conditioned and behaving animal."[75] But in this book, her target is no longer totalitarianism only. Her broader concern is with how the freedom instantiated by the ancient Greek ideal of a polis of equals has increasingly given way to an unfreedom associated with the predominance of what she calls society or the social. For Arendt, society "excludes the possibility of action," the properly political activity that differentiates humans from animals, and "expects from each of its members a certain kind of behavior, imposing innumerable and various rules, all of which tend to 'normalize' its members, to make them behave, to exclude spontaneous action or outstanding achievement."[76] The reference here is not only to the new kind of human being imagined by Soviet theory (and in a different sense by Nazi practice) but also to the conformity that seemed to her increasingly enjoined in the West.

In other words, if behaviorism is for Arendt a kind of limit case of manipulation, it's also the logical terminus of the modern West's form of pressure toward good behavior. The present-day "society of jobholders," she writes,

demands of its members a sheer automatic functioning, as though individual life had actually been submerged in the over-all life process of the species and the only active decision required of the individual were to let go, so to speak, to abandon his individuality, the still individually sensed pain and trouble of living, and acquiesce in a dazed, "tranquilized," functional type of behavior. The trouble with modern theories of behaviorism is not that they are wrong but that they could become true, that they actually are the best possible conceptualization of certain obvious trends in modern society.[77]

Disturbed, like many of her contemporaries, by the rise of what Herbert Marcuse would call "one-dimensional man," Arendt distantly evokes (with her allusion to tranquilized behavior) the *soma*-damped inhabitants of Huxley's *Brave New World*.

Yet if Huxley recurs to a vision of domination by bosses and managers who use conditioning to control a population of slaves, Arendt ventures that the frightening culmination of the social's ascent may take a different form:

> As we know from the most social form of government, that is, from bureaucracy (the last stage of government in the nation-state just as one-man rule in benevolent despotism and absolutism was its first), the rule by nobody is not necessarily no-rule; it may indeed . . . even turn out to be one of its cruelest and most tyrannical versions.[78]

A few pages later, Arendt will go on to equate "society's victory in the modern age" with "its early substitution of behavior for action and its eventual substitution of bureaucracy, the rule of nobody, for personal rulership."[79] And so where Huxley sees conditioning, that most radical instrument of the transformative vision, as convenient to the purposes of would-be human overlords, Arendt (along with Zamyatin, at least as viewed from some angles) sees it as serving a potentially headless collectivity that would be no less oppressive, no less stifling of individual capacity and autonomy. "What we traditionally call state and government," she remarks, "gives place here to pure administration—a state of affairs which Marx rightly predicted as the 'withering away of the state,' though he was wrong in assuming that only a revolution could bring it about, and even more wrong when he believed that this complete victory of society would mean the eventual emergence of the 'realm of freedom.'"[80]

We'll revisit "pure administration" at length in chapter 3. Here, we need to note that it's not merely a fear of the subsumption of the individual by bureaucracy, collectivity, and the species to which Arendt gives voice. As the passages just cited indicate, the project of bringing modern people to a condition of perfect uniformity is for her inseparable from a project of breaking the individual into constituent elements. Total domination is possible only where all persons are reduced to "bundles of reactions" that "can be exchanged at random for any other." And this is to say that the transformative vision here seems to reach yet another dramatic endpoint, another culmination within the larger culmination represented by schemes of total conditioning. In Arendt's representation, the transformative regime's subjects become less than people not merely in being subject to some vaguely defined dehumanization but in the more concrete sense that they're dissolved into elements capable, in theory, of being organized in any manner the system might ordain. We've already remarked how some of the problems utopia has confronted arise from people's double status as its instruments and its beneficiaries, its means and its ends; under totalitarian regimes as Arendt understands them, human beings do no more than furnish the material of the organization. The units in play no longer being persons but reactions, even the project of organizing people qua integral persons seems, at this extreme of the transformative vision, to disappear.

This sense in which the disappearance of freedom implies a disappearance of people sets the stage for a consideration of justice that will occupy us at the close of this chapter. Before proceeding to that inquiry, however, we need to dwell a little longer with the other half of Skinner's fraught pairing, dignity. That Arendt's critique speaks to matters of freedom can hardly be doubted. But it should be clear that it is, in a way, still more deeply concerned with human dignity in the sense of worth, what Kant called *Würde*. For Arendt, again, the camps move "not only to exterminate people and degrade human beings" but also to transform "the human personality into a mere thing, into something that even animals are not." And the same applies, mutatis mutandis, to the satire mounted by *Brave New World*. If Huxley's critique is predicated on utopia's threat to personal liberty, it's still more powerfully predicated on utopia's threat to human value.

Indeed we may find it hard to imagine how Huxley's future people could meaningfully enjoy freedom without being very different from the way they are—say, at least minimally more alert and accomplished. With the exception of the aberrant main characters, the Brave New Worldians are shallow, unambitious, unoriginal, and passionless, their vapidity compounded or foregrounded by the unchallenging forms of recreation they're permitted ("Electro-magnetic Golf . . . Centrifugal Bumble-puppy" [212]) and the mnemonics they recite as guides to conduct ("a gramme is better than a damn" [61]). Huxley even leaves open the possibility that the aridity of souls in this world results more from triviality of culture than from the killing of contingency in early experience; he permits us to ask whether these existences seem vacuous less because they can never pass beyond the bounds set for them by the World State than because they resemble too closely the culture-industry-fed lives of the early twentieth century. (The inhabitants of Skinner's paradise of conditioning, Walden Two, notably direct a portion of their leisure time to high-cultural pursuits.) Whatever we may conclude about the cause of these characters' limitedness, it's clear that Huxley has fashioned his socially obedient characters to elicit readerly contempt. His implication that their world isn't worth very much is grounded in the implication that their lives lack significance individually.

As we've seen, the Skinner of *Beyond Freedom and Dignity* offers a surprising take on some of our basic assumptions about human value, and this on two related fronts above all. He illuminates how value is tethered to mysteriousness by observing that we "stand in awe of the inexplicable"—that in common understandings, any "evidence that a person's behavior may be attributed to external circumstances seems to threaten his dignity or worth." And he illuminates how value is tethered to admiration for putatively self-generated action in remarking that his own kind of program "seems demeaning because nothing is eventually left for which autonomous man can take credit." Skinner takes on the question of what value lives would possess in a radically transformative utopia, in other words, by suggesting that traditional reasons for valuing lives in nonutopian circumstances are based on a set of misapprehensions.

Although *Utopia and Its Enemies* was published before *Beyond Freedom and Dignity*, Kateb characterizes Skinner's challenge to antiutopians in just this way. In his telling, Skinner's "aspirations disturb two images of man that have been cherished for centuries." The first of these, which relates to freedom, is of "an essentially mysterious being . . . , not fully explicable by his milieu, having at least a small core of unaccountable volition, and capable of some spontaneous (unpredicted, unpredictable) behavior . . . ; at the very least, capable of resisting the combined force of his endowment and his milieu in order to determine his own character, his own self" (146). The second, which relates to dignity or *Würde*, is of "a being who, rationally comprehending the requirements of the moral law, attains, through his own efforts, a measure of moral excellence, using his conscience against his temptation, toughened and refined in the process and therewith granted a full appreciation of what it is to be good" (147).

Having thus focused the question of worth around the problem of moral virtue, Kateb goes on to assess hostile appraisals of Skinner. He replies first to a critique leveled by Joseph Wood Krutch in *The Measure of Man* (1954), casting Krutch as prey to a "fondness for being at the mercy of chance or the unknown which we have already noted in the antiutopian mentality" (150). In Kateb's account, Krutch evades the point that it would seem "only reasonable to see how" culture influences "the formation of character," to "move into a position where the cultural environment, to the fullest degree possible, is made to stop working in our despite and 'behind our backs'" (151). In other words, Krutch ultimately chooses ignorance over knowledge and thus clings to the first image of the human that Skinner contests. With respect to the second image, Kateb allows that Skinner proposes to "make it easier for people to be good" by conditioning them "so perfectly that whatever they desire is licit and whatever is required of them they do without strain" (159). But he also calls into question what he identifies as the antiutopian assumption that "the very concept of virtue is incompatible with ease" (172). For Kateb, goodness can never be in danger of "becom[ing] automatic" (172), even under a thorough application of Skinner's principles, and it can hardly be bad for early training to permit people to be virtuous with less agony.[81]

Kateb does acknowledge that there's a "threat of moral flaccidity in a safe and harmonious utopia" (115–16) and that "in the utopian sensibility there is generally present some strong predilection for the neat and tidy, for the ordered and arranged" (119). But if we can identify "a utopian estheticism of order and repose and literal-mindedness (similar, but only in part, to the utopian estheticism attacked by Karl Popper)" (120),[82] we can also discern "an antiutopian estheticism that answers to it and that may be even more reprehensible"—one that "shows its callous disposition" in the "delight in takes in observing the flux of events, and in the preference it has, at its extremest, for being at the mercy of chance and the unknown. . . . The world is thought to move for its sport: life becomes a succession of scenes and men are taken for characters" (120–21). For Kateb, antiutopian insistence on the value of struggle and suffering—which then becomes integral to the worth of the struggler and sufferer—amounts to a spectatorial pleasure that is itself unethical. At one point, Kateb quotes Williams James's observation, from "The Moral Equivalent of War" (1910), that "the possibility of violent death [is] the soul of all romance" (quoted at 116); it's precisely this kind of romanticizing that draws Kateb's scorn.

In other words, the antiutopian position Kateb counters here holds that a materially or morally easy existence can never be an authentic one. Kateb doesn't refer to authenticity explicitly in *Utopia and Its Enemies*, but the concept covers many of the antiutopian desiderata he interrogates, and it was one much in public circulation by 1963 thanks in part to the popular dissemination of ideas from Martin Heidegger, Jean-Paul Sartre, and Simone de Beauvoir. Authenticity was, moreover, explicitly important to Arendt and Marcuse, whose debts to Heidegger shaped their alarm at the immersive conditioning they saw as enforced both by the culture of consumerism and by the capitalist workplace.[83] In Arendt's framing, as we've seen, the postwar "society of job-holders" requires "of its members a sheer automatic functioning" and in this shows how "modern theories of behaviorism" are "the best possible conceptualization of certain obvious trends in modern society." Critiquing the Western culture of consumption and conformism in *One-Dimensional Man* (1964), Marcuse would decry the creation of "false" needs—needs that, imposed "upon the individual by particular social interests in his repression," eventuate in "euphoria in unhappiness" and serve "to arrest the development of the ability . . . to recognize the disease of the whole."[84]

Yet the desideratum of authenticity was also subject to powerful critique in these years, as, for example, in Theodor Adorno's scathing takedown of Heidegger in *The Jargon of Authenticity*, which saw print the same year Marcuse published *One-Dimensional Man*. The critical take on authenticity that most closely resonates with *Utopia and Its Enemies*, however, came in the form of a 1971 book that, like Kateb's, lives at the border between ethical inquiry and literary history. Lionel Trilling's project in *Sincerity and Authenticity* was, first, to trace how a criterion of sincerity—"the avoidance of being false to any man through being true to one's own self"—emerged in European and American imaginative writing since the Renaissance, then to examine how this criterion was displaced, in a process beginning in earnest a little before 1900, by a demand for authenticity.[85] Compared to sincerity, Trilling writes, authenticity suggests "a more strenuous moral experience,"

> a more exigent conception of the self and of what being true to it consists in, . . . a less acceptant and genial view of the social circumstances of life. At the behest of the criterion of authenticity, much that was once thought to make up the very fabric of culture has come to seem of little account, mere fantasy or ritual, or downright falsification. Conversely, much that culture traditionally condemned and sought to exclude is accorded a considerable moral authority by reason of the authenticity claimed for it, for example, disorder, violence, unreason.[86]

At one point, Trilling describes the rise, in the nineteenth century, of the concept of culture as "a unitary complex of interacting assumptions, modes of thought, habits, and styles, which are connected in secret as well as overt ways with the practical arrangements of society and which, because they are not often brought to consciousness, are usually unopposed in their influence over men's lives." For the devotee of authenticity, according to Trilling, this massive constraint might valiantly be opposed by "the perpetration of acts of unprecedented power and mastery" that would "startle" the "dull pain of the social world and make it move and live" and in this "retrieve the human spirit from its acquiescence in non-being."[87] Thus framed, of course, the ambition of authenticity neatly comports with the twin desiderata that Skinner and Kateb saw antiutopians as elevating. Acts of unprecedented power and mastery startling the dull pain of the social world speak very clearly to the desiderata of autonomy and spontaneity, of exercise of will and mysteriousness, that the ascent of utopia might be thought to imperil.

Taken in its historical context, Trilling's description also hints, of course, at how authenticity could seem threatened by social visions whose transformative character arises simply from their providing too much material stability. Authenticity's privileging of hardship, adventure, and recalcitrance may range itself against resignation to the view that human beings will be shaped decisively by the array of external forces that impinge on them, but as Kateb suggests it can also oppose the idea that humans *should* be spared species of pain and danger that provide opportunities for valiant struggle. As we've already seen to some extent in Huxley, Arendt, and Marcuse, a particularly serious and proximate form of this threat could appear to be posed by consumer society, the traps of which would include not only false needs, dull conformity, distraction from serious art, and withering of serious involvement in political life but also sheer removal from the character-building features of tough necessity.

The imminent prosperity trumpeted by an ascendant American business sector was, however, only one contributor to expectations that a new era of abundance might be on its way in the third quarter of the twentieth century; no less important, clearly, was the prospect of universal provision that came with the welfare state.[88] That this promise was legible as a transformative utopian one is indicated by Kateb's way of framing *Utopia and Its Enemies* as a whole. For he begins the book by casting it as a defense against recent attacks on utopia that "stem from the belief that the world sometime soon (unbearably soon) will have at its disposal . . . the material presuppositions of a way of life commonly described as 'utopian.' Such a prospect, one would have thought, would be a cause for gladness" (1), but to Kateb's dismay it has unleashed efforts to expose "both the insufficiency of utopian ideals and the unacceptability of arrangements thought necessary to the realization of those ideals" (1). For those Kateb sets out to critique, what's intolerable about the new world dawning is ultimately the threat to authenticity posed by a breadth of provision that, in doing away with many forms of adversity, would unacceptably restrict people's capacity for moral heroism.

The connection between prospects of abundance and anxiety about transformative designs' shaping power also materializes in a number of twentieth-century fictions that, in one way or another, pit meaningfully real experience against utopian arrangements whose strong direction of human life courses leave small space for danger and want. One such text is the first of three that Kateb describes, early in *Utopia and Its Enemies*, as together containing "almost every fear that utopian ends arouse" (20). Along with *We* and *Brave New World*, Kateb names E. M. Forster's 1909 story, "The Machine Stops," which anticipates in remarkably diagrammatic ways anxieties that would later coalesce around the figure of inauthenticity.[89]

The protagonist of "The Machine Stops" is a woman named Vashti, who, like the other people of her age, lives in a single room in a vast honeycomb beneath the surface of the earth. Like her fellows, Vashti rarely leaves that room, since within it all needs are met at the touch of a button. An encompassing entity known as "the Machine" provides food, drink, light, ventilation, and entertainment: one can push a button that somehow "produce[s] literature"; one can hear whatever music one desires at any time; and there's no need to go visiting other people physically, since one's thousands of friends communicate with one through "speaking-tubes" and "blue optic plate[s]."[90] One can even listen to a friend give a lecture, an especially appealing pastime because in Vashti's world, lectures about things—such as Vashti's own presentation on "Music during the Australian period" (91)—are often preferred to the things in themselves.

A general rage for mediation is indeed characteristic of Vashti and her fellows. In the world of the Machine, the only things that matter, at least to advanced thinkers such as herself, are ideas; any stimuli deemed unproductive of ideas (for example, views of the Himalayas, the Caucasus, and Greece that she sees on a reluctantly undertaken journey by airship) are dismissed as a waste of time, and even ideas can appear threatening if insufficiently removed from immediate experience. One of the most admired lecturers in the world of the Machine is warmly applauded when he advises, "Let your ideas be second-hand, and if possible tenth-hand, for then they will be far removed from that disturbing element—direct observation" (114). Such counsel accords perfectly with the "terrors of direct experience" (97) that afflict Vashti more than once during her air travel, as it does with her society's lack of concern about the optic plates' incapacity to give more than a hazy sense of the other speaker's face. "The imponderable bloom" of expressive nuance, "declared by a discredited philosophy to be the actual essence of intercourse, was rightly ignored by the Machine, just as the imponderable bloom of the grape was ignored by the manufacturers of artificial fruit. Something 'good enough' had long since been accepted by our race" (93).

The counterweight to Vashti's acceptance of mediation and mediocrity is her son Kuno, who for most of the tale lives on the other side of the world, where the Machine has placed him (that is, under what was once England, whereas Vashti lives beneath what had been Sumatra). Kuno horrifies his mother first by telling her of his desire to walk on the surface of the earth without leave—a wish strongly at odds with the social norms Vashti upholds—and then by telling her that he has actually done so. Eventually, however, they come to a convergence of views. After some years, the Machine falls apart; and in the apocalyptic close, at which the Machine succumbs to "disintegration . . . accompanied by horrible cracks and rumbling" (121), they physically touch—Kuno having recently been transferred to a room not far from Vashti's own. They also weep together

> for humanity. . . . Man, . . . the noblest of all creatures visible, . . . was dying, strangled in the garments that he had woven. Century after century had he toiled, and here was his reward. Truly the garment had seemed heavenly at first . . . and heavenly it had been so long as man could shed it at will and live by the essence that is his soul, and the essence, equally divine, that is his body. The sin against the body—it was for that they wept in chief . . .

—[the body, which had become] white pap, the home of ideas as colour-less, last sloshy stirrings of a spirit that had grasped the stars. (122–23)

"The Machine Stops" thus limns quite plainly a number of the "fear[s] that utopian ends arouse." In Forster's tale, the specter of domination by machines, actual and social, is bound up with the loss of corporeal joy and of bodily vulnerability: Kuno reports that he prepared for his adventure by engaging in physical exercise (another violation of the social norms of his world) and in the course of his journey risked at least two forms of fatal accident, electrocu-tion and a fall in a daring jump. Linked to both these depletions of experience and the menace of machine authority is also the threat of abundance itself, which here takes the form of a provision so cloying that the ending of the novel, gruesome as it is, also reads as a breath of fresh air, an escape into op-portunity. Deprivation (of security, first and foremost, but also of other mate-rial comforts) by this point seems a release from a kind of poverty paradoxi-cally brought on by the capacity to have every desire instantly fulfilled. What perhaps most damns Vashti's far-too-well-supplied life, however, is her and her friends' captivation by mediation, which we might describe as an active em-brace of inauthenticity that doesn't simply reflect the condition of the world of the Machine but, as it were, goes it one better.

In its conjoining of inauthenticity, material security, and distancing from unmediated reality, "The Machine Stops" looks forward to, indeed provided a template for, a line of subsequent fictions, extending into the present, in which ever more dramatic extensions of utopian transformative ambition result in ever more fearful dilutions of experience. In this line of (for the most part antiutopian) writing, the central worry is, to put it simply, that a life too care-fully orchestrated and too comfortable must become bloodless, vicarious, virtual, or unreal. But the orchestration can take many forms, as can the dimi-nution. It will be useful for us to examine a few later specimens of this genre before closing out this section, since taken together with Forster, Zamyatin, and Huxley, they help us gain additional purchase on the question of how justice fares in transformative utopias.

We can begin with Robert Graves's *Seven Days in New Crete* (also published in the United States as *Watch the North Wind Rise*). In this 1949 novel, Edward Venn-Thomas, an English poet of the present day (of the 1940s) is transported to a future whose affect and decor evoke the gentle-tempered neomedievalism of William Morris. His first impression of this future's atmosphere is that it's "goody-goody," and for the most part he has small reason to change his verdict: its inhabitants are extremely polite to each other, obedient to rules (some of them very peculiar), and lacking in a sense of humor as we would understand it. War has been reduced to contests played with staves between villages; as in

Morris, there's no money, and people go to market to take just what they need. Men treat women "as the superior sex." Over the course of the novel, those closest to the visitor suffer a series of ghastly fates, which events are finally explained toward the close, when it's revealed that the all-powerful Goddess who presides over human history has brought Venn-Thomas to the future precisely in order to disrupt its too-comfortable way of living. In a departing speech delivered under the impulse of "a divine afflatus," Venn-Thomas tells the inhabitants of the future, "She [the Goddess] summoned me from the past, a seed of trouble, to endow you with a harvest of trouble, since true love and wisdom spring only from calamity."[91]

Readers today will mostly wince their way through Graves's novel thanks to the recurrence of a casual misogyny inseparable from its narrator's repeated discovery that he's the object of rampant female sexual desire. But a reader sympathetic to the kind of arguments made by Kateb in *Utopia and Its Enemies* may find scarcely less hard to take the complacency with which Graves delivers the moral that the highest human values are incompatible with ease. Graves does permit Venn-Thomas to admire the ways of the future in limited respects: "Yet what dignified old men and women, what serene girls, what handsome, courteous young men were seated all around me at their lager and pretzels." But his early verdict that "life here's a little too good to be true" is enforced by an ongoing withholding of dignity from most of the inhabitants of the future. There are exceptions, but in the main the men in the novel read as weaklings, the women as overbearing, and nearly everyone as lacking in the intensity that is the gift of a harder world. As the character Quant remarks to Venn-Thomas in a familiar antiutopian refrain, "We have lived what your age . . . called 'the good life,' and that is a very easy life indeed. . . . But somehow that's not enough."[92]

A version of the same tale, in some ways painted in even broader strokes, can be found in Lois Lowry's popular young-adult novel, *The Giver* (1993), which was made into a film in 2014. As in *Seven Days in New Crete*, the inhabitants of the future community described are gentle and respectful to each other in their daily interactions and are also meticulous followers of rules— violations of which may be easily detected, since the governing committee of Elders can listen in on the conversations of any household. The protagonist of the novel, an adolescent named Jonas, is chosen to become the next Receiver— the holder of memories for the community and indeed the only person permitted a serious knowledge of the past. The present Receiver trains Jonas by transferring memories to him, and in this way Jonas learns about real pain and real love, of which his fellows are all deprived. Just as Graves allows that there are some good things about this muted future, so Lowry presents the utopians as not immune to pleasure and fellow feeling and gives a glimpse of the horrors of war, violence, and greed that characterize the nonutopian world. Nonetheless, the strongly urged takeaway of *The Giver*—enhanced by the revelation that the people of this nice world are in fact radical eugenicists who know nothing of the warm pleasures of Christmas or of grandparents, which echoes Venn-Thomas's discovery that the New Cretans practice ritual murder—is that there cannot be love or real feeling of any kind without pain. Were there any doubt that an attenuation of experience is at issue here, Lowry reinforces the point by revealing that no members of the community, save the Receivers, are able to perceive color—the faculty having been done away with long ago because it interferes with the social desideratum of "Sameness."[93]

If *The Giver* presents a sort of nightmare version of parents and educators who try to promote respect and sharing by indoctrination and surveillance, the slightly later young-adult fiction *Feed* (2002) presents a nightmare version of corporations that try to promote products by indoctrination and surveillance in other forms. The horrible future M. T. Anderson depicts in this sharp-witted novel is by no means utopian in the manner of Graves or Lowry: people aren't particularly gentle in their interactions; social inequality, both within and across national boundaries, is the order of the day; climate change seems on the verge of making life unlivable for everyone; and adolescent sociality is fraught, as it is in our world, with emotional insecurity. What makes the earth of Anderson's novel (slightly) different from our own is that on it, data are pushed into each person's brain (or at least into the brains of all those who can afford it) directly, via a feed. The feed permits a kind of telepathic communication with others on the network and immediate access to information in the manner of the internet, and like the internet, it pushes a constant stream of advertising: "They were wearing these tachyon shorts so you couldn't barely look at them, which were $789.99 according to the feed, and they were on sale for like $699 at the Zone, and could be shipped to the hotel for an additional $78.95, and that was just one great thing that people were wearing."[94] *Feed* thus renders transformative utopia-dystopia in a manner reminiscent of *Brave New World* (and to a lesser degree "The Machine Stops"), presenting not a society of authentically fulfilled people but one in which persistent proclamation of the availability of happiness is bound up with relentless exposure to carefully designed stimuli. The protagonist, Titus, finds a way to something like real love and care by the end of the novel, but for most members of his society, it seems, a lack of meaningful human interaction is bound up with a technologically grounded virtualizing of existence.

Versions of such virtualizing also appear in other utopian, dystopian, and antiutopian fictions of the 1990s and 2000s. One of the infernal devices surfacing in Octavia Butler's *Parable of the Talents* (1998), for example, is the "dream-mask," which makes computer-stimulated and guided dreams available to the public. . . . Each one offered wearers a whole series of adventures in which they could identify with any of several characters. They could live their character's fictional life complete with realistic sensation. They could submerge themselves in other, simpler, happier lives. The poor could enjoy the illusion of wealth, the ugly could be beautiful, the sick could be healthy, the timid could be bold.[95]

Yet even the dreammasks are just "cheap kid's toys," in the words of the late-appearing character Len Ross, in comparison to the yet more engulfing virtual rooms that permit those within them to create and visit other realities: "fourteenth-century China, present-day Argentina, Greenland in any imagined distant future, or one of the distant worlds circling Alpha Centauri." Len's mother became addicted to "her virtual room—her own private fantasy universe," Len recounts, fashioning "more obliging versions" of anyone who failed to indulge her and increasingly shunning contact "with real people with real egos of their own."[96]

Needless to say, the v-room and the dreammask read as distortions of utopia in which the achievement of the just new order for all is replaced by escape for the individual user—and also, perhaps, as projections of the bad conscience of the utopian engineer (wondering whether an achieved utopia would compromise human authenticity) or the crafter of utopian fictions (wondering to what extent these made-up worlds tempt readers to unhealthy isolation). Walter Mosley evokes this same concern in describing the effects of the highly addictive drug Pulse in his linked collection of stories, *Futureland* (2001). The substance alters

> the structure of the pleasure centers of the brain, temporarily allowing consciousness some measure of control over dreams. With just the right amount, a pulsar, as the users called themselves, could create a complex fantasy, build a whole world and live in it for what seemed like days, weeks. . . . Pulsars' minds drifted into passionate love affairs and musical performances that lasted for days. Many lost interest in the world around them, making better worlds in their unconscious minds. And to make matters worse, or better from a profit point of view, it turned out that after four or five uses, the brain collapsed in on itself without regular ingestion of the drug. It was an addiction from which death was the only withdrawal.[97]

In a kind of bookend to the briefly sketched seductions of Pulse, a character in one of the last stories of *Futureland* ends up absorbed in a different kind of virtuality. Mortally injured but saved by the godlike operating system Un Fitt,

Neil Hawthorne learns that until a new body can be found for him (and it's by no means clear how long this will take), he'll live within Un Fitt's matrix as a kind of sensing intelligence. His first reaction to the news is a "hysterical shudder of claustrophobia." A moment after, however, he discovers that his new life has a remarkable benefit: he can now have, virtually and immersively, experiences he had longed for in the past: "What had been a void was suddenly a vast panorama of the sea, the Pacific Ocean, Neil knew instinctively. It was the prehistoric coastline that he'd yearned for since childhood."[98] Where Pulse is the gateway to death, Un Fitt is the harbor of life—though Neil is no less in thrall to his virtual experience than is the Pulse addict. [99]

Of course, the most widely discussed representation of such virtualizing in recent decades is to be found in *The Matrix*. In the world of this 1999 film, a person's life can be a lie from beginning to end, inasmuch as human beings are attached from birth to feeds imparting experiences that are felt but not otherwise real. Neo, the film's protagonist, improbably breaks through to his real body, but most spend their lives in suspension, never perceiving anything that's not simulacral. In its moment, *The Matrix* proved of high interest not only to cultural critics but also to philosophers, for whom it offered a way of introducing nonphilosophers to important problems in epistemology and ethics. One of these was the puzzle of how and whether we can be sure we aren't simply, in Hilary Putnam's resonant phrase of 1982, "brains in vats." Another, more relevant to us here, was whether we would be right to choose an existence of pleasant but unreal experience over a less happy existence in which our experiences are actual. In the film, the character Cypher, who has learned the truth about the Matrix, chooses to go back in, resuming his earlier ignorance of his experiences' unreality. "I know," he says, "that this steak doesn't exist. I know that when I put it in my mouth, the Matrix is telling my brain that it is juicy and delicious." But in the long run, he concludes, "Ignorance is bliss."[100] Most philosophers writing on Cypher's choice assume that it's wrong and seek to explain why; a few take another line, observing, for example, that a "benevolently generated" Matrix would have much to recommend it and indeed be preferable to a life of misery and struggle outside.[101]

The relevant innovations of the seven fictions we've just visited can, roughly at least, be placed on a spectrum of experiential attenuation: on one end would fall *Seven Days in New Crete*, whose characters enjoy the least virtual version of living, on the other *The Matrix*, where for most human beings the virtual is all there is. A moment's reflection will make clear, further, that the infernal systems of most tendentially antiutopian fictions (including Zamyatin's and Huxley's) can be placed on such a continuum as well, since all activate an anxiety that a strongly designed transformative system—whether developed with beneficent or nefarious intent—will result in a radical diminution of authenticity. In "The Machine Stops," *Brave New World*, *We*, *The Giver*, and *The Matrix*, a social arrangement effectively loyal to the Owenian insight that "the character of man is . . . always formed for him" results not only in the stifling of vigorous action that preoccupies the antiutopians critiqued by Kateb but also in a possible depletion of something like reality and, by extension, of value. Their authors—and in less enveloping ways Graves, Anderson, Butler, and Mosley as well—invite the reader to ask what a manner of living can finally be good for if the living in it is, in some important sense, unreal.

Recipients of Justice

Virtually this same question is the subject of a thought experiment frequently cited by philosophers contemplating *The Matrix*—a thought experiment that, as it happens, was imagined in a book whose topic is utopia and justice. In *Anarchy, State, and Utopia* (1974), Robert Nozick offered a libertarian rejoinder to Rawls's *A Theory of Justice*, published three years earlier, countering Rawls's normative defense of a state that might engage in extensive economic redistribution with a normative argument for a minimal state concerned almost solely with protecting people from each other. We'll return to Nozick's speculations about truly utopian social organization in chapter 3; what will detain us here is the thought experiment in question, which falls in the midst of a treatment of animal rights and the problem of how feelings might be counted in a utilitarian calculus.[102]

Nozick writes,

> Suppose there were an experience machine that would give you any experience you desired. Superduper neuropsychologists could stimulate your brain so that you would think and feel you were writing a great novel, or making a friend, or reading an interesting book. All the time you would be floating in a tank, with electrodes attached to your brain. Should you plug into this machine for life, preprogramming your life experiences?. . . . While in the tank you won't know that you're there; you'll think that it's all actually happening. . . . Would you plug in? *What else can matter to us, other than how our lives feel from the inside?*[103]

Nozick enumerates several reasons why we might not plug in. We might refrain because "we want to *do* certain things, and not just have the experience of doing them"; or because "we want to *be* a certain way, be a certain sort of person" rather than a tank-floating "indeterminate blob"; or because we don't want to be limited "to a man-made reality, to a world no deeper or more important than that which people can construct." And should we be offered still more sophisticated machines that would overcome these objections, as, for example, a "transformation machine" that would permit one "to become as one would wish," we would still likely reject them, because they would seem to be "living our lives for us." "Perhaps what we desire," Nozick concludes, "is to live (an active verb) ourselves, in contact with reality."[104]

Nozick does not mention Huxley, Skinner, Kateb, Arendt, or Trilling (let alone Forster, Zamyatin, or Graves) in *Anarchy, State, and Utopia*. Yet it's not hard to see how his experience machine resonates with questions that link all of these writers, along with the post-1974 authors just discussed—questions about the fate of authenticity under a radically transformative regime. The source of all stimuli for the human beings plugged into it, Nozick's device evokes the provisioning Machine of Forster's story, of course, as well as the contented blankness of the "cyphers" in *We* and, at a remove, the conditioning presented negatively by Huxley and Arendt and affirmatively by Skinner. In addition, it takes the mediatedness or vicariousness that seems always one of utopia's dangers to what would seem the unsurpassable limit of *The Matrix*, thus posing in the hardest possible form the question of whether authenticity in living mustn't finally prove—Skinner's demurral notwithstanding—a criterion for a genuinely ideal society.

Of course, the machine Nozick imagines, unlike the machine in *The Matrix*, neither operates through the whole of a person's life nor rules an entire group of people. But suppose we take it upon ourselves to imagine something like the social equivalent of this machine: a society whose conditioning is so complete and thorough that every person who lives in it would have experiences that are essentially predetermined (and, let us add, free of pain and misery). With such an imagined arrangement, we would surely arrive at the ne plus ultra of the transformative utopia (and perhaps of the dexterous managerial utopia as well), the most radical imaginable version of the system we've tracked from More through Condorcet, Owen, and Marx and up to Forster, Huxley, Skinner, and later writers. In our thought experiment, the perfectly engineered social mechanism would ensure that all citizens are not only secure and content but also—because conditioned with an eye only toward their well-being—free of the exploitative and malevolent forms of conditioning Skinner condemns. For someone taking Skinner's and Kateb's view that the ideal of authenticity wielded against utopia is finally a chimera or an unethical aesthetic preference, it's not immediately clear what in the arrangement here conceived would be problematic. What ethical objections could a partisan of utopia who regards the criterion of authenticity with skepticism raise against this notional society?

Before answering this question, we must note that there are at least two perspectives from which the idea of such a society might *not* be troubling. One would be that of pure utilitarianism. If the existence of such a society puts more happiness (or some other good) into the universe—and indeed it would appear to put in a great deal—then from the standpoint of an unbending utilitarianism it would have to be endorsed. The other position that might not find such a society worrisome would be one that takes the well-functioning state (or some other efficient collective) or the survival of a culture as its ultimate telos. If our notional society is a state or a culture, then the predeterminedness of its members' individual experiences should present no problem of value for someone willing to accord state or culture such preeminence.

This latter view may well be that of the shadowy authorities in *We*, and it has, of course, historically been a stance on value taken by real people, just as strict utilitarianism has. Arendt's analysis of the concentration camps, as synecdoches of totalitarianism generally, bids to be recalled here: in her formulation, again, the camps undertook "the ghastly experiment of eliminating, under scientifically controlled conditions, spontaneity itself as an expression of human behavior." Having predetermined the experiences of those who inhabit it, our notional utopia of radical conditioning would be marked by precisely such a foreclosure of spontaneity, though where the totalitarian regime would be interested mainly in repression, our imagined society's intentions would be benign and its citizens happy. For Skinner in his long evolutionary view, meanwhile, the "survival of a culture" is a "value to be taken into account in addition to personal and social goods. . . . A culture, like a species, is selected by its adaptation to an environment. . . . A new practice may weaken a culture . . . or strengthen it" (*Beyond* 129–30). Whatever drives individuals to strive to preserve their culture, the "simple fact," for Skinner, "is that a culture which *for any reason* induces its members to work for its survival . . . is more likely to survive. Survival is the only value according to which a culture is eventually to be judged," we've already seen him remarking, "and any practice that furthers survival has survival value by definition" (*Beyond* 136). From the point of view of a culture, individual spontaneity may not be of particular moment.

Yet it's precisely this foreclosure of spontaneity that points to the larger reason why many, even observers not much exercised by utopia's threats to authenticity, would find this extreme of the transformative utopia hard to endorse. If each person's existence in such a society is merely the living out of a plan, the performance of an already written script, it would seem difficult to regard such existences as meaningful, at least in the way human lives are normally thought to be meaningful, unless (again) one holds the utilitarian or collectivity-privileging views just named. Otherwise, a society of people who merely enact a preset program may seem radically supererogatory, a kind of unnecessary replication in the realm of the actual of what has already been arranged in idea by the masterful social engineer. The problem here is oddly less one of dematerialization, of some *unreality* of the inauthentic, than of pointless materialization.

The terror that a whole society of people might be condemned to the radical secondariness of merely executing a scheme is, arguably, the most substantive terror of *We* and *Brave New World*. Beyond or beneath any judgment on the hollowness of life as lived in these antiutopias, we can discern in these texts a fear of planning that has become its own end and accordingly produces humans as mere instruments or tokens of its realization. This point is rendered especially vivid by the capacity of the Hatcheries, in the latter novel, to germinate beings who are completely identical, "standard men and women; in uniform batches. The whole of a small factory staffed with the products of a single bokanovskified egg" (18). As the Director, his voice "almost tremulous with enthusiasm," exclaims, "Ninety-six identical twins working ninety-six identical machines!" (18).[105] From the point of view of freedom, the horror here may be that the dronelike people produced have no autonomy from the moment of birth to the moment of death. But from the point of view of value, the horror is that these duplicate human beings seem to lack something that even the most degraded people in our own world can claim, a worth predicated on the development of capacities and life narratives that are not wholly foreordained.

A no less fascinating rendering of the horror of mere duplication appears in *The Blithedale Romance*—perhaps not all that surprisingly, since as we observed in chapter 1, Hawthorne's 1852 fiction may be considered one of the great meditations on utopia (and other lattices of human relation) as fate. Gazing from his hotel room window at a "row of fashionable dwellings," the narrator, Miles Coverdale, reflects,

> Here, it must be confessed, there was a general sameness. From the upper-story to the first floor, they were so much alike that I could only conceive of the inhabitants as cut out on one identical pattern. . . . It seemed hardly worth while for more than one of those families to be in existence, since they all had the same glimpse of the sky, all looked into the same area, all received just their equal share of sunshine through the front windows, and all listened to precisely the same noises of the street on which they boarded. Men are so much alike, in their nature, that they grow intolerable unless varied by their circumstances.[106]

"It seemed hardly worth while for more than one of those families to be in existence": like Huxley's bokanovskified egg, these existences that simply duplicate one another invite a particularly disturbing question about value: what can be the worth of a human life that lacks (at least a modicum of) distinctiveness? As in *Brave New World* also, this anxiety about the value of replicative lives can be taken as a kind of figure for anxiety about the value of lives that seem merely to play out a utopian script—even though Coverdale implies that the sameness of those in the fashionable dwellings contrasts with "the distinctness of separate characters" to which he "had recently been accustomed," presumably in Blithedale.[107] In the case of actual duplicates, one human life seems supererogatorily to repeat another; in the case of utopia, each human life seems supererogatorily to bring into reality what was already planned down to the last detail.

Of course, the antiutopia of *Brave New World* is far more radically transformative than the stab at a utopian community undertaken by the characters of *Blithedale*. Yet precisely for this reason, the Hawthorne example suggests that something of the repulsion engendered by our notional society of radical conditioning will filter into perceptions of much less rigid utopias. After all, any occurrence of a behavior elicited by a social organization designed *to* elicit that behavior can be understood as merely executing what has been prearranged: the specter of profound meaninglessness, of a vacuous enacting of the already planned, may to some degree haunt renderings of any utopians' lives. And it's just here, of course, that we return—but now armed with some additional insight—to the anxiety about authenticity that so often dogs utopia. At this point, we can discern at work in such anxiety, in addition to the suspicion of attenuation anatomized by Kateb and Skinner, a suspicion that the strongly transformative utopia is a place in which human life becomes secondary to, even purely instrumental to, the goal of perpetuating utopia. Earlier, we saw Arendt worrying about instrumentalization under totalitarian regimes that reduce people to "bundles of reactions"; here we can observe that radical preprogramming would constitute a similar reduction, transforming humans into pure means and in this abolishing persons in a robust sense.

The radically conditioned society (but also less extreme utopias, wherever they appear to partake of the radically conditioned society's presetting of human life courses) would seem, then, to reverse the relation between utopia and persons that gives utopia its rationale. In our ordinary understanding, relations among people are a problem to which utopia provides a solution. But in the case of the radically experience-determining society, the sequence seems to run the other way, with the system in place first and the people following (in the sense, again, that their lives are fully determined by that system). Thus the value problem that arises when we imagine a society of thoroughly preprogrammed experience may not only be that we desire, in Nozick's words, "to live (an active verb) ourselves, in contact with reality." It may also be that entirely planned experience would lack a robust *we* to do any desiring. In the ultraradically conditioned society, there would be, in a manner of speaking, no people preexisting that society whose relations would be *arranged* by the system; rather, the system would create people whose lives are determined, in advance, down to the last stroke.

What this suggests is that utopia may only have meaning where persons are understood as existing, in some logical or deep-structural sense, in advance of or apart from the utopian resolution. To acknowledge this isn't to suggest that utopia is ripe for unmasking as the creature of some dogmatic liberalism in which the only bearer of value is the atomized or wholly self-interested individual. Nor is it to grant primacy to individual-centered views of what's good for society over communitarian ones. It's rather to recall once more, but in a fresh context, that for utopia, human beings have always been a special kind of given—not only the means and material of the ideal society but also the ends that ideal organization serves. The *nomos* or right allocation that utopian *nemesis* calls forth requires individuals who can receive things, who can figure as the beneficiaries of the excellent social organization utopia provides. As we move toward the condition of our thought experiment, in which all experience is preprogrammed, however, the system seems very dramatically to give over the project of figuring out how to arrange things for the good of recipients in favor of the project of fashioning the recipients *tout court*. With the molding of subjects down to the last detail, the very possibility of *nomos* as right allotment or apportionment, the very possibility of justice, threatens to dissolve.

These considerations in turn bring us back to the interface between utopia and justice that we began to consider in chapter 1. For they show us that justice resembles utopia in two ways. Like utopia, justice seems to have meaning only where we can imagine persons, or at least value-bearing beings of some kind, structurally or logically preexisting the system that imparts a right arrangement to things. And like utopia, justice may be understood as problem-solving, as fundamentally reparative.

To take the first point first: as many theorists have noted, it seems obvious that for justice to exist, there must be recipients of justice. It's hard to imagine justice prevailing absent beings to whom justice can be rendered or where the beings in question would have no relation to each other. (If there were only one entity in the universe, it would be hard to say that said entity could receive justice or be treated unjustly, just as it would be hard to imagine that entity, or the arrangement of the universe containing it, being just or unjust.) Michael Walzer captures this intuition when he writes in *Spheres of Justice* (1983) that the "problem that justice poses is . . . to distribute goods to a host of Xs in ways that are responsive to their concrete, integrated selves. Justice, that is, begins with persons. More than this, it begins with persons-in-the-social-world."[108]

What Walzer is specifically taking issue with here is Rawls's celebrated thought experiment in *A Theory of Justice*—that imagining of the "original position" that we encountered in chapter 1 and to which we'll turn again in chapter 3—wherein judgments about justice as fairness would be made by people with no knowledge of the circumstances into which they'll be born or of what abilities they'll possess. Rawls has been charged by others in addition to Walzer with ignoring the essential shaping power of the relations and systems, including identity categories, that inevitably attach to us in the real world; he has also been faulted for privileging the self-interested individual subject in a way that betrays a damaging limitation by assumptions derived from Western philosophies. Rawls and some of his defenders have responded by emphasizing that the original position is, above all, a heuristic we can use to think through what we mean by fairness as a political matter,[109] but what matters for our purposes here is that for Rawls as for Walzer, justice pertains fundamentally to persons. Indeed one of the reasons why questions about personhood under various conceptualizations of justice have received so much theoretical attention in recent decades is surely that subjects of justice assume such striking priority in Rawls's thought experiment. One of the most important intuitions in post-Rawlsian justice theory is that if justice is to have meaning—if it's to have, so to speak, any work to do—there must be beings who remain conceptually prior to, or in excess of, the system of justice itself.

To come to the second commonality shared by utopia and justice: it's usually agreed that for justice to be salient, there must be some problem of relations for it to settle or remediate. In the *Summa Theologica*, Aquinas observes that "since justice . . . implies equality, it denotes essentially relation to another, for a thing is equal, not to itself, but to another," and that "inasmuch as it belongs to justice to rectify human acts, . . . this otherness which justice demands must needs be between beings capable of action."[110] In book 8 of the *Nicomachean Ethics*, Aristotle had noted long before that "when people are friends, they have no need of justice,"[111] and David Hume would develop this point in a number of his works, including *A Treatise of Human Nature*, where he observes that

> justice takes its rise from human conventions . . . intended as a remedy to some inconveniences, which proceed from the concurrence of certain *qualities* of the human mind with the *situation* of external objects. The qualities of the mind are *selfishness* and *limited generosity*: And the situation of external objects is their *easy change*, joined to their *scarcity* in comparison of the wants and desires of men. . . . If every man had a tender regard for another, or if nature supplied abundantly all our wants and desires, . . . the jealousy of interest, which justice supposes, could no longer have place. . . . Encrease to a sufficient degree the benevolence of men, or the bounty of nature, and you render justice useless, by supplying its place with much nobler virtues, and more valuable blessings.[112]

Hume thus prizes benevolence and generosity while consigning justice to the role of a "cautious, jealous virtue," a sad necessity for a nonarcadian world.

Rawls opens his *Theory* by commending justice as "the first virtue of social institutions," as we saw in chapter 1; yet he also draws on Hume to assert that there must be "circumstances of justice," which he defines as "the normal conditions under which human cooperation is both possible and necessary."[113] In his critique of Rawls, *Liberalism and the Limits of Justice*, Michael Sandel makes much of this tension, arguing that in spite of Rawls's wish to make justice primary for all societies, the existence of empirical situations in which justice is unnecessary (such as the loving family) means that "justice can be primary only for those societies beset by sufficient discord to make the accommodation of conflicting interests and aims the overriding moral and political consideration. . . . Justice appears as a remedial virtue, whose moral advantage consists in the repair it works on fallen conditions."[114]

Rawls would surely agree, however, that the requirement that there be circumstances of justice (if justice is to have meaning) illuminates how justice is a righting of what is not apposite. The reason Dike-Astraea is never at home on Earth is that justice depends to a peculiar degree on the existence (or at least the imaginability) of its own absence—seems, again, a condition whose rightness can only emerge in contrast to some specter of wrong. Thus is justice tightly linked, as we've seen, with *nemesis*: it's very hard to imagine justice mattering apart from indignation against injustice. Like utopia, it seems to depend for its cogency upon the existence (at least notional) of a state of affairs that it can correct and upon the existence of beings who may benefit from the excellence of the *nomos* without being fully subsumed by it.[115]

Margaret Cavendish captures something of this aspect of utopia in her exhilarating fantasy of 1666, *The Blazing World*. There, the Empress, having been "perswaded by the Duchess" (Cavendish's own quasi-avatar in the tale) "to make an imaginary World of her own," and having then "finished it, and framed all kinds of Creatures proper and useful for it, strengthened it with good Laws, and beautified it with Arts and Sciences," finds she has nothing left to do, unless she were to make "some alterations in the Blazing-World, she lived in, which yet she could hardly do, by reason it was so well ordered that it could not be mended; for it was governed without secret and deceiving Policy; neither was there any ambition, factions, malicious detractions, civil dissentions, or home-bred quarrels, divisions in Religion, Foreign Wars, &c. but all the people lived in a peaceful society, united Tranquility, and Religious Conformity." There's nothing to alter; yet when, just a few sentences later, the Duchess observes that the Empress rules "a peaceable, quiet, and obedient world," the latter replies, "'Tis true, . . . but although it is a peaceable and obedient world, yet the Government thereof is rather a trouble, then [*sic*] a pleasure; for order cannot be without industry, contrivance and direction."[116] It's as though Cavendish recognizes that the first passage threatens to transform utopia into arcadia, then modifies it with the second to keep the work of justice, as it were, in view.

And indeed the Empress's words point to a third quality that justice and utopia share: that of having always an uneasy association with perfection. Arrangements can be more just or less just, to be sure, and one can think of justice in this or that degree; yet justice always and also names a *nomos* in which all relations would stand in rightness. Similarly, debates about the definition of utopia (and about the relation between utopian desire and various forms of perfectionism) affirm that if utopia can be thought of as a less than total improvement over existing conditions, the name of utopia inevitably gestures as well toward a perfected social order. As the foregoing pages have intimated, however, perfection is not just constitutive of justice and utopia but also a problem for them because perfection narrowly construed may sort ill with a certain open-endedness associated with the value of human lives.

In this respect, it bears noting that the idea of "life plans" has been important to many theorists of the justice-person relationship—especially in the wake of Rawls, who uses the term of "plan of life" to name the course an actual individual will pursue.[117] For Sandel, summarizing Rawls's debt to Hume, the leading "subjective" circumstance of justice is that "each person has a distinctive life plan, or conception of the good, which he regards as worthy of advancement."[118] In *Imperfection and Impartiality* (1999), the political theorist Marcel Wissenburg includes among six criteria for being a recipient of justice a "freedom of mind (autonomy) and freedom of action (agency)" associated with the "capacity for developing and executing plans of life."[119] Scholars such as Martha Nussbaum have meanwhile addressed problems in social justice theory by advancing a notion of "capabilities equality," according to which what must be equalized for just distribution to obtain are neither resources per se nor the degrees of well-being resources might sustain but rather, in Alexander Kaufman's words, "the person's freedoms to *be* or *do* certain fundamentally important things."[120]

In the earlier parts of this chapter, we tracked the rough historical ascendance of what we've been calling the transformative kind of utopia as against what we've been calling the managerial. At the close of that survey, we encountered a kind of paradox in which the most thoroughly transformative utopia would undo itself precisely by operating perfectly—by predetermining its inhabitants' life courses so fully as to leave no scope for individually developed life plans or self-realization, no real freedom to be or do. Here, in other words, questions of freedom came to seem indistinguishable from questions of value, not because liberty as such proved a pure good but because the freedom to be and do emerged as a necessary condition of the meaningful being and doing that many would say brings value to life. What we can now see is that the counterindignation engendered by utopias of radical determination is legible as a fear of an end to justice that would take the form not of ultimate *injustice* but of a kind of radical nonjustice, a condition wherein there would no longer be any possibility of rightness because there would be no persons, in excess of the system itself, whose circumstances might be set right. And we can see as well how this kind of misgiving will be portable to reactions against less radically transformative utopias.

As moments in Owen, Wilde, Kateb, and other writers we've encountered also suggest, however, the transformative utopia—like theories of justice that advocate very active redistribution or other vigorous institutional interventions—may possibly be redeemed from the charge that it unduly compromises freedom if it places its emphasis on positive rather than negative liberty. Utopia and schemes of justice may seem less worryingly meddlesome, that is, where the perfection they aspire to is understood as what we might call, by no means euphoniously, a capabilities perfection—one that doesn't predetermine the courses of lives but in the highest degree makes more or richer courses possible. A way to mitigate the tainting of less extreme utopian visions by the most radically and nightmarishly transformative ones, in other words, would be to stress that more designed fashioning of utopia's conditions might mean more options, not fewer, for its inhabitants. Where utopia sets up possibilities rather than dictating results, the circumstances of justice might remain generatively active indeed. There would still be justice to attend to, in the midst of perfection.

3

Workers in Motion

The Time and Place of the Worker

To think of utopia in terms of *nomos* and *nemesis*, it might seem, must be primarily to think of it as directed to the proper distributing of goods, material and otherwise, that society has produced. Yet as anyone who has read much utopian writing knows, the arrangement with which ideal societies tend to be yet more reliably and immediately concerned is the distribution of roles in production and administration—in other words, the allotting of labor and position, condition and status. This concern is traceable back, in Western utopian writing, to Plato's *Republic*, which for Ernst Bloch, as we saw in chapter 1, conjures an order in which people appear "as pedestals, walls, and windows, where all of them are only free to be supporting, protective, and illuminating in the ranked limb structure."[1] Bloch's architectural metaphor captures well the rigidity, even the claustrophobia, of Plato's prescriptions; yet as we'll see in the following pages, it would be a mistake to associate the utopian structuring of productive roles solely with the kind of stasis that "arrangement" may at first call to mind. Indeed one of the main observations of this final chapter is that utopian imagining has been profoundly animated by questions pertaining to the value of human mobility, understood both in terms of actual movement from place to place and as a figure for other forms of freedom.

The *Republic* begins with, and in its subtitle presents itself as, an inquiry into the nature of *dikaiosune*—δικαιοσύνη, "doing right"—whose translation as "justice" can be misleading in many contexts but has been much to the purpose in our explorations here (and whose relationship to *nomos* we reviewed in chapter 1). As the dialogue unfolds, Socrates presses the idea that the essence of *dikaiosune*/justice lies in hewing to the proper distribution of occupations. In book 4, at a key moment, he persuades Adeimantus and Glaucon that "justice is the requirement we laid down at the beginning as of universal application when we founded our state. . . . that in our state one man was to do one job, the job he was naturally most suited for." Justice "consists in minding your own business and not interfering with other people"; it means "keeping what is properly one's own and doing's one own job."[2] In other words, if the essential practice of a worthy state is the doing of what's right—if what's proper turns out to be what's proper—this disclosure is saved from tautology by its pivoting on the more specific, and by no means self-evident, claim that each person is naturally fitted to one occupation.

Socrates does not actually argue for this view. In the opening sections of the *Republic*, he recurs to the value of persons' and things' fitness to a given task in the course of making other points and then, in the middle of book 2, tells Adeimantus and Glaucon, "as you were speaking, it occurred to me that . . . no two of us are born exactly alike. We have different natural aptitudes, which fit us for different jobs" and hence "we do better to exercise one skill" than "to try to practise several." His interlocutors accede to these points without further discussion, so that when in book 3 Socrates refers to "the principles we adopted earlier, that one man does only one job well, and that if he tries to take on a number of jobs, the division of effort will mean that he will fail to make his mark at any of them," he's referring back to assertions that were acknowledged to be empirically apt rather than to conclusions logically demonstrated.[3]

It's on the basis of these principles, in any case, that Socrates excludes from the ideal state those who would assume the voices of various characters when performing poetry. Beginning with the threat that the virtuous rulers of society would fail to fulfill their function should they practice impersonating the nonvirtuous (or persons who fill other social roles), he concludes that the ideal state he imagines is the only one

> in which we shall find (for example) the shoemaker sticking to his shoemaking and not turning pilot as well, the farmer sticking to his farming and not taking on court work into the bargain, and the soldier sticking to his soldiering and not running a business as well, and so on. . . . So if we are visited in our state by someone who has the skill to transform himself into all sorts of characters and represent all sorts of things, . . . we . . . shall tell him that he and his kind have no place in our city, their presence being forbidden by our code.[4]

In *The Politics of Aesthetics: The Distribution of the Sensible* (*Le Partage du sensible: Esthétique et politique*), first published in French in 2000, Jacques Rancière offers a noteworthy take on this moment and its antecedents in the *Republic*. Plato, he observes,

> states that artisans cannot be put in charge of the shared or common elements of the community because they do *not have the time* to devote

themselves to anything other than their work. They cannot be *somewhere else* because *work will not wait*. The distribution of the sensible reveals who can have a share in what is common to the community based on what they do and on the time and space in which this activity is performed.[5]

If in the *Republic* "the principle of a well-organized community is that each person only does the one thing that they were destined to do by their 'nature,'" the "mimetician brings confusion to this distribution: he is a man of duplication, a worker who does two things at once," who "provides a public stage for the 'private' principle of work. . . . It is this redistribution of the sensible that constitutes his noxiousness, even more than the danger of simulacra weakening souls." This then leads to one of the central contentions of Rancière's work: that there is "an 'aesthetics' at the core of politics that has nothing to do with [Walter] Benjamin's discussion of the 'aestheticization of politics' specific to the 'age of the masses.' . . . It is a delimitation of spaces and times, of the visible and the invisible, of speech and noise, that simultaneously determines the place and the stakes of politics as a form of experience."[6]

Examining arguments by Wai Chee Dimock and Elaine Scarry in chapter 1, we noted that if the distributive ordering of justice seems profoundly linked to symmetries or other patterns associated with aesthetic experience, the reason is that both convey a sense of rightness, of apposite arrangement. What Rancière brings out is that Plato's utopia is predicated on an ideal of rightness that's quite emphatically aesthetic and political at once, and in a manner that has to do not only with the satisfactions of elegant structures but also with our apprehension of social reality as something like a visible entity. The mimetician disrupts Plato's state not only by violating the rule of one person–one occupation in the abstract but also by seeming to perform that violation, by appearing in a particular place as a kind of embodiment of the disruption unleashed by the claim to be in two places (that is, to hold two social positions) simultaneously.

In a passage from his "Ten Theses on Politics" (first published in English in 2001 and retranslated for the 2010 collection *Dissensus: On Politics and Aesthetics*) that we saw part of in chapter 1, Rancière evokes the *nomos* explicitly in this context. He explains that what he calls the *partage du sensible* is

> the dividing-up of the world and of people, the *nemeïn* upon which the *nomoi* of the community are founded [*la découpe du monde et de monde, le nemeïn sur lequel se fondent les nomoï de la communauté*]. This partition should be understood in the double sense of the word: on the one hand, as that which separates and excludes; on the other, as that which allows participation. . . .

The essence of the police lies in a partition of the sensible that is characterized by the absence of void and of supplement [*L'essence de la police est
d'être un partage du sensible caractérisé par l'absence de vide et de supplément*]:
society here is made up of groups tied to specific modes of doing, to places
in which these occupations are exercised, and to modes of being corresponding to these occupations and these places. . . . The essence of politics
consists in disturbing this arrangement by supplementing it with a part of
those without part, identified with the whole of the community. . . . Politics, before all else, is an intervention in the visible and the sayable.[7]

In Rancière's construction, the *nemeïn* that founds society is quite clearly not
an allotment of goods or rewards but a fundamental distribution of roles, of
places in society. And in this construction, politics is a disruption of whatever
nomos prevails, a movement of some of the previously marginalized toward
some recognition, a violation of prior restrictions on who may speak where,
on who may be seen when. Politics consists in the unsettling of the formerly
orderly space associated with the police; it's "the instituting of a dispute over
the distribution of the sensible, over that *nemeïn* that founds every *nomos* of
the community."[8]

What Plato seeks to do, however, is to *counter* the disruptive force that is
politics as Rancière defines it. Indeed in inaugurating political philosophy,
Plato

> founds an archi-politics understood as a law that unifies the "occupations" of
> the city-state, its "ethos," (i.e. its way of inhabiting an abode) and its *nomos* (as
> law but also as the specific "tone" according to which this *ethos* reveals it-
> self). . . . And political philosophy . . . is fated to have to re-identify politics
> and police, to cancel out politics through the gesture of founding it.[9]

The history of political thought and indeed political practice, for Rancière, is
the history of attempts to contain politics, to reestablish a condition of stasis
in the teeth of the redistributions politics would perform (its bringing to visibility of those who had before been invisible). For Rancière, then, the utopian
text we call the *Republic* offers crucial insight into all political societies, not just
ideal imagined ones. And this is so not because the ideal society of the *Republic*
stands as the first great emancipatory alternative to the constraints of extant
social orders in Western writing but rather because Plato's ideal society *also*
embodies the conservative dream of an absolute end to political contestation,
to the dispute over *nemeïn* and indeed to social mobility.

It would seem, then, that Rancière makes a striking case for the salience of
the eternal tension between utopia conceived as a liberatory alternative to

what-is and utopia as a coercive, totalizing ordering whose soi-disant ideality brooks no disruption of its structures. And indeed he writes in *The Politics of Aesthetics*, as we saw in chapter 1,

> Utopia is, in one respect, the unacceptable, a no-place, the extreme point of a polemical reconfiguration of the sensible, which breaks down the categories that define what is considered to be obvious. However, it is also the configuration of a proper place, a non-polemical distribution of the sensible universe where what one sees, what one says, and what one makes or does are rigorously adapted to one another.[10]

We might even say that Rancière brings out how these two faces of utopia align with the two faces of *nomos* we considered earlier—or, more precisely, with the two ends of the spectrum of meanings that the term could have for the ancient Greeks. At one end, as we noted, *nomos* touches on ideal *dike*, a perfect justice not seen on Earth since some golden age and hence a conviction that things should be otherwise than they are in this badly arranged world. At the other end, however, *nomos* fades into custom or mere social convention, the rightness of what's generally regarded as right, the way things are done here and now. Like *nomos*, utopia can imply either the essence of conservatism or its opposite, depending on whether one is thinking of it as a social order that once brought into being must never substantially change (because to fall away from it would be to fall away from perfection) or as a radical alternative, not presently existing, to the world at hand.

Rancière's vision of politics, along with his writing's most intimate contacts with utopia, is grounded in not one but two historical scenes. If part of his inquiry pivots on a rereading of the fifth- and fourth-century BCE Athens of Plato and Aristotle, a crucial frame for that rereading is furnished by nineteenth-century France. In one of his earliest books, 1981's *La Nuit des prolétaires* (translated into English as *Nights of Labor*, 1989, and republished in the same translation but with a new preface by Rancière as *Proletarian Nights*, 2012), Rancière examines written records of some early nineteenth-century workers who used their precious nonlaboring hours "to learn or dream or debate or write," to imagine alternatives to the prevailing order—and in this violated, in a particularly resonant way, the rule of one person–one job.[11] The volume thus proposes, in Rancière's words from the original 1981 preface, to give a "history of . . . nights snatched from the normal round of work and repose . . . in which our characters prepare and dream and already live the impossible suspension of the ancestral hierarchy subordinating those dedicated to manual labor to those who have been given the privilege of thinking."[12]

In other words, Rancière can be seen as analyzing Plato through the lens of his interest in the lived predicament of nineteenth-century workers—a concern that was in turn rooted in his experiences of Paris in 1968 and his break with Althusserian Marxism at around that time. As Rancière himself attests, he felt impelled, above all, to question a "jealous concern to preserve popular, plebeian, or proletarian purity" that he discerned in dominant strains of French Marxism—a sentimentalizing ideal according to which the worker should remain a pure worker, unsullied by the theoretical occupations of the intellectual vanguard.[13] In other words, Rancière frames *La Nuit des prolétaires* in terms of the same problem that would fix his attention in Plato, that of the worker having no time to think because the work will not wait.

In the case of the French workers of the nineteenth century, however, the problem wasn't only one of prescription from above (manual workers *should* not engage in the work of thinking) but also one of lived experience below— practical limitations on free time, and the feeling of passing one's life in futility. On the first page of his 1981 preface, Rancière writes, of the "few dozen or hundred laborers in their twenties around 1830" who are his subject,

> What they found intolerable was not exactly the poverty, the low wages, the uncomfortable housing, or the ever-present specter of hunger. It was something more basic: the anguish of time shot every day working up wood or iron, sewing clothes or stitching footwear, for no other purpose than to maintain indefinitely the forces of servitude with those of domination; the humiliating absurdity of having to go out begging, day after day, for this labor in which one's life was lost.[14]

This anguish could, however, be productively sharpened when visions of other worlds came to impinge, as through contact with the lives of the rich, or through philosophical reading, or through "Saint-Simonian preaching sessions" from which a seamstress might return (here Rancière quotes a letter of one Desirée Véret from 1831) "filled with admiration . . . for the grandeur of the ideas and the unselfishness of the apostles."[15] At such a moment, the pre-scribed distribution of the sensible is disrupted: the worker begins to become something other than the sentimentalized proletarian unstained by theory. And what effects this disruption is, we might say, the worker's coming to per-ceive glimmers of utopia. Rancière's account thus contains a certain Blochian and Benjaminian dimension, even though Rancière doesn't mention the for-mer in *La Nuit* and elsewhere positions his own theory as a version of the politics-aesthetic relation quite different from Benjamin's.

Most significant for our purposes, in this, is that the stealing of time seems the most stinging humiliation to which the worker is subject, or rather the humiliation that grounds all the others because it seems to abrogate space for thought itself (including the contemplation of injustice, the impression that *dike* seems to have fled this world). Of course, the documents Rancière examines are hardly the only ones from the period that speak to this point. An exceptionally distilled rendering of the stealing of workers' moments appears, for example, in Thomas Hood's poem "The Song of the Shirt," which was first published in the Christmas 1843 number of *Punch* and quickly became "a national sensation."[16] Hood was neither a member of the working classes nor an activist as such, but his (sentimental, to be sure) poem fixes on a theft of time so absolute that the worker is able to indulge in only one personal activity, or expression: lamentation. And this because lamenting is the single thing one can also do while laboring.

The voice of the poem is a needlewoman who, "With fingers weary and worn, / With eyelids heavy and red," sings of the horrible conditions of her labor while "Plying her needle and thread": "Work! work! work! / While the cock is crowing aloof! / And work—work—work, / Till the stars shine through the roof!" In the poem's climactic stanza, she cries

> Oh but for one short hour!
>   A respite however brief!
> No blessed leisure for Love or Hope,
>   But only time for Grief!
> A little weeping would ease my heart,
>   But in their briny bed
> My tears must stop, for every drop
>   Hinders needle and thread![17]

The poem's clear lesson to this point has been that the cruelest feature of this woman's servitude is its unremittingness; here, she follows the previous stanza's note that she has not an hour to enjoy the countryside (as she used to) with the lament that she lacks even the leisure to weep. While there's room for mournful song because singing can accompany stitching, there's none for love or hope, or even for that somatic expression of pain to which presumably all people are entitled, the shedding of tears. Every drop hinders needle and thread.

If this is how the world of the nineteenth-century laborer is to be interpreted, how is that world to be changed? What would the ideal alternative look like? A famous passage from Karl Marx and Friedrich Engels's *The German Ideology*—none of which was published before 1924, as earlier noted, but which was written in 1845–46 (and thus not long after "The Song of the Shirt")—seems to supply an answer:

> And finally, the division of labour offers us the first example of the fact that, . . . as long as a cleavage exists between the particular and the common interest, . . . man's own deed becomes an alien power opposed to him,

which enslaves him instead of being controlled by him. For as soon as the division of labour comes into being, each man has a particular, exclusive sphere of activity, which is forced upon him and from which he cannot escape. He is a hunter, a fisherman, a herdsman, or a critical critic, and must remain so if he does not want to lose his means of livelihood; whereas in communist society, where nobody has one exclusive sphere of activity but each can become accomplished in any branch he wishes, society regulates the general production and thus makes it possible for me to do one thing today and another tomorrow, to hunt in the morning, fish in the afternoon, rear cattle in the evening, criticise after dinner, just as I have a mind [*wie ich gerade Lust habe*], without ever becoming hunter, fisherman, shepherd or critic.

This fixation of social activity, this consolidation of what we ourselves produce into a material power above us, growing out of our control, thwarting our expectations, bringing to naught our calculations, is one of the chief factors in historical development up till now.[18]

As several critics have noted, the best-known words in this much cited passage—"to do one thing today and another tomorrow, to hunt in the morning, fish in the afternoon, rear cattle in the evening, criticise after dinner, just as I have a mind, without ever becoming hunter, fisherman, shepherd or critic"—are unusual within Marx's corpus for their evocation of what daily life might actually be like under an achieved communism. And indeed one compelling reading of the manuscript evidence, by Terrell Carver, holds that Marx, evidently antipathetic to Engels's pastoral fantasia, added the phrases about criticism as a way of signaling his disdain on the manuscript page.[19] Still, it's precisely the passage's utopian allure that helps account for the fact that many readers who know nothing else of *The German Ideology* know this quotation. The particulars it conjures accord with convictions about the good life that many would undoubtedly share, including a belief in the value of being able to exercise one's powers in a variety of ways. In other words, one of the features that make the passage appealing is its rebuke to the confidence of the *Republic* on the matter of one person–one job.

Of course, insofar as this passage calls up work's capacity to be intrinsically satisfying, it points at once to a line of thinking prominent among Victorian social critics (Thomas Carlyle, John Ruskin, William Morris) and to theoretical Marxism's continuing concern with alienation and reification. Yet if the passage gestures toward work-derived fulfillment as such, it does so only implicitly. What it explicitly presents as the benefit of communist society is the freedom to choose one's occupation, not just in the sense of career or profession but in the sense of activity in which one is engaged at a given time.

Removed from its context, "just as I have a mind" may suggest the airiness of whim, but within the larger passage, this phrase puts before us the irreplaceable good of freedom to select one's work. The misery associated with the division of labor, here, proceeds less from possible dissatisfaction with one's work per se than from a sense of constraint, while the joy of work is, above all, the joy of being able to decide what activity one will undertake, even from moment to moment.

It's as if, in other words, Marx and Engels were responding to precisely the worker grievances that Rancière emphasizes in *Proletarian Nights*, the "anguish of time shot every day" and the humiliation "of having to go out begging . . . for this labor in which one's life was lost." In *The German Ideology* passage, just as in Rancière, the bitterest and most basic wrong takes the form of constraints on labor that are bound up with constraints on time and that instantiate constraint more generally: "Each man has a particular, exclusive sphere of activity, which is forced upon him and from which he cannot escape." We might indeed say that one of the accomplishments of this rendering of the communist quotidian is to fuse elegantly the two great desiderata of freedom and happiness, whose tendency to raise competing claims has so often engendered problems for the utopian imagination. The "fixation of social activity, [the] consolidation of what we ourselves produce into an objective power above us, growing out of our control" is the essence of unfreedom, and it's also the sheerest unhappiness. Libertarian polemicists might envy the finesse with which this passage persuades us that freedom is an affective good.

A further rhetorical wiliness is at work here, however, inasmuch as Marx and Engels make the freedom to choose one's occupation at a given moment look at once so humble that it seems not much to ask for and so significant that one wonders how any utopia could do without it. Of course, the freedom to choose one's occupation just as one has a mind, moment to moment, would seem a quite radical freedom in a modern society, given the complexities of conditions of production. Yet as we'll see, variants of this fantasy have loomed large in utopias at least since Fourier, with significant consequences not only for utopia's rendering of the interplay between freedom and happiness but also for its claim to realize a general condition of justice.

For the moment, however, we might notice two things: first, that utopian writing has not always ascribed great value to the freedom to switch occupations, let alone to other forms of mobility available to workers; second, that the topos of workers moving *is* foundational to the utopian genre. And this latter not only by virtue of Plato but, still more emphatically, by virtue of Thomas More. For if utopia as a modern genre can be said to originate with a single socioeconomic spectacle, that spectacle would be the one of workers on the move in the early sixteenth century—or rather, of the formerly employed on the move, looking for work, not finding it, resorting to stealing, and being hanged in the end.

Here's a longer version of the passage partly quoted in chapter 2 of this study in which More's narrator Raphael Hythlodaeus discusses the situation of early sixteenth-century England:

> For look in what parts of the realm doth grow the finest and therefore dear-est wool, there noblemen and gentlemen, yea and certain abbots . . . not contenting themselves with the yearly revenues and profits that were wont to grow to their forefathers . . . leave no ground for tillage: they enclose all into pasture. . . . Therefore that one covetous and insatiable cormorant . . . may compass about and enclose many thousand acres of ground together within one pale or hedge, the husbandmen be thrust out of their own . . . : By one means . . . or by other, either by hook or crook, they must needs depart away, poor, silly, wretched souls, men, women, husbands, wives, fa-therless children, widows, woeful mothers, with their young babes, and their whole households small in substance and much in number, as hus-bandry requireth many hands. Away they trudge, I say, out of their known and accustomed houses, finding no places to rest in. . . . And when they have wandered abroad till [what they have] be spent, what can they else do but steal, and then just pardy be hanged, or else go about a-begging? And yet then also they be cast in prison as vagabonds, because they go about and work not, whom no man will set a-work, though they never so willingly offer themselves thereto.[20]

Among the contemporary social problems on which part 1 of *Utopia* fo-cuses, criminality is the first and the most lengthily discussed. And at this crucial juncture, Hythlodaeus attributes most thievery to the desperation pro-duced by the enclosure of formerly common lands for sheep pasturing, an appropriation spurred by the high market value of English wool. This early phase of enclosure (often conducted at will by large landowners, in contrast to the legislative enclosure that prevailed in the eighteenth and nineteenth centuries) was part of the larger set of transformations of economic life that Marx, in chapter 26 of *Capital*, volume 1, dubbed "primitive accumulation"—in Richard Halpern's summary, "the various means by which fractions of the late feudal producing classes, including peasants and some small artisans, were dispossessed or otherwise deprived of the means of economic production by which they sustained themselves and thus became available for employment as landless or 'free' laborers."[21]

In part 1 of *Utopia*, Hythlodaeus argues that the problems of thievery and vagabondage in England may be solved by halting the practice of enclosure—which recommendation evokes Tudor efforts, before and after, to limit enclosure by acts of law—and by the provision of full employment for farmers and artisans. As to the question of how to punish thievery when it nonetheless asserts itself, Hythlodaeus describes the wise arrangements of the Polylerites, who condemn thieves "to be common labourers," not imprisoned ("unless the theft be very heinous") but set "at large, labouring in the common works" (28). If the condemned "refuse labour, or go slowly and slackly to their work," they're chained and whipped, but otherwise "they live without check or rebuke. Every night they be called in by name, and be locked in their chambers" (28). The punished thieves are also "apparelled in one colour" and have "the tip of the one ear" cut off for easy identification, and their shire of residence is disclosed by "several and distinct badges which to cast away is death" (29). Hythlodaeus notes approvingly, "By this means they never lack work, and besides the gaining of their meat and drink, every one of them bringeth daily something into the common treasury" (29).

In Utopia itself, as described in chapter 2, work is also provided to all so that there's no incitement to vagabondage. But more than that, Utopia's rules and institutions are built on the principles that everyone must work and that people must, for the most part, stay put. We learn early on that "the chief and almost the only office of the Syphogrants"—the magistrates annually chosen by "thirty family or farms" to govern and represent them—"is to see and take heed that no man sit idle" (55, 57). A man must have permission from his father and consent from his wife to travel in his own county, and when traveling receives no food until he has performed a due share of labor in the visited region. Utopians are not permitted to depart the bounds of their own shire without a special license (though such is "easily obtain[ed]" [67]), and in any case there's little incentive to go moving about, since the fifty-four shire towns of utopia are all more or less the same: "As for their cities, whoso knoweth one of them knoweth them all" (52). Hythlodaeus thus invites his audience to see "how little liberty" the Utopians "have to loiter," being "in the present sight and under the eyes of every man" (68). Even the Syphogrants, who are technically exempt from labor, "exempt not themselves, to the intent that they may rather by their example provoke others to work" (60).

More's solution to the problem of need-caused thievery is thus in one sense structurally rigorous, a sort of (theoretically) benevolent *contrapasso*. The real-world problem requiring utopian remedy is a historical unfreedom associated with unwanted mobility among laborers; in Utopia, employment is certain and mobility minimal. Where the cause for concern in the real England lay in workers forcibly deprived of their commons, lacking work, and on the move, More presents an alternative in which everything is in common, there's extremely full employment, and travel is greatly restricted. This plan answers the wish and more, so to speak. As Halpern writes, "Utopia's fully productive citizens are the direct antitypes of English vagrants, as is suggested by their very names. If the residents of book 2 are 'Utopians' because they live in a place called 'Nowhere,' the vagrants of book 1 are also 'utopian' in the very different sense that they have nowhere to live."[22]

More is hardly alone among utopian writers, of course, in grounding a heightened positive freedom in a certain curtailment of what we would call negative freedom—in proposing an enforced stability that permits people to develop more richly by freeing them from precarity and abuse. And in his Utopia, this richer development may occur both in and outside the domain of work. Utopia's strictures on physical movement and against idleness are counterbalanced by a fair amount of freedom in choosing one's occupation: "Besides husbandry, . . . every one of them learneth or other several and particular science as his own proper craft," and if a Utopian be drawn to a different one, "he is by adoption put into a family of that occupation he doth most fantasy. . . . Yea, and if any person when he hath learned one craft be desirous to learn also another, he is likewise suffered and permitted" (57). The Utopians also prize leisure. Holding that "to be wearied from early in the morning to late in the evening with continual work" is "worse than the miserable and wretched condition of bondmen" (57–58), they labor only three hours before noon and three after dinner,[23] giving eight hours to sleep and devoting their remaining time to rest, eating, and other wholesome activities such as music, attendance at lectures, and "contemplation . . . of science liberal" (58). (Vices such as gambling, and "riot or slothfulness," are not tolerated, however; free time must be bestowed "well and thriftily" [58]). The foundation of human flourishing in Utopia is, then, a system of fully mandated labor characterized by flexibility as to individual forms and a productivity high enough to preclude anyone's needing to labor more than six hours a day.

The main reason productivity is so high is not, however, that the Utopian apparatus is highly efficient (though it does seem to be that).[24] Rather, what makes it possible for everyone to have leisure is a distribution of labor under which no one is excused from work. According to Hythlodaeus, the non-Utopian world of the here and now is populated by numerous species of idlers, including many or most women, priests, and gentlemen, as well as beggars who are in fact able to do honest work. There are also many whose forms of work generate nothing useful for the commonwealth. Were it the case, however, that all who are "now busied about unprofitable occupations . . . were set to profitable occupations, you easily perceive how little time would be enough, yea, and too much, to store us with all things that may be requisite either for necessity or for commodity" (59–60).

This is not to say that for *Utopia*, injustice in the real world is precisely a matter of unequal distribution of labor. Rather, injustice arises in a mismatch between labor contributed and benefits derived:

> For what justice is this [*Nam quae haec iustitia est*], that a rich gold-smith or an usurer or, to be short, any of them which either do nothing at all, or else that which they do is such that it is not very necessary to the commonwealth, should have a pleasant and wealthy living, either by idle-ness or by unnecessary business, when in the meantime poor labourers . . . should yet get so hard and poor a living and live so wretched and miser-able a life, that the state and condition of the labouring beasts may seem much better and wealthier. . . . Is not this an unjust and unkind public weal [*An non haec iniqua est et ingrata respublica*], which giveth great fees and rewards to gentlemen, as they call them. . . . And yet besides this the rich men, not only by private fraud but also by common laws, do every day pluck and snatch away from the poor some part of their daily living. So whereas it seemed unjust to recompense with unkindness their pains that have been beneficial to the public, now they have to this their wrong and unjust dealing (which is yet a much worse point) given the name of justice, yea, and that by force of a law [*ita quod ante uidebatur iniustum, optime de Republica meritas pessimam referre gratiam, hoc isti deprauatum etiam fecerunt, tum prouulgata lege iustitiam*]. (120–21)[25]

Utopia's corrective to real-world injustice, again, takes the form of a realloca-tion in what we might call zero-sum terms: redistributing labor in society, so to speak moving work from the laborers to the idlers, gives everyone in Utopia security and leisure. Halpern identifies excess as the bête noire of Utopia[26]; we might refine this further to say that the Utopian solution is to redistribute excess—excess of leisure and also excess of goods—for the good of all.[27] Full employment, a radically egalitarian *nomos* on the side of the distribution of labor, is a solution to the problem not only of the idle poor but also of the idle rich.

This plank of utopian thinking would live well beyond *Utopia* itself. Accord-ing to J. K. Fuz, "the problem of full-employment" was the "central idea of almost all Utopias" of the period following Francis Bacon's *New Atlantis* of 1629 and lasting through Robert Wallace's 1761 *Various Prospects of Mankind, Nature, and Providence*. And it gave rise to schemes for ensuring not just that all would have work but that all work would meet real needs. The author of *A Description of the Famous Kingdome of Macaria* (1641), understood by Fuz to be Samuel Hartlib but now believed to be Gabriel Plattes, "proposed a reform to adjust the supply of tradesmen to demand by manipulations with the prescribed time of apprenticeship" as well as "a governmentally organized and subsidized emigration of the surplus population, adapted to yearly needs and possibilities."[28] Hartlib himself would propose, in *Considerations Tending to the Happy Accomplishment of England's Reformation in Church and State* (1647, not properly speaking a utopian fiction), an Office of Accommodations "envisaged," in J. C. Davis's words, "as a clearing house for economic information and as a kind of labour exchange." The office would, that is, be "an Engine to reduce all into some Order which is confused."[29]

In *The Law of Freedom in Platform; or, True Magistracy Restored* (1652), Gerrard Winstanley (for whom, in Davis's words, "the only freedom that mattered was freedom from economic insecurity"[30]), advocated provision of common lands upon which any who would work might work and also, as the "fundamental material structure of his new society," an "institution of public storehouses or depots" that would "obviate the need for buying and selling commodities in markets."[31] Meanwhile overseers would manage "the transfer of youths from one trade to another" and all would be required to perform manual labor up to the age of forty, after which those who wished could remove themselves "to state service," and in any case "those over sixty" would "automatically become general overseers."[32] In *Various Prospects*, Wallace would propose a propertyless ideal society in which decisions about labor are made collectively, declaring that "idleness must be banished, universal industry must be introduced and preserved, labour must be properly and equitably distributed; every one must be obliged to do his part, and the earth must be cultivated by the united labours of all its inhabitants acting in concert, and carrying on a joint design."[33]

Though the "full-employment reformers"—Plattes, Rowland Vaughan, Peter Chamberlen, Peter Cornelius Plockhoy, and John Bellers—certainly did want to reduce indigence and unemployment among the poor, they were, according to Davis, seeking "a release from idleness in the name of work, as much as a release from indigence in the name of sustenance." And this release was "but one aspect of a demand for the full employment of all resources."[34] In utopian and quasi-utopian discourse of the sixteenth and seventeenth centuries in England, in other words, full employment as desideratum tended to mean not merely that all would have the opportunity to work but that none, at least among the relatively young and healthy, would have the opportunity not to work. Quite in line with Halpern's representation of More, moreover, it was associated not just with a banishing of certain forms of exchange but also with a banishing of excess and a bringing of order out of chaos.[35]

In what's now the most famous of seventeenth-century English outlines of an ideal society, *The Commonwealth of Oceana* (1656), James Harrington notes in passing that if in raising a man nature "does not stand safe, and so that she may set him to some good and useful work, he spits fire, and blows up castles;

for where there is life, there must be motion or work; and the work of idleness is mischief, but the work of industry is health."[36] *Oceana* is not significantly concerned with the employment of the masses; its effort is rather to imagine a republican government proof from concentration of power in the hands of the few. But Harrington's opinion here (which leads off a discussion of education in Oceana) illustrates again how it was possible to regard a freedom from waste and excess as the distinguishing or definitional marker of a well-ordered society, of an apposite *nomos*.[37] With the proper arrangement in place, there would be no superabundant energies to go into, for example, the kind of self-enrichment whose terminus would be the deprivation of the many at the hands of the few (and thus precisely what Harrington sought to prevent, the consolidation of power by one segment of society).

In framing his description of the actual workings of his ideal Oceana, Harrington observes that in "the institution or building of a commonwealth, the first work . . . can be no other than fitting and distributing the materials. The materials of a commonwealth are the people, and the people of Oceana were distributed by casting them into certain divisions, regarding their quality, their age, their wealth, and the places of their residence or habitation." Harrington goes on to remark that "there is nothing so like the first call of beautiful order out of chaos and confusion, as the architecture of a well-ordered commonwealth,"[38] thus evoking Plato as characterized by Bloch ("people as pedestals, walls, and windows") and by Rancière (for whom Harrington's phrase might stand as precisely that which the action of politics unsettles). Harrington's architectonic figures are not, however, rooted in a metaphysical commitment to one person–one job, but rather based upon a conviction that where various interests remain in dynamic tension with each other, society will be more stable—will indeed operate more or less smoothly no matter what individuals (driven by their own self-interested desires) should do to disrupt it.

Thus in a remarkable passage from his *Discourse upon This Saying: The Spirit of the Nation is not yet to be trusted with Liberty* (1659) cited by both Davis and Robert Appelbaum, Harrington describes a mummer's show he had seen in Italy in which the

> Cooks were all Cats and Kitlings, set in such Frames, so ty'd and so ordered that the poor creatures could make no Motion to get loose, but the same caused one to turn the Spit, another to baste the Meat, a third to skim the Pot and a fourth to make Green-Sauce.
>
> If the Frame of your commonwealth be not such, as causeth every one to perform his certain Function as necessarily as did the Cat to make Green-Sauce, it is not right.[39]

Whatever their individual inclinations, the felines nonetheless, by force of the contraption's ingenious design, prepare the dish. In this tableau, the "right" frame of the commonwealth emerges not as a *nomos* where the rule of one person–one job prevails, as in Plato, but rather in a design so perfect that the peculiarities of the individual actor become immaterial. The system cannot be ruined by individual caprice or ineptitude, which is to say that we have here an especially strong version of the managerial as opposed to the transformative utopia (though Harrington's concerns are narrower than most utopians'). "Throughout his work," Davis observes, "Harrington reiterates the proposition that a perfect commonwealth is not so much one that provides its citizens with opportunities for virtue, as one that is inviolable to their propensity to sin. . . . The citizen participates in a set of rituals designed to reduce his moral responsibility rather than enhance it."[40]

The idea of a *nomos*-machine immune to the failings of its human components or operators would eventually prove crucial to the visions of the "utopian socialists" and their heirs, where it would be closely tied to the desideratum of full employment. A case in point is that of Henri de Saint-Simon, the reception of whose doctrines by workers in early nineteenth-century France forms one of the largest topics of *La Nuit des prolétaires*. In reaction against prevailing social arrangements that, in his view, entrusted the incompetent leisured with the crucial decisions confronting the state—those pertaining to the economic and scientific development that would eventually usher in an ideal world—Saint-Simon envisioned a regime in which those decisions would be made by the kinds of people he called *industriels*: scientists, artists, and workers. Under his plan, administrators would merely conduct the routine business of management, and even the decision makers would fulfill their aims not by applying a subjective creativity to the advancement of society's interests but by discerning what is, objectively, the best course of action.[41]

The sovereignty exercised "by the social body itself," according to Saint-Simon in his *Deuxième extrait de mon ouvrage sur l'organisation sociale* (published in *L'Organisateur* in 1820),

consists not in an arbitrary opinion established in law by the mass, but in a principle derived from the very nature of things, whose justice men have only to recognise and whose necessity they have only to proclaim. In such a situation the citizens charged with the various social functions, even the highest, only perform, from a certain point of view, subordinate roles, since their functions, however important they are, involve no more than following a course which they themselves have not chosen. Furthermore, the aim and object of such an organisation is so clear, so settled, that there is no longer any room for the arbitrariness of men, or even of laws, because both can be exercised only in the realm of uncertainty which is, so to speak, their natural element. The act of governing, in the sense of commanding, then plays no or almost no part.[42]

In the society Saint-Simon envisions, policy questions—about what enterprises are to be pursued, how to pursue them with the least expense, and so on—are "eminently positive and answerable; decisions can only be the result of scientific demonstrations, absolutely independent of all human will, which may be discussed by all those educated to understand them."[43] And

> because in such a system all social functions have a positive character and a clearly determined object, the capacity required in order to fulfil them is so clear, so easy to ascertain that there could never be any indecision on the subject, and every citizen must naturally tend to confine himself to the role for which he is most suited. . . . In this situation the three principal disadvantages of the present political system—arbitrariness, incapacity, and intrigue—will be seen to disappear all at once.[44]

If in Plato the one person–one job rule appears as a technical demand buttressed by metaphysical intuitions about what is right, it reads in Saint-Simon as a more purely technical, or technocratic, imperative. To be sure, an end to unemployment is one of the pillars of the liberation of workers that Saint-Simon envisions: his 1820 *Considérations sur les mesures à prendre pour terminer la révolution*, for example, mandates a securing of "the existence of the proletariat by providing work for all fit men, and relief for the sick," while in the postscript to his address to the king in his 1821 *Du système industriel*, he similarly calls for "the provision of work for all persons who have no other means of existence."[45] But while the Saint-Simonian gospel offers workers participation in the direction of the State and the chance to work, in effect, for their own benefit, it's at best ambiguously directed to the disruption of the *nomos* of one person–one role.[46]

Among the "three great utopians" Engels identified in *Anti-Dühring* (1878; Engels 30), however, it was neither Saint-Simon nor Robert Owen who brought to the fore the freedom in choice of work adumbrated in "hunt in the morning, fish in the afternoon, rear cattle in the evening, criticise after dinner, just as I have a mind." It was rather the remaining member of that triad, Charles Fourier, who asserted not only that full employment could be imagined absent the constraint of one person–one job but also that frequent changes of occupation are crucial to human thriving. Although Fourier did assert the virtues of microspecialization in one sense—members of the pear-growing "series," for example, will be variously expert in mealy pears, compact pears, medlars and abnormally soft pears, or any of four other categories[47]—he would also devote much ingenuity to varying the workday. In his "Théorie de l'Unité Univer-selle," originally published (as "L'Association domestique agricole") in 1822, for example, Fourier observes that nature "demands variety in industry as in all other things" and lists among the seven conditions that must be fulfilled, if "associative labor" is to be attractive, that "the industrial sessions be varied about eight times a day, it being impossible to sustain enthusiasm longer than an hour and a half or two hours in the exercise of agricultural or manufacturing labour" and that "in this distribution, each one, man, woman, or child, be in full enjoyment of the right to labour or the right to engage in such branch of labour as they may please to select, provided they give proof of integrity and ability."[48]

The means by which work is to be coordinated, given this need for change, is far more extravagantly baroque than the reader unused to Fourierian habits of thought would likely imagine. All members of the "Phalanx," Fourier writes in a manuscript eventually published in 1851, will gather at nightfall each day "to plan the activities of the following days." And there they will encounter "much more animation and intrigue . . . than there is at the stock exchanges of London or Amsterdam. For every individual must go to the Exchange to ar-range his work and pleasure sessions for the following days. . . . Assuming that 1200 individuals are present, and that each has twenty sessions to arrange, this means that in the meeting as a whole there are 24,000 transactions to be concluded"—all of them conducted via a complicated system of signals com-municated over iron wires.[49]

The Fourierian exchanges thus evoke earlier imaginings of bureaus that would connect those needing work with work needing to get done—Hartlib's Office of Accommodations, for example, or a proposal by Owen for a national information service that would report on labor availability.[50] In Fourier, though, the system is staggeringly elaborate, and this elaborateness is part of the pleasure: the organization of work takes on the quality of a festival, and the quondam anxiety of precarity is transformed into a delicious suspense in wheeling and dealing. The inhabitants of Fourier's utopia don't enjoy the full spontaneity of the future communists of *The German Ideology*: they can't quite hunt in the morning, fish in the afternoon, rear cattle in the evening, criticise after dinner, just as they have a mind. But any slight conflict between freedom and happiness on this score is in theory compensated by the perverse gratifica-tion that attends small impediments to perfect spontaneity in Fourier's system.[51]

Saint-Simon and Fourier thus present two different understandings of how the *nemein* of occupations and positions in society can serve the goal of doing away with cycles of unemployment and poverty. In Saint-Simon, the rooting of the ideal society in expertise, such that each locus in the vast system must be occupied by a person possessing the requisite knowledge and aptitudes (which will lead that person to the one objectively correct decision), implies that rapid shifting from one role to another would be fatal to the whole organization. In Fourier, by contrast, individual whim is a donnée whose harnessing itself supports the new golden age. Indeed the phalansteries' precipitation of a mobility in occupation over time, but always within their confined demesnes, reads as a synecdoche for the Fourieran domestication of impulses that might otherwise be excessive and destabilizing. Where Saint-Simon looks forward to the banishment of "arbitrariness, incapacity, and intrigue" from the political, Fourier puts the first and third to work and suggests that doing so will take care of the second. He thus breaks especially visibly with two key assumptions of the Platonic *nomos*: that perfect social organization will distribute one place to each person and that one's position within the social order must be predicated upon what kind of labor one performs.

As it happens, this same contrast—between an expertise-driven ideal society favoring something like one person–one job and a more pastoral utopia that rejects that rule in the name of human flourishing—can be observed in two texts of the later nineteenth century whose dialogue with each other we have touched on more than once already: Edward Bellamy's *Looking Backward* and William Morris's *News from Nowhere*. In Bellamy's future United States, new technologies of communication and data management permit the distribution of work assignments on a scale far larger than that of the Fourierian exchanges. As Dr. Leete explains to Julian West, owing "to the vast scale on which industry is organized, with coordinate establishments in every part of the country," his society is "able by exchanges and transfers to fit every man . . . with the sort of work he can do best."[52] Thanks to this fluidity of information, which grounds a fluidity of labor and of production, "overproduction in special lines . . . is impossible now"; and even were there by "an error of judgment excessive production of some commodity," the "consequent slackening or cessation of production in that line" would throw "nobody out of employment," the workers therein being "at once found occupation in some other department of the vast workshop. . . . With us it is the business of the administration to keep in constant employment every ounce of available capital and labor in the country" (162).

Yet this technological speed does not serve a Fourierist scheme of changes of work at whim. Though "every worker is allowed," with some limitations, "to volunteer for another industry," frequent "and merely capricious changes of occupation are not encouraged or even permitted" (62), and the national administration's rigorous matching of aptitude to job is complemented by an equally rigorous correlation of recognition to result. The industries of Bellamy's future society divide "their workers into first, second, and third grades, according to ability, and these grades are in many cases subdivided into first and second classes." Periodic regradings permit those with more experience to move up, with the privileges of a higher grade including priority of choice in specialization and the wearing of a finer badge (gold for first, silver for second, iron for third) (93–94). There are other inducements to better work too: all receive equal material compensation, but the "value of a man's services to society fixes his rank in it. Compared with the effort of our social arrangements in impelling men to be zealous in business," Leete tells West, "we deem the object lessons of biting poverty and wanton luxury on which you depended a device as weak and uncertain as it was barbaric" (78).

In other words, Bellamy heads off the threat that full employment and equal income might eliminate the incentive to good work by preserving a form of stratification by contribution. Moreover, work is straightforwardly compulsory—"A man able to do duty, and persistently refusing, is sentenced to solitary imprisonment on bread and water till he consents" (95)[53]—and the industrial army is unapologetically conscriptive: "We have no wars now, . . . but in order to protect every citizen against hunger, cold, and nakedness, and provide for all his physical and mental needs, the function is assumed of directing his industry for a term of years" (55–56). Of course, the passive construction in this last remark signals an awareness, on Bellamy's part, that not every reader will think it wise to pay for the positive freedoms of utopia by surrendering negative ones. Not everyone will find the good of full employment worth the price of a massive centralization of control over choice, time, and manner of labor, and even those otherwise attracted to Bellamy's utopia might be put off by its authoritarian character.

In *News from Nowhere*, Morris rejects not only Bellamy's urban siting of utopia and preference for social hierarchy but also, tellingly, the rule of one person–one job. His utopia grants people unrestrained freedom in choosing their work, and this not for years but more or less every day, since labor is organized cooperatively and may be redistributed spontaneously by the workers themselves. Indeed the very first conversation between two utopians witnessed by Morris's narrator, William Guest, concerns precisely the kind of exchange of tasks that, in the better future, curves responsibility toward inclination. When Dick, the first person Guest meets in the future London, offers to serve as "showman" of the "new world," Guest worries that this will take him away from his responsibilities. But Dick assures him that playing cicerone will give him "the opportunity of doing a good turn to a friend of [his] who wants to take [his] work"—at which he summons that friend, Bob, with a "little silver bugle-horn." On appearing, Bob greets him with, "Am I to have my work or rather your work?", and the two trade promised employments.[54] The rest of *News from Nowhere* is consistent with this opening, its dominant note being a high freedom of choice in work made possible by a diminution of the need for specialists, a general consciousness of work's necessity to satisfaction in life, and an implication that in this realm of easy plenty, no one need work unduly hard.

It would be difficult to say whether the freedom to move about physically in order to choose one's work is, in Morris's utopia, primarily a literal good or a metaphor for a more abstract freedom. The physical journey on which Morris takes his readers—travel by carriage and foot and then (slowly, soothingly) by boat—embodies the ease and lack of constraint that characterize life in this beautiful future. It marks a contrast not only to Bellamy's relatively static narrative, in which West remains in Boston for the duration, but also to most prior utopias, where, whatever the quality of the journey *to* the ideal place, the sensation of moving at a certain pace through the revealed new world does not seem crucial to the text's effects. On returning from Morris's utopia, however, one may feel that being denied its leisurely free movement would be a genuine impoverishment. The worker of the future fantasized in *The German Ideology* can change occupations at will but does not evidently enjoy the latitude to change locations; after some time in Morris's utopia, one may feel that Marx and Engels's future communist is, on this key point, rather deprived.

If *News from Nowhere* thus intimates that the freedom to choose one's work and the freedom to move as one will are profoundly connected, it reinforces this moral by sketching a utopian organization under which choosing one's location *is* in effect choosing one's occupation (for the day). Plato insists, per Rancière, that the worker "cannot be *somewhere else* because *work will not wait*"; Morris grants that work (the harvest, emblematically) won't wait but sketches a society in which the worker *can* be somewhere else—not in two places at once, but somewhere other than she was, say, earlier that week— because work in another place will call. The contrast to the Victorian England depicted in "The Song of the Shirt," where the worker controls not a moment of her time and is deprived of the pleasure even of walking about for refreshment, could hardly be starker.

And as if to underscore this very point, Morris craftily repurposes Hood's "Song" in *News from Nowhere*. At one juncture in the narrative, the raconteur Hammond explains to Guest that "some memory" of the old terrible slum life of east London does abide with the utopians, inasmuch as an annual May Day feast commemorates the clearing of the slums. And

> on that occasion the custom is for the prettiest girls to sing some of the old revolutionary songs, and those which were the groans of the discontent [*sic*], once so hopeless, on the very spots where those terrible crimes of class murder were committed day by day for so many years. To a man like me, who has studied the past so diligently, it is a curious and touching

sight to see some beautiful girl, daintily clad, and crowned with flowers from the neighbouring meadows . . . to hear the terrible words of threatening and lamentation coming from her sweet and beautiful lips, and she unconscious of their real meaning: to hear her, for instance, singing Hood's Song of the Shirt, and to think that all the time she does not understand what it is all about—a tragedy grown inconceivable to her and her listeners.[55]

In need of a song to represent "tragedy grown inconceivable" to his future Englanders, Morris turns to one that depicts a society diametrically opposite to their own utopia, where life is lived in the beautiful countryside and people's moments and hours are very emphatically theirs to dispose of as they will. Among major nineteenth-century utopian designs (Fourier's included), that of *News from Nowhere* presents perhaps the most radical antithesis to Plato's prescription for justice, the rule of one person–one job. And if Morris's utopia seems one in which liberty reaches its acme, this is so only partly because anarchy is its mode of organization. It's also, clearly, because the fruit of this anarchist arrangement is a more or less full control over time and place for every worker, which is to say for every person.

Freedom through Administration

That inhabitants of an ideal society would enjoy the freedom to choose their work, in the short term as well as the long, and that they would enjoy uninhibited freedom of movement: if these ideas gained a serious foothold in utopian discourse in the nineteenth century, they took center stage in the first decade of the twentieth in fictions by H. G. Wells and Aleksandr Bogdanov. In Wells's *A Modern Utopia*, which we considered in relation to Bellamy and Morris in chapter 1, and in Bogdanov's 1908 novel *Red Star*, freedom in employment and freedom of movement are supported not by a benevolent anarchy, as in Morris, but by accelerated transfers of information that recall Bellamy while also speaking to the evolution of real-world technologies, especially the telephone and the telegraph. Further, these two dreamed-of forms of freedom point, as we'll see, to the dream of a third, one that might be described as more radical, more fundamental, or both.

On the other Earth Wells describes in *A Modern Utopia*—the nonidentical double of our own planet, where every person on our world has a doppelganger but society is organized on quite a different plan—employment seems anything but arduous and can indeed, as we'll see in a moment, have a Morrisian flavor. Yet the means of finding work needing doing isn't the word of mouth that prevails in *News from Nowhere*. Rather, it's a bureaucratic resource, furnished by the World State and evocative of the national coordination limned in Bellamy and the employment exchanges of Fourier and Owen. When the citizen of utopia cannot find work, Wells's narrator explains, that citizen will head "to a neat and business-like post-office" and state

> his case to a civil and intelligent official. In any sane State the economic conditions of every quarter of the earth will be watched as constantly as its meteorological phases, and a daily map of the country within a radius of three or four hundred miles showing all the places where labour is needed will hang upon the post-office wall. To this his attention will be directed. The man out of work will decide to try his luck in this place or that, and the public servant, the official, will make a note of his name, verify his identity . . . and issue passes for travel and coupons for any necessary inn accommodation on his way to the chosen destination. . . . Such a free change of locality once or twice a year from a region of restricted employment to a region of labour shortage will be among the general privileges of the Utopian citizen.[56]

The narrator of *A Modern Utopia* and his companion, "the botanist," at one point avail themselves of this resource and are sent to Lucerne, where "there is a demand for comparatively unskilled labour in carving wood" (112). Although the workplace they find there is called a factory, it's a lovely one—indeed so attractive that in later years, whenever the narrator smells resin, he recalls "the open end of the shed looking out upon the lake, the blue-green lake, the boats mirrored in the water, and far and high beyond . . . the atmospheric fairyland of the mountains of Glarus" (151). Nor does work in this place mean operating heavy equipment. Rather, the toy animals produced by the "factory" are "made in the rough by machinery, and then finished by hand, because the work of unskillful but interested men—and really it is an extremely amusing employment—is found to give a personality and interest to these objects no machine can ever attain" (150). Thus does Wells dispose of any conflict between the handicraft advocated by Morris and his own hopes for a future improved by technology.

Yet Wells's language notably distances his utopia from the kind of vision that numbers satisfying work among the principal requirements of a good life. The finishing of the toys is "an extremely amusing employment," not a way of meeting the soul's profoundest needs, and *A Modern Utopia* in general eschews the sanctification of labor promoted by Victorian enthusiasts. Wells even takes an explicit dig at Ruskin's famous scheme, in 1874, for putting Oxford undergraduates (one of whom was Oscar Wilde) in touch with the blessings of manual labor by having them build a road:

> Road-making under Mr. Ruskin's auspices was a joy at Oxford no doubt, and a distinction, and it still remains a distinction; it proved the least

contagious of practices. And Hawthorne did not find bodily toil anything more than the curse the Bible says it is, at Brook Farm.

> . . . A certain amount of bodily or mental exercise, a considerable amount of doing things under the direction of one's free imagination is quite another matter. . . . But now that the new conditions physical science is bringing about . . . supply the hope that all routine work may be made automatic, it is becoming conceivable that presently there may be no need for anyone to toil habitually at all; that a labouring class—that is to say a class of workers without personal initiative—will become unnecessary to the world of men. (72–73)

Wells's narrator further erodes the moral-existential glamor of labor with his description of the affective atmosphere at the Lucerne factory. The hearty good fellowship in collective endeavor so integral to *News from Nowhere* goes unmentioned, and indeed the narrator undercuts any inference that "personal initiative" will be found to be ubiquitous among utopians. "We carvers—who are the riffraff of Utopia—work in a long shed together," he explains, "nominally by time; we must keep at the job for the length of the spell, but we are expected to finish a certain number of toys for each spell of work." Yet while the "rules of the game as between employer and employed in this particular industry hang on the wall behind" them, "any man who has skill or humour is presently making his own bargain with our employer more or less above that datum line" (150–51). In utopia, it seems, at least some workers take a healthy interest in bending the rules, and in some quarters there may even be something suspect about the person who seems to love work too zealously. Except for the Samurai—figures evocative of Plato's guardians who run the World State—the citizens of *A Modern Utopia* manifest little zeal for contributing to the collective good, at least in what glimpses of them we receive. They seem rather to accede to work for reasons ranging from mellow enjoyment to sheer resignation to Adam's curse. But if work isn't the core satisfaction in life in Wells's ideal society, what is?

The narrator points to an answer in the first substantial generalization he delivers:

> I submit that to the modern-minded man it can be no sort of Utopia worth desiring that does not give the utmost freedom of going to and fro. Free movement is to many people one of the greatest of life's privileges—to go wherever the spirit moves them, to wander and see—and though they have every comfort, every security, every virtuous discipline, they will still be unhappy if that is denied them. (31)

A discussion of privacy follows, after which the narrator returns to the matter of utopian peregrination. "It is now our terrestrial experience that whenever economic and political developments set a class free to travel, that class at once begins to travel"; and on this basis, he posits that "in the modern Utopia travel must be in the common texture of life" (36). By means of "double railways or monorails or what not" the utopian will "travel about the earth from one chief point to another at a speed of two or three hundred miles or more an hour," and this "will abolish the greater distances" (37).

Nor will utopian mobility be limited to temporary excursions. On the contrary, the "population of Utopia will be a migratory population beyond any earthly precedent, not simply a travelling population, but migratory" (39). In the real world of the early twentieth century, people already change their "habitations with a growing frequency and facility," so that "to Sir Thomas More we should seem a breed of nomads" (39); Utopia will see a heightening of this happy trend.[57] Indeed the goal of full employment itself will be fulfilled in a manner that accommodates the peregrine impulse, the State "stand[ing] . . . as the reserve employer of labour" in such a way as to support the universal urge to see the world (97). A not wholly dissimilar estimate of the importance of movement appears in Charlotte Perkins Gilman's *Herland*, published ten years after Wells's novel: to the narrator Van's talk of couples pairing off in "'homes' of their own," the Herlander Celis explains, "Our work takes us all around the country. . . . We cannot live in one place all the time."[58]

Yet Wells's utopia doesn't bestow liberty of movement without imposing other tolls on freedom. As we've seen, the "free change of locality" in work that "will be among the general privileges of the Utopian citizen" is limited to "once or twice a year" and depends on the citizen's furnishing identification to the official in the "neat and business-like post-office." Further, the worker must carry proper documentation on his journey to new employment, which is to say that travel is in one sense as restricted in Wells's modern utopia as it was in More's early modern one (and that Wells in his way anticipates the hardening of the international passport regime during and after World War I[59]). Nor does Wells's World State monitor its citizens solely by means of documents carried on the person. The narrator of *A Modern Utopia* ventures that in the future every individual "could be given a distinct formula, a number or 'scientific name'" based on "thumb-marks" and "inalterable physical characteristics," all of these catalogued in a "great main index" of transparent cards that could easily be copied, photographically, and would be stored "in a vast series of buildings." A "little army of attendants would be at work upon this index day and night" and there would also be "a system of other indices with cross references to the main one, arranged under names, under professional qualifications, under diseases, crimes and the like" (113).

Thus, Wells concludes, would "the inventory of the State . . . watch its every man. . . . Such a record is inevitable if a Modern Utopia is to be achieved" (114). For many, of course, this would be a chillingly high price to pay for enhanced opportunities for travel, and the narrator acknowledges that to liberals, "brought up to be against the Government on principle, this organised clairvoyance will be the most hateful of dreams." He adds, however, that such liberal mistrust is based on an old assumption that "the more powerful the government the worse it was," whereas in the modern utopia, government is benevolent, its goodness ensured by the upstandingness of the carefully cultivated, public-spirited Samurai. If we now turn to Bogdanov's *Red Star*, published three years after *A Modern Utopia*, we can see how a vast, efficient, and benign system for matching workers to jobs might permit a society to be ideal without its managers being faultless.

Red Star has been called the first Bolshevik utopia, not least because Bogdanov was a prominent early Bolshevik theorist whose ideas would enjoy enormous influence in the eventual Soviet Union. In the wake of the Russian Revolution of 1905, radical elements had been relegated to the political margins; *Red Star* was part of Bogdanov's effort to reenergize the cause in this unpromising time. In the words of Richard Stites, introducing Charles Rougle's English translation of the text, Bogdanov "was the first in Russian fiction to combine a technical utopia, grounded in the latest scientific theories of the time, with the ideas of revolutionary Marxism," and his novel's success was enormous, particularly after 1917.[60] "Well received in Party circles after the Revolution"[61] it was reprinted at least five times in the Soviet Union,[62] including reissues in 1918 and 1922[63] and a run of 120,000 copies in 1929;[64] it also enjoyed a stage adaptation by the Proletcult theater in 1920.[65] It seems quite likely, moreover, that in writing it, Bogdanov was influenced by *A Modern Utopia*. According to Mark B. Adams, Bogdanov likely "read Wells's scientific romances and, in particular, his utopia," since these works "were well known and widely published in Europe and even in Russia, where the popular weekly *Vokrug sveta* regularly serialized new works by Wells in Russian translation as soon as they appeared."[66]

Red Star tells the story of a dedicated communist earthling named Leonid who, spirited to Mars, encounters a functioning society of the kind Bogdanov imagined for a Bolshevik Russia. The most memorable innovation of the Martian society appears halfway through the novel. Having been shown a Martian factory, which is cleaner and quieter than any on Earth and populated by workers captivated by their tasks, Leonid asks his Martian guides how production is organized. In reply, they lead him to a set of "small cubical building[s]" whose black walls are

> covered with rows of shiny white signs showing tables of production statistics. . . . On the first of them . . . was the following:
> "The machine-building industry has a surplus of 968,757 man-hours daily, of which 11,325 hours are of skilled labor. The surplus at this factory is 753 hours, of which 29 hours are of skilled labor.

"There is no labor shortage in the following industries: agriculture, chemical, excavations, mining," and so on, in a long alphabetic list of various branches of industry.[67]

Thus indicating where there are labor shortages and surpluses, these tables permit the worker to exchange her present occupation for a different one if she so desires. Menni, Leonid's chief mentor among the Martians, explains:

> The figures change every hour. . . . In the course of an hour several thousand workers announce that they want to change jobs. The central statistical apparatus takes constant note of this, transmitting the data hourly to all branches of industry. . . . The Institute of Statistics . . . computes the difference between the existing and the desired situation for each vocational area and communicates the result to all places of employment. Equilibrium is soon established by a stream of volunteers. (65–66)

Thus does Bogdanov's Martian utopia—offering its own improvements upon the employment offices of Wells and harking back, through them, to the labor exchanges of Fourier and even Hartlib—solve the twin problems of constraints upon workers' ability to choose their kind of work and variations in labor availability that lead to production slowdowns and unemployment. Menni explains that it wasn't always the case that workers had complete discretion on this front: two hundred years earlier, "when collective labor just barely managed to satisfy the needs of society, statistics had to be very exact, and labor could not be distributed with complete freedom." But new inventions have permitted "the transition to a system in which each individual is perfectly free to choose his own occupation" (67). The present arrangement obliges no individual "to take it upon himself to restore the equilibrium" of the system: "Everyone takes these figures into consideration when making their own plans, but they cannot be guided by them alone. . . . The statistics continually affect *mass* transfers of labor, but each individual is free to do as he chooses" (68).[68]

Further, Menni's explanations suggest that changes of occupation can transpire at a brisk pace on communist Mars. Where in Bellamy, as in More, such a change might happen only once or twice in a worker's lifetime, Bogdanov's Martian worker, like Wells's but much faster, can switch jobs virtually on a whim. The paradigmatic worker here is not the ironsmith or the doctor, whose skills are honed over many years and whose sense of identity may be much bound up with a profession or trade, but rather the factory laborer who has no need to identify with an occupation temporarily adopted. This immunity to subsumption by one's work is in fact reflected in the attitudes of the workers in the factory, who strike Leonid as "inquisitive, learned observers who had no real part in all that was going on around them. It was as if they simply found it interesting to watch how the enormous chunks of metal glided out beneath the transparent dome" (64).

Red Star thus offers something like the "just as I have a mind" of The German Ideology but with different parameters: where the inhabitant of Engels and Marx's communist future inhabits one place and changes occupations at will (hunting, fishing, herding, or criticizing, but not apparently relocating), this echo of gentlemanly prerogative is replaced on Bogdanov's Mars by a condition in which a change of job implies a change of venue. Certainly, we need to be careful not to overstate Bogdanov's investment in freedom of this kind for the individual worker. Red Star was, after all, a communist text issuing in a culture where the virtue of synchronizing the self to the collective had historically commanded far greater allegiance than it had in, for example, the liberal culture of Britain, and in the novel, the glory of Mars lies in its shining collectivity, not the pleasantness of each laboring day. At the same time, Menni clearly deems the convergence of collective benefit and individual preference in his society important enough to mark as one of his world's happy features. While freedom in work may not be the Martian social organization's paramount virtue, it's a virtue, and one that must heighten that utopia's attractiveness for the reader who prefers a collective in harmony with its members' desires.

Taken together, then, A Modern Utopia and Red Star attest to the significance, for utopian imagining in the early twentieth century, of a dream of liberation predicated on a vast central apparatus for managing information about production and labor. Such an emancipatory vision may strike twenty-first-century readers as extremely strange, given our contemporary tendency to associate centralization with domination: as Fredric Jameson notes in Archaeologies of the Future, the excitement generated by "the valorization of the Plan . . . in the 1920s and 1930s, at the beginning of the Soviet experiment, has been completely forgotten," and we might say the same for Bolshevik enthusiasms circa 1908.[69] Yet (as Jameson continues), the "centralization mostly today repudiated in the name of a decentralization now associated with democracy was not always oppressive" and utopian writers "have been divided on the matter" of whether centralization is a good thing for the ideal society (164).

Of course, the dream of Wells and Bogdanov is the more comprehensible when viewed against the backdrop of new technologies (real and hypothetical) for moving people from place to place, of (imaginably) vast advances in data management, and of a reconceptualizing of norms of living that both kinds of technologies could sponsor. Why should new plans for the ideal society *not* hold out the promise of a liberty of movement unknown, even in dreaming, to previous ages? Why should such a promise *not* be linked with the dream of freedom in choice of occupation? Even the antitechnological utopia of Morris, with its picaresque changes of scene, had intimated how the capacity to change one's location at will, once thought of, might be hard to omit from utopians' perquisites. How could a utopia be modern, really, *without* divesting humanity of what Wells calls the "old fixity" of location taken for granted by More?

Further inspection, however, discloses something else at stake in the figure of the job-changing worker in Wells and Bogdanov—another kind of freedom in addition to those of choice of occupation and choice of location. To see how the radical worker mobility we've been considering here wasn't about work and mobility only, we'll do well to turn to some of the writings in which Bogdanov and his fellow Bolsheviks envision not a fictional Martian order but a communist future on Earth. We can start with *A Short Course of Economic Science*, published in 1897 and written by Bogdanov himself.

Having devoted most of this lengthy work to a Marxist history of economic and social organization, Bogdanov turns in his final section to socialist society, where "production is *consciously and systematically organised by society as a whole*."[70] Such a form of organization will have for its center, Bogdanov explains, "a gigantic *statistical bureau* based on exact calculation for the purpose of distributing labour power and instruments of labour"[71]—just the kind of institution that he would soon depict in *Red Star*. He then goes on to explain that this bureau's activity will not imply "the old authoritarian centralism, but . . . a scientific centralism"[72]; and following the lead of Engels, who declared in *Anti-Dühring* that there would be no state as such in the classless society of perfected communism, Bogdanov stresses that those

> who think that the "State form," *i.e.,* a legal organisation, must be preserved in the new society because certain compulsory laws are necessary, like that requiring each one to work a certain number of hours per day for society, are mistaken. . . . The distribution of labour in society will be guaranteed on the one hand by the teachings of science and those who express them— the technical organisers of labour acting solely in the name of science, but having no power—and on the other by the power of the social sense which will bind men and women into one labour family by the sincere desire to do everything for the welfare of all.[73]

This same point is made repeatedly in writings by Bogdanov's fellow Bolshevik theorists—and political rivals—Nikolai Bukharin and V. I. Lenin. In *The ABC of Communism*, which was first published in 1920 and became the best-selling Soviet political primer of the decade,[74] for example, Bukharin and his coauthor Yevgeni Preobrazhensky answer the question of how a complex society can "be set in motion without any administration" by asserting that the

> main direction will be entrusted to various kinds of book-keeping offices or statistical bureaux. . . . Inasmuch as . . . all will understand . . . that life goes easier when everything is done according to a prearranged plan and when the social order is like a well-oiled machine, all will work in accordance with the indications of these statistical bureaux. There will be no need for special ministers of State, for police and prisons, for laws and decrees. . . . Just as in an orchestra all the performers watch the conductor's baton and act accordingly, so here all will consult the statistical reports and will direct their work accordingly.
>
> . . . In these statistical bureaux one person will work to-day, another tomorrow. The bureaucracy, the permanent officialdom, will disappear. The State will die out. . . .
>
> . . . Within a few decades there will be quite a new world, with new people and new customs.[75]

In *The State and Revolution* (1918), Lenin similarly argues that in creating "large-scale production, factories, railways, the postal service, telephones and so forth," capitalism has reduced most "of the functions of the old 'state power'" to such "simple operations of registering, filing, and checking that these functions will become entirely accessible to all literate people, . . . performable for an ordinary 'workman's wages' and . . . stripped of every shadow of association with privilege or peremptory command."[76] This passage suggests that Wells's rendering of the utopian work distribution center as a "post-office" was not the eccentricity we might at first take it for—and it also grounds Jameson's suggestion in *An American Utopia* (2016) that the post office could fill the "role of a parallel and non-state power" balancing the state's authority in a utopia for our own time.[77] Like Wells, it would seem, Lenin saw in the postal service evidence that a vast and complex apparatus could be managed (at least at the lower levels) by people of no singular ability.

Yet where Wells would insist on the continuing importance of experts in a transformed society, Lenin here saw grounds for thinking that the culture of specialists set apart from other workers, against which he elsewhere rails, could come to an end entirely. In communist society, there would be no separate administrative class—that is, no governing class—because, as Lenin observes, "the *mass* of the population will rise to the level of taking an *independent* part not only in voting and elections *but also in everyday administration*. Under socialism, *everyone* will administrate in turn and will soon become accustomed to no one administrating."[78] This extirpation of the administrative class is legible as, among other things, an extension of the desideratum, for the individual worker, of not being confined to one kind of work. "Under communism," write Bukharin and Preobrazhensky earlier in *ABC*, "there will not be permanent managers of factories, nor will there be persons who do one and the same kind of work throughout their lives"; rather, "people receive a many-sided culture, and find themselves at home in various branches of production: to-day I work in an administrative capacity, I reckon up how many felt boots or how many French rolls must be produced during the following month; to-morrow I shall be working in a soap factory, next month perhaps in a steam laundry, and the month after in an electric power station."[79] Thus is the kind of fluidity in occupation adumbrated in *The German Ideology* rendered in more Bogdanovian, less pastoral terms, and with the addition that remaining in a single occupation will be one work-related freedom that *cannot* be permitted.

It wasn't rotation alone, however, that the Bolsheviks saw as making for a heightened liberty from administrative oppression. The further suggestion is that even on a given day or at a given hour, those who hold the administrative role will have almost no need, and perhaps no capacity, to coerce. Once the system of book-keeping offices or statistical bureaux is established, those who work as administrators will issue not orders but, in Bukharin's diction, simple "indications." Because all will understand the benefits of cooperation— because a "social sense . . . will bind men and women into one labour family by the sincere desire to do everything for the welfare of all"—only information will be required; there will be no need for "peremptory command." Administration is here reduced to the thinnest layer of functionality, to a kind of pure facilitation in which questions of enforcement are irrelevant.

In so proposing, again, the Bolsheviks take up a line from Engels, who had insisted in the third part of *Anti-Dühring* that when the state at last "becomes the real representative of the whole of society, it renders itself unnecessary. . . . State interference in social relations becomes, in one domain after another, superfluous, and then dies out of itself; the government of persons is replaced by the administration of things, and by the conduct of processes of production. The state is not 'abolished.' *It dies out.*" Engels acknowledges in turn, here, a debt to Saint-Simon, whom he credits with already plainly expressing, in 1816, "the idea of the future conversion of political rule over men into an administration of things and a direction of processes of production—that is to say, the 'abolition of the state,' about which recently there has been so much noise."[80] Lenin, for his part, moves in *The State and Revolution* to rescue the celebrated *Anti-Dühring* passage from misinterpretation "advantageous only to the bourgeoisie" and later links it up with Marx's famous phrase from the *Critique of the Gotha Program* (1875): "The state will be able to wither away completely when society fulfils the rule: 'From each according to his ability, to each according to his needs,' i.e., when people have become so accustomed to observing the fundamental rules of social intercourse and when their labour becomes so productive that they will voluntarily work *according to their ability*. 'The narrow horizon of bourgeois right' which compels one to calculate with the coldheartedness of a Shylock whether one has not worked half an hour more than somebody else, this narrow horizon will then be crossed."[81]

These texts make evident that Lenin and his fellow Bolsheviks envision the transfer of the means of production as resulting in not one but two transformations that will permit a new day in work conditions to dawn. First, there will be an upwelling of voluntary contribution to the labor required by the new society—fruit of the ascendant "social sense" that binds "men and women into one labour family," of the newly ubiquitous and easy "observing [of] the fundamental rules of social intercourse." (One feels here the long hand of Nikolai Chernyshevsky's *What Is to Be Done?*, which we encountered in chapter 2, and which optimistically ties new social arrangements to old virtues of civility and self-sacrifice.) Second, there will be the abolition of the governing class, which in this context means that managers will no longer be able to impose their will over subordinates. These two developments mean that the exercise of power by people over other people will become both impossible and unnecessary.

With these considerations before us, we're in a better position to see what the radical occupational mobility of *Red Star* further implies. For in their way of limning the communist future, Bogdanov, Bukharin, and Lenin suggest that what matters in the operation of the Martian Institute of Statistics is not only the speed with which the Martian worker can move to a new job but also the absence, or at least the relative invisibility, of oversight of such changes by individual functionaries. The Martian worker appears to switch jobs without anyone else judging or approving of, let alone interfering with, her decision; indeed it's almost as though no one meaningfully *sees* the worker's choice at all. The statistical flows that smooth out the variability introduced by individuals' selections, coupled with a universal understanding that "work is a natural need for the mature member of . . . society" (Bogdanov, *Red* 66) and a shared fidelity to the project of the collective's flourishing, means not only that there will be no permanent class of bosses on Mars but, again, that there will be no coercion in work—which is to say, given the centrality of work distribution to the Bolshevik program, no coercion whatever. The dream incarnated in the mobile Martian worker is one not just of radical mobility but of a world in which no person exercises power over another.

Bogdanov, Bukharin, and Lenin indeed frame the problem solved by communist society as a problem of domination between people. To lack freedom, in their construction, is to be subject to another's will; once again adapting

Sartre's *"L'enfer, c'est les autres,"* we might say that in their view unfreedom is other people. Or as Lenin himself puts it: under achieved communism, the "need for violence against people in general, for the *subordination* of one person to another, of one section of the population to another, will vanish altogether since people will *become accustomed* to observing the elementary conditions of social life *without violence* and *without subordination.*"[82] Relieved of "capitalist slavery, of countless horrors, savageries, absurdities and infamies of capitalist exploitation, people will gradually *become accustomed* to observing the elementary rules of social intercourse that have been known for ages and repeated for thousands of years in all copybooks—and to observing them without force, without compulsion, without subordination, without the special apparatus for compulsion called the state."[83] The echoes of thinkers such as Rousseau, Condorcet, and Wilde are quite clear (even if Lenin's reference to violence calls up his own conviction of the necessity of force when conditions are nonideal): new social arrangements will strip away all that has led people to be less than their best selves. And this productive ascesis here has an additional result: the end of domination.

Insofar as the radical mobility of workers in *Red Star* stands as a synecdoche for a larger freedom from coercion by persons, it might seem that Bogdanov's concerns are finally at something of a remove from Wells's. Unlike Bogdanov's Mars, again, Wells's modern utopia is managed by an elite evocative of the guardians in Plato's *Republic*, and Wells goes out of his way to distinguish his utopian vision from the kinds that worry about the dominance of a governing class: "It would seem that Aristotle's idea of a rotation of rulers, an idea that crops up again in Harrington's *Oceana*, that first Utopia of 'the sovereign people' . . . , gets little respect in Utopia. The tendency is to give a practically permanent tenure to good men" (207). Yet in truth there's a surprising commonality of disposition between the Bolshevik future, in which the administrative class disappears, and the Wellsian future, in which the administrative class is reified beyond anything in the world we know. For although the Samurai are charged with setting policy for the modern utopia, the relatively ascetic "Rule" under which they're required to live means that they enjoy a smaller range of material rewards and even perhaps of pleasures than other members of society; like Plato's custodians, they cannot become an aristocracy in any material sense. Their class is, so to speak, rigidly delimited by its directive function, which is to say that administration here approaches from another direction the ideal of pure administering adumbrated in *Red Star*.

More to the point, however, *A Modern Utopia* intimates how unfreedom is other people in a fashion of its own—namely, by excluding from its narrative all social units, and even interpersonal relationships, that exhibit meaningful permanence. A novel of roads and inns rather than homes or halls, it outdoes even *News from Nowhere* in its commitment to the pleasures of uncommitted wandering. Morris's fiction at least shows its utopians living together, in households that, though voluntarily assembled, are not without whiffs of domestic tension; by contrast, Wells's narrator tells us that in his utopia, "autonomy of the household has been reduced far below terrestrial conditions by hotels and clubs, and all sorts of cooperative expedients" (147) and that the "solitary house may prove to be very rare" (149).

The antipathy of *A Modern Utopia* to human entanglements is then clinched, in a double sense, by the figure of the botanist—who, as we saw in chapter 1, both wallows in stories of human entanglement and constitutes such an entanglement for the novel's narrator. Particularly annoying to the narrator, as we've seen, is that melancholy sidekick's recurrence to an amorous disappointment back on Earth. "This thing perpetually happens to me," the narrator complains, "this intrusion of something small and irrelevant and alive upon my great impressions. . . . This man, on my first night in Utopia, talks and talks and talks of his poor little love affair" (43). Wells does present the botanist as something more than a pure foil: his valuing of human intimacy and pain counters the utopia's (and the narrator's) chilly distance from same, and at the climax, he's permitted to rise to temporarily unanswered eloquence. (The narrator having asserted that the botanist's earthly emotion has no place in utopia, being just "a scar from the earth," the botanist plangently retorts, "And what are we all but scars? What is life but a scarring? . . . We live to be scarred . . . ! We are the scars of the past!" [237].) The last pages of the novel, however, largely privilege the narrator's view, and the general disposition of *A Modern Utopia* remains a sort of upbeat aversion to enmeshing human relations.[84]

If the Wells of *A Modern Utopia* and the Bolsheviks share a hope that the most oppressive features of social life might be eliminated by giant administrative systems, they share as well an optimism anent the centralization that would accompany those systems. We've already encountered Wells's fondness for a World State epitomized by its one vast index of everyone's identifying information; we've seen, too, Bogdanov's enthusiasm for not "the old authoritarian centralism, but . . . a scientific centralism." For Wells, what keeps this centralization from becoming despotic is the good faith of the Samurai; for the Bolsheviks, again, it's a faith that under communism, *bureaucracy*—the holding of power by a distinct administrative class—will be no more. In *The State and Revolution*, Lenin prophesies that the "workers, having conquered political power, will smash the old bureaucratic apparatus" and that under the new order, "everyone may become a 'bureaucrat' for a time and therefore . . . *nobody* may be able to become a 'bureaucrat.'"[85] The disappearance of bureaucracy means the end of inefficient administration because it means the end of inadequate and self-interested human actors' capacity to disrupt the algorithm with arbitrariness, irrelevant considerations, and injustice.

Discussing Laura Riding's vision of a utopian social organization in *The Poetry of the Possible: Spontaneity, Modernism, and the Multitude,* Joel Nickels observes that questions about spontaneous governance

> belong to a tradition of thought that extends from the anarcho-syndicalist theories of the early twentieth century to multitude theorists such as Hardt and Negri.... The unique features of this intellectual tradition are its hostility to what Rudolf Rocker calls "bureaucratic ossification"—including that of Bolshevik Russia—and its belief that the regulative apparatuses of the state could be replaced with "the administration of public affairs on the basis of free agreement" [this a quotation from Rocker's *Anarcho-Syndicalism*]. Of course, imagining administrative organs that would be porous, changeable, and participatory enough that they would not harden into bureaucratic fixtures is the central problem of this tendency in political theory.[86]

Nickels then goes on to sketch Riding's effort, in her 1938 project *The World and Ourselves,* "to imagine a form of social organization that could absorb the administrative functions of the state without adopting its anonymity and bureaucratic rationality." For Riding, writes Nickels, "the basis of such a process would be self-governing community companies that would no longer make a distinction between public administration and private commitment," that "would be modeled on the 'company of friends'" and thus "integrate material production and affective exchange."[87]

This account furnishes an illuminating contrast, within a larger similitude, to the vision of the Bolshevik theorists. Lenin and company were certainly as antipathetic to bureaucratic ossification as Riding and Rocker, at least qua theorists, and any sharp distinction between public and private was preemptively rendered out of court for them by values both Russian and communist. Still, their optimism that altruistic devotion to the common project would naturally arise in all workers had to be shored up, as it were, by prescriptions for rotation and so on that would counter any failure of the hoped-for enlightenment. And if their theoretical positionings of administration in opposition to bureaucracy imply a hearty fellow feeling not requiring articulation, the frontal rhetoric of those positionings points not to warm affective exchange but to a desirable *de*personalization—an elision of the capacity of fallible individual actors either to disrupt the system or to subject other workers to unfair treatment.

As Nickels's "'bureaucratic ossification'—including that of Bolshevik Russia" recalls, however, the dream of a centralization resisting the fall into bureaucracy would go so strikingly unrealized in the Soviet state that the latter would become a byword for bureaucratic hypertrophy. "During the earliest months and years following the Russian Revolution of 1917," writes Seymour Melman, "industrial workers who had organized themselves in enterprise- and industry-wide soviets, or workers' councils, played a certain role in government operations and policy-making," but this role diminished "as the Communist Party, during and after the years of civil war, underwent a transformation."[88] Even in early 1918, according to Robert Service, "factory-workshop committees were subordinated to the trade unions, and these in their turn to the government"; by the summer of 1918, "the soviets themselves in the provinces were being strictly supervised by the central authorities. Working-class strikers were designated as hooligans; and, when peasants refused to release grain to the towns, the requisitioning of supplies began."[89]

Of course, these and other developments ran directly athwart Lenin's emphasis, in *The State and Revolution*, on "local initiative, mass participation and popular self-determination."[90] But Lenin—that "irascible proponent of altruistic work," in Anna Feldman Leibovich's words[91]—found his ideals for the communist order sorely tested from the moment he rose to power. The "grim facts of the day—workers' strikes, their desertion of the workplace, and the fall in production—bore bitter testimony to the illusory nature of Lenin's vision of the communist ethic of work"[92] even if they could be seen as perversely affirming Lenin's insistence back in "What Is to Be Done?" (1902) that workers on their own, sans a Marxist vanguard, could scarcely be trusted to develop a properly revolutionary politics. By the end of 1920, according to Richard Day, the "danger of bureaucratic degeneration had already become apparent," and "Lenin understood that the Soviet state could not embody 'the collective reason of the working class,' as Bukharin maintained. For the working class, as Bukharin admitted, was internally differentiated according to levels of class consciousness."[93]

The Soviet government's efforts to limit the liberties of workers would grow increasingly draconian. The years of War Communism (1918–21) were marked by a massive outflow of people in search of food to the countryside; then the years of the New Economic Policy (1921–28) saw a massive movement in the other direction, which created so much urban unemployment that the government had, in the words of the sociologist Arvid Brodersen, "to take stern measures in order to stop the migration—prohibition of entry into cities; registration of unemployment only by individuals who had previously been employed in industry; making an individual's access to the labor market dependent upon his being a member of a trade union," even as the unions themselves were stripped of independent powers.[94]

The ability of workers to move about at will was then further restricted in succeeding years, as authorities continued to face a staggering level of labor turnover. A party decree of October 1930 made six months' unemployment the punishment for leaving one's job without a license, and in ensuing years the carrot of material incentives as well as the stick of penalties (as severe as incarceration) were widely deployed. Domestic passports for urban and industrial workers over sixteen were introduced in 1932 and 1940,[95] and in June 1940, as Donald Filtzer recounts, the Stalin regime "took the bold step of making both job changing and absenteeism criminal offences. Absenteeism, which now embraced any unauthorized loss of work time of more than 20 minutes within the working day . . ., condemned the offender to . . . up to six months' corrective labour at his or her current enterprise at reduced pay."[96] Further, with the Soviet entry into World War II, those who were classified as working in defense industries—an increasingly capacious category—were considered to have been mobilized, so that anyone failing to perform as required in these jobs could face "a military tribunal, and if convicted would go to a labour camp for between five and eight years."[97] These regulations continued to be enforced and were "in certain respects even augmented" in the postwar years.[98] And yet throughout there was a high incidence of violations of these regulations, and quite a number of convictions.[99]

If the largest irony of Bolshevik governance was thus that the state grew exponentially even as its waning was proclaimed, the most striking synecdoche of theory's failure to become practice lay in the radical restriction of workers' capacity to decide what work they would do, and where, and when.[100] Here, utopia's people problem—the difficulties unleashed by persons' double role, in utopia, as ends and means—surfaces in notably concrete form. An implication running through Bolshevik theory, we might say, was that those who would benefit from the new social sense would quickly come to discern those benefits and then achieve that sense (as if the managerial utopia's incentivizing and the transformative utopia's transformation of character were to be synched at last, the former leading immediately to the latter). The reasons why the theory was not borne out in practice in the Soviet case were many, but it's surely fair to say that the vision of worker mobility realized on Bogdanov's Mars was partly undone, on Earth, by workers' very desire for mobility.

This dispiriting consideration would seem to be a significant backdrop of the most Bogdanovian utopia published during the Cold War. Ursula Le Guin's 1974 novel, *The Dispossessed*, doesn't quite hew to the familiar utopian format in which a visitor to the happy society receives an education in why it functions so brilliantly; rather, it tells about utopia, or the effort to sustain something like utopia, using a focalizer who visits a world that is, by most measures, far less utopian than is his own. We learn that a century and a half before the events of the novel, a large group of revolutionaries was permitted to migrate from their home planet, Urras, to that planet's moon or sister planet,

Anarres—there to build an anarchist society if they could. And they have. Following the teachings of the great innovator and revolutionary Odo, the Anarresti live completely without property; indeed they use "propertarian" as a term of abuse (to be hurled against anyone who seems bent on claiming individual possession of anything), and they pull together in an arduous struggle with the natural conditions of their world, which lacks the abundant resources of Urras. The novel proper begins with the journey to Urras of an Anarresti scientist named Shevek, the first such return in history and one that has generated much controversy among the Anarresti. Over the course of the novel, sections detailing Shevek's meeting with the Urrasti (in which he and they learn more about their respective worlds) alternate with flashbacks that tell the story of Shevek's life.

Clearly, the Anarresti experiment is meant to evoke communist, communal, anarchist, and utopian projects, large and small, seen in our own nineteenth and twentieth centuries. In setting the Anarresti against Urrasti skeptics who resemble naturalizers of capitalism in our world, Le Guin recalls movingly how such experiments had continuously to defend themselves against claims that they could never be sustained and how they required for their survival a continuing fervor for the experiment itself. What will most detain us here, however, is the likeness, well noted by Phillip Wegner, between the Anarresti method of work distribution and that of Bogdanov's Mars.[101] On Anarres, assignments are dispensed by the Division of Labor Office, or Divlab, which resembles closely the Martian Institute of Statistics. In a flashback chapter, Shevek visits Divlab, which,

> with its computer and its huge task of coordination, occupied a whole square. . . . Inside, Central Posting was . . . very full of people and activity, the walls covered with posting notices and directions as to which desk or department to go to for this business or that. . . . The human/computer network of files in Divlab was set up with admirable efficiency. It did not take the clerk five minutes to get the desired information sorted out from the enormous, continual input and outgo of information concerning every job being done, every position wanted, every workman needed, and the priorities of each in the general economy of the worldwide society.[102]

As Anarres is, at least roughly speaking, a functioning anarchy, it has no state or government as such, no apparatus to which Divlab would be officially subordinate. But as Shevek explains to one of his Urrasti hosts, there is "a network of administration and management" called "PDC, Production and Distribution Coordination," that coordinates "all syndicates, federatives, and individuals who do productive work." The components or members of PDC "do not govern persons; they administer production," and hence have "no authority either to support . . . or to prevent" Shevek's unprecedented trip to Urras. They can only tell him and his supporters "the public opinion of [them]—where [they] stand in the social conscience" (76). The Bolshevik dream inherited partly from Engels and Saint-Simon appears here quite forthrightly: at least nominally, Anarres replaces the government of persons with the administration of things.

On Anarres, as on Bogdanov's Mars and Wells's alternative Earth, this handling of big data supports a high mobility in work. Divlab seems extremely effective in determining what tasks need to be done where, and meanwhile all Anarresti enjoy, at least nominally, freedom of choice of occupation in the short term and the long. Answering an Urrasti's question about who does the dirty jobs on Anarres, Shevek explains that everyone must take them on for a time, though no one need do so "for very long, unless he likes the work" (149). Pressed on whether a person can refuse an order, Shevek then elaborates, "It's not an order. . . . He goes to Divlab . . . and says, I want to do such and such, what have you got? And they tell him where there are jobs" (149). Asked further why anyone accepts a dirty job though not compelled to, Shevek offers as Anarresti reasons the value of work done in common, the appeal of any break from routine, and also the "challenge. . . . Where there's no money the real motives are clearer, maybe. People like to do things. They like to do them well. . . . They can . . . show off. . . . Work is done for work's sake. It is the last pleasure of life. The private conscience knows that. And also the social conscience, the opinion of one's neighbors. There is no other reward, on Anarres, no other law. One's own pleasure, and the respect of one's fellows. That is all" (150). The relatively rare Anarresti who "won't cooperate" by doing needed work is mocked, beaten, or otherwise excluded from sociality by the local community; when such a person grows tired of this treatment, she moves on. Those who do this "all their lives" have a special name, *Nuchnibi* (150).[103]

As in Bogdanov, people are impelled to labor both by the immediate satisfaction of work and by dedication to the project of keeping the just society going; we'll turn to the additional matter Shevek mentions, "the opinion of one's neighbors," shortly. For the moment, however, we need to notice that contribution to the collective labor required on Anarres carries costs of a kind that does not appear in Bogdanov or Wells. It emerges that one of the most serious downsides of life on Anarres is the geographical displacement often entailed by a fresh work posting, which can lead to the dissolution of friendships and romantic relationships. "A couple that undertook partnership did so knowing that they might be separated at any time by the exigencies of labor distribution," and while "Divlab . . . tried to keep couples together, and to reunite them as soon as possible on request . . . it could not always be done." An Anarresti grows up "knowing labor distribution as a major factor of life, an immediate, permanent social necessity; whereas conjugality was a personal matter, a choice that could be made only within the larger choice" (245–46). The difficulty of maintaining bonds long-distance is heightened by a prejudice against "unnecessary writing or calling" (which in the Anarresti view "smack[s] of privatism, of egoizing"), so that although fidelity sometimes strengthens attachments, overall "an Anarresti tended to look for his friends where he was, not where he had been" (251).[104]

The narrator's rendering here is then borne out by the plot of the novel, quite a number of whose turns prove to be driven by postings. Shevek's parents are separated by the wishes of the Central Institute of Engineering, which wants his mother but not his father (26–27); Shevek loses contact with his friends from adolescence when postings take them to different areas; he's parted from his lover (and the mother of his child), Takver, for four years, after an emergency posting calls her to a distant laboratory. Anarresti enjoy a notional freedom to choose their work, then, but their practical control over their lives is curtailed by a state of affairs less like that of Bogdanov's perfected Mars than like the earlier stage alluded to by Menni, "when collective labor just barely managed to satisfy the needs of society . . . and labor could not be distributed with complete freedom."

Yet this imperfection of the system pales, in terms of destructiveness to many Anarrestis' thriving, before another one: its ultimate inability stave off the unfreedom that is other people. Anarres by no means exudes the antipathy to intimate connection that we find in A Modern Utopia; on the contrary, Le Guin makes clear that one of the great achievements of its society lies in its privileging of human relationships over investments in things—in the profound authenticity of Anarresti bonds, hard though these may be to maintain. But Anarres also illustrates with matchless clarity the anarchist-Bolshevik point that constraint may be found to be social, indeed intersubjective, in its essence. In The Dispossessed, the anarchist society does hold together, and it leaves its members free from naked exercises of governmental authority. But coercion takes root there anyway, as its main characters come to recognize, and this coercion is grounded in people in an extraordinarily stark way.

For it turns out that if devotion to the Odonian project is one reason work assignments are always accepted on Anarresti, another and more powerful one is an absolutely smothering peer pressure, a force of public opinion that the novel's reader increasingly experiences as regrettable and ugly. This force of opinion is even harnessed by some to consolidate immediate power over others, though such power implicitly remains fragile and limited. Ruminating on how the nefarious Sabul (a colleague at the Central Institute of Sciences) has been able to force Shevek to share credit for work that's entirely Shevek's own, Shevek's friend Bedap urges,

Sabul uses you where he can, and where he can't, he prevents you from publishing, from teaching, even from working. Right? In other words, he has power over you. Where does he get it from? Not from vested authority, there isn't any. Not from intellectual excellence, he hasn't any. He gets it from the innate cowardice of the average human mind. Public opinion! That's the power structure he's part of, and knows how to use. The unadmitted, inadmissible government that rules Odonian society by stifling the individual mind. (165)

As ventriloquized by Bedap, Le Guin's conclusion is that maintaining a society from which power remains absent would require a constant vigilance against the "human will to dominance," which is "as central in human beings as the impulse to mutual aid is" (168).[105]

It bears stressing that as taken by Le Guin, this is not a conservative position, though it may call to mind rightist asseverations that progressive schemes neglect fallible human nature. An often mournful but not a despairing novel, *The Dispossessed* seems a compound of nostalgia for the old dream that inspired the Bolsheviks' anarchist predecessors; critique of some of that dream's premises; and preservation of the hope that, creatively reconstituted, the dream might somehow survive.[106] Le Guin takes no delight in suggesting that even extremely committed and intelligent anarchists might have trouble keeping their society power-free, indeed stresses that the waning of "anarchy" in the sense of a deliberately instituted and maintained style of (non)government might be permitted or hastened by the decline of "anarchy" in the sense of a relatively disorganized condition. Stability, Bedap tells Shevek in the diagnosis just quoted in part, "gives scope to the authoritarian impulse. In the early years of the Settlement we were aware of that, on the lookout for it. People discriminated very carefully between administering things and governing people. They did it so well that we forgot that the will to dominance is as central to human beings as the impulse to mutual aid is" (166–67). Further on, Shevek will tell Takver, "Bedap was right: every emergency, every labor draft even, tends to leave behind it an increment of bureaucratic machinery," so that the worker's ability to choose her own way quietly vanishes: "We're ashamed to say we've refused a posting. . . . we *obey*. We fear being outcast, being called lazy, dysfunctional, egoizing. . . . We have created crime, just as the propertarians did" (329–30).

In *Archaeologies of the Future,* Jameson questions Le Guin's "qualification of Anarres as an 'anarchist' Utopia. Thereby she doubtless intends to differentiate its decentralized organization from the classical Soviet model, without taking into account the importance of the 'withering away of the state' in Marxism also" (278). But surely this is to miss how Le Guin's narrative speaks to the difficulty of getting the state to wither away, precisely as this was illustrated in the historical Soviet Union. The actual Soviet attempt to eradicate the unfreedom that is other people, which appeared to have ended not with the emancipation of the worker but with the intensification of bureaucracy, was surely one of the real-world developments, between Bogdanov's moment and Le Guin's, that shaped the timbre of *The Dispossessed*. In this sense, Le Guin's novel can be read as the terminus, or epitaph, of an emancipatory dream in which choice of work, choice of location, and freedom from coercion by other people variously intersect and constellate—a dream that begins with the full-employment reformers of the seventeenth century (or even with More) and continues through Harrington, Saint-Simon, Fourier, Marx and Engels, Morris, Wells, Bogdanov, and the early theorists of Bolshevism, at a minimum.

This genealogy of a particular hope for humanity is of more than genealogical interest, however. For it also illuminates some broader questions pertaining to utopian justice. Let us recall that whether or not a given utopia incorporates centralization as such, utopias conceived in any concreteness may be distinguished from other imaginings of a perfect world—Edens, pastorals, Lands of Cockaigne, millenarian kingdoms—by their grounding in a total plan (even if this be a scheme for functioning anarchy) designed to solve problems besetting human society. This has always made utopias seem suspect on the score of freedom. Yet what *Red Star* and our other texts highlight is that a kernel of radical freedom could imaginably be contained within what would seem this most alarmingly coercive aspect of utopian imagining. The wager of utopia is that design itself can give birth to freedom *precisely by* being a strong design—a "well-oiled machine," to use Bukharin's handy expression—that leaves no scope for the caprices or self-interest of individual operatives and functionaries.[107]

In one sense, the preceding treatment of unfreedom as a matter of persons might have sounded odd: what, one might ask, can freedom or unfreedom be, apart from other people?[108] Yet the coerciveness with which utopia has traditionally been charged is not so anthropocentric or, we might better say, so intersubjective. The alarm provoked by utopia has often, that is, had less to do with the submission of some of its inhabitants to others than with the submission of all to the plan, the design, the machine, or (a point to which B. F. Skinner gestures in *Walden Two*), the original engineer. In chapter 2, we saw how Arendt (along with, in certain ways, Zamyatin and Forster) articulates one form of this alarm: the fear of a society where there are oppressed without even oppressors, in which effectively no one pulls the strings in spite of a condition of utter domination. Bringing Arendt's concern to bear here, we can see that what utopias—or at least what Russell Jacoby calls "blue print utopias," in contradistinction to "iconoclastic utopias"[109]—may seem to offer is an

exchange of freedoms: in return for continuous submission to the plan, liberation from unpredictable coercion by other people.

Of course, most utopias do rely on governors who may wield considerable
individual authority. Pre-nineteenth-century utopias, especially, feature rulers,
heads of families, and the like who exercise a great deal of control over the lives
of their subordinates, and in Bellamy's *Looking Backward*, a fiercely merito-
cratic system is sustained by a powerful managerial hierarchy. It bears noting,
however, that utopias rarely depict holders of authority who use their powers
for ill. And if we ask why such dangerous governors rarely materialize in utopia
(and when they do are efficiently relieved of their authority), the answer is
clear: the utopian design doesn't permit their continuing to hold power for
long or, more usually, doesn't permit such flawed types to obtain power in the
first place. Utopia's educational arrangements produce only wise and good
people; or its meritocracy ensures that only the best will rise to supervisory
positions; or its electoral system permits swift recall of inadequate officers; or
utopians are so admirably self-governing that leaders (if there are any) have
no need to compel obedience; or new conditions of production extinguish the
class of permanent administrators. Whatever the reason, the decisions made
by utopia's decision makers are the right and just ones, and often the products
less of individual creativity than of a well designed system acting through those
representatives (see again Harrington, Saint-Simon, and Engels). Bogdanov's
vision of administration reduced to pure facilitation can thus be understood not
as an extreme among utopian forms of arrangement but rather as a distillation
or intensification of what utopias have perhaps always effectively promised.

This is not, of course, to argue that human beings would be wise to choose
the more abstract unfreedom of submission to utopian design over the more
quotidian and perhaps tangible unfreedom of subjection to others. Among the
many problems with such a view is that subordination to the utopian plan
could only be truly innocent of the latter form of coercion if every inhabitant
of utopia agreed that submission to the design is preferable to any alternative
and if the system were one that could truly forestall every reentry of power
relations. The point here is rather that to charge utopia with an abolition of
freedom generally, as many antiutopian commentators have, is to miss how it
bids to open up freedom in one direction even if it closes down options in
another.

But utopia is by no means alone in proposing liberation along these lines.
If the idea of a sociopolitical arrangement in which the damaging caprices of
human actors are mitigated or eliminated by a larger system sounds familiar,
this may be because it's also to be found, and rather more visibly, in theoretical
schema other than utopian ones. In fact, this kind of dream is associated with
at least two other ways of thinking about ideal arrangements that, far from

bearing the generally leftist associations of utopianism, have been allied, especially recently, with positions at the other end of the political spectrum.

The first of these is the principle of the "rule of law"—in which, to use John
Adams's celebrated language from the Massachusetts Constitution, the desideratum is a "government of laws and not of men." This ideal, whose theorization descends from John Locke, Montesquieu, and the *Federalist Papers*, is very
precisely built upon the conviction that unfreedom is other people. For its
advocates, "to live under the rule of law is not to be subject to the unpredictable vagaries of other individuals," is "to be shielded from the familiar human
weaknesses of bias, passion, prejudice, error, ignorance, cupidity, or whim."[110]
Few devotees of the rule of law would assert that submission to it implies no
unfreedom whatever. But they accept this relatively abstract sacrifice of freedom as preferable, on the whole, to the ordinarily more concrete and intimate
unfreedom that might come with subjection to the inclinations of others.

Where the rule of law differs most dramatically from utopia, apart from its
tendency to self-limitation, is in its general aversion to exercises of governmen-
tality designed to heighten social prosperity or to enhance forms of equality
apart from political and legal equality. If the rule of law appeals especially to
libertarians, this is because it seems to work against fetters on the individual,
whereas utopia seems to stress the individual's embeddedness in webs of social
relations and may even subordinate the individual's needs or desires to those
of the collective. Yet to the degree that the rule of law presents itself as more
than an austere principle—as the foundation of a clearly preferable social
order in some robust sense—it has a certain deep affinity with utopian
imagining.

This point is in a manner confirmed by the very genealogy of the rule of
law. For the source of Adams's formulation is none other than *Oceana*, wherein
Harrington famously declares, "Government (to define it *de jure*, or according
to ancient prudence) is an art whereby a civil society of men is instituted and
preserved upon the foundation of common right or interest; or, to follow Aristotle and Livy, it is the empire of laws, and not of men."[111] We might indeed
say that both *Oceana* and Harrington's tableau of the Cats and Kitlings, where
the machine works so perfectly that it can't be marred by the inclinations of
individual agents, participate in two traditions or corpuses, those of utopia and
the rule of law—and thereby illuminate the usually occluded relation between
them. We might also find telling, with respect to our consideration of utopia's
connections to *nomos*, *nemein*, and *nemesis*, the alternative name for the rule
of law: *nomocracy*. The semantic peregrinations of *nomos*—from proper allotment to right ordering of persons and things to law itself—in their way underscore the continuity between utopian rightness of arrangement and the rule
of law's defense against individual caprice.

The other line of thinking that may come to mind when we speak of a system that bequeaths liberty and prosperity by transcending the faults of individual human agents is that associated with the notion of the "invisible hand"—with the assumption that a superior social result will be obtained when actors (especially economic actors) pursue their individual self-interest rather than aiming consciously at the collective good. Of course, political positions that depend on versions of the invisible hand, like commitments to the rule of law, stand at a remove from what we conventionally call utopian speculation in a number of crucial ways. Evident centralization is ordinarily anathema to them; they have no consistent objection to intersubjective relations of power; and where utopians may aspire to a strong social plan invulnerable to damage from erring individual executors, those who subscribe to invisible-hand optimism hold that however aberrant a human action may look in isolation, the sum of such actions will sustain and validate the larger system. In laissez-faire economics, of course, this larger system will be some version of the market whose prerogatives aren't artificially checked. Yet invisible-hand thinking obviously does meet up with utopian thinking in its conviction that desirable social ends can be achieved via the operation of a mechanism that, once set running, takes care of all exigencies. Like some strains of utopianism, at least, it puts its faith in a kind of machine or giant algorithm—though here that device or constellation of formulae may ultimately be complex beyond human reckoning.[112]

At the present time, invisible-hand thinking enjoys wide discussion not only among proponents and antagonists of "free" markets as such but also in defenses of, and attacks on, that composite of theories, practices, policies, institutions, and values known as *neoliberalism*. As numerous commentators have pointed out, this term has in recent years come to seem ever more necessary and ever more problematic, at once crucial and misleading. It can seem indispensable inasmuch as it captures how policy shifts and ideological configurations coming into their own in the Reagan-Thatcher years were grounded in a set of economic principles—vigorously liberal under some acceptations of "liberal" but not under others—developed in the middle of the twentieth century. But the term is also ungainly in that the myriad positions it's said to encompass sometimes conflict with each other, in that rhetoric privileging invisible-hand views may be at odds with practices of "neoliberal" institutions, and in that contemporary invisible-hand ideologies don't always align, in truth, with the earlier theories from which they claim descent.[113]

Nonetheless, most would agree that the discursive ubiquity of *neoliberalism* highlights how invisible-hand thinking has quite effectively pushed against the kinds of programs and policies that have grounded the welfare state. And it is precisely this that puts in one more surprising light the early twentieth-century dream of a freedom and happiness sponsored by a *nomos* transcending human fallibility. We may be tempted to regard this dream as a curiosity only a very different time could germinate, a vision discredited by history and of small residual interest to theory. But a glance at the invisible hand's long hand should make us think again.

Archipelagic Dreams

"On the day when he reached the thirtieth year of his personal life Voshchev was discharged from the small machine factory where he had earned the means of his existence. The dismissal notice stated that he was being separated from his job because of his increasing loss of powers and tendency to stop and think amidst the general flow of work."[114] So begins Andrei Platonov's remarkable novel *The Foundation Pit*, written in 1929–30 though not published in the Soviet Union until 1987. *The Foundation Pit* is a satire, tonally rueful and gentle but the more devastating for that, on the elusiveness of Bolshevism's utopian aspirations. Its characters struggle to make sense of communist metaphysics in the world that confronts them, their faith in collectivization and other tenets of the new society simultaneously touching, admirable, and appalling—as when, early in the novel, the workman Safronov asks another character, "But why does the field lie there so sadly, Nikit? Is there misery inside the whole world, and we're the only ones with the five-year plan inside us?" (40). The pausing to think for which Voshchev is fired is precisely in this vein: asked by the "trade union committee" what was occupying him, Voshchev says that he was thinking "about the plan of life"; asked what he thought this meditation could accomplish, he answers, "I could have thought up something like happiness, and spiritual meaning would improve productivity" (5).

Of the several wayward strands of Soviet utopian hope addressed in *The Foundation Pit*, the one to which Voshchev's firing gestures most directly is the vision of workers choosing where they'll labor and what kind of work they'll do—which, as we've seen, was bound up with hope for an end of submission to other persons and thus the end of domination in general. In beginning with Voshchev's dismissal, *The Foundation Pit* signals the departure, or at least the radical deferral, of this dream. Who would have thought that achieved communism—or even the "transitional phase" on the way there, the "dictatorship of the proletariat"—would see a thoughtful man "separated from his job" because he had paused to think? The several pages that follow then extend Platonov's effective rendering of how the ambitions encoded in Bogdanov's *Mars* have gone unrealized. In the wake of his termination, Voshchev must leave the place he has lived and see what employment he can find elsewhere, which is to say that in direct contrast to the volitionally mobile worker of *Red Star*, Voshchev becomes itinerant against his will.

Fortunately, he does find work in the next town—though this is thanks not to the efficiency of the Soviet work-allocating machine but rather to a hitch in its operation (albeit one that could be considered a sign of the overall success of the late economic transformation). Responding to Voshchev's appeal for work, Safronov tells him that "maybe he would do, since people, like materials, were now hard to get. The union deputy had been combing all the towns and empty places around for days, looking for some landless poor that could be turned into permanent workers, but he seldom brought anyone. Everybody was living and working" (15). A little later, the engineer Prushevsky will tell the excavator Chiklin, "The Labor Exchange promised to send fifty men, and I asked for a hundred" (18–19), while Pashkin, the "chairman of the Area Trade Union Council" (27), will tell the worker Kozlov, "there is a shortage of proletariat nowadays" (29). So it is that Voshchev joins a crew digging a foundation pit for a giant "common building" (16) where "the entire local proletariat would come to live" (16)—after which transition the "small one-family homes" would be "vacated and impermeably overgrown with vegetation, and the remaining, withered humans of forgotten times would gradually breathe their last in them" (16–17).

This anticipated gathering of the whole community in one huge structure embodies not just Soviet collectivization, of course, but utopian imagining in general, which in so many instances reposes hope in common housing and giant refectories, in the supersession of the individual property owner and the monadic family. As we've seen already in this chapter, however, concern with the movement of workers and, more generally, with freedoms associated with choice of place may be scarcely less integral to utopia than are fixed architectures. To focus on utopia's obsession with arrangement in a static sense (its invention of routines and orders, its design of buildings and cities) is to lose sight of its sustained interest in the possibility that an essential component of the best life could be the ability to move—to change tasks, to switch homes, to exchange one community for another.

Yet the character of that interest hasn't remained fixed over time. Dimly adumbrated, at best, in More, it has taken a variety of forms in later writers through the Bolsheviks and beyond. If *The Foundation Pit* (written in advance of the cruelest Soviet decrees limiting worker mobility) appears as a partly proleptic elegy for whatever ambitions Bolshevik theory may have had in this area, Le Guin's *Dispossessed* can look, as we've seen, like a requiem for the same from the other side of the twentieth century—a reflection on the pragmatic difficulties of sustaining an anarchist society, certainly, but also a valediction to the Soviet experiment. After the moment of Le Guin's novel, utopian writers certainly remained interested in liberty of movement. But as will be argued here, the nature of their investments altered markedly enough to make it possible to think of our own phase of utopian imagining as having commenced between forty and fifty years ago.

In *Archaeologies of the Future*, Jameson proposes just such a dating for the last great shift in the character of utopian fiction, venturing that "the great feminist Utopias of the 1960s and 1970s were somehow the last traditional ones" and that "a kind of break can then be posited for the emergence of Thatcherism and the crisis of socialism" (216). In *An American Utopia*, he keeps this dating but slightly reweights his reasoning on cause, proposing that "the end of utopian production" was witnessed by "Ernest Callenbach's great *Ecotopia* of 1975" and that what led to the dissipation of traditional utopia was less the triumph of deregulation under Reagan and Thatcher than the rise of "an anti-institutional and anarchist preponderance on the left whose causes are clearly multiple," but which notably include a continuous interrogation of power, founded "in the work of Michel Foucault and others," that eventuates in "a quasi-paranoid fear of any form of political or social organization" (1–2).[115] In the pages that follow, we'll see why Jameson's hypotheses in this area, though in certain ways incontestable, need to be supplemented with attention to certain features of human movement in our world. This point might be made via attention to any of scores of writers, but two theorists and two novelists should prove sufficient to our purposes.

We can begin with one of the theorists. In chapter 2, we visited briefly with the political philosopher Robert Nozick, whose *Anarchy, State, and Utopia*, published in 1974, countered John Rawls's *A Theory of Justice* with an argument that "a minimal state," limited to certain duties of protection, "is justified"; that "any more extensive state . . . is unjustified"; and that "the minimal state is inspiring as well as right" (ix). What we need to notice here is that Nozick stops well short of saying that all people will experience a minimally intervening regime as the one that best suits them. Axiomatically solicitous for the rights of the individual, Nozick acknowledges that while some will prefer a society of quite limited government, others will prefer other kinds of arrangements, even ones that look more like Rawls's. Of course, the "best of all possible worlds for me will not be the best of all possible worlds for you."[116] And thus in the last section of his book, Nozick asks how we can possibly imagine utopia, given that people are different. What kind of social organization, he asks, could be ideal for, all at the same time, "Wittgenstein, Elizabeth Taylor, Bertrand Russell, . . . Yogi Berra, Allen Ginsburg [*sic*], . . . Hugh Heffner, Socrates, Henry Ford, . . . Gandhi, Sir Edmund Hillary, . . . Bobby Fischer, Emma Goldman, . . . you, and your parents" (310)?

No one "kind of life" would be "best for each of these people" (310), clearly. And more generally, "there will be *no* way to satisfy all of the values of more than one person, if only *one* set of values can be satisfied" (309). If, however, "there is a diverse range of communities, then (putting it roughly) more persons will be able to come closer to how they want to live, than if there is only one kind of community" available to them (309). And thus the most truly utopian arrangement would be one in which the individual is able to choose among many societies, all arranged in different ways:

> Utopia will consist of utopias, of many different and divergent communities in which people lead different kinds of lives under different arrangements. Some kinds of communities will be more attractive to most than others; communities will wax and wane. People will leave some for others or spend their whole lives in one. Utopia is a framework for utopias, a place where people are at liberty to join together voluntarily to pursue and attempt to realize their own vision of the good life in the ideal community but where no one can *impose* his own utopian vision upon others. . . . Utopia is meta-utopia: the environment in which utopian experiments may be tried out. (312)

"The framework for utopia that we have described," Nozick concludes, "is equivalent to the minimal state." And "this morally favored state, the only morally legitimate state, the only morally tolerable one, we now see is the one that best realizes the utopian aspirations of untold dreamers and visionaries" (333).

Again, Nozick is careful to stress that although his utopian framework "is libertarian and laissez-faire, *individual communities within it need not be,* and perhaps no community within it will choose to be so" (320). What makes the metautopia acceptable from his libertarian perspective, indeed as nearly ideal as any imagined social organization can be, is nothing intrinsic to the communities themselves but rather the utopian's freedom to exchange arrangements that feel uncongenial for ones that seem more suitable. Given that communities will in the end be spatially or geographically delimited, this implies absolute freedom to change one's physical location. And thus although Nozick is little interested in conditions of labor or the movements of workers, a particular kind of freedom of movement is of the highest importance to his scheme. Metautopia requires absolute freedom of emigration (coupled, of course, with absolute freedom of immigration, although the latter is left implicit). Launching his discussion of the utopian framework, Nozick indeed invites us to "call a world which all rational inhabitants may leave for any other world they can imagine . . . an *association*; and . . . a world in which some rational inhabitants are not permitted to emigrate to some of the associations they can imagine, an *east-berlin*" (301).

Nozick's proposal for metautopia has more recently been taken up by the second theorist to be considered here—one whose quite different political position makes the more noteworthy his recourse to Nozick at the, or rather a, culmination of many years and pages of reflection on utopia. This theorist is Jameson himself. In the final chapter of the first half of 2005's *Archaeologies*—that is, at the end of the part of the volume that presents new writing—Jameson cites the passage in which Nozick posits as utopia "a framework for utopias" (quoted at 217) and pairs it with another scheme for a "multiplicity of Utopian communities scattered across the globe" advanced by Yona Friedman in the 1975 book *Utopies réalisables* (219). In Friedman, as summarized by Jameson, we find utopias "each following its own Absolute," nothing in the mold "of a world state or of some higher-level United Nations or *ekumen* which would somehow unify mankind" (219). Friedman's utopias are linked solely by infrastructure, and one of the "two fundamental mechanisms of this new global Utopian system" is "the right of migration" (219).[117]

Building upon Nozick and Friedman, Jameson proposes that we "think of our autonomous and non-communicating Utopias—which can range from wandering tribes and settled villages all the way to great city-states or regional ecologies—as so many islands: a Utopian archipelago, islands in the net, a constellation of discontinuous centers, themselves internally decentered" (221). What matters in this model is less the ability to change jobs and locations within a given demesne (as in the Fourieran phalanstery or Bogdanov's Mars) than the ability to move beyond a border, to enter (literally or metaphorically) a new territory where different modes of organization hold sway. As in *Anarchy, State, and Utopia*, the vision is much bound up with a mobility that is also a certain power of self-determination, though for Jameson the self and its community will always in an important sense be internally riven. The federalist vision he describes would, writes Jameson, accord with "the great lesson of Fourier" that the collective will and perhaps ought to have "productive inner conflicts and compacts or conspiracies" (223); it would accommodate or harness "the supreme social force of envy" and guarantee "on a permanent or structural basis that inner gap or béance in the subject which is normally overlooked or misrecognized" (223). If "Utopias can correspond" to the multiplicity inside each of us, "they will assuredly be Delanyian ones"—a characterization we'll revisit in a moment—"a Bakhtinian polyphony run wild" (214).

For Jameson, such a vision "goes a long way towards palliating . . . objections to the closure of the system as a whole" (223) and moreover pushes against capitalism even in its globalized phase by "mak[ing] the enlargement and expansion necessary to capital impossible" (220).[118] Still, Jameson worries that this kind of framework might not be sustainable because it would be incapable of serving as a cathexis in the way the figure of the nation can: it may be that "Federalism cannot be invested with the desire associated with the lost, indeed the impossible object" (225). Of even greater concern, however, is that such a scheme may ultimately fail to make the future the "radical and systemic break with the present" that Jameson believes a utopia must embody if it's to be really meaningful (228). Thus he concludes that the archipelago might best be understood as an "ornament and spatial decoration" exhibiting not the radically disruptive work of the Imagination but rather "the operation of what we have called Utopian Fancy" (229)—an operation whose importance is not to be underestimated, however, given that it has become Fancy's role "to elaborate schemes by which capitalism is ameliorated or neutralized, or socialism is constructed in the mind" (55).

Whatever the merits of this assessment of the archipelago, we should pause here to register that the archipelagic vision of a world of different communities freely entered and freely exited marks a departure from the long history of representations in which utopia is either a bounded enclave set off from societies less perfectly arranged or a world-sized state in itself. The former style of utopia reaches back at least to More's Utopia, so conspicuously divided from the mainland, and persists through the New Atlantis, Swift's Houyhnhnmland, Gilman's Herland, and many more incarnations, right up to actual intentional communities operating today. The latter tradition has often been assumed to be a more recent innovation: for Northrop Frye, writing in "Varieties of Literary Utopias" in 1965, for example, the possibility of the isolated utopia began to vanish when it was recognized, "from about 1850 on, that technology tends to unify the whole world."[119]

Against this idea of a sharp historical turn, certainly, it has been well argued that utopia in the West has always had an expansionist aspect. According to Doyne Dawson, writing on Hippodamus of Miletus, the fifth century BCE architect who "probably planned the town" of Thurii in present-day Calabria, "Utopianism was a by-product of colonization, which made it uniquely Greek."[120] Bloch asserts in the second volume of *The Principle of Hope* that utopia moved beyond the island or city-state model with the advent of Stoic literature, which imagined a "programme of world-citizenship, which here means the *unity of the human race*"; for the Stoics, it was not military power but "the universal element, the oecumene, which made Rome so seductive."[121] Still, the call of the world-state–sized utopia does seem to have become harder to resist beginning in the nineteenth century.

In 1849's *Revolution in the Mind and Practice of the Human Race*, to take one example, Robert Owen imagines his proposed "rational townships" of five hundred to three thousand persons covering the globe: "As these Townships increase in number, unions of them, federatively united, shall be formed in circles of tens, hundreds, and thousands, etc.; until they shall extend over Europe, and afterwards to all other parts of the world, uniting all in one great republic, with one interest."[122] In *Looking Backward*, Leete tells West, "You must understand that we all look forward to an eventual unification of the world as one nation" (105), and for the Wells of *A Modern Utopia*, nothing "less than a planet will serve the purpose of a modern Utopia. Time was when a mountain valley or an island seemed to promise sufficient isolation for a polity to maintain itself intact from outward force. . . . But the whole trend of modern thought is against the permanence of any such enclosures. . . . World State, therefore, it must be" (15). As Wegner notes, Bogdanov was unwilling "to accept a model of a social totality (and history) confined by the borders of the nation-state" because one of the foundations of his socialism was a supersession of national divisions.[123] And even Skinner is far from restricting the ambitions of Walden Two to one enclave, his Frazier rather noting that at their present rate of growth and subdivision into new communities, the Walden experiments could in thirty years "absorb the whole country many times over."[124]

For Nozick, the idea of utopia as a framework of communities permitting free emigration from one to the other is simply a logical solution to the problem for freedom presented by persons' differing ideas about what makes a good life. As we've seen, however, Jameson situates his thinking more historically: just before introducing Nozick and Friedman, he offers his above-quoted view of the break that follows the feminist utopias of the 1960s and 1970s and calls up "the emergence of a world-wide late capitalism from its modernist integument, from which it bursts in the form of full-blown globalization and postmodernity" (216). For Jameson, what came on the scene after this, as Kim Stanley Robinson's *Mars* trilogy and other texts illustrate, is "a new formal tendency, in which it is not the representation of Utopia, but rather the conflict of all possible Utopias, and the arguments about the nature and desirability of Utopia as such, which move to the center of attention. . . . What is Utopian becomes, then, not the commitment to a specific machinery or blueprint, but rather the commitment to imagining possible Utopias as such, in their greatest variety of forms" (216–17). Thus while the proposal for a utopian archipelago may, per Nozick, possess a certain internal logic or a transcendental commonsensicalness, Jameson encourages us to consider what historical developments helped prepare the ground for such a conception's evolution and dissemination.

Again, the one that suggests itself most immediately is globalization as a phenomenon of capitalism itself, which seems to make at once imperative and nearly impossible the thinking of how, in Jameson's words, "any kind of local unit, from city to nation-state," could "possibly resist the overwhelming power of the global market forces, let alone delink from the latter and reconquer its autonomy and self-sufficiency" (215). As Patrick Hayden and Chamsy el-Ojeili remark in the introduction to their 2009 collection *Globalization and Utopia*, globalization seems both to furnish "a distinct mode of utopian representation" and to portend "a threatening dystopian predicament." On the one side, there's the vision of "the utopia of a 'world without borders', encompassing truly free trade, high-tech production, progressive equalization between nations," the "emergence of a cosmopolitan order of multilateral negotiation, human rights, peace, and global governance," and "a global village of mutual understanding and constructive interchange." On the other, there's the specter of a "growing polarization of wealth, the global rule of multinational corporations, and a profit-above-all drive that threatens life on the planet" as well as "a 'new imperialism' centered on US military might and plans for a 'new American Century'" marked by "cultural imperialism, Westoxification, and Coca-colonization." A similar tension meanwhile informs views of human agency: on the one hand, globalization may be "associated with the idea of a blockage of the utopian imaginary," the idea that people are no longer capable of forging the future in a strategic or deliberate way, while on the other, it may support a resurgence of efforts to resist the dominance of capitalism by specifically utopian thinking.[125]

We'll return to globalization shortly. Here, however, we need to note that at least two other real-world phenomena of the last half century appear to bear on the archipelagic model's emergence and allure. One is, again, the collapse of the Soviet utopian experiment, which can be described equally meaningfully as post-1960s or post-1989, and which under the aegis of various rhetorics and master narratives helped make decentralization appear a more attractive path to utopian freedom than any scheme marked by vestiges of a centralizing impulse. The other is the call for liberty of lifestyle that exploded into American public discourse in the 1960s and went on to become a staple of progressivism—a legacy of the counterculture that would be crucial to, yet of course remains conceptually distinguishable from, the emergence of identity politics.

The question of lifestyle figures particularly strongly in the first of the two novels we'll want to consider here: *Trouble on Triton: An Ambiguous Heterotopia* (originally published in 1976 under the title *Triton*), which Samuel R. Delany wrote, or rather revised in draft, partly in response to *The Dispossessed*.[126] Here, as in Le Guin, movement from place to place is a central trope as well as a central plot element. But the world, or rather the solar system, Delany depicts in *Triton* differs crucially from the Anarresti model in that its promise of liberation isn't tethered to a single administrative apparatus. Rather than being restricted to one country or even one planet, the people in Delany's future have, within limits, the option to move from world to world, the solar system as a whole here evoking Jameson's and Nozick's federalist arrangement (although as we'll see, it's very far from free of conflict between component units). It's not clear what fraction of the overall population of the solar system in *Triton* has the financial means or the legal ability to emigrate, but evidently many are able to exercise some discretion about whether to live on patriarchal Earth; on feminist but also perhaps authoritarian Mars; on Earth's moon; or on any of the habitable moons of Jupiter, Saturn, or Neptune (including Neptune's Triton). The novel's protagonist, Bron, grew up on Mars but now calls Triton home.

Crucial for our purposes is that those living on the outer worlds enjoy ample individual freedom, especially around matters of self-display, living situation, gender, and sexuality. On Triton, one can report to work wearing a mask and cape one day and naked the next; one can make one's home in a gay co-op, a straight co-op, a mixed co-op, a large family compound, or any of many other configurations; one can change one's sex through surgery easily performed; one can even change the gender direction of one's sexual desire with a similarly straightforward visit to a government-funded clinic. There's also a good deal of latitude in choice of work, as Triton boasts more or less full employment under normal conditions. In the aforementioned chapter of *Archaeologies,* Jameson writes that any new formal utopian solution would

> need to take into account both the historic originalities of late capitalism— its cybernetic technology as well as its globalizing dynamics—and the emergence, as well, of new subjectivities such as the surcharge of multiple or "parcellated" subject positions characteristic of postmodernity . . . according to which we are black in one context, and intellectual in another, a woman in another. (214)

It's surely with *Triton* in mind that Jameson then adds the remark already quoted: "if Utopias can correspond to this kind of multiplicity, then they will assuredly be Delanyian ones, a Bakhtinian polyphony run wild" (214).

As we'll see, Delany does introduce into this idyll eruptions of precarity that are of high significance to the novel's overall purport. For the moment, however, we can simply note again that *Triton* reads as a colorful evocation of something like the utopian archipelago, one in which a degree of choice *among* communities is doubled by a rich array of choices *within* (at least some of) those communities. If Le Guin's Anarres evokes the old Soviet administration, Delany's outer solar system, at least, looks like an archipelago of Santa Cruzes— and Castros-back-in-the-day. Most inhabitants of the outer moons seem to relish the freedom to change their gender and their desires at will.

Bron, however, is more doubtful. Indeed at one point in the novel, he gives vent to a version of a complaint often voiced against utopias that provide their inhabitants a wide array of choices about how to live—that this plenitude can leave one adrift:

> Somewhere, in your sector or in mine, in this unit or in that one, there it is: pleasure, community, respect—all you have to do is know the kind, and how much of it, and to what extent you want it. That's all. . . . But what happens to those of us who *don't* know? What happens to those of us who have problems and don't know *why* we have the problems we do? What happens to the ones of us in whom even the part that wants has lost, through atrophy, all connection with articulate reason. Decide what you like and go get it? Well, what about the ones of us who only know what we *don't* like?[127]

Delany is too thoughtful a writer to suggest that utopia must make everyone unhappy; many on the outer worlds *do* seem to achieve a certain contentment. But not Bron, who in the last part of *Trouble* makes a bid to gain new understanding, and concomitant fulfillment, by crossing the boundary of gender. He becomes a woman. Alas, this new commitment has nothing of the hoped-for effect, at least not by the novel's end. Bron finds herself stuck in place emotionally, living a life that's relatively stable materially but by no means satisfying: "Here I am, she thought, as she had done from time to time ever since she'd come from Mars: Here I am, on Triton, and again I am lost in some hopeless tangle of confusion, trouble, and distress."[128]

The lesson of Bron, whose transition to femaleness at the close of the novel echoes her earlier move from Mars to Triton, would thus seem to be that crossing boundaries—whether of gender or of planet—may get you somewhere, but won't do so necessarily. And in putting forward this lesson, we might say, Delany looks somewhat beyond, or askance at, the hopes that Nozick and Jameson pin to border crossing—holds out a fantasy of unlimited movement only to assert the limits of that dream in two interrelated ways. First, as just mentioned, he represents achieved crossing or passage as less than necessarily liberating or fulfilling, asking whether there are fundamental limitations to any effort to build a society responsive to the multiplicity—and the elusiveness—of human desires. Second, he plants in the middle of the novel an interplanetary war that renders travel between enemy worlds temporarily hazardous and eventuates in minor economic disruption and horrific casualties. Bron is surprised when another character has trouble finding a job, and then even more surprised when he himself is required to take a two-week furlough[129]; things get yet more grim when actual hostilities eventuate in a staggering loss of life. In other words, Delany injects into his "ambiguous heterotopia," as the subtitle of the novel has it, a dose of nonutopian reality, including an evocation of at least one kind of limit to border crossing that occurs in our own world. And in this he points to a historical problem haunting, as we might say, the dream of the utopian archipelago.

For the most obviously appropriate term for the movement from world to world just described is, of course, *migration*. And with that term before us, we come to the profound historical irony attending the emergence of the idea of the archipelago as a resolution to problems bedeviling the utopian totality. If we ask what real-world developments pertinent to utopia are evoked by the anxieties of *Triton*, we might think not only of the winding down of the Soviet experiment, the increasing recognition of freedom in lifestyle choice as a social virtue, and confirmations of American economic insecurity that began to arrive in number in the 1970s but also of the severing, under the sign of what we call globalization, of the old link between emigration and freedom.

Of course, no historical phase of border crossing can be associated with emancipation *tout court*. The Middle Passage, the Great Migration within the United States, the waves of European migration to the United States: the first was compulsion, the other two intricate interweavings of emancipation and dire economic constraint. Nonetheless, there's an important sense in which globalization changes the game. As a concept or a structure that helps us apprehend contemporary reality, globalization recasts migration less as a passage from old to new than as one from same to same, a transition from one capitalist topography to another that will prove no less capitalist and often similarly exploitative. The historical irony shadowing Nozick's and Jameson's formulations, then, lies in the fact that movement across boundaries has, in recent decades, come ever more signally to emblematize not liberation but its opposite. We might say that even as the Soviet denouement seemed to be rendering less tenable the dream of utopian emancipation through the nation-state, what might have seemed a viable replacement for it—the dream of emancipation through border crossing—was already being undermined by the reality of global labor "flows." It's surprising that this point has so far not attracted more attention from scholars of utopia, many of whom have recognized in other ways that globalization has changed the terms on which utopia can be conceived.

Triton registers this effect obliquely and anticipatorily; any number of more recent novels register it more directly. Immigrant communities, radical and painful dislocations, or both loom large in dystopian or quasi-dystopian fictions otherwise as different from each other as Octavia Butler's *Parable of the Sower* (1993) and *Parable of the Talents* (1998), Nalo Hopkinson's *Brown Girl in the Ring* (1998) and *Midnight Robber* (2000), Romesh Gunesekera's *Heaven's Edge*, (2000), Margaret Atwood's *Oryx and Crake* (2003), Amitav Ghosh's *The Hungry Tide* (2005), and Cormac McCarthy's *The Road* (2009). Tying the collapse of one or another version of a good or at least adequate society to unsought displacement, these texts illustrate not only how the idea of utopia has been under strain in a general way since the crises of the 1970s but also how movement in particular has come to read, at least some of the time, not as release from a constricting society but as a condition of deprivation. To be sure, the emergence in these same years of mobility studies and critiques of sedentarist metaphysics have challenged the normativization of non-nomadic lifestyles, and the fictions just named do find ways of celebrating resilience on the road. But it must be said that their frequently grim picaresques depict the hardships of unchosen displacement far more vividly than they do any satisfactions therein, and often in ways that make settled communities in our own world seem the lost havens of a golden age.

One text that illustrates especially cogently utopia's character in the present era of migration is Chang-Rae Lee's On Such a Full Sea (2014). Lee sets his story in a future United States given over to three distinct kinds of communities. First, there are the "Charter villages"—fiercely gated sanctuaries of the affluent.[130] Here, residents enjoy a high level of material well-being but are also threatened by what goes on outside their walls (about which more in a moment) and beset by a sort of intensified version of the anxieties attributed to the prosperous American middle class at least since Sinclair Lewis's Babbitt. The inhabitants of the Charter villages worry about social position, material standing, and, above all, their children's ability to succeed in a competitive work environment. Second, there are the "production settlements," which quite explicitly serve the Charter villages (148). Equally gated, they provide the food and perhaps other goods required by their more affluent counterparts; and while these communities seem to enjoy a comparable level of stability, their standard of living is far lower and their political position clearly subordinate. The novel's protagonist, a young woman named Fan, begins as a resident of one such community, B-Mor, whose specialties are vegetables and fish. Fan initially works as a diver in the fish-raising tanks.[131]

These first two kinds of communities are connected by "secured, fenced" highways for which users pay steep tolls (40). And what both the communities and the tollways are guarded from is the general lawlessness that prevails everywhere else. For the third kind of society in Lee's future United States, if it can be called a society, is that of the "open counties," where people survive by forming compounds, running small businesses they protect with firearms, or joining or submitting to local police forces that operate as extortion rings. Where the Charter villages are populated mainly by white people who resemble upper-middle-class whites in our own time, those who live in the open counties read as poor whites, country people, brutal and brutalized versions of rural blue-collar Americans today. But who, then, are the inhabitants of the second kind of community, the production settlements?

In the case of B-Mor at least, they're migrants. For B-Mor is a future Baltimore in which white flight and money flight have been nearly absolute instead of partial. Those with the means to do so long ago decamped from the crumbling city, and most of the remaining poor were relocated. But a power described only as one of "the federated companies" (21) repopulated the quondam Baltimore with people from "Xixu City," a town in "New China" that had been "made uninhabitable by the surrounding farms and factories and power plants and mining operations," its "water fouled beyond all known methods of treatment" (19). Deposited in their new home on another continent, the emigrant Chinese set about rebuilding, and by the time of the novel's action, Baltimore, now B-Mor, is again operational.[132]

Thus the setup, unfolded piecemeal over the novel's first chapters. The main action of the narrative is then relatively simple and picaresque. Learning that her boyfriend Reg has left B-Mor under mysterious circumstances, Fan lights out for the open counties on her own, where she has a series of mostly harrowing adventures, eventually making her way to a Charter village where she endures further trials. Her story is told by a "we" who may be a small group of seasoned residents of B-Mor or one person adopting a certain aura of the collective. The narrating "we" describe how Fan has become a legend in B-Mor and insert reports of B-Mor's recent history into their imagining of what happened to her. ("Imagining," because it's hard to see how they could have any actual knowledge of Fan's doings.)

Lee's novel contains a number of elements that recall prior fictions such as *Parable of the Sower, Oryx and Crake,* and especially *Midnight Robber.* Like B-Mor, the Toussaint of Hopkinson's 2000 novel is an in-some-ways utopian community populated by nonwhite people, and like Fan, that tale's heroine Tan-Tan (who becomes a justice-dealing robber queen) leaves the community and embarks on a journey that finds her using her wits and her strength to survive in extremely dangerous circumstances. Further, while Toussaint isn't explicitly a service community, it's a domain established by a business entity—a planet transformed two hundred years before the start of Tan-Tan's narrative when "the Marryshow Corporation sink them Earth Engine Number 127 down into it like God entering he woman," as one of the novel's narrators tells us.[133] Toussaint further resembles B-Mor in representing, at least for some of its inhabitants, a kind of modest utopia, one that inspires a certain pride in what the present generation's ancestors have been able to achieve.

There are differences between B-Mor and Toussaint, however. Among the B-Moreans themselves, inequalities seem less sharp than they are among the inhabitants of Toussaint, and there seems in B-Mor a stronger sense of partici-pation in a communal project. More to the point for us here, Lee emphasizes more strongly than does Hopkinson how the place the heroine departs from is already a migrant *destination*—how in leaving B-Mor, Fan abandons an en-tity that could be described as what remains of the utopian dream. In this sense, the world of *On Such a Full Sea*, still more emphatically than that of *Midnight Robber*, is one in which the dream of utopian worker mobility is at once retained and lost, or rather retained in a manner that reads as loss.

Indeed the scattered walled enclaves in Lee's novel present a kind of grim parody of Nozick's and Jameson's utopian archipelago—one in which emigra-tion in the manner of Fan is not a way of finding like-minded souls and a congenial style of life but rather a staggeringly dangerous undertaking holding scant promise of social or material, let alone spiritual, gain. Fan becomes a leg-end at least in part because few if any before her had taken their chances with the open counties by choice; in emigrating at the behest of her own desire, she's distinctive in, rather than representative of, her world. We can say, then, that if *Triton* presents early intimations of the limits of a utopian dream grounded in border crossing, *On Such a Full Sea* puts a nail in that dream's coffin. Or, rather, that it offers a far more thorough elegy for that dream, one deepened by forty more years of witness to what migration would come to signify.

This point is notably underscored by a minor character in the novel, Mala. A "helper"—cook, all-around servant—who works in a Charter residence in which Fan also briefly comes to serve, Mala is "an Asian of some kind" but with dark skin and wiry hair suggesting that she is not "of New Chinese Blood"; Fan speculates that she may be a holdover from a failed experiment in "bringing in groups from places like Vietnam and Indonesia and the Philippines" (200). Mala spends twenty days out of each twenty-one-day cycle working for her Charter employers—having the twenty-first, only, to spend with her own hus-band and daughters in the open counties. Mala's "schedule for the last seven-teen years" (201) gestures unmistakably to the phenomenon, in our own world, of workers who devote much of their lives to earning money for family members in their home countries whom they rarely see—a phenomenon fre-quently illustrated, in public discourse on the issue, by accounts of Filipina domestic employees.

Yet if Lee's novel reads as another elegy for the dream that freedom might be realized in some mobility of the worker, it's not only elegiac any more than Le Guin's *Dispossessed* is. For it suggests, by its most impressive formal maneu-ver, how utopian hopes once pinned to migration and the utopian archipelago might be replaced by hopes of another kind. As noted above, the "we" who narrate the novel interweave two kinds of stories, now relating Fan's adven-tures, now relating what has lately transpired in B-Mor. They tell us, for example, that after Fan and Reg departed, "freshly painted portraits" of them would sometimes appear "on the side of a row house or fence, hastily done in the night and clearly by different hands" (17). They observe that goods and health care have become more expensive; they report changing hairstyles, a rise in suicides, a brief collapse in the market for fish. And they describe how, recently, the B-Moreans have pushed back against the authorities, apparently gaining some concessions. There are "outbreak[s] of vandalism and im-promptu public protest" as people exhort "one another to bring about change" (278, 280), then "demonstrations that are no longer just spontaneous . . . or stray," including a meeting at which speakers protest a diminution of the al-ready tiny percentage of B-Mor children who are admitted, upon testing by examination at age twelve (183), to a life in the Charter world (337–38). At last—in response either to the disturbances themselves or to a relative tran-quility that takes hold as demand for B-Mor goods rebounds—"the director-ate, or some other body, we can't be sure," reverses "some of the more disheart-ening measures of recent times, foremost being restrictions on health clinic visits . . . and the qualification for Charter promotion." There is also "an unpre-cedented round of new, if modest, public works" (389).

At first, it's difficult to tell whether the "we" telling the story are reporting events in B-Mor roughly as they happen or setting them down at a later junc-ture. For much of the novel, the reader will likely assume the latter—that they're unfolding their tale more or less at one go, and that the incidents in B-Mor had all already occurred by the time they set pen to paper (or fingers to keyboard) or began talking. Eventually, however, it becomes clear that the narrating "we" have been giving their account in installments, and that the new events in B-Mor are occurring in between (or somehow alongside) their bouts of telling Fan's story. The effect of this revelation is to impress the more firmly on the reader that B-Mor is less static than one might expect such a utopia/dystopia to be. The changes that occur over the course of the narration bespeak both precarity and glimmers of hope, B-Mor continuing to evolve even if there seems no immediate prospect of an amendment in the overall scheme of things. "There was so little of this voicing before, and now that there is much more, we see it takes as many forms as there are people" (339): it becomes clear to the B-Moreans "that where we are does not wholly comfort us. And perhaps never truly has" (343). The migrant refuge proves definitively *not* utopia, but out of this very recognition comes the thought that perhaps a genuinely com-forting place can be fought for.

Meanwhile, Fan remains in a crucial sense static, in spite of her many star-tling adventures. Certainly, she's a very mobile worker, adroit at dispatching fresh kinds of tasks as they come before her; and certainly, her journey is still continuing at novel's end. Yet her tale conspicuously lacks a strong forward momentum, and it associates freedom with movement only in an attenuated way: she repeatedly extricates herself from scrapes and traps, but these little liberations in no way evoke the liberty enjoyed by mobile workers in Morris, Wells, and Bogdanov or that Nozick and Jameson affiliate with the crosser of boundaries. If there is utopian promise in the novel, again, it seems embodied not in Fan's journey so much as in her legend's capacity to stir something in B-Mor's people. At one point, thinking of Fan, the narrating "we" reflect that "every once in a while there are figures" whom others seem devoted to helping, who lead others to "want to see them succeed" and indeed "draw our energies so steadily and thoroughly that only toward the finish of events can we recognize the extent of our exertions, and how those exertions in sum might have taken the form of a movement" (263). The last word of the passage captures eloquently what we might call the transfer of trajectory in *On Such a Full Sea*: Fan's movement doesn't bring her to utopia, but it inspires a movement back home that strives to make a corporation-fashioned *nomos* much better than it has been.

Lee's novel thus suggests a certain passage of utopian hope, or longing, from the figure of the worker in motion to that of the situated collective. *On Such a Full Sea* is certainly a road novel, but it's not one in which utopia lies at the end of the road. It's rather one that suggests an end *for* the road—a fading, as one of utopia's privileged figures and dreams, of the freedom to choose where one works. As the narrating "we" adjure in the book's final words,

> Don't hurry, Fan.
> Stay put for now.
> We'll find a way.
> You need not come back for us. (407)

A Global *Nomos*

We can refine this picture of the recent fate of aspirations associated with worker mobility a bit further, however. For if the character of migration around the turn of the twenty-first century has dampened some forms of indignation having a utopian aspect, it has clearly stimulated others. Around the world, varieties of *nemesis* (in the sense we've been using that term) have emerged in response to injustices associated with emigration and the treatment of migrants in receiving countries. Indignation about abuses perpetrated by immigration and naturalization authorities, about failures to honor undocumented persons' basic rights, about exploitation in even the least compromised guest-worker programs, and about the "repatriation" even of children who have never lived in their parents' countries of origin is by now a familiar response not only to individual regimes worldwide but also to the whole post-Westphalian structure of national sovereignty, which seems in numerous ways unequal to the realities of people on the move that it has itself helped create.

Such indignation doesn't always have a utopian character, of course. The immediately staggering immiseration of both individuals and groups on the move, coupled with the magnitude of what we might (adapting Bruce Robbins's resonant phrase "the sweatshop sublime") call the migration sublime, can make speculation about how global labor flows would *ideally* be accommodated feel like a luxury for which there's scant occasion and less time. And yet there has come into circulation in recent decades a powerfully evocative term, prominent in public discourse and at the same time constitutive of a particular domain of scholarly inquiry, that points directly to hopes for a rearrangement of the world under which the political and economic wrongs that have given rise to, and included various aspects of, mass migration would be remedied. This term is *global justice*.

In its broadest acceptation, *global justice* has come to name something like a goal of equity for people worldwide that activists, policy makers, and others may work toward—has, in the words of Huw L. Williams and Carl Death, become a significant term in the areas of "human rights, just war, humanitarian intervention, terrorism, economic injustice, gender justice, immigration, environmental issues, health issues and natural resources" as well as "international law" and more. Moreover, it has come to point to a vast international ensemble of efforts toward this goal. The movement for global justice "is often described as a 'movement of movements,'" Williams and Death note, "or a network of organizations and campaigns who loosely coalesce around opposition to war, neoliberal globalization, and the global governance of the World Trade Organization, International Monetary Fund, World Bank, and so on. . . . Those who mobilize under the banner of global justice tend to have a radical political outlook, and protest repertoires include marches, sit-ins and occupations, petitions (increasingly online), and mass gatherings such as the World Social Forum."[134] As the foregoing would suggest, what arguably most links those who identify their activities with global justice goals is antagonism to the inequitable distribution of power, wealth, resources, and opportunities between the global North and the global South, or between the most affluent nations and regions of the world and the rest.

The very term *global justice* suggests how the range of struggles undertaken on these fronts are impelled by a spirit of utopian *nemesis*—not only because in setting themselves against injustice at all, they evoke a damaged *nomos*, a wrong arrangement of things, but also because the modifier *global* points to an aspiration toward totality, a setting right on the largest scale. Of course, people acting in the name of global justice have been able to oppose particular forms of exploitation, inequality, and violence without having specific utopian designs in mind: the *global* in *global justice movement* can be understood as betokening the extent of the movement rather than the envelopingness or perfection of the justice sought.

More tightly bound up with utopian totality, at least in certain ways, is the second and narrower sense of *global justice* that has entered discourse in recent years. This acceptation of the term refers to a domain of political theory that tries to leverage points of normative consensus about justice, fairness, and responsibility into a rethinking of transnational political and economic arrangements. In a 2015 article for the *Stanford Encyclopedia of Philosophy*,[135] Gillian Brock explains that in "the domain of global justice, theorists do not seek *primarily* to define justice between states or nations"—that would be the concern of what has come to be called "international justice"—but rather "drill down through the state shell and inquire about what justice among human beings consists in."[136]

Global justice in this second sense—which will here be called *global justice theory* whenever there could be any chance of confusion with *global justice* in the first and broader sense—is generally agreed to have emerged as an effort to scale up to the level of the world the principles Rawls enumerates for a just society in his 1971 *A Theory of Justice*. As we've seen, Rawls there conducts a thought experiment in which persons having no knowledge of what conditions they'll be born into—"No one knows his place in society, his class position or social status; nor does he know his fortune in the distribution of natural assets and abilities, his intelligence and strength, and the like"—would try to achieve consensus on how society should be arranged if it's to be just.[137] Rawls concludes that they would agree on a small number of principles, including the principle that each person must "have an equal right to the most extensive total system of equal basic liberties compatible with a similar system of liberty for all" (302) and the "difference principle," which states essentially "that the social order is not to establish and secure the more attractive prospects of those better off unless doing so is to the advantage of those less fortunate" (75). As should be evident from this précis, Rawls's theory offers a kind of moral basis for pillars of the liberal democratic order in the twentieth century, supporting both a high degree of liberty and a certain redistribution of social goods within a market economy.

Given that it's not immediately clear why justice's moral demands should halt at the boundaries of community, society, or state, it's perhaps no surprise that scholars who found Rawls's *A Theory of Justice* compelling soon began to ask why the obligation to fairness shouldn't extend across the world as a whole.[138] In his detailed 1973 examination of Rawls, *The Liberal Theory of Justice*, Brian Barry argued that on Rawls's own terms, the minimum acceptable for the worst off "should not depend capriciously upon the good luck of being born into a rich society or the ill luck of being born into a poor one. . . . From the standpoint of the 'original position' the question of distribution between societies dwarfs into relative insignificance any question of distribution within societies."[139] A more extensive intervention in this area came with 1979's *Political Theory and International Relations*, in which Charles Beitz imagined, as Barry effectively had, representatives of various nations conferring under the auspices of an "international original position." Beitz argued, in line with Barry, that the "parties would view the distribution of resources much as Rawls says the parties to the domestic original-position deliberations view the distribution of natural talents"—that is, as "arbitrary from a moral point view." Indeed they would see the natural distribution of resources as even more purely arbitrary than the distribution of talents, because the possession of resources is not conventionally held to be constitutive of an individual's personhood.[140]

Beitz also observed that given the political and economic interdependence of the nations of the contemporary world, which "produces benefits and burdens that would not exist if national economies were autarkic," the effect of "confining principles of social justice to domestic societies" is to tax "poor nations so that others may benefit from living in 'just' regimes."[141] In his 1989 *Realizing Rawls*, Thomas Pogge would note similarly that the world order, which produces immense disadvantages for inhabitants of poorer nations, is "imposed not by fate or nature but by other, more advantaged participants." This means that "our current global institutional scheme is unjust"—that "as advantaged participants in this order we [inhabitants of wealthier nations] share a collective responsibility for its injustice," and so "ought to use our more advantaged political and economic position to work for global institutional reforms."[142] In the related 1992 article "Cosmopolitanism and Sovereignty," Pogge argued—on behalf of the "cosmopolitan" view as against that of "communitarian" political philosophers—that the injustice of the present economic order is "wrong for its more affluent participants to perpetuate . . . quite independently of whether we and the starving are united by a communal bond or committed to sharing resources with one another, just as murdering a person is wrong irrespective of such considerations."[143]

In an important 1987 essay, "Aliens and Citizens: The Case for Open Borders," meanwhile, Joseph Carens argued that "citizenship in Western liberal democracies is the modern equivalent of feudal privilege—an inherited status that greatly enhances one's life chances," and that consequently "borders should generally be open and . . . people should normally be free to leave their country of origin and settle in another, subject only to the sorts of constraints that bind current citizens in their new country." According to Carens, "many of the reasons that make [Rawls's] original position useful in thinking about questions of justice within a given society also make it useful for thinking about justice across different societies. . . . Whether one is a citizen of a rich nation or a poor one, whether one is already a citizen of a particular state or an alien who wishes to become a citizen—this is the sort of specific contingency that could set people at odds. A fair procedure for choosing principles of justice must therefore exclude knowledge of these circumstances, just as it excludes knowledge of one's race or sex or social class. We should therefore take a global, not a national, view of the original position."[144]

These lines of thinking thus resonating widely among political philosophers, Rawls's own intervention in this arena was much anticipated. But *The Law of Peoples*, published in book form in 1999, came as a disappointment to those believing that the principles of *A Theory of Justice* demanded extension across national boundaries. For here Rawls seemed to assert that the moral imperatives of justice within a society, as he had articulated them, do *not* fully translate across societies. In *The Law of Peoples*, Rawls does imagine a "second original position," but in this case the representatives who confer on fundamental principles from behind a veil of ignorance represent not individuals but "peoples."[145] And for the Rawls of *Law*, "liberal peoples" (23)—whom we might imagine embracing the principles outlined in *A Theory of Justice* and who, it would seem, the *Theory* is aimed at persuading—must tolerate "decent" nonliberal societies, by which he means societies whose "basic institutions meet certain specified conditions of political right and justice and lead its people to honor a reasonable and just law for the Society of Peoples" (59–60).

It's on this basis that Rawls opposes claims made by cosmopolitan theorists for the global extension of the principles of *A Theory of Justice*. Addressing Beitz's arguments in favor of a redistribution of resources, in particular, Rawls argues that "a global egalitarian principle" in the cosmopolitan vein has no cutoff point—would leave the obligations of more affluent nations effectively endless—whereas a "duty of assistance," which he favors, has such a cutoff—namely, when "the world's poor . . . are either free and equal citizens of a reasonably liberal society or members of a decent hierarchical society." And this political criterion is the essential one, for Rawls, not only as a matter of theory but also as a matter of practice, since "the crucial element in how a country fares is its political culture . . . and not its level of resources" (117). In other words, poorer "peoples" have mainly themselves to blame for international inequities; the leading culprit is not differences in natural resources, let alone military, legal, political, financial, or other actions taken by wealthier and more powerful nations. Summarizing "the contrast between the Law of Peoples and a cosmopolitan view," Rawls writes, "The ultimate concern of a cosmopolitan view is the well-being of individuals and not the justice of societies. . . . It is concerned . . . with whether the well-being of the globally worst-off person can be improved. What is important to the Law of Peoples is the justice and stability for the right reasons of liberal and decent societies, living as members of a Society of well-ordered Peoples" (119–20). As cosmopolitans themselves would agree, the primary subject and recipient of justice in cosmopolitan thinking has traditionally been the person, whereas the subject of the Law of Peoples is peoples.[146]

One reason Rawls rejects cosmopolitanism is that "if all societies were required to be liberal, then the ideal of political liberalism would fail to express due toleration for other acceptable ways (if such there are, as I assume) of ordering society" (59). It has not gone unremarked that global justice theory originated as, and arguably largely remains, the creation of Western intellectuals rather than on-the-ground activists or non-Western intellectuals, and a number of critiques have faulted it for paternalism, illegitimate universalizing, and other features linked with modes of thought understood as indissolubly bound to the West. There has also been extensive debate about whether and to what degree cosmopolitanism is tainted by, or even a form of, Western imperialism. We'll return to these points in a moment, but here it bears noting that in *Law*, Rawls seems to try to address this critique by asserting that the Law of Peoples is not "ethnocentric" since it "asks of other societies only what they can reasonably grant without submitting to a position of inferiority or domination. . . . [It] does not require decent societies to abandon or modify their religious institutions and adopt liberal ones. [Other societies] cannot argue that being in a relation of equality with other peoples is a western idea!" (122). In the context of the anticosmopolitanism of *Law* as a whole, this unusually defensive exclamation point suggests that one thing Rawls very much wants to avoid is seeming to choose an endemically Western privileging of individuals as subjects of justice over other views of the claims of persons and collectives.[147]

As many critics of *The Law of Peoples* have argued, however, it's hard to see how one can hold that the rules of justice one believes in are morally binding while also deferring to the possibility of other moral systems—in other words, to other notions of justice.[148] Not surprisingly, therefore, the publication of the book did little to inhibit the project of global justice theory. In its wake, in fact, earlier contributors to the debates refined and expanded their arguments and additional scholars joined the conversation. Beitz described Rawls as holding that "the international realm has its own, distinctive form of distributive justice whose principles differ in content and foundation from those that apply within individual societies," and asked "why one should believe that structural differences between the international and the domestic realms generate reasons for action that differ in this way."[149] Pogge argued that "institutional interconnections" under globalization "render obsolete the idea that countries can peacefully agree to disagree about justice, each committing itself to a conception of justice appropriate to its history, culture, population size and density, natural environment, geopolitical context, and stage of development." And he asked why, if the difference principle is unacceptable internationally because "it is unacceptable for one people to bear certain costs of decisions made by another," this "ground should not analogously disqualify the difference principle for national societies as well. Why is it not likewise unacceptable for one province, township, or family to bear such costs of decisions made by another?"[150] Carens would develop his views at greatest length in a 2013 study to which we'll turn in a moment.

Other scholars advanced further counterarguments to Rawls. In *Scales of Justice: Reimagining Political Space in a Globalizing World* (2009), Nancy Fraser argued that while the "assumption that obligations of distributive justice applied only among fellow citizens" has had a long history, this "'Westphalian' framing of justice" is today "in dispute."[151] In *Global Justice: A Cosmopolitan Account*, Brock moved to show how valid policy proposals in the areas of global poverty, basic liberties, humanitarian intervention, immigration, and the world economic order can be derived from cosmopolitan theory and also shape that theory in return.[152] In *The Birthright Lottery: Citizenship and Global Inequality*, Ayelet Shachar elaborated, without extensively referring to prior global justice work and in a more specifically legal framework, an argument similar to Carens's construing of citizenship as analogous to feudal privilege. Noting the extraordinary differences between the most affluent nations and the least on metrics such as life expectancy, health outcomes, educational attainment, and income, she observed that "citizenship laws ... perpetuate and reify dramatically differentiated life prospects by reliance on morally arbitrary circumstances of birth, while at the same time camouflaging these crucial distributive consequences by appealing to the presumed naturalness of birth based membership."[153]

In recent years, scholars have adopted various critical approaches in order to loosen global justice theory's tight focus on quantitative inequality between poor and rich nations and to move past post-Rawlsian debates in which the default moral subject is the privileged inhabitant of the global North. Neera Chandhoke, for example, has noted (invoking an earlier critique by Steven Smith) how "liberal egalitarian compassion-based theories of social relations" devalue "the rational perspective and agency of those who are defined as having 'bad fated' conditions through no fault of their own"; she highlights how "human agency, which is a *constitutive* aspect of justice" may be sidelined where people in less affluent nations are treated as recipients of redistributed resources only, not as contributors to more just outcomes.[154] Brooke Ackerly has stressed that "taking responsibility for injustice . . . entails taking responsibility for how we take responsibility for injustice"—that it must not "further entrench or, worse, legitimate the hierarchies of injustice."[155] Margaret Kohn has observed that if global justice literature orients itself, as it has tended to do, to the question "What do we owe to distant others?," it relies on a "we" that problematically "conflates two positions: the normative theorist and the ethico-political agent." She invites her reader to reflect on how the question "changes if posed like this: 'What do distant others (e.g., the rich in wealthy countries) owe to us?'"[156]

Kohn's challenge appears in the recent volume *Empire, Race and Global Justice*, edited by Duncan Bell, which exemplifies a larger movement toward challenging earlier global justice theory's failure to devote significant attention to questions of imperialism and race. One of the important themes that emerges across several of the collection's essays is that the Rawlsian provenance of the field—oriented to ideal normative considerations in a framework of transnational distributive injustice at a moment of present time—has prevented it from engaging with problems of restorative justice (such as reparations) rooted in the history of imperial and racist exploitation.[157] Another recurring theme, evocative of earlier critiques of cosmopolitanism, is that global justice theory's overwhelming emphasis on individual moral responsibility has limited its engagement with philosophical traditions of the very global "others" it sets out to assist—traditions that may elevate different, in many cases more visibly communal, priorities.[158] Yet a third thread in the collection concerns migration. Inés Valdez advocates for a prioritizing of the transnational, which unlike vocabularies of the global highlights "how the encounter of distinct forms of political and economic structures such as colonialism, slavery, and migration result in instances of domination that do not track neatly the division between the West and the non-West."[159] Anne Phillips argues similarly that if debates about global justice have found "little resonance amongst scholars in the post-colonial world," this is because in "asking whether principles of domestic egalitarian justice can or should be applied to the global realm," they presume "a separation that is already challenged by patterns of global migration."[160]

Why the question of migration has not always seemed paramount in global justice theory is not hard to discern. In *A Theory of Justice*, Rawls is concerned with how benefits ought to be allocated and never with the physical movements of persons[161]; rooted as it was in Rawls, the global justice literature evidently found its natural starting point in differentials that seemed to call out for remedy via wealth redistribution or institutional rearrangement. We might say that the very boundedness of the society that forms its horizon of inquiry puts Rawls's *Theory* deep within the tradition of sedentarist metaphysics—a point Rawls in a way confirms in *The Law of Peoples* when he quotes approvingly Michael Walzer's assumption that "a world of deracinated men and women" would be an unequivocal evil (quoted at 39).

Migration and related matters did, however, begin to draw more attention in the 2000s, especially after interventions by scholars such as Seyla Benhabib. In *The Rights of Others: Aliens, Residents, and Citizens* (2004), which includes a critique of *The Law of Peoples*, Benhabib asserted that while "recent attempts to develop theories of global justice have been curiously silent on the matter of migration," in fact "transnational migrations, and the constitutional as well as policy issues suggested by the movement of peoples across state borders, are central to interstate relations and therefore to a normative theory of global justice." In Benhabib's view, "a cosmopolitan theory of justice cannot be restricted to schemes of *just distribution* on a global scale, but must also incorporate a vision of *just membership*" that entails recognizing refugees' moral claims, establishing porous borders for immigration, and protecting "the right of every human being to 'have rights,' that is, to be a *legal person*, entitled to certain inalienable rights, regardless of the status of their political membership."[162] In her 2012 *Human Rights, Migration, and Social Conflict*, to take another example, Ariadna Estévez proposed, as "a scholar based in the periphery, in a major migrant-sending country," an "epistemological decolonization of liberal ideas of global justice that shifts the emphasis from abstract morals to specific material aspects of the human rights of individuals and groups" and focuses "on the human rights of a specific, rather than a generic, type of individual—the modern migrant."[163]

As we've seen, Carens's early work stands as an exception to the rule that global justice theory tended to background migration questions, and his more recent *Ethics of Immigration* (2013) advances the most expansive of theoretical arguments for open borders. In the book's initial chapters, Carens adopts, so as to be able to pursue normative inquiries around pressing policy questions, the conventional presupposition that states are "morally entitled to exercise considerable discretionary control over the admission of immigrants."[164] In the later chapters, however, he elaborates his own claim "that discretionary control over immigration is incompatible with fundamental democratic principles and that justice requires open borders" (10). Most significant for our purposes here is Carens's particular response to theorists who believe in "bounded justice"—that is, that "the demands of justice arise primarily within the context of a state" (256). Against this view, Carens asks, "Why does the way the world is organized raise questions of justice?" (258), and answers,

Because that structure itself is coercively imposed. Human beings enter a world in which they are subject to the authority of a particular state and have no right to move to any other state only because that is the way we human beings have organized the world. . . . The current organization is maintained through the use of force, implicit and explicit. So, we are entitled, indeed obliged, to ask whether this coercively imposed structure can be justified to those who are subject to it. (258)

"For most people," that is, "membership in the cooperative scheme of a particular community is not the result of some choice that they made as an individual but is an accident of birth. That is acceptable as a basis for the initial assignment of membership, . . . but not for the exclusion of those who want to join" (282).[165] For Carens, the justness of open borders would, all other things being equal, be beyond debate, which leaves the burden of moral proof in the closed-open debate with those who would insist on the validity of present (discretionary) arrangements.[166]

Arguments such as these illustrate particularly clearly how global justice theory, though in certain respects quite removed from anything like the idea of the utopian archipelago, also converges with it in significant ways. Being itself an ideal arrangement, the metautopia or archipelago imagined by Nozick and Jameson may be assumed to be perfectly free of the problems global justice attempts to address, including material inequality, limitations on mobility, and war and other incursions by one state or unit into others' affairs. This isn't to say that the archipelago itself solves these problems, of course; it's rather to note that their having been overcome is a given of the construct. Nozick and Jameson envision the utopian archipelago not as a remedy for want but as a remedy for unfreedom, and particularly for unfreedom with respect to lifestyle. Yet for this freedom to be possible, reasonable levels of comfort and security would have to be on offer everywhere. It seems hardly to need saying that the utopian archipelago would cease to be utopian if some communities suffered dire material want: were the net, as Jameson calls it, to include a community not utopian in these terms, the net itself would no longer be utopia. Nor is this merely a quibble about nomenclature. In practice, large discrepancies in quality of life between units of the archipelago would surely function as they do in our own world, impelling people otherwise uninterested in changing their habitation to relocate for reasons of security and subsistence, and this potentially to communities whose cultural and social arrangements might be sharply at odds with their preferences or beliefs.

Further, as some of the foregoing quotations hint, something like the utopian archipelago always hovers close at hand in global justice theory, though it's never mentioned by name. In the quotation just given, for example, Carens asserts that while membership in a given community may be assigned at birth, the accident of birth can't morally be a reason for excluding a person from membership in a community that person might wish to join later on. In other words, justice itself, in any world, would demand the kind of freedom of membership that prevails in the utopian archipelago. The only just organization of communities would be one essentially governed by the utopian archipelago's membership rules, and correspondingly the utopian archipelago can be understood as that order of communities whose membership rules are (the only) just ones.

This becomes particularly evident, of course, where global justice theory engages questions about migration. In *The Law of Peoples*, Rawls determines that "the problem of immigration . . . is eliminated as a serious problem in a realistic utopia" because the "numerous causes of immigration . . . would disappear in the Society of liberal and decent Peoples" (8–9). "Persecution of religious and ethnic minorities" and "political oppression of various forms" would no longer be factors, nor would "population pressure," since its causes, including "the inequality and subjection of women," would be remedied. Even famines could cease to be significant, given that they're "often themselves in large part caused by political failures and the absence of decent government" (9). Far less absurd analyses in this vein have been advanced by other contributors to debates on global justice. Brock, for example, points to empirical confirmations that people would move in fairly limited numbers were border controls abolished, while Ryan Pevnick remarks that most people build their lives in one community and stay there, and Shachar avers sweepingly that in "a world" where there were "no significant political and wealth variations among bounded membership units," nothing would "be gained by tampering with the existing membership structures," since there would be "no motivation for change or migration."[167] Even Carens acknowledges that in a just world, with significantly reduced "economic inequalities between states," people "would be less likely to feel that they had to move out of economic necessity and so would presumably be less inclined to move to a society with a very different culture and way of life, unless they were attracted by these differences" (*Ethics*, 291).

Of course, this is a very significant "unless." For Nozick and Jameson, writing on the utopian archipelago, freedom of choice with regard to values, lifestyle, and (in Nozick) political organization would be essential to the utopian condition. And as we've seen, such freedom is essential to justice for some global justice theorists as well. Benhabib notes that in "the majority of cases, the root causes of migration are poverty, famine, persecution . . . , ethnocide, genocide, civil wars, earthquakes, pestilence, and the like," but she also observes that "individuals may feel that their understanding of the good, be it for moral, political, religious, artistic, or scientific reasons, obliges them to leave the society into which they were born and to join another society. This implies that individuals . . . ought to have a right to leave their societies. Emigration must be a fundamental liberty in a Rawlsian scheme, for otherwise his conception of the person becomes incoherent. The language of a 'complete and closed society' is incompatible with the liberal vision of persons and their liberties."[168]

Carens demands, similarly,

> What if I don't like the "people" into whom I am born? Perhaps I reject all their fundamental values (and accept those of some other "people"). If we recognize the moral equality of all human beings, we should presumably have to explain why assigning someone to a "people" at birth (with a right to leave but no right of admittance elsewhere) adequately respects this moral equality, given the vast consequences of such an assignment for one's life chances and one's life projects. (*Ethics*, 268)[169]

Having thus pointedly gestured to Rawls's valuing, in *A Theory of Justice*, of plans of life, Carens continues, "Why can't one have the right to change 'peoples'? Of course, one can if another 'people' is willing to let one in, but why should it be entirely up to them? I think that the reason that Rawls does not see any of these issues as a serious problem, at least in the sense of something that requires discussion, is that he is implicitly seeing individuals as having moral claims only as members, not as human beings" (268). In other words, for both Benhabib and Carens, the significant problem with Rawls's take on immigration is that, like *The Law of Peoples* and anticosmopolitan positions generally, it replaces *persons* as the ultimate recipients of justice with another entity—in this case, *members* of a given people or polity.

As these quotations also highlight, the global justice argument for porous or open borders is finally two-pronged. One prong of the case, again, is that if apportionment is to be just, people cannot be punished for being born into the wrong territory. The other, adopted by some though not all advocates of open borders, is that freedom of movement is a basic right. Of course, even a policy of open borders wouldn't by itself be enough to secure ideal justice along these lines, since many people lack the means to cross borders if they wish to. But suppose a world in which anyone wishing to migrate would be supplied with the means as well as the right to do so—a world of full mobility, we might say, where "mobility" names not movement as such but the capacity to relocate according to one's wishes. To regard such a world as a solution to the moral problem of inequalities arising from geographical birthright would be, very precisely, to see a route to moral success in the conversion of the world into an entity or framework functionally single with respect to the right of movement—precisely what the utopian archipelago is in raw structural terms.

What's perhaps a little surprising about this convergence of global justice ideals with the utopian archipelago is that it proves, on inspection, not so much a swerve away from a Rawlsian privileging of concerns about distribution within an essentially static *nomos* as a natural consequence of global justice's Rawlsian roots. How is this so? As we've seen, the problem that fundamentally propels Rawls's reflections in *A Theory of Justice* is the arbitrariness, from a moral standpoint, of inequities attendant on accidents of birth, which leads him to claim that reasonable people, behind the veil of ignorance, would try to move society toward justice and away from this arbitrariness by adhering to the difference principle. As we've also seen, the question of birthright remains the fundamental one for global justice theorists such as Carens and Shachar: if a genuinely fair arrangement is one in which ascriptive inequality is minimized—that is, in which the accidents of birth circumstances are countered as far as possible—then disadvantaging by geography must be among the wrongs addressed by any truly just social arrangement. As Shachar puts it, "Citizenship laws, which mark the literal delineation between insider and outsider, member and nonmember, have coercive effects that are felt by those on *both* sides of this boundary. On both the literal and metaphorical planes, membership-defining principles represent a category of laws that simply cannot be categorized as having effects borne only, or even primarily, by their beneficiaries; their coercive authority is also felt with major force by those whom they exclude."[170]

In other words, the inequities with which global justice foundationally concerns itself are inequities imposed (or rendered durable) by national boundaries. In global justice theory, strategies for the remediation of unfairness, whether or not they concern borders directly, are in effect always compensatory for disadvantages incurred by being born within one set of borders rather than another. This means that such strategies are directed at disadvantages imposed by any condition short of a capacity for full mobility—which means in turn that *immigration and emigration rules are already forms of apportionment on a global scale.* That these rules establish a global arrangement by which benefits are allotted is indeed one of global justice theory's central revelations.[171]

From this perspective, justice concerns are related to migration in a sense that goes much deeper than, and extends far beyond, questions about fairness in matters such as border controls and citizenship. What becomes clear is that immigration and emigration rules abide at the very root of international questions of justice because these rules collectively establish a *nomos* of and for the globe. And this would be true even were open borders the rule. Open or closed or something in between, anarchic indifference or impenetrable walls or another arrangement entirely: as long as there are borders at all, some set of policies and practices will govern borders and thus instate a *nomos*, whether or not those who frame the policies understand themselves as prescribing for the world in this way. We might therefore discern in the indignation under-girding both global justice theory and global justice activism the *nemesis* appropriate to this *nomos*, a *nomos* of apportionment by the setting of national boundaries, which subtend and imply boundaries of membership.

The foregoing considerations thus present another instance of a phenomenon we've encountered repeatedly over the course of this study: a tight imbrication of utopia, *nomos*, justice, and persons that explains why efforts to address justice's claims can swiftly lead to, or be understood as versions of, thinking about utopia (construed as a society in which right arrangement prevails). Indeed we can discern in the discourse of global justice an especially literal illustration of the point that what utopia names is an imagined rectification of the unjust ordering of things, a renovated *nomos* in which people receive what's due them. Seen through the global justice lens, the geographical position of a given human subject is an exceptionally powerfully determinant of that subject's options in life; for cosmopolitan global justice theorists, the highest level of fairness would be one in which such a position is no longer so strongly determinative. And for open-borders cosmopolitans in particular, the highest level of fairness would be one in which such a position is in no way constrained by immigration law.[172]

If global justice theory highlights a sense in which the capacity to move is tightly linked with justice writ large, however, it has seemed largely to pass over something attended to by many of the utopian writers we've considered in this chapter. What seems notably missing from these discussions is strong consideration of how choice of occupation (again in the sense of both career and task at a given moment) might be a valuable component of life in an ideally just society. A vision of work as something of intrinsic qualitative interest seems to hang on only insofar as the freedom to seek genuinely desirable employment might be silently included among the distributed benefits whose imbalance would be rectified by open borders or some other protocol tending toward a more just *nomos*.

To be sure, those invested in global justice have concerned themselves extensively with the conditions of labor, migrant and otherwise. Activists around the world have taken on employers, governments, and NGOs over the exploitation and silencing of industrial and domestic workers, and the plight of workers has been important in some domains of normative thinking about global justice. Carens, for example, argues against the view that it's "morally acceptable for a democratic state to have one set of rules regarding working conditions for citizens and permanent residents and a different set of rules for workers who are present on a temporary basis" or undocumented (*Ethics* 115, 142).

Scholars have also made the point that while in theory, restrictive migration regimes may be out of line with neoliberalism's opposition to limits on economic border crossing (as in trade restrictions and barriers to international financial transactions), in practice, migration controls in various ways support neoliberal imperatives, especially by creating work forces that can be poorly treated.[173] More generally, commentators have noted how the problem of exploitation of migrant workers has contributed to a shift in human rights discourse, from an initial emphasis on protecting citizens from abuse by their own states' regimes to a concern with the rights of nonmembers as well as members in any state.[174]

That global justice theory and its kin have been more concerned with abuse of the worker than with the potential value or satisfactions of work is, again, quite understandable given the present state of the world. Only a fraction of work-oriented migration is impelled by the urge to find jobs or activities that are deeply satisfying; most is driven by the urge to find some work instead of no work, less brutal labor instead of more brutal, better paid employment instead of poorly paid. But this is to say that work's very position within the configuration of migration- and border-related injustices tends to lead to its framing as a necessary evil, a means for obtaining other goods rather than a meaningful part of life experience whose particular features—including, for example, how readily one occupation may be exchanged for another over the course of a day or a span of years—would loom large in assessing the rightness of a given *nomos*.

The effectively compulsory character of much migration, which we saw shadowing *Trouble on Triton* and infusing *On Such a Full Sea*, has thus contributed not only in the realm of utopian fiction but also in other domains to the challenge of continuing to conceive of rewarding work (and discretion over one's work) as an important ideal. Moreover, in an irony we've already noted in examining Delany and Lee, the injustices associated with migration and borders have made it particularly difficult to hold in view the connection, ascendant in later nineteenth- and early twentieth-century utopian writing, between satisfying work and freedom of movement. In the frame of reference established by dilemmas of contemporary migration, in which work is consigned to the realm of drudgery and basic survival, work's own contribution to utopian fulfillment appears to have evaporated.

This passing of worker mobility from the scene of utopian imagining receives a remarkable epitaph, as it were, in Jameson's most recent venture into extended utopian speculation: *An American Utopia: Dual Power and the Universal Army*, already cited in this chapter. The volume begins with a long essay in which Jameson advances an outline for just what his title names, which hundred-page proposal is then followed by responses from nine other writers (including the editor of the book, Slavoj Žižek) and a final word from Jameson himself. It would be an understatement to say that Jameson's proposal for a future utopian United States is a surprising one. For the centerpiece of his plan is the institution of conscription for all Americans between the ages of sixteen and fifty or sixty (28).

Everyone goes into the army, then, though this is not an army that fights, or at least not an army that only fights. Rather, or in addition, it's an army of social provision, along the lines of Bellamy's industrial army but with a yet more democratizing slant. It does all the work that has to be done to keep people materially comfortable, and everyone in the aforementioned age range must contribute to the effort (29). But the time commitment for each person is modest. "I envisage," Jameson writes, "a utopia of the double life, in which social reproduction, albeit only involving a few hours a day, is performed in work clothes and in teams, a little like going for army reserve duty. These shifts could be vertical or horizontal, that is, a shift every morning or night, or else a concentrated period of several weeks followed by an equal stretch of what we used to call free time" (83; see also 59).

Jameson posits at least three major benefits to this scheme. The first of these is full employment, which he marks as "the highest social priority" of his utopian system: "everything must be planned in order to secure it" (45). In this, *An American Utopia* clearly bears the imprint of the 2008 financial crash, when precarity moved front and center in the minds of scholars thinking about how people might live in the future. Yet as we've seen, the desideratum of full employment has been crucial to utopian thinking at least since More, and meanwhile the threat of diminishing opportunities for work remains acute as technologies of automation continue to develop and climate change portends ever more unstable markets and ever vaster waves of migration. Jameson's absolute privileging of full employment, after so many intricate analyses of the utopian imagination from countless other angles, therefore reads as an indication that what utopia has for centuries really looked toward, as its negative other, is precisely the jobless future.

A second benefit of the proposal, in Jameson's construction, stems from the fact that the army is by his account an institution in which people from all strata of society and all identity groups mix on essentially equal terms (the military hierarchy itself notwithstanding). In Jameson's phrasing, "the army is the first glimpse of a classless society" (61; see also 95–96), and in his American utopia it offers a path to the end of social classes (85–87). But the end of classes and of class warfare cannot, Jameson hastens to insist, imply the end of social antagonism. We've seen how in *Archaeologies of the Future* he invokes Fourier to suggest that utopia ought to be hospitable to conflicts within and between people, to mark the productivity of the collective's "inner conflicts and compacts or conspiracies" (223). In *An American Utopia*, he treats more expansively the assumption that envy and antagonism won't disappear in any human society, and that indeed subjects themselves are so divided in their desires that no social organization can hope to provide contentment in some ongoing sense. "Too often forgotten in the conventional stereotype of utopia as an edulcorated conflict-free zone of social peace and harmony," he writes, is "the necessarily antagonistic nature of individual life and experience in a classless society. 'Classless' in this context means the elimination of collective antagonism and thereby, inevitably, the heightening of individual ones" (63).

What Jameson's American utopia would do, then, is replace large inter-group aggressions that destabilize our world with temporary individual animosities and fluid interfactional hostilities that could even be imagined as fun. This last idea may not seem so farfetched to those who have spent any time with Fourier, who arranges his utopian "phalanxes" to just such an end, and indeed Jameson cites Fourier approvingly in this context as well: "Just as Bellamy is the tutelary deity of the universal army and its infrastructure, so Fourier becomes that of a realm of freedom, of culture and its superstructures, and to my mind the only thinker who has thus far discovered the way for a collectivity or a multiplicity to coordinate the ineradicable individualities which make it up" (81). Jameson even imagines, with his tongue surely somewhat in his cheek, "a new kind of institution, destined to supplant traditional government and its agencies and to articulate the superstructural or cultural level of our new society in a post- or trans-Fourieresque spirit": a "Psychoanalytic Placement Bureau" that "will, in conjunction with unimaginably complex computer systems, handle and organize all forms of employment as well as all manner of personal and collective therapies." This bureau "will eventually replace government and political structures equally, the state thereby withering away into some enormous group therapy" (81–82). Antagonisms, then, will beautifully persist, but they'll by no means be disruptive of utopia. Jameson's heir to the offices of Hartlib, Wells, Bogdanov, and Le Guin will manage them in such a way as to make the *nomos* of utopia one in which both work and therapy are rightly allocated.

The third benefit Jameson imagines is simply that in this utopia one may, in one's considerable spare time, do anything one likes. "In the world of the superstructure," which is essentially that of leisure time as opposed to the time of mandated labor, "the individual is as free to be a recluse as a party person, to practice hobbies or to live out existence as a couch potato, to be a family man or professional mother, to volunteer for hospital work or to climb mountains or to struggle with drug addiction. . . . The superstructure is a matter of invention; and to begin with, one expects its practitioners to distinguish their choices by the most extravagant garments" (83; see also 93). This mention of extravagant garments may seem oddly gratuitous at first, but its relevance becomes obvious once we recognize that Delany's *Trouble on Triton* is much on Jameson's mind in *An American Utopia*—that indeed Delany represents the third tutelary deity of Jameson's scheme, doing for the pluralization of lifestyle choices what Bellamy does for the industrial army and Fourier for festively managed antagonism.

We might pause here to observe that this picture of doing what one likes should, in one way, elicit enthusiasm from thinkers in Nozick's line. To be able to live as one wishes to live might be construed as the essential libertarian desideratum, and in any case it's just what the utopian archipelago is designed to make possible. But Nozick would, of course, have problems with Jameson's American utopia for reasons in addition to its grounding in a very nonminimal statelike apparatus. Another fatal difficulty, from a Nozickian perspective, would be that it omits something crucial to the utopian archipelago: the liberty to choose the political structure under which one lives. Some may favor liberal democracy in a more or less republican form; others may enjoy quasianarchistic communities; still others may believe that authoritarian rigidity suits them best. Jameson's utopia doesn't seem to leave a great deal of room for choice on this score, and while Nozick isn't mentioned in *An American Utopia*, some of Jameson's respondents in the volume decry the absence of political process and contestation in his proposal.[175]

Quite apart from the apparent excision of form of government from the array of lifestyle parameters that might be chosen, however, it's clear that something significant has happened to Jameson's vision between *Archaeologies of the Future* in 2005 and *An American Utopia* in 2016. The utopian archipelago has been replaced, in the later rendering, by a formation whose emancipatory possibilities are associated not, or not mainly, with the right to pass freely across borders but rather with the disposition of one's nonworking hours. Unlimited control over part (but not all) of one's time, we might say, has replaced unlimited movement through space as the ground of freedom.[176] And in this context, it's noteworthy that when Jameson explicitly invokes *Trouble on Triton*, he refers to a form of liberty in that novel's solar system that's neither the possibility of migration from world to world nor the outer worlds' general permissiveness respecting self-fashioning.

For it happens that a few of Bron's adventures occur in a part of Triton "where no law officially held." Each "Outer Satellite city had set aside" such a lawless quarter, "since, as the Mars sociologist who first advocated it had pointed out, most cities develop, of necessity, such a neighborhood anyway. These sectors fulfilled a complex range of functions in the cities' psychological, political, and economic ecology."[177] Near the end of the main essay of *An American Utopia*, accordingly, Jameson proposes an "adoption of Samuel

Delany's magnificent institution (in his utopian novel *Triton*) of a so-called 'unlicensed sector,' where no law exists and anything goes" (94), even hazarding that something like this domain's function in Delany might prove to be "the role of the city itself, as its form survives the great transformation" (94) to utopia.[178] Perhaps, Jameson muses, big cities could be wrested "away from their states" and made into "universal terrains that belong to everybody and to no one: places of anonymous collective wealth and of orgiastic yet cosmopolitan celebration, where troops of open-mouthed yokels mingle with city slickers, with lots of pickpocketing and outright fistfights" (89).

In this last evocative image, Jameson may seem to channel the kind of yearning for authenticity-through-violence that has often served, as we saw in chapter 2, as a premise of antiutopian critique. But Jameson doesn't present authenticity as an explicit rationale for his suggestion: his point isn't that antagonism makes human life vital or worthwhile (though this may be intimated tonally) but rather that it's an aspect of human intersubjectivity that simply won't disappear. Nor is it his idea that antagonism should run rampant or that it should be acknowledged as crucial to the conditions and processes that govern human destinies on a large scale. It's rather that the expression of antagonism should be given a place, along with countless other forms of spontaneity, within a larger structure that won't be disrupted by its occurrence. Of course, this thought illustrates as well as any proposal in the history of utopian imagining how the utopian *nomos* must be a genuine form of arrangement, a real structure, without being so inflexible as to preclude that capacity for the unexpected that makes people recipients as well as instruments of justice.

But there's another sense, more tuned to our present moment and the matters treated in this chapter, in which it's telling that the feature of Bron's solar system extracted for *An American Utopia* is a hyperutopian anarchic, or libertarian, enclave within utopia itself. For Jameson's move here instantiates again the contraction of scale, or shift in emphasis, that we've already posited as an effect of migration's recent visibilities. Back in the scheme of the utopian archipelago from *Archaeologies*, utopianness was affiliated with vastness: it inhered in people's liberty to range about the entire world at will, which is to say that when Jameson there suggested the virtues of "Delanyian" utopias that would "correspond to" the multiplicity in each of us, he was surely pointing not only to the endless restyling of self permitted in *Trouble on Triton* but also to the archipelago of worlds in that novel's solar system. In the scheme of *An American Utopia*, by contrast, utopianness at its purest subsists in a bounded zone of radical freedom surrounded by the relatively less free realm in which everyone serves in the universal army.

All of this doesn't mean, of course, that the receding of the utopian archipelago follows as by *logical* necessity from the specter of migration under globalization. However far from emancipatory migration may look under current conditions, it remains possible to imagine a utopian archipelago founded on a good form of migration—a world in which numerous communities coexist without armed conflict and people can pass freely from one to another, choosing the society they will. Utopia is, after all, utopian, a realm of unbridled speculation in which it's not necessary to lay out every step toward, or element in, the achievement of the ideal. It does seem, however, that predicaments of immigration and emigration as we know them have led to rethinkings both of the meaning of work in utopia and of how utopia's borders might be drawn. In today's migration environment, again, what most drives people from place to place is labor demand or lack thereof, not a quest for more fulfilling work or enthusiasm for new experiences or even a strong urge to live under different arrangements, though these desires may factor in. How very tempting, then, to redraw utopia's boundaries once more, and this time in a way that consigns work to the realm of necessity, while leaving to leisure hours the nurture of the soul.

Coda

AT THE CLOSE of this study's second chapter, we saw how a question pointed to by experience machines such as those in Robert Nozick's *Anarchy, State, and Utopia* and the film *The Matrix* could lead us to an insight about the subjects of justice. Suppose we imagine a society full of consistently contented and happy beings whose every experience in life has been preprogrammed. Why, even if those beings inhabit a nonvirtual reality and have genuine contact with each other, would many of us not think their society a valuable addition to the universe? Why would many of us regard so thoroughly designed a social organization as something other than a valid utopia, even as an antiutopia or a dystopia of a particularly horrifying kind?

The answer I proposed was that the existences of those in this preprogrammed society, being in effect materializations of a plan already worked out to the last detail, would seem in some deep sense pointless, supererogatory. From there, I went on to argue that for utopia to have meaning, it must have component members (persons or other entities) it can do right by—who in some sense stand apart from it, preexist it conceptually if not actually. I suggested, too, that this intuition about utopia converges with the widely held view that for justice to prevail, there must be recipients of justice: persons—or nonhuman beings, or families, or communities, or systems—who can be described as having what they ought to have in a sense distinct from the interests of the overarching whole. And I proposed that this in turn implies that utopia always signifies a rectification of injustice or of potential injustice—a righting of what is, or could be, wrong for those who live within it.

In the third chapter of this study, we turned to versions of Nozick's claim, also made in *Anarchy, State, and Utopia*, that the only truly ideal social configuration would be a metautopia in which people freely choose their communities: "Utopia will consist of utopias, of many different and divergent communities in which people lead different kinds of lives under different arrangements. . . . Utopia is a framework for utopias, a place where people are at liberty to join together voluntarily to pursue and attempt to realize their own vision of the good life in the ideal community but where no one can *impose* his own utopian vision upon others. . . . Utopia is meta-utopia: the environment in which utopian experiments may be tried out."[1] In the course of chapter 3, I tried to show how this formulation, which Fredric Jameson adapted under the name of "the utopian archipelago," makes its presence felt in utopian imagining of the last half century or so. I also posited, however, that the persuasiveness of this dream of a world in which one might migrate freely to the community that best suits one has at the same time been undercut by the conditions of migration in our own world, which betoken liberty far less often than they do compulsion and exploitation.

The experience machine and the metautopia appear nearly three hundred pages apart from each other in *Anarchy, State, and Utopia*, and Nozick nowhere explicitly connects them. Yet it's not hard to see how they're linked. For both address what may be the most intractable of the problems that human beings themselves present for the utopian imagination: the variety of human desires and convictions about what's right and good. In any kind of community—even ones in which people's beliefs are strongly shaped by custom and tradition, even ones whose members are strongly disposed toward compromise and consensus—there's always the chance that the social fabric will be tested or rent by differing views of what's satisfying and proper. There's always the possibility that one or another member of the group will find its ways contemptible, immoral, unsatisfying, or otherwise unbearable. And this means, as has been remarked frequently in the literature on utopia, that social arrangements one person might find utopian can easily seem hellish to someone else. Even the utopian archipelago cannot be ideal in the fullest sense, since in not containing an infinite number of communities, it cannot provide precisely what each and every member would choose (though from the point of view Nozick articulates, it offers the best that can be imagined).

What we can notice here is that the *Matrix*-like experience machine and the preprogrammed society offer a solution to the problem of the variety of human wishes and convictions just as the utopian archipelago does, even if this solution isn't their most striking feature. The experience machine solves the problem by making it unnecessary for people to interact with each other at all: in it, each subject's world includes no other real inhabitants, which means that there's no shared life whose contours would be subject to dispute. The preprogrammed society (which arguably takes to an antiutopian extreme what I dubbed, in chapter 2, the transformative utopia) solves the problem by predetermining its inhabitants' every urge and principle. The inhabitants of such a society would all want and commend the same things, or they would want and commend different things in a way that never leads to social friction.

But can we imagine another alternative? Can we imagine a utopia that would retain the virtues of the experience machine, the preprogrammed society, and the utopian archipelago without suffering from their drawbacks? Can we conceive of an order of things that would really be utopian yet in which people would develop as they do in our own world—that is, in unpredictable, nonpreordained ways—and in which their desires and convictions would in some meaningful sense come from themselves rather than the algorithms of social engineers? Can we envision an ideal organization that not only sustains this freedom but also allows its inhabitants to shape it politically, to change its institutional structures and frameworks of sovereignty? And can we imagine an organization that would, in addition, grant each member of society some form of utopian fulfillment—some immersive satisfaction—without mandating the kind of isolation from other members that's the price of the virtual rooms in Octavia Butler's *Parable of the Talents*, of the pods in *The Matrix*, and of the drug Pulse in Walter Mosley's *Futureland*?

As it happens, just such a utopia, or framework for utopia, is envisioned in a text published a few years after *Talents*, *The Matrix*, and *Futureland*—this one by a writer often hailed as a leader in the reinvention of utopian fiction, yet who on at least one occasion declared a mistrust of such fiction on the ground that it so often succumbs to the problem we've just been considering. This writer is Butler herself. "I don't like most utopia stories," she notes in the afterword to one of two newer tales published in the 2005 reissue of *Bloodchild and Other Stories* (originally 1995), "because I don't believe them for a moment. It seems inevitable that my utopia would be someone else's hell."[2] Of the text that afterword accompanies, however, she writes: "'The Book of Martha' is my utopia story" (214). And in that work, her title character develops an ingenious solution to the problem of the variety of human desires and values.

Martha Bes is a forty-three-year-old novelist living in Seattle to whom God appears one day. God explains that Martha has been chosen to "help humankind to survive its greedy, murderous, wasteful adolescence"—to help it "find less destructive, more peaceful, sustainable ways to live" (192). She will, God tells her, have all the divine power at her command—"What you decide should be done with humankind *will* be done" (200)—though in discussion her commission narrows to "one important change" and one only (197). Martha at first considers limiting the birth rate, but problems with this idea emerge as she and God revolve it, leading her to ask a version of the question that, as we saw in chapter 2, has always dogged transformative utopias: "Are you saying that if . . . if humanity is changed, it won't be humanity any more?" (200, ellipsis Butler's). God indicates that it will not, and moreover that changing humanity, as by limiting its fertility, could lead to its destruction.

Martha presses on, finally putting the question that most directly anticipates Butler's afterword: "What, exactly, do you want? A utopia? Because I
don't believe in them. I don't believe it's possible to arrange a society so that
everyone is content, everyone has what he or she wants" (202). God, as it turns
out, agrees: Utopia isn't possible "for more than a few moments," he says, since
that's "how long it would take for someone to decide that he wanted what his
neighbor had—or that he wanted his neighbor as a slave of one kind or another, or that he wanted his neighbor dead" (202). But God also explains that
he isn't asking for a utopia. He just wants Martha to help humankind: "Fewer
wars, less covetousness, more forethought and care with the environment. . . .
What might cause that?" (202–3, ellipsis Butler's).

At last, Martha has her idea. In the changed world, people

"would have their own personal best of all possible worlds during their
dreams. The dreams should be much more realistic and intense than most
dreams are now. Whatever people love to do most, they should dream
about doing it, and the dreams should change to keep up with their individual interests. Whatever grabs their attention, whatever they desire, they
can have it in their sleep. In fact, they can't avoid having it. Nothing should
be able to keep the dreams away—not drugs, not surgery, not anything.
And the dreams should satisfy much more deeply, more thoroughly, than
reality can. I mean, the satisfaction should be in the dreaming, not in trying
to make the dream real."

God smiled. "Why?"

"I want them to have the only possible utopia." Martha thought for a
moment. "Each person will have a private, perfect utopia every night—or
an imperfect one. If they crave conflict and struggle, they get that. If they
want peace and love, they get that. Whatever they want or need comes to
them. I think if people go to a . . . well, a private heaven every night, it
might take the edge off their willingness to spend their waking hours
trying to dominate or destroy one another." She hesitated. "Won't it?"
(203–4, ellipsis Butler's)

God and Martha consider some of the negatives that might attend this arrangement, especially a dulling of interest in the real world that would liken
the dreaming to addiction. Martha doesn't want the dreams to "take away"
people's "self-respect," just for them to "slow things down a little. A little less
aggression, as you said, less covetousness. Nothing slows people down like
satisfaction, and this satisfaction will come every night" (205). Just to make
sure that removal from the shared world doesn't ensue, she finally requests a
rider: the dream must "teach—or at least promote—more thoughtfulness
when people are awake, promote more concern for real consequences" (211).

God agrees to the addition, and so the thing is done, though the story ends before we see anything of the altered world.

One feature of "The Book of Martha" worth noting immediately is how multiply, if also subtly, its main character exemplifies the figure of the indignant engineer whose centrality to the imagining of utopia we noted in chapter 1. To be sure, the presiding affect of Butler's story seems ruefulness more than indignation: neither Martha nor God fiercely rages at the folly of humans or their systems, and when God remarks, "Nothing ever works smoothly with humankind," Martha perceives that God "like[s] that"—harbors a sort of amused affection for humankind's conflictual ways (211). Yet disappointment in humanity is the bass note of the tale. Humankind's adolescence is again "greedy, murderous, wasteful"; humans are "well on the way to destroying billions of themselves by greatly changing the ability of the earth to sustain them" (193); Martha's charge, as she formulates it at one point, is to "put a stop to war and environmental destruction" (199). And racial and patriarchal domination make their presence felt too: Martha, who's Black, is at first unable to see God as other than a bearded white man (the pronoun remains "he" for the first twenty of the story's twenty-five pages), and when, toward the end, she asks why it has taken time for her to see God as a Black woman, God replies, "As I've told you, you see what your life has prepared you to see" (209). Altogether, the irresponsibility of humankind, which in its way seems to delight God, issues in a far from delightful human record, and *nemesis* is Martha's operating position.

Martha is also marked as a rearranger of things, a design engineer, in at least two ways. For one thing, she's by trade a novelist, an orchestrator of fictional human destinies, which may be one reason God chooses her for the crucial work. Further, Martha's very name associates her with putting things in good order. The Martha of the gospels—called up inescapably by the title of Butler's story, which gives a Martha her own book—is known for two things. One, recounted in the eleventh and twelfth chapters of John, is being a sister of Lazarus. This in itself heightens the allusive density of Butler's text inasmuch as Martha Bes presides over a sort of resurrection of humankind—which also allies her with the figure of Noah, about whom Martha asks midway through her dialogue with the divinity. ("Was there really a Noah?" [201]. God answers, chillingly in Martha's view, that while there was never "one man dealing with a worldwide flood," there "have been a number of people who've had to deal with smaller disasters," including the dying of most of those around them [201].)

The biblical Martha's other major association, however, is with domestic management; indeed Roman Catholic hagiography appoints her the patron saint of servants, cooks, and housekeepers. "Now it came to pass, as they went," records the King James Version of Luke 10:38–42, that Jesus entered into a certain village: and a certain woman named Martha received him into her house. And she had a sister called Mary, which also sat at Jesus' feet, and heard his word. But Martha was cumbered about much serving, and came to him, and said, Lord, dost thou not care that my sister hath left me to serve alone? bid her therefore that she help me. And Jesus answered and said unto her, Martha, Martha, thou art careful and troubled about many things: But one thing is needful: and Mary hath chosen that good part, which shall not be taken away from her.

In Butler's "Book of Martha," God chooses not Mary but rather the one cumbered with serving and careful and troubled about the management of the household—a figure, further, whose name in Aramaic signifies the mistress of the house. In other words, the utopian reconfigurer of Butler's "Book of Martha" is a woman whose name and biblical lineage associate her with oversight of the *oikos*, with making sure that things are set to rights and rightly set. Another text that reverberates here is thus Gilman's *Herland*, where, in a transvaluation of values that makes features of women's work the path to an ideal society, utopia appears as a kind of vastly expanded household, superintended by women whose genius for arranging social institutions, as for designing things that enhance the quality of daily life, far exceeds anything in the world of men.

What the Martha of Butler's story crucially manages, as we've seen, is the problem of how utopia can contain people holding many different views about what utopia must contain. In Martha's design, people enjoy, in their dreams, versions of what Joshua Kotin calls "utopias of one"[3]—but again without being drawn away from the shared world by that enjoyment. Unlike the pods to which characters in *The Matrix* are consigned, Martha's "only possible utopia" doesn't prevent people from coming together in a common reality. Unlike the transformative utopia taken to its fanatically determined limit (and unlike the suspension in the virtual of *The Matrix* as well), it avoids the pointlessness of preprogrammed existence. And unlike Mosley's Pulse and Butler's own virtual rooms, it repels rather than creates addiction to isolation. Moreover, Martha's scheme shows little likelihood of changing humanity so profoundly that "it won't be humanity any more." In response to her expressed hope that people will be "a lot more awake and aware when they are awake, a lot less susceptible to lies, peer pressure, and self-delusion," God cautions, "None of this will make them perfect, Martha" (211). From the point of view just described, this is reassuring.

In addition, Martha's solution abrogates the utopian archipelago's requirement that one physically relocate in order to find a community whose values, opportunities, and pleasures suit one. This is an important point in its favor, for even were movement from place to place breathtakingly easy in the archipelago, relocating to a community more to one's taste could mean severing ties with family and friends who choose to stay behind, with groups and subcommunities that perforce have to remain more rooted. The archipelago makes small concession to the fact of human bonds; it relies on a more or less atomistic construction of the individual that many might find ethically or theoretically unappealing. Martha's utopia doesn't ask that one depart from loved ones, local haunts, beloved places and things in order to achieve a more suitable way of living. And we may therefore wonder whether, in limning a metautopia that mandates no physical transplantation at all, "The Book of Martha"—published the same year as *Archaeologies of the Future*—doesn't to some degree partake of the skepticism about the migratory utopia that we've detected in other twenty-first-century writing.

What makes this possibility the more plausible is that the other story added to the 2005 edition of *Bloodchild* juxtaposes a refraction of the utopian archipelago to highly foregrounded predicaments of migration and unfreedom in work. Like "The Book of Martha," "Amnesty" tells the tale of a woman who hopes to help all humankind—in this case a Noah figure whose actual name is Noah Cannon. Moreover, just as "The Book of Martha" manages to lay out the condition of the whole world in a few exchanges between Martha and God (supplemented by Martha's thoughts) over what seem a few hours of experienced time, so "Amnesty" paints the state of its Earth through a series of exchanges between Noah and a few interlocutors (supplemented by Noah's thoughts) over a similar span. Yet the circumstances under which Noah imagines performing her rescue work could hardly be more different.

Over the course of "Amnesty," we learn that some decades before the moment of the story, Earth was invaded by alien beings who arrived in spaceships, settled themselves in the world's deserts, and achieved complete domination over humankind—principally, it turns out, by making clear their capacity to wipe out all human life. These beings Noah calls "the Communities." The Communities are not organisms, but groups of organisms that travel together: they may be roughly half the size of a room and in some configurations resemble a bunch of branches, though at other times they resemble "spiny stone[s]" (150). As Noah explains to her human listeners in the interchange that makes up most of the story, "Each Community contains several hundred individuals—an intelligent multitude. But that's wrong too, really. The individuals can't really survive independently, but they can leave one community and move temporarily or permanently to another. They are products of a completely different evolution. When I look at them, I see what you've all seen: outer branches and then darkness. Flashes of light and movement within" (162).

Noah has a special relationship to the Communities. In their first years on Earth, the Communities had abducted a number of human beings in order to study them; plucked from her bedroom at the age of eleven, Noah was for the next dozen years subjected to the Communities' experiments and examinations. These were often horrifically painful, because the Communities only slowly learned to appreciate that humans are intelligent beings capable of suffering in ways the Communities cannot. Noah recounts the tortures the Communities inflicted on her without detectable anger, however—indeed with a certain compassion for the limits of the Communities' understanding that infuriates most of the humans to whom she's relating her experience. This is understandable, since most humans chafe in their subjugation to the alien invaders, unfathomable beings who have not only taken over Earth but also engaged in mineral-resource extraction and other enterprises that may (so the story hints) have led to the collapse of human economies.

For her own part, Noah judges humans more harshly than she does the Communities. During her detention, the aliens had sometimes hurt her directly, but "most of the time, the people actually hurting me were other human beings. . . . Some of us were more likely than others to be violent. Then there were those of us who would have been thugs even without the Communities' help. They were quick enough to take advantage of any chance to exercise a little power, get a little pleasure by making another person suffer" (164). There was worse to come, however. Upon her release by the Communities, Noah was detained by the US military, which subjected her to inquisitions evocative of the Communities' but less redeemable: "The only difference between the way they treated me and the way the aliens treated me during the early years of my captivity was that the so-called human beings knew when they were hurting me. They questioned me day and night, threatened me, drugged me, all in an effort to get me to give them information I didn't have. They'd keep me awake for days on end, keep me awake until I couldn't think, couldn't tell what was real and what wasn't" (170).

Toward the end of "Amnesty," Noah reveals to her human auditors that the Communities don't need human beings in order to survive but do have other cause to value them. For reasons obscure to both species, a Community's enfolding of a human can induce in both a feeling of tranquility and joy. Indeed earlier in the story, when Noah is so enfolded, Butler describes her experience thus:

> She couldn't see at all. . . . She felt herself surrounded by what felt like long, dry fibers, fronds, rounded fruits of various sizes, and other things that produced less identifiable sensations. She was at once touched, stroked, m[a]ssaged, compressed in the strangely comfortable, peaceful way that she

had come to look forward to whenever she was employed. She was turned and handled as though she weighed nothing. In fact, after a few moments, she felt weightless. She had lost all sense of direction, yet she felt totally secure, clasped by entities that had nothing resembling human limbs. Why this was pleasurable, she never understood, but for twelve years of captivity, it had been her only dependable comfort. (151–52)

Noah reveals that this holding has become for the Communities not just a curious experience but something difficult to do without: "We're an addictive drug" (179).

Humans' use as a resource by another form of intelligent being, here, certainly recalls other fictions such as *The Matrix*. But where in that film, the nonhumans who dominate are homegrown products of human hubris, in "Amnesty," they've journeyed to Earth from another world. And "Amnesty" very clearly engages fears and anxieties associated with migration. Quite often in venting their hatred of the Communities, Noah's human interlocutors use a rhetoric familiar from populist antimigrant hostility: "I'm angry that these things, these weeds can invade us, wreck our economies, send the whole world into a depression just by showing up. They do whatever they want to us, and instead of killing them, all I can do is ask them for a job!" (160); "They come to our world and we have to learn their language" (177); "They've still got no right to it [territory on Earth]. . . . It's ours, not theirs" (181). The Communities cannot, however, return whence they came, at least not soon: "They're here to stay. . . . There's no 'away' for them—not for several generations anyway. Their ship was a one-way transport" (167), Noah explains. "Some day," she allows, "some of them will leave. They'll build and use ships that are part multigenerational and part sleeper," but that will be "maybe a thousand of years from now" (182). The Communities are effectively refugees.

Insofar as Butler's chosen title relates to elements within the story, it points to Noah's state of feeling with respect to the Colonies: though she tells her hearers, "I don't forgive them. . . . They haven't asked for my forgiveness and I wouldn't know how to give it if they did" (168), she clearly abides with the Communities without nurturing grave resentment. But "Amnesty" points another way, of course, being the term opponents of progressive immigration reform use to deride paths to stability or legal citizenship for undocumented immigrants. One of the many ironies or strangenesses of "Amnesty"—which has the feel of a kaleidoscope in which standard counters of political contention around migration are shaken into unusual configurations—is that its title links policies that, in our world, benefit nearly powerless undocumented arrivals with a kind of generosity that issues, in Butler's, from a nearly powerless native of the destination place.

Part of what makes this alignment possible in Butler's story, of course, is that the alien arrivals are not just refugees but also colonists. The Communities don't ask to join the human society of Earth but instead conquer the planet, and while they limit their residence to land areas that suit them (which are conveniently those that least suit most human beings), they make clear their capacity to place humanity in their thrall. The author also of *Kindred*, which celebrated 1979 novel features a contemporary Black woman repeatedly teleported back to the antebellum South, Butler doesn't need to paint the Communities' domination in heavy strokes to make clear that since their appearance, Earth has become a scene of subjection.

But another feature of the Communities, in addition to their status as both refugees and colonists, calls migration to mind. According to Noah, as we've seen, the Communities' individual members cannot survive on their own, but it does appear that a given member may exchange one Community for a different one. The Communities read not only as migrants, then, but also as sending and receiving societies, destinations and points of departure for their component entities. And if this movement is volitional, as is suggested faintly by Noah's note that "they can leave one community and move temporarily or permanently to another," then the Communities may, collectively, evoke the kind of political meta-arrangement we've been considering under the name of the utopian archipelago. For a reader sympathetic to the idea of utopia who's also of strong communitarian inclinations, the Communities might even hold a certain attraction, made up as they seem to be of intelligent members who cannot live in isolation from their fellows.

It turns out, however, that whatever the Communities' whispers of utopian mystique, they're probably not utopias for those who compose them. Certainly, the Communities are quite successful by some measures: Noah has "never seen a dead" one, though she has "seen a couple of them have what you might call internal revolution. The entities of those Communities scattered to join other Communities. I'm not sure whether that was death, reproduction, or both" (182). Yet in explaining to her human hearers why few of the Communities she has encountered are interested in her personal history, Noah delivers a significant aside: "They have problems enough among themselves. What humans do to other humans outside their bubbles is usually not that important to them" (175). Butler's reader finally has no way of assessing the virtues, let alone the justice, of the Communities' internal arrangements.

As if all this weren't enough to make the Communities less than prodigious as utopian models for early twenty-first-century readers—that is, readers living in an age of violently accelerating wealth disparities, barely restrained corporate predation, and neoliberal doctrines ascendant in policy regimes across the globe—there is, in addition, the fact that the Communities represent an employer class. In fact, "Amnesty" is set entirely in a place of work, part of its power as well its wit arising from its manner of interweaving banalities of the office with the Communities' outrageous unlikeness to anything in the world of Butler's readers. The first part of the story describes Noah's meeting with two Communities, one "globular, easily twelve feet high" and looking, to Noah's eye, "a little like a great, black, moss-enshrouded bush with . . . a canopy of irregularly-shaped leaves, shaggy mosses, and twisted vines . . . in serious need of pruning," the other "a somewhat smaller, better-maintained-looking dense, black bush" (149). But these beings also have other names. The first is a "subcontractor" and the second is Noah's "employer," who at this moment is hiring Noah out (150).

Moreover, the conversation with her fellow humans that takes up the rest of the tale is an information session for applicants seeking employment with the Communities. The work Noah performs for the subcontractor is of a kind that some of the applicants she's meeting "might wind up doing someday, and yet that job—translator and personnel officer for the Communities—and the fact that she could do it was their reason for distrusting her" (156). In this second of its two parts, as in the first, "Amnesty" gains a frisson of comedy from its placement of extraterrestrial invaders in familiar corporate frames: "But what does a contract mean to things that come from another star system?", asks one recruit; another, "Translator, do you truly believe they will consider themselves bound by anything they sign? Although without hands, God knows how they manage to sign anything." Noah replies patiently that they can make marks that serve as signatures, that they "spent a great deal of their time and wealth in this country with translators, lawyers, and politicians, working things out so that each Community was counted as a legal 'person,' whose individual mark would be accepted," and that "for twenty years since then, they've honored their contracts" (157). This fidelity would, of course, make the Communities more honorable than most colonists in human history, even if their legal success also calls to mind the "corporate personhood" that would attract so much attention a few years after the publication of "Amnesty," in the wake of the US Supreme Court's verdict in *Citizens United v. Federal Election Commission*.

Butler's practice, in "Amnesty," of infusing what may seem the most mundane exchanges with high significance extends to the story's final lines:

> Thera Collier stared at her bleakly. "But . . . but there must be something we can do, some way to fight."
> Noah stood up, pushed her comfortable chair away.
> "I don't think so," she said. "Your employers are waiting. Shall we join them?" (184, ellipsis Butler's)

The story ends, it would seem, on a note of resignation as mortifying as it is dry. There will, Noah affirms, be no escape from the subjugation, at once colonial and corporate, imposed by the Communities, and the choice for her hearers implied in her last words is one between working for these overlords and recommencing an employment search that will likely end, at best, with a job that pays far less well.[4] Moreover, Noah's final question highlights how working for the Communities really means joining them—and this in a way that's life-changing and intimate (employees must live in the Communities' territorial "bubbles"; employees must learn to be physically enfolded) yet unaccompanied by anything like full membership (employees remain, in this sense as in others, guest workers).

Further, Noah's last words bring together in striking fashion two of the données we've seen utopia negotiating throughout this study: the necessity of labor and the necessity of living together. "Your employers are waiting. Shall we join them?": having just dismissed the possibility of fighting invaders who are themselves powerless to vacate the planet, Noah seems in these sentences to fuse the demands of work and the burdens of socialization under the sign of the inescapable—and thus firmly to extinguish any last glimmers of utopia the story might have been thought to contain. In this, "Amnesty" reads as a sort of eloquent contrast to Jameson's *An American Utopia*, which concludes, with respect both to work and to social interaction, that although utopia will have to propitiate necessity, it can also circumscribe it. On the side of work, Jameson's concession takes the form of labor mandated under the auspices of the universal army, while a foothold in the realm of freedom is proffered in the form of leisure hours spent in any way the utopian citizen may desire. On the side of social interactions, the concession is that antagonism will be recognized as a permanent feature of human life, but utopia also keeps the consequences of antagonism within bounds, enmities being, if plentiful, happily so, subsisting in small interchanges and individual relations rather than threatening utopia's overarching peace.

The submission to necessity that follows from the Communities' addiction to human beings, on the other hand, manages, impressively, to amalgamate the drudgery of work at its least appealing with the slog of living with others at their most unnerving. The Communities' particular extraction of affective labor perhaps even replicates in another register the theme we saw threading through *The Blithedale Romance* in chapter 1: Hell is other people, and worse hell is when they bind themselves to you as your fate. This point then finally returns us to what may seem the most melancholy suspicion of the "The Book of Martha": that utopia might only be available in isolation from others—and hence not utopia in the fullest, most longed-for sense.

Yet neither story is quite as unhopeful as these distillations suggest. Both in fact hold open the prospect of a much better world, and in both the path to that world is illuminated not by a master planner intent on implementing a final infallible system but by a dreamer whose sense of *nemesis* impels her to lay a groundwork, to give future beings the best possible chance of fashioning a better way of living for themselves. In "Amnesty," Noah takes for her life's project that of helping human beings and the Communities to understand each other, to work together in addressing their shared fate in spite of strong reasons for mistrust on both sides: "Community by Community, human by human," Noah tells her employer, she will endeavor "to make them think. I want to tell them what human governments won't tell them. I want to vote for peace between your people and mine by telling the truth. I don't know whether my efforts will do any good, in the long run, but I have to try" (155). This is a slender hope, as Noah acknowledges, and it's undercut by at least two characters in the story: the employer, who tells Noah, "You cannot change your people or mine" (155), and Noah herself, who regards with disdain a recruit who seems naively optimistic about sharing between the species. (On this applicant's venturing, "If we honor them, maybe they will take us to heaven with them," Noah suppresses "an urge to hit the woman" [182]). Yet Butler has elsewhere permitted a protagonist to realize a staggeringly ambitious vision against what might be called, in a double sense, astronomical odds. Thinking of Lauren Olamina from *Parable of the Talents*, we may wonder whether Noah Cannon's determination might not carry the day.

And on this front, a further aspect of the staging of necessity in "Amnesty" solicits our attention. We've seen how the necessity of work and the necessity of living together are fused in the Communities' willingness to pay for a certain kind of contact with human beings; we've seen, too, how this fusion can be taken as helping to render more remote the prospect of anything like genuinely utopian bonhomie. Yet there's another side to this coin. Humans are sought by the Communities not for their labor in any traditional sense—not for what they can produce materially or perform in the way of other tasks supporting survival—but rather for their capacity to stimulate certain feelings when they're hugged. Within such a configuration of desire, the border between necessity and luxury grows fuzzy, and not only for the Communities themselves, because the touching is pleasant and indeed uniquely transporting for the human enfolded. We might perhaps discern in this strange communion, then, a hint of the old dream—articulated by William Morris and so many others—of a regime in which labor is a conspicuously fulfilling part of life. To be sure, the touching in question must read from one perspective as a perversion of that dream, situated as it is within the oppressive hierarchy of Communities and humans. But what if, as Noah hopes, social relations change for the better (as they always do in utopia)? In a context of trust and even collaboration between Communities and humans, this work-pleasure, this feeling-labor, might be a little utopian after all.

"The Book of Martha," meanwhile, puts forward the hope that humankind, which even God describes as being in its adolescence, will in time become wiser and less self-destructive. If in "Amnesty" community seems at once a hard fact and a chance for growth—a donnée that constricts but also perhaps opens up—the same holds true in "Martha," if in a different and as it were still less metaphorical sense. In chapter 1, we saw not only how living together justly has proven an insuperable challenge for human beings but also how dwelling on human limitation in this area can eventuate in a ferocious misanthropy—a *saeva indignatio*, a kind of *nemesis* that leads not to utopian imagining but to blanketing satire. Against such estimates of human depravity, however, "The Book of Martha" sets the possibility that humankind may yet prove not an obstacle to justice but rather (with one great nudge from an indignant engineer who, at story's end and at her request, is permitted to forget what she has done) the way forward to that condition in which all and each have what they ought to have. Perhaps people can be not only the ends utopia serves but also—really—the means to get there.

Butler's story proposes, that is, that given enough satisfaction in dreams, human beings—fractious and recalcitrant as they are—might be able to build a fine world together, collaborating in the building as they go, negotiating and conferring, allowing and assisting. If "people go to a . . . well, a private heaven every night," this "might take the edge off their willingness to spend their waking hours trying to dominate or destroy one another." In Hesiod's *Theogony*, Nemesis is a child of dreadful Night described as "the bane of / Mortals," and among Night's other horrific progeny are the Oneiroi, "the legions of Nightmares."[5] But we can imagine—on the other side of the mirror, as it were—these children of Night having a different character, another valence. We can imagine a Book of Martha, say, in which a happier dreaming and a more charitable *nemesis* work together, for good.

NOTES

Introduction

1. Thomas Hardy, *Tess of the d'Urbervilles* (London: Penguin, 1978), 69–70.

2. Hardy, *Tess*, 70.

3. As Matthew Beaumont notes, *Looking Backward* sold two hundred thousand copies in the United States in its first year in print and would go on to sell at least three hundred thousand more by Bellamy's death in 1898. Beaumont, *Utopia Ltd.: Ideologies of Social Dreaming in England, 1870–1900* (Leiden: Brill, 2005), 1; and Beaumont, *The Spectre of Utopia: Utopian and Science Fictions at the Fin de Siècle* (Oxford: Peter Lang, 2012), 31. Meanwhile a hundred thousand copies had sold in Britain by 1890 (*Utopia Ltd.* 1–2, *Spectre* 31), and *Looking Backward* became the first work of American fiction since Harriet Beecher Stowe's *Uncle Tom's Cabin* to attain sales of more than a million overall (*Utopia Ltd.* 189, *Spectre* 27).

In his monumental *Utopia and Anti-utopia in Modern Times* (Oxford: Basil Blackwell, 1987), on which Beaumont partly draws, Krishan Kumar recalls, too, that *Looking Backward* was "translated, usually within a year or two of initial publication, into every major language in the world," read "not only in England, France, Germany, Russia and Italy, but also in Australia, India, Indonesia, Japan, South Africa and many other countries" (133). *Looking Backward* inspired "The Bellamy Library of Fact and Fiction," a series of reprinted classics of radical political writing (*Spectres* 121–50) and the establishment of Bellamy societies on both sides of the Atlantic. See on this also Michael Robertson, *The Last Utopians* (Princeton, NJ: Princeton University Press, 2018), 66.

Looking Backward also unleashed a torrent of further utopian writing. Between 1889 and 1900, according to Kumar, at least sixty-two "utopias and novels influenced by Bellamy were published, most of them in the United States, but several also in Britain and Germany" (*Utopia and Anti-utopia* 135). According to Darko Suvin in *Metamorphoses of Science Fiction* (New Haven, CT: Yale University Press, 1979), between one hundred and two hundred "utopian tales expounding or satirizing social democracy, state regulation of economy, a Populist capitalism, or various uncouth combinations thereof were published in the United States from 1888 to the first World War" (178). And according to Robertson, citing Lyman Tower Sargent's 1988 annotated bibliography of British and American utopian literature, "more English-language works—over five hundred—were published in the quarter-century following the appearance of Bellamy's novel than had appeared in the nearly four hundred years between More and Bellamy" (4).

4. In *The Shaping of Tess of the D'Urbervilles* (Oxford: Clarendon, 1975), J. T. Laird argues from manuscript evidence for "the existence of an Ur-novel during the period from at least as early as October 1888 until November 1889" (6).The mention of a "blighted" world already appears in that Ur-text, as a later note in Laird reveals (73).

5. Michael Millgate, *Thomas Hardy: A Biography Revisited* (Oxford: Oxford University Press, 2000), 293.

6. Oscar Wilde, *Complete Works* (New York: Perennial Library, 1989), 1089, 1084. Often omitted, however, is the continuation of the thought about utopia: "And when Humanity lands there, it looks out, and seeing a better country, sets sail. Progress is the realisation of Utopias."

7. As Lawrence Danson notes in *Wilde's Intentions: The Artist in His Criticism* (Oxford: Clarendon, 1997), *Tess of the D'Urbervilles* shared both a publisher and a book designer with *Intentions*, the 1891 volume by Wilde in which "The Soul of Man" was first reprinted. The publisher was James Ripley Osgood of Osgood McIlvaine, and the designer was Charles Ricketts (21). As Danson observes, "Osgood saw Wilde as a marketable author, comparable in sales appeals to Thomas Hardy" at this time—and the two "belonged together because they were two of the most dangerous writers in England" (22). Indeed in 1895, Wilde and Hardy would both feel the wrath of the conservative British public—Wilde at his trials, Hardy on the publication of *Jude the Obscure*.

8. Samuel Beckett, *Endgame* (New York: Grove, 1958), 21–23.

9. Fredric Jameson, *Archaeologies of the Future: The Desire Called Utopia and Other Science Fictions* (London: Verso, 2005), 42–43.

10. Russell Jacoby, *Picture Imperfect: Utopian Thought for an Anti-utopian Age* (New York: Columbia University Press, 2005), xiv, xv.

11. J. K. Fuz, *Welfare Economics in English Utopias* (The Hague: Martinus Nijhoff, 1952), 3.

12. "One of the fundamental tasks of the State," write Deleuze and Guattari in *A Thousand Plateaus: Capitalism and Schizophrenia* (trans. Brian Massumi; Minneapolis: University of Minnesota Press, 1987), "is to striate the space over which it reigns, or to utilize smooth spaces as a means of communication in the service of striated space. It is a vital concern of every State not only to vanquish nomadism but to control migrations" (385).

13. This is not to imply that many utopias concern themselves with smooth space as such. For Deleuze and Guattari, the regulation of labor flows would very much be part of the work of striation.

14. Lisa Malkki, "National Geographic: The Rooting of Peoples and the Territorialization of National Identity among Scholars and Refugees," *Cultural Anthropology* 7.1 (1992): 31; Timothy Cresswell, *On the Move: Mobility in the Modern Western World* (New York: Routledge, 2006), 26–42.

15. Krishan Kumar, *Utopianism* (Minneapolis: University of Minnesota Press, 1991), 33. Kumar goes on to explain that while other "varieties of the ideal society or the perfect condition of humanity are to be found in abundance in non-Western societies, usually embedded in religious cosmologies," nowhere in these societies "do we find the practice of writing utopias, of criticizing them, of developing and transforming their themes and exploring new possibilities within them. . . . Only for China has it seriously ever been claimed that there is something approaching an indigenous utopian tradition. . . . But on inspection it turns out that what we are presented with are predominantly primitivist conceptions whose central feature is a lost Golden Age" (*Utopianism* 33). Thus Kumar in 1991; according to Lyman Tower Sargent in his own *Utopianism: A Very Short Introduction* (Oxford: Oxford University Press, 2010), "Today, most scholars disagree and argue that such traditions existed in most cultures, noting such traditions in Buddhist, Confucian, and Taoist China, Buddhist and Hindu India, the Islamic countries of the Middle East, Buddhist Southeast Asia, and Buddhist and Shinto Japan" (67).

For more extended considerations of non-Western utopian writing, see, for example, Adam Seligman, ed., *Order and Transcendence: The Role of Utopias and the Dynamics of Civilizations* (Leiden: E. J. Brill, 1989); Douwe Fokkema, *Perfect Worlds: Utopian Fiction in China and the West* (Amsterdam: Amsterdam University Press, 2011); and two essays from Gregory Claeys's *Cambridge Companion to Utopian Literature* (Cambridge: Cambridge University Press, 2010): Sargent's "Colonial and Postcolonial Utopias" (200–222) and Jacqueline Dutton's "'Non-Western' Utopian Traditions" (223–58). Whether any non-Western texts appearing before a particular date can be called utopian seems ultimately to depend on how utopia is defined and, no less crucially, on how "the West" is defined. In future, it may be useful in many contexts to take to heart Dutton's point that "with its historically West-centered description of theory and practice, the concept of utopia may no longer be broad enough to encompass the full scope of social dreamings" and adopt her suggestion of "intercultural imaginaries of the ideal" as "a more appropriate and neutral term" for scholarship (224).

16. Jameson, *Archaeologies*, xvi.

17. Conservativism's relation to utopia has been discussed by, among others, Karl Mannheim in *Ideology and Utopia*, trans. Louis Wirth and Edward Shils (San Diego: Harvest, n.d.; first published in German in 1929); and Hayden White in *Metahistory* (Baltimore, MD: Johns Hopkins University Press, 1973). Ruth Levitas rebuts the claim that "right-wing utopias are not properly to be considered utopias" in *The Concept of Utopia* (Oxford: Peter Lang, 2010; first published 1990 by Philip Allan), 215.

18. Fredric Jameson, *The Seeds of Time* (New York: Columbia University Press, 1994), xii.

19. Langston Hughes, *Collected Poems* (New York: Knopf, 1995), 190–91.

20. Bodys Isek Kingelez, "Propos Recueillis par André Magnin Kinshasa, Paris, 2000," in *Bodys Isek Kingelez* (Ostfildern-Ruit, Germany: Hatje Cantz, 2001), 98, 100.

21. A reading of Kingelez appears, for example, in the 2009 volume titled *Utopias,* edited by Richard Noble and published in the Whitechapel Gallery-MIT Press Documents of Art series.

22. Kingelez, "Propos," 100.

23. Bodys Isek Kingelez, "La Ville Fantôme 1995–96," in *Bodys Isek Kingelez* (2001), 101; Okwui Enwezor, "Trickster Urbanism: The Architectural Simulations of Bodys Isek Kingelez," in *Bodys Isek Kingelez* (2001), 93–94.

24. Erica Perlmutter Jones, "Imagining Heterotopia: Kinshasa and the Urban Simulations of Bodys Isek Kingelez" (master's thesis, UCLA, 2008), viii.

25. Chika Okeke-Agulu, "On Kingelez's Audacious Objects," in *Bodys Isek Kingelez*, ed. Sarah Suzuki (New York: Museum of Modern Art, 2018), 34.

26. Bodys Isek Kingelez, "The Essential Framework of the Structures Making Up the Town of Kimbembele-Ihunga (Kimbéville)," in Suzuki, *Bodys Isek Kingelez*, 50–51.

27. Seth Brodsky, *From 1989; or, European Music and the Modernist Unconscious* (Berkeley: University of California Press, 2017), 188.

28. Tim Rutherford-Johnson, "The Ghost of the Avant-garde," *The Guardian*, April 23, 2012, theguardian.com/music/musicblog/2012/apr/23/luigi-nono-future-creative-utopia.

29. Quoted in Brodsky, 190.

30. The piece's subtitle represents it as a "madrigal for multiple 'travelers' with Gidon Kremer." The word for "travelers" here is *caminantes*, which, as Brodsky notes, "alludes to a phrase

that permeates—or, better, haunts—virtually all of Nono's last works: 'Caminante, no hay caminos, hay que caminar' [Wanderer, . . . there are no roads, one has to wander]" (187), which Nono saw on the wall of a monastery in Toledo. Brodsky quotes the violinist Miranda Cuckson's sense that in performance of the piece, musicians and audience "temporarily take on the condition of those 'displaced by war: emigrants, refugees, "alien" residents'" (190).

31. In *Utopia in Performance* (Ann Arbor: University of Michigan, 2005), Jill Dolan argues that "live performance provides a place where people come together, embodied and passionate, to share experiences of meaning making and imagination that can describe or capture fleeting intimations of a better world" (2). She also coins the term "utopian performatives" for moments in which audiences are lifted "slightly above the present, into a hopeful feeling of what the world might be like if every moment of our lives were as emotionally voluminous, generous, aesthetically striking, and intersubjectively intense" (5). In *Cruising Utopia: The Then and There of Queer Futurity* (New York: New York University Press, 2009), José Muñoz refers to a "utopian performativity" that would be a "manifestation of a 'doing' that is on the horizon, a mode of possibility. Performance, seen as utopian performativity, is imbued with a sense of potentiality" (99). *La Lontananza* certainly partakes of the utopian performative in these senses; I'm suggesting that its title brings specificity to this general condition of performance by inviting the audience to wonder how the experience of the piece might represent utopia quasi-mimetically.

Chapter 1. Utopian *Nemesis*

1. The 1802 text, as it appears in Gregory Claeys's anthology, *Utopias of the British Enlightenment*, is cited here except as noted. The full title of the 1802 version is *Bruce's Voyage to Naples, and Journey Up Mount Vesuvius; Giving an Account of the Strange Disaster which Happened on His Arrival at the Summit: the Discovery of the Central World; with the Laws, Customs, and Manners, of that Nation, Described; Their Swift and Peculiar Mode of Travelling; the Wonderful Riches, Virtue, and Knowledge, the Inhabitants Possess; the Author's Travels in that Country; and the Friendly Reception He Met with from Its Sovereign and His People.* The subtitle of the 1755 version is similarly lengthy.

2. Anonymous, *Bruce's Voyage to Naples*, in *Utopias of the British Enlightenment*, ed. Gregory Claeys (Cambridge: Cambridge University Press, 1994), 251, 267. Further citations will be given parenthetically in the text.

3. Heinrich Lausberg, *Handbook of Literary Rhetoric: A Foundation for Literary Studies*, trans. Matthew T. Bliss, Annemiek Jansen, and David E. Orton (Leiden: Brill, 1998), 204–7.

4. Jonathan Swift, *Gulliver's Travels and Other Writings*, ed. Louis A. Landa (Boston: Houghton Mifflin, 1960), 48. Further citations will be given parenthetically in the text.

5. Anonymous, *A Voyage to the World in the Centre of the Earth* (London: S. Crowder and H. Woodgate, 1755), 20.

6. *Gulliver's Travels* and *Bruce's Voyage* are also linked in presenting ideal societies with one signally disturbing feature: a willingness to contemplate eradication of those incorrigible beings known as humans. In book 4 of the former, Gulliver famously recalls Houyhnhnm deliberations about whether to exterminate the Yahoos, by castration of all the young of the species or by other means (218–20). Bruce, meanwhile, reports that the descendants of (literally fallen) former surface dwellers, who have been permitted to occupy their own quarter in the mid-Earth empire, have become a threat to that empire, upon which the rulers decide that all the Earth

males will be castrated, the females having the option either of living "with their husbands" or "marry[ing] among the central inhabitants." The aim, in other words, is "to extirpate the whole race" of immigrants from the surface (286).

7. Claude Rawson, *Swift's Angers* (Cambridge: Cambridge University Press, 2014), 239, 3, 2, 2, 4, 267.

8. Juvenal, "Satires," in *Juvenal and Persius*, trans. G. G. Ramsay (London: William Heinemann, 1940), 5. (Latin: "Satires," in *Juvenal and Persius* [London: William Heinemann, 1940], 4 [line 30].)

9. In *The Practice of Satire in England, 1658–1770* (Baltimore, MD: Johns Hopkins University Press, 2013), Ashley Marshall quotes Thomas Gilbert's 1749 *Satire on All Parties* to note that among period commentators, a common claim was that "the satirist is compelled by 'generous indignation'—by a resistance to wrongdoing that every good man should feel 'when he reflects on the Insolence of Exalted Vice, which has a pernicious Effect on the Community'" (62). Back in *The Anatomy of Melancholy* (1621), Robert Burton had remarked that "'tis a most difficult thing to keep an even tone, a perpetual tenor, and not sometimes to lash out; *difficile est satiram non scribere*, there be so many objects to divert, inward perturbations to molest, and the very best may sometimes err" (123). Burton, *The Anatomy of Melancholy* (New York: New York Review Books, 2001).

10. Andrew Stauffer, *Anger, Revolution, and Romanticism* (Cambridge: Cambridge University Press, 2005), 38–42. As Stauffer further refines it, political contestation in the 1790s "evoked two traditions of anger, traceable to Juvenal on the one hand and Seneca on the other. . . . For Seneca, anger is furious rage: irrational, worse than pointless. . . . The typical contributor to political debate in the 1790s claimed he was angry in the Juvenalian manner *at the fact that* his opponents were angry in the Senecan" (40–41).

11. John Barrell, *English Literature in History, 1730–80: An Equal, Wide Survey* (London: Hutchinson, 1983), 32–33.

12. Juvenal, 251, 247–49, 85, 9. (Latin: Juvenal 250, 246–48, 84, 8 [lines 13.64–66, 13.26–30, 6.19–20, 1.85–86].)

13. Anonymous, *A Voyage*, 132.

14. Glenn Negley and J. Max Patrick, *The Quest for Utopia: An Anthology of Imaginary Societies* (New York: Henry Schuman, 1952), 5–6.

15. Darko Suvin, *Metamorphoses of Science Fiction* (New Haven, CT: Yale University Press, 1979), 54–55.

16. Krishan Kumar, *Utopia and Anti-utopia in Modern Times* (Oxford: Basil Blackwell, 1987), 124–25.

17. Similarly, Hythlodaeus rails in part 1 against kings who would beggar their people and answers this defalcation twice: first with an anecdote of the Macarians, whose king "is bound by a solemn oath that he shall never at any time have in his treasury above a thousand pound of gold or silver" (40), then in part 2 by recalling a Utopian statute designed to prevent that country's (elected) leaders from "conspir[ing] together to oppress the people by tyranny, and to change the state of the weal-public" (56). Thomas More, *Utopia*, trans. Ralph Robinson, in *Three Early Modern Utopias*, ed. Susan Bruce (Oxford: Oxford University Press, 1999). The Robinson translation of More's Latin used is (a modernized version of) the second edition, published in 1556.

18. More, *Utopia*, 76. Further citations will be given parenthetically in the text.

19. Ernst Bloch, *The Principle of Hope* (Cambridge: MIT Press, 1995), 2:543. Bloch would go on to challenge this very distinction in his *Natural Law and Human Dignity* of 1961.

20. The complete conceit of the text's authorship is a step more baroque still. The author's preface, dated "December 26, 2000," marks West as the fictional creation of a twenty-first-century scholar who wishes to help readers in his own age "who, while desiring to gain a more definite idea of the social contrasts between the nineteenth and twentieth centuries, are daunted by the formal aspect of the histories which treat the subject. . . . The author has sought to alleviate the instructive quality of the book by casting it in the form of a romantic narrative." Edward Bellamy, *Looking Backward: 2000–1887* (New York: Signet, 1960), xxi. Further citations will be given parenthetically in the text.

21. In *The Last Utopians* (Princeton, NJ: Princeton University Press, 2018), Michael Robertson observes of Bellamy's allegory, "[N]o one is responsible for the unjust system; everyone is equally a victim; the coach was not designed but simply sprang into existence" (62). This is true, strictly speaking, but the self-pluming of the wealthy in the figuration, along with their superior material comfort, makes them victims rather less easy to sympathize with.

22. William Morris, *News from Nowhere and Other Writings* (London: Penguin, 1993), 79. Further citations will be given parenthetically in the text.

23. H. G. Wells, *A Modern Utopia*, (London: Penguin, 2005), 237, 242. Further citations will be given parenthetically in the text.

24. In *Ideology and Utopia* (trans. Louis Wirth and Edward Shils [San Diego: Harvest, n.d.]), Karl Mannheim argues that "the conservative mentality as such has no utopia" but also frames that mentality as a reaction against a liberal progressive Enlightenment that "appealed to free will and kept alive the feeling of being indeterminate and unconditioned. . . . If one wishes to formulate the central achievement of conservatism in a single sentence, it could be said that in conscious contrast to the liberal outlook, it gave positive emphasis to the notion of the determinateness of our behaviour" (229). The socialist utopia then represents "a peculiar assimilation of the conservative sense of determinism into the progressive utopia which strives to remake the world. . . . For the socialists . . . it is the social structure which becomes the most influential force in the historical moment, and its formative powers (in a glorified form) are regarded as the determinant factors of" historical development (242).

25. Pauline Hopkins, *Of One Blood; or, the Hidden Self* (New York: Washington Square Press, 2004), 58. Further citations will be given parenthetically in the text.

26. Quoted in Robert A. Hill and R. Kent Rasmussen, afterword to *Black Empire*, by George Schuyler (Boston: Northeastern University Press, 1991), 260.

27. Schuyler, *Black Empire*, 166. Further citations will be given parenthetically in the text.

28. Stuart Christie, "Trickster Gone Golfing: Vizenor's *Heirs of Columbus* and the Chelh-ten-em Development Controversy," *American Indian Quarterly* 21.3 (1997): 370. Christie notes critically that Vizenor refers neither to the struggle of the local Lummi People with efforts to develop the land of Chelh-ten-em/Point Roberts nor—Vizenor's own emphasis on the trickster figure notwithstanding—to the "local trickster idiom" (374).

29. Mat Johnson, *Pym* (New York: Spiegel and Grau, 2010), 28, 25. Further citations will be given parenthetically in the text.

30. Griggs's Imperium does lay out a "plan of action" for the seizing of Texas and Louisiana (251), which can certainly be imagined as a claimed homeland, if not a reclaimed one in the sense of Africa in *Black Empire*. Moreover the Imperium, boasting seven and a half million

members and extending covertly across the South and perhaps beyond, represents itself as "another government, complete in every detail, exercising the sovereign right of life and death over its subjects, . . . maintained and organized within the United States for many years" (190). Nonetheless, the capitol of this government, disguised as Thomas Jefferson College in Waco, Texas, reads as a bounded utopian enclave in a manner that contrasts with the extensiveness of the Imperium's reach in the white-dominated United States. Sutton Griggs, *Imperium in Imperio: A Study of the Negro Race Problem* (Project Gutenberg ebook #15454, 2005).

31. *Oxford English Dictionary* online, s.v. "indignation," accessed January 22, 2020. See also the *Oxford Latin Dictionary* (1982), s.v. "indignor" 1, "To regard with indignation, take offence at, resent, disdain."

32. *Oxford Latin Dictionary*, s.v. "dignus" 1, 2.

33. Elizabeth Forbis, *Municipal Virtues in the Roman Empire* (Stuttgart: B. G. Teubner, 1996), 24. The *Oxford Latin Dictionary* also notes the derivation from "decet," s.v. "dignus." And see also in the *Oxford Latin Dictionary*, s.v. "decet" 1, 3, 4: "To add grace to, adorn, become"; "To accord with approved standards of taste or behaviour, be proper, be right"; "It is right, proper, fitting, etc."

34. F. E. J. Valpy, *An Etymological Dictionary of the Latin Language* (London: A. J. Valpy, 1828), 124.

35. Melissa Lane, introduction to *The Republic*, 2nd ed, by Plato, trans. Desmond Lee (London: Penguin, 2007), xx.

36. Ernst Bloch, *Natural Law and Human Dignity*, trans. Dennis J. Schmidt (Cambridge: MIT Press, 1986), 40.

37. Aristotle, *Politics*, trans. Ernest Barker (New York: Oxford University Press, 1958), 258; Aristotle, *Nicomachean Ethics*, trans. Robert C. Bartlett and Susan D. Collins (Chicago: University of Chicago Press, 2011), 99–100.

38. Plato, *Republic*, 137, 138, 152–53.

39. Bloch, *Principle of Hope*, 2:487–88.

40. Aristotle, *Politics*, 7.

41. John Rawls, *A Theory of Justice* (Cambridge: Harvard University Press, 1971), 3. Further citations will be given parenthetically in the text.

42. Wai Chee Dimock, *Residues of Justice* (Berkeley: University of California Press, 1996), 4. Further citations will be given parenthetically in the text.

43. Elaine Scarry, *On Beauty and Being Just* (Princeton, NJ: Princeton University Press, 1999), 78. Further citations will be given parenthetically in the text.

44. Dimock notably calls upon a rather similar Augustine—one for whom "our love of the world, our capacity to enjoy it, . . . enabled us to love God" (131)—before turning to Jonathan Edwards.

45. "Aristotle points to money as a necessary (if regrettable) instrument," writes Dimock, "for 'money, acting as a measure, makes goods commensurate and equates them.' . . . [Aristotle's] own understanding of justice turns out to be surprisingly modest, carrying with it always a definitional disclaimer, a conscious shying away from any presumed totality. . . . It is this scrupulous restraint on Aristotle's part—his refusal to 'cover' the field, as it were—that is progressively eroded in the ascendancy of justice as a philosophical concept, an ascendancy most powerfully shaped by Kant and most powerfully exemplified, in our own time, by John Rawls" (3–4). On the passage from the *Nicomachean Ethics* to which Dimock refers, see note 54, below.

46. In *Cruel Optimism* (Durham, NC: Duke University Press, 2011), Lauren Berlant remarks that "justice itself is a technology of deferral or patience that keeps people engrossed politically,

when they are, in the ongoing drama of optimism and disappointment" (184). We might say that a sense that justice can at best be approached asymptotically can issue in either of two opposed positions: where it modulates into resignation, it can work against active engagement; but it can also underwrite a willingness to press on even if a social or political goal hasn't been achieved when or as desired.

47. Susan Bruce, explanatory notes to *Three Early Modern Utopias*, 229.

48. Guillaume Budé, "Guillaume Budé to his English friend Thomas Lupset: Greeting," in Bruce, *Three Early Modern Utopias*, 140. Budé's reference to early writers' definition of Justice "as the power who assigns each his due" does not hark back to Aristotle only. Also alluded to here, undoubtedly, is the *City of God*, in book 19 of which Augustine critiques Cicero's vision of justice in *On the Republic*. Augustine begins by affirming, in line with Aristotle and Cicero, that "what is rightly done is justly done"; that "where there is no justice, there is no commonwealth"; that "Justice is the virtue which accords to each and every man what is his due" (469). Augustine goes on, however, to argue that Rome had never been a genuine commonwealth because true justice—*uera justitia*—can only obtain where the true God is served. Saint Augustine, *City of God*, abridged ed., trans. Gerald G. Walsh, Demetrius B. Zema, Grace Monahan, and Daniel J. Honan (New York: Image, 1958).

In *On the Trinity*, meanwhile, Augustine asserts, in Robert Dodaro's phrasing in *Christ and the Just Society in Augustine* (Cambridge: Cambridge University Press, 2004), that as Christians' understanding of justice deepens, they "no longer regard the virtue as obliging them to measure what they owe to one another according to the classical definition" but rather "understand that justice obliges them to love their neighbour" (158), in line with the Pauline injunction, "Let no one owe anything except to love one another" (Romans 13:8, quoted in Dodaro 158). More, who lectured on the *City of God*, notably makes love a key quality of Utopia: "They live together lovingly," Hythlodaeus reports (93).

49. Budé, 142.

50. Fredric Jameson, *The Seeds of Time* (New York: Columbia University Press, 1994), 56.

51. Fredric Jameson, *Archaeologies of the Future: The Desire Called Utopia and Other Science Fictions* (London: Verso, 2005), xiii. Further citations will be given parenthetically within the text.

52. Russell Jacoby, *Picture Imperfect: Utopian Thought for an Anti-utopian Age* (New York: Columbia University Press, 2005), xiv–xvi.

53. Aristotle, *Politics*, 6–7.

54. Aristotle perhaps plays on the double sense of *nomos* as both right apportionment and law or custom in *Nicomachean Ethics* 5 when he explains that although money does not serve as a perfect measure of commensurability between unlike things, it serves well enough: "But money has become, by agreement, a kind of exchangeable representative of need; and on account of this it has its name [*nomisma*, literally 'legal currency'], because it exists not by nature but by law [*nomos*]. . . . Now, in truth, it is impossible for things that differ greatly from one another to become commensurable, but it is possible, to a sufficient degree, in relation to need. So there must be some one thing [that serves as a measure], and this is based on a presupposition; hence it is called 'legal currency' [*nomisma*]." Aristotle, *Nicomachean Ethics*, 101–2. (Bracketed insertions by the translators.)

55. Ernest Barker, introduction to Aristotle, *Politics*, trans. Ernest Barker (New York: Oxford University Press, 1958), lxxi.

56. Helmut Berking, *Sociology of Giving*, trans. Patrick Camillier (London: SAGE, 1999), 69.

57. Richard Seaford, *Money and the Early Greek Mind: Homer, Philosophy, Tragedy* (Cambridge: Cambridge University Press, 2004), 49.

58. Ronald Bogue, *Deleuze's Way* (Aldershot, UK: Ashgate, 2007), 125.

59. Martin Ostwald, *Nomos and the Beginnings of the Athenian Democracy* (Oxford: Clarendon, 1969), 7, 7 54.

60. Ostwald, 62, 64, 67, 68.

61. Ostwald frequently associates *nomos* with what we call *norms*, a term that nicely captures the sense of what's generally expected in a given society as well as the way *nomos* flirts with, but often seems less than anchored in, transcendence. In *Critique, Norm, and Utopia* (New York: Columbia University Press, 1986), Seyla Benhabib suggests that "norm and utopia are concepts referring to two visions of politics, which I also name the 'politics of fulfillment' and the 'politics of transfiguration.' . . . While norms have the task of articulating the demands of justice and human worthiness, utopias portray modes of friendship, solidarity, and human happiness. Despite their essential tension, a critical social theory is only rich enough to address us in the present, insofar as it can do justice to both moments" (13). Benhabib's definitions, which descend in their way from Bloch, are certainly apposite on their own terms, but it should be clear that the present study considers justice in a sense that reaches beyond the narrowly normative while also arguing that utopia is normative in a crucial sense.

62. In *The* Nomos *of the Earth* (1950), *nomos* names something like the condition of the geopolitical order at a given time, Schmitt basing his usage on what he takes to be the essential Greek sense of *nomos* as "the immediate form in which the political and social order of a people becomes spatially visible," as "a matter of the fundamental process of apportioning space that is essential to every historical epoch." Carl Schmitt, *The* Nomos *of the Earth in the International Law of the* Jus Public Europaeum, trans. G. L. Ulmen (New York: Telos, 2003), 70, 78. See also 67–79 and 236–50 for Schmitt's fuller elaboration of the meanings of *nomos*. In a 2005 issue of the *South Atlantic Quarterly* (104.2) devoted to Schmitt's relevance for the twenty-first century, Carlos A. Otero, in "From the *Nomos* to the Meridian," focuses on the few references to utopia that appear in *The Nomos of Earth*. According to Otero, Schmitt regards utopia as an "extreme danger" because "it takes place as the rupture of the physis-nomos continuity, as the separation of orientation and order. The binding property of the nomos becomes diluted on the one hand by a technical process of accelerated and irreversible delocalization, and on the other by an endless dialogue about the 'ought to be,' a dialogue that is merely rhetoric, tinged by impotence and inconsistencies" (385).

Schmitt's construction would later furnish an important context for Agamben's celebrated naming of the concentration camp as "the new biopolitical *nomos* of the planet" in *Homo Sacer: Sovereign Power and Bare Life* (Stanford, CA: Stanford University Press, 1998; first published in Italian in 1995), 176. In *The Sacred Canopy: Elements of a Sociological Theory of Religion* (New York: Doubleday, 1967), Berger developed a theory of religion and secularization using an idea of *nomos* as a socially generated ordering of experience "internalized" by the individual "in the course of socialization" and "thus appropriated by the individual to become his own subjective ordering of experience" (21). Cover would adapt Berger and others in turn for his celebrated 1983 article "Nomos and Narrative." Building from the premise that we each "inhabit a *nomos*"—"a normative universe" in which "the rules and principles of justice, the formal institutions of the law, and the conventions of a social order" play only a small (if nonetheless important) part—Cover developed a linked set of provocations that has spurred rafts of subsequent scholarship on matters such as law's relation to narrative and conflicts between the norms of a national community and those of communities within the nation (such as self-defined religious minorities). "The Supreme Court, 1982 Term—Foreword: Nomos and Narrative," *Harvard Law Review* 97.1 (1983): 4. Scholars of the rule of law, meanwhile, have used *nomocracy* to refer to government characterized by adherence to law in preference to the discretion of persons, especially in the wake of Oakeshott's deployment of the term in 1975's *On Human Conduct.*

If these writers tended to stress the implication of norms and ordering in *nomos,* others more fully exploited the term's association with distribution or justice. In his "Letter on Humanism" of 1947, Heidegger used *nomos*—as "not only law but more originally the assignment contained in the dispensation of being"—to assert the priority of humans' finding "the way to their abode in the truth of being" over the instituting of rules. Martin Heidegger, *Pathmarks* (Cambridge: Cambridge University Press, 1998), "Letter," trans. Frank A. Capuzzi (274).

In *Difference and Repetition* (1968), Deleuze exploited the double pointing of *nomos* both to law and to pasture or nomadism to conceive of "a completely other distribution which must be called nomadic, a nomad *nomos,* without property, enclosure, or measure" (45–46). This idea of a prelegal *nomos* would reappear in his and Guattari's *A Thousand Plateaus* (1980) and would contribute to their development of the interrelated concepts of nomadism, smooth space, and the rhizome. In his treatment of the gift in *Given Time* (1991), Derrida invoked *nomos* as "the law of distribution (*nemein*), the law of sharing or partition [*partage*]" (6) at the heart of *oikonomia*—the management of the household, but also economy, economics, and circulation—and marked *nomos* as that which, with *logos,* is "sent into crisis by the madness of the gift" (35). Gilles Deleuze, *Difference and Repetition,* trans. Paul Patton (London: Continuum, 2001); Gilles Deleuze and Félix Guattari, *A Thousand Plateaus,* trans. Brian Massumi (Minneapolis: University of Minnesota Press, 1987); Jacques Derrida, *Given Time: I. Counterfeit Money,* trans. Peggy Kamuf (Chicago: University of Chicago Press, 1992).

63. Jacques Rancière, *Dissensus: On Politics and Aesthetics* (London: Continuum, 2010), 36–37.

64. Jacques Rancière, *The Politics of Aesthetics: The Distribution of the Sensible,* trans. Gabriel Rockhill (London: Continuum, 2004), 40.

65. Jean-Luc Nancy, *The Creation of the World; or, Globalization* (Albany: State University of New York Press, 2007), 109–10.

66. Nancy, 112.

67. Of course, it can be argued that even thinking of justice as a rightness impossible to achieve in this world or as a form of indignation that can never be quieted fails to absolve justice of problems that arise if it's associated with adequation at all. In *The Undercommons: Fugitive Planning and Black Study* (Wivenhoe: Minor Compositions, 2013), Stefano Harney and Fred Moten frame a meditation in this line with reference to the appalling trap of consumer credit and debt, especially student debt: "They say we have too much debt. We need better credit, more credit, less spending. They offer us credit repair, credit counseling, micro-credit, personal financial planning" (61), but when credit is restored, we enter a realm of "restorative justice" that's "always the renewed reign of credit, a reign of terror, a hail of obligations to be met, measured, meted, endured. Justice is only possible where debt never obliges, never demands, never equals credit, payment, payback" (63). In *Just Responsibility: A Human Rights Theory of Global Justice* (Oxford: Oxford University Press, 2018), Brooke Ackerly argues that "distributive,

restorative, and reciprocity" notions of justice characterize injustice as a relationship mediated by a particular currency "such as income and wealth or human rights," but "when "the currency and *not* the political relationship among people becomes the site of discussion of injustice, the scope of global justice is incomplete" (78–79).

68. Michael Hornum, *Nemesis, the Roman State, and the Games* (Leiden: E. J. Brill, 1993), 6. Further citations will be given parenthetically in the text.

69. Bernard Williams, *Shame and Necessity* (Berkeley: University of California Press, 2008; first published 1993), 80.

70. The Chicago Homer online, ed. Ahuvia Kahane and Martin Mueller, *Iliad* 3.156–57; *Odyssey* 2.136–37; *Odyssey* 14.284.

71. Richard Seaford, *Money and the Early Greek Mind: Homer, Philosophy, Tragedy* (Cambridge: Cambridge University Press, 2004), 50.

72. The Chicago Homer online, *Odyssey* 6.188–89.

73. Jennifer Larson, *Ancient Greek Cults: A Guide* (New York: Routledge, 2007), 180.

74. The Chicago Homer online, *Works and Days*, 197–201.

75. *Oxford English Dictionary* online, s.v. "nemesis," accessed January 22, 2020.

76. One notable exception here is Philip Roth, who brought *Indignation* and *Nemesis* together as the titles of two short novels (2008 and 2010) in a quartet eventually published under the title *Nemeses* (New York: Library of America, 2013). Later made into a film directed by James Schamus, *Indignation* concerns a Jewish college student's outrage at demands placed on him by his dean as well as the dean's outrage at the behavior of students. *Nemesis* sets a story of (what may or may not be) pursuit by a force of outraged justice amid an imaginary polio epidemic gripping Newark in the summer of 1944. (Polio did sweep through areas of that city in 1916 and 1952, but not 1944.)

77. In response to this caveat (in this study), Matthew Roller observes that we *can* say with assurance that when Greeks of the Classical and Hellenistic period (for whom *nomos* would, in the first instance, mean "statute") read Homer, they could see how semantic clusters around *nomos* and *nemein* were working in that early text—where *nomos* clearly does not mean "law" *tout court*.

78. Thinking of utopia in terms of a *nemesis* that seeks an unrealizable *nomos*, a perfect justice, perhaps helps us understand why Joshua Kotin's formulation of "utopias of one," in his 2018 study of that name, feels paradoxical but not intuitively inadmissible. Kotin takes up writers who respond to failures of political imagination in the real world by, in his telling, constructing works of art that maintain a kind of perfection in denying admission to anyone but the writer (including the reader): "Utopias of one are exclusive—and, in most cases, inimitable." *Utopias of One* (Princeton, NJ: Princeton University Press, 2018), 2. With Nancy in mind, we might say that what makes it possible to consider such a construction in utopian terms is the thought that such a monadic utopia would at least achieve justice for its particular (the author) and thus realize an aspiration that any real-world social configuration would be hard pressed to manage.

Two recent studies, Nathan Waddell's *Modernist Nowheres: Politics and Utopia in Early Modernist Writing, 1900–1920* (Houndmills: Palgrave, 2012) and Anahid Nersessian's *Utopia, Limited: Romanticism and Adjustment* (Cambridge: Harvard University Press, 2015), resemble Kotin's not only in that they focus on utopian dimensions of texts that are not utopias in any traditional sense but also in emphasizing failure or limitation. For Waddell, "utopian desire . . . is a desire that unites a search for a particular (and therefore subjective) view of social justice and happiness with a questioning or rejection of the present which is *so* passionate it leaves unclear the road to a better tomorrow or a reclaimed past" (13). Nersessian discerns a paradigm in writings of or around Romanticism in which "the perfect world" is reconstituted "as a place where grief, loss, suffering, and habits of self-denial . . . become essential to the idea of utopia per se" (2) and in which we're invited to "discover finitude as a mode of utopian longing that can be tender and mild, but also elated, impassioned, even euphoric" (24). In one sense, the positive limitedness these critics describe is closer than Kotin's formulation is to the Nancy-inflected rendering of utopia as impossible justice we've been considering here. Waddell and Nersessian highlight how there may be a tacit element of exuberance (picked up by Nancy) in the consideration of a justice that can be striven for in spite of impossibility. At the same time, however, Nersessian's paradigm seems distant from Nancyan impossible justice insofar as it seems disburdened of *nemesis*, of an urgent sense that the world is blighted in a metaphysically ultimate way.

79. Francis Bacon, *New Atlantis*, in Bruce, *Three Early Modern Utopias*, 182–83; Marge Piercy, *Woman on the Edge of Time* (New York: Fawcett, 1977; first published 1976), 163; Margaret Cavendish, Duchess of Newcastle, *The Description of a New World, Called the Blazing World* (Peterborough, Canada: Broadview, 2016), 65, 146; Norman Rush, *Mating* (New York: Knopf, 1981), 188, 215.

80. B. F. Skinner, *Walden Two* (New York: Macmillan, 1976; first published 1948), 15, 26, 19.

81. Charlotte Perkins Gilman, *Herland, The Yellow Wall-Paper, and Selected Writings* (New York: Penguin, 1999), 64, 68. Further citations will be given parenthetically in the text.

82. Charlotte Perkins Gilman, *Women and Economics* (New York: Harper, 1966), 61.

83. Quoted in Hill and Rasmussen, 260.

84. Nor is this effect limited to technological invention alone. As Alex Zamalin observes in his recent *Black Utopia: The History of an Idea from Black Nationalism to Afrofuturism* (New York: Columbia University Press, 2019), Schuyler's novel also "undermined white supremacist narratives of black *political* passivity," giving "reality to the utopian potential of black power by representing black people as agents in their destiny and racial identity as a source of resistance" (73, emphasis added). We might also note in this context that in "Sultana's Dream," published by Rokeya Sakhawat Hossain in *The Indian Ladies' Magazine* in 1905, the guide who introduces the narrator to a utopia of women anticipates Schuyler not only by exhibiting utopia's use of solar power but also by explaining that it was not by means of arms that male domination was ended but "by brain," women's brains being "somewhat quicker than men's." Rokeya Sakhawat Hossain, *Sultana's Dream and Padmarag*, trans. Barnita Bagchi (New Delhi: Penguin India, 2005), 9.

85. The founding and arrangement of Utopia More describes speaks to Doyne Dawson's argument that the "tradition of utopian planning that Aristotle attempts to summarize in *Politics* 2 was . . . associated with the practical planning activities that always accompanied the foundation of new colonies" around the Mediterranean by Greek settlers. In other words, Dawson argues, "utopianism was a by-product of colonization" (21) that "helped to define the polis and imparted to Greek political life and thought much of their distinctive character" (22). Further, the veneration of Utopus evokes what Dawson calls the "colonial cult of the *oikistes*, the founder of the city," which made "it easy to think of a city as the product of conscious design and the work of a single individual . . . preferably designated by the Delphic oracle. . . . He would mark out the site, divide the land into plots for the settlers, and set aside sacred places for the gods. . . . The need to divide the land as equally as possible promoted regular urban design" (22). Doyne Dawson, *Cities of the Gods: Communist Utopias in Greek Thought* (Oxford: Oxford University Press, 1992).

86. In "Art from Nowhere: The Academy in Utopia" (in *The Age of Projects*, ed. Maximilian Novak [Toronto: University of Toronto Press, 2008]), Albert Boime takes up utopian fictions' concern with "the possibilities of the ideal city. Starting with Thomas More, and his almost four-square city on the hill, Amaurot, utopias have been consistently visualized as symmetrical urban spaces. [Lewis] Mumford's trenchant reading of these spaces as ultimately authoritarian has a compelling logic, though utopian authors pretended to re-enact in the fictive romances an earthly harmony reflective of cosmic order. Notions of the good life were inevitably bound up with the urban environment and the conveniences it provided. In this utopian view, the city also represented the creation of human intelligence as opposed to the rustic or primitive paradise" (223).

87. This deep connection between planning and imputable eccentricity is well emblematized by the ancient figure of Hippodamus of Miletus, who for Bloch highlights in addition the close "contact between architectural and political planning in general" (*Principle* 2:738). In the *Politics*, Aristotle notes that Hippodamus, who "invented the planning of towns in separate quarters, and laid out the Peiraeus with regular roads" was "the first man without practical experience of politics who attempted to handle the theme of the best form of constitution"—and that in his personal life, he "was led into some eccentricity by a desire to attract attention," as by keeping "his hair long and expensively adorned" and wearing "expensively decorated" robes "made from a cheap but warm material . . . in summer time as well as in winter" (68).

88. Jameson does admit, with respect to Imagination and Fancy, that "as with all dualisms, the terms keep swapping places ceaselessly, in an alternation in which . . . what counted as Imagination and overarching form unexpectedly turns into a play of wit and ingenious artifice, while the formerly decorative principle unexpectedly assumes an architectonic function" (54). But this admission seems primarily designed to set the stage for the historically specific reversal with which Jameson's chapter culminates. At the close, Jameson posits that now that capitalism has effaced "beyond any recall but the nostalgic kind that simpler pastoral or village existence on which earlier Utopias were able to draw for their account of utopian daily life," Fancy's task is rendered immeasurably more complex, while Imagination's is simplified. Imagination must now either live with a capitalism that's truly ubiquitous or advocate straightforwardly for its socialist alternative, whereas Fancy "begins tireless[ly] to elaborate schemes by which capitalism is ameliorated or neutralized, or socialism is constructed in the mind" (55).

89. Plato, *Republic*, 161.

90. In the greeting to Peter Giles that precedes *Utopia*, More wonders whether he ought to risk publishing, since "the natures of men be so diverse, the phantasies of some so wayward, their minds so unkind, their judgements so corrupt" that those who follow "their own sensual pleasures and carnal lusts, may seem to be in a much better state" than those who vex themselves with the "publishing of something, that may be either great profit or pleasure to others, which others nevertheless will disdainfully, scornfully, and unkindly accept the same" (8). Additional complaints about unresponsive and ungrateful readerships follow.

91. Joan Thirsk, *Economic Policy and Projects: The Development of a Consumer Society in Early Modern England* (Oxford: Clarendon, 1978), 1, 17.

92. Maximilian Novak, introduction to Novak, *Age of Projects*, 6–7.

93. Quoted in Novak, *Age of Projects*, 1.

94. Novak, *Age of Projects*, 3–4.

95. Kimberly Latta, "'Wandering Ghosts of Trade Whymsies': Projects, Gender, Commerce, and Imagination in the Mind of Daniel Defoe," in Novak, *Age of Projects*, 141. For still more

recent treatments of projectors and the ridicule or suspicion they engendered, see, for example, Jessica Ratcliff, "Art to Cheat the Common-Weale: Inventors, Projectors, and Patentees in English Satire, ca. 1630–1670," *Technology and Culture* 53.2 (2012): 337–65; David Alff, "Swift's Solar Gourds and the Rhetoric of Projection," *Eighteenth-Century Studies* 47.3 (2014): 245–60; Mordechai Feingold, "Projectors and Learned Projects in Early Modern England," *The Seventeenth Century* 32.1 (2017): 63–79; and Koji Yamamoto, *Taming Capitalism before Its Triumph: Public Service, Distrust, and "Projecting" in Early Modern England* (Oxford: Oxford University Press, 2018).

96. Anita McConnell, "Thomas Northmore," *Oxford Dictionary of National Biography* online, https://doi.org/10.1093/ref:odnb/20332.

97. Thomas Northmore, *Memoirs of Planetes*, in Claeys, *Utopias of the British Enlightenment*, 139.

98. Robert Owen, *A New View of Society and Other Writings* (London: Penguin, 1991), 220.

99. Mary E. Bradley Lane, *Mizora: A World of Women* (Lincoln, NE: University of Nebraska Press, 1999), 44, 111.

100. Richard Whiteing, *The Island; or, the Adventures of a Person of Quality* (New York: Century, 1899), 167, 201.

101. Octavia Butler, *Parable of the Talents* (New York: Grand Central, 2000), 177, 177, 179, 138, 309, 405.

102. Ernst Bloch, *The Principle of Hope* (Cambridge: MIT Press, 1995), 1:3. (German: Ernst Bloch, *Das Prinzip Hoffnung* [Frankfurt: Suhrkamp, 1959], 1:1.)

103. Bloch, *Principle*, 1:432. Bloch later notes, however, that if for "thousands of years this hope of the social utopias in particular was passed off as particularly unworldly and much laughed at," things changed with the arrival of Soviet Marxism: when "this sort of thing actually started to begin in a vast country, instead of on a dream island . . . the laughter stopped" (2:582).

104. Bloch, *Principle*, 1:435.

105. Gregory Claeys, *Thomas Paine: Political and Social Thought* (Boston: Unwin Hyman, 1989), 157.

106. Bloch, *Principle*, 1:440.

107. Huxley, *Letters* (New York: Harper and Row, 1969), 351.

108. Mannheim, *Ideology and Utopia*, 233–35.

109. Alexander Pope, *Poetical Works* (London: Oxford University Press, 1966).

110. Nathaniel Hawthorne, *The Blithedale Romance* (New York: Penguin, 1986), 1–2. Further citations will be given parenthetically in the text.

111. A further catalogue of instances of mockery, ridicule, and less pointed raillery in *Blithedale* can be found in James E. Caron, "Comic Laughter in *The Blithedale Romance*: Miles Coverdale and the Idea of the Gentleman Humorist," *Nathaniel Hawthorne Review* 39.2 (2013): 4–35.

112. Many readers of *Blithedale* have pointed out that its characters are drawn the more tightly to each other by forms of amorous and erotic attraction variously admitted and obscured. As Michael Colacurcio observes, in an essay tracing many of these paths of passion, "though all the characters are in the grip of sexual desire, most of them are using it as a way to manipulate other people. Sublimation, as we might think, in its very worst form. And this at a community dedicated to the happy premise that love can teach us to cooperate." "Nobody's Protest Novel: Art and Politics in *The Blithedale Romance*," *Nathaniel Hawthorne Review* 34.1–2 (2008): 26.

Chapter 2. Shaping Utopians

1. Condorcet, *Political Writings* (Cambridge: Cambridge University Press, 2012; *Sketch*, trans. June Barraclough), 140. Further citations will be give parenthetically in the text.

2. Though as Karl Mannheim notes in *Ideology and Utopia* (trans. Louis Wirth and Edward Shils [San Diego: Harvest, n.d.]), Condorcet does at least concede "relative validity to these tentative stages which precede a state of perfection" (223).

3. J. K. Fuz, *Welfare Economics in English Utopias* (The Hague: Martinus Nijhoff, 1952), 3.

4. Fredric Jameson, *Archaeologies of the Future: The Desire Called Utopia and Other Science Fictions* (London: Verso, 2005), 168. Further citations will be given parenthetically in the text.

5. Edward Bellamy, *Looking Backward: 2000–1887* (New York: Signet, 1960), 56. Further citations will be given parenthetically in the text.

6. Quoted in Krishan Kumar, *Utopia and Anti-utopia in Modern Times* (Oxford: Basil Blackwell, 1987), 28.

7. At the close of that novel, the children of Earth set off for the stars, having evolved into beings quite unlike humans have been up to that point.

8. Quoted in Kumar, *Utopia and Anti-utopia*, 29. In his magisterial study, Kumar cites this passage amid a discussion of how the classical utopias, as both H. G. Wells and Judith Shklar noted, were "attacks on the radical theory of original sin." Utopia need not quite hold with Wells that "man, on the whole, is good" (since such a viewpoint, "carried to an extreme, . . . would . . . make utopia redundant," as Kumar observes), but it is essential to utopia that "human nature should be seen as almost infinitely malleable. . . . There should, above all, not be such intrinsic checks and obstacles to human perfectibility as to doom the utopian enterprise from the start" (28).

9. J. C. Davis, "Thomas More's *Utopia*: Sources, Legacy, and Interpretation," in *The Cambridge Companion to Utopian Literature* (Cambridge: Cambridge University Press, 2010), 36.

10. Thomas More, *Utopia*, trans. Ralph Robinson, in *Three Early Modern Utopias*, ed. Susan Bruce (Oxford: Oxford University Press, 1999), 42. Further citations will be given parenthetically in the text.

11. Albert O. Hirschman, *The Passions and the Interests* (Princeton, NJ: Princeton University Press, 2013; originally published 1977), 20.

12. Graham Hammill, *The Mosaic Constitution: Political Ideology from Machiavelli to Milton* (Chicago: University of Chicago Press, 2012), 162.

13. Quoted in Hirschman, *Passions and the Interests*, 22.

14. Francis Bacon, *New Atlantis*, in Bruce, *Three Early Modern Utopias*, 173.

15. Bacon, *New Atlantis*, 175.

16. Anonymous, *The Island of Content; or, A New Paradise Discovered*, in Claeys, *Utopias of the British Enlightenment*, 13–14.

17. Charles Gide, introduction to *Selections from the Work of Fourier*, trans. Julia Franklin (London: Swan Sonnenschein, 1901), 18.

18. Charles Fourier, *Design for Utopia: Selected Writings*, trans. Julia Franklin (New York: Schocken, 1971), 183.

19. Fourier, *Design*, 189. (French: Charles Fourier, *Théorie de l'unité universelle*, vol. 3 [Paris: Societé pour la Propagation et pour la Réalisation de la Théorie de Fourier, 1841], 517.)

20. Latin: Thomas More, *The Utopia of Thomas More* (London: Oxford University Press/ Henry Frowde, 1895), 175.

21. For Žižek in *The Sublime Object of Ideology* (London: Verso, 1989), "they know very well what they are doing, but they are still doing it," a phrase drawn from Peter Sloterdijk (29), aptly represents the character of ideology as distilled in what Žižek calls the "cynical position" (28–35). In 1991's *For They Know Not What They Do: Enjoyment as a Political Factor* (London: Verso), Žižek finds in the essential phrase of disavowal, "I know, but nevertheless" a capturing of "the relationship of knowledge and belief that determines our everyday ideological horizon: the gap between (real) *knowledge* and (symbolic) *belief*" (241).

22. Plato, *The Republic*, 2nd ed., trans. Desmond Lee (London: Penguin, 2007), 98.

23. Robert Burton, *The Anatomy of Melancholy* (New York: New York Review Books, 2001), 83.

24. Rhiannon Evans, *Utopia Antiqua: Readings of the Golden Age and Decline at Rome* (London: Routledge, 2008), 24.

25. This particular leap in time invites a historical clarification: that this study doesn't in fact take the position that there was no utopian thinking in the West between antiquity and More. Many writers, from Winstanley and Wallace to Condorcet and the Bolshevik theoreticians we'll visit in chapter 3, were eminently utopian thinkers in their planning for ideal societies even if they didn't produce utopian fictions as such, and there was clearly utopian thinking in something like this sense in the Middle Ages (though under a stricter definitional regime, it could perhaps be called protoutopian or parautopian). See, for treatments of medieval utopian directions, Rosemary Horrox and Sarah Rees Jones's collection *Pragmatic Utopias: Ideals and Communities, 1200–1630* (Cambridge: Cambridge University Press, 2001) as well as Karma Lochrie's *Nowhere in the Middle Ages* (Philadelphia: University of Pennsylvania Press, 2016).

It bears recalling in particular that there were strong strains of utopianism in some millenarianisms. Indeed as Gregory Claeys helpfully proposes, utopian thought can be regarded as having three phases: "the mythical, the religious, and the positive . . . or institutional," the first two of which "link the afterlife to this life, while the third mostly does not, though it may offer a secular equivalent to salvation." *Searching for Utopia: The History of an Idea* (New York: Thames and Hudson, 2011), 8. In *Ideology and Utopia*, Mannheim proposes that a decisive turning point for utopian thought and social reform came when "'Chiliasm' joined forces with the active demands of the oppressed strata of society"—a union anticipated in the teaching of Joachim of Fiore in the twelfth century and emerging fully with "the Hussites, and then in Thomas Münzer and the Anabaptists" (211–12).

26. Fuz, *Welfare Economics*, 51. (Fuz's phrasing.)

27. Fuz, *Welfare Economics*, 69. (Fuz's phrasing.)

28. James Burgh, *An Account of the First Settlement, Laws, Form of Government, and Police, of the Cessares, A People of South America*, in Claeys, *Utopias of the British Enlightenment*, 109.

29. Thomas Northmore, *Memoirs of the Planetes*, in Claeys, *Utopias of the British Enlightenment*, 180–81.

30. Jean-Jacques Rousseau, *The Major Political Writings*, trans. John T. Scott (Chicago: University of Chicago Press, 2012), 73. (French: Jean-Jacques Rousseau, *Discours sur l'origine et les fondements de l'inégalité parmi les hommes* [Paris: Gallimard, 1969], 73.)

31. Rousseau, *Major Political Writings*, 88.

32. Rousseau, *Major Political Writings*, 88.

33. Jean-Jacques Rousseau, *Emile; or, On Education*, trans. Allan Bloom (New York: Basic Books, 1979), 153.

34. Respecting the enlightenment of recent times, Condorcet writes in the ninth epoch of the *Sketch*, "Nor did men any longer dare to divide humanity into two races, the one fated to rule, the other to obey, the one to deceive, the other to be deceived. They had to recognise that all men have an equal right to be informed on all that concerns them, and that none of the authorities established by men over themselves has the right to hide from them one single truth. These principles, which the noble Sydney paid for with his blood, and on which Locke set the authority of his name, were later developed by Rousseau with greater precision, breadth and energy, and he deserves renown for having established them among the truths that it is no longer permissible to forget or to combat" (93).

35. Turgot is still credited with inspiring later eighteenth-century thinkers to imagine a progressive development of humankind rooted in the accumulation of knowledge. Richard Price and Joseph Priestley, who imagined progress culminating in the Millennium, took the part of the Revolution (as emblem of progress) in the "Revolution Controversy" of the 1790s. Price also published on human perfectibility in sermons and meditations such as *The Evidence for a Future Period of Improvement in the State of Mankind* (1787), while Priestley wrote several histories designed to demonstrate the forward march of humanity. In their massive 1979 survey, *Utopian Thought in the Western World* (Cambridge: Harvard University Press), Frank E. and Fritzie P. Manuel argue that Condorcet marks a milestone in this movement toward optimism about the malleability of character and the perfectibility of human beings by dint of the coherence of his *Sketch*. Where the writings of Turgot, Price, and Priestley "were too sketchy and dispersed ever to become popular," Condorcet's text "was the form in which the eighteenth-century idea of progress was generally assimilated by Western thought" (491).

36. Robert Owen, *Selected Works* (London: William Pickering, 1993), 1:33.

37. Owen, *Works*, 1: 48.

38. Robert P. Sutton, *Communal Utopias and the American Experience: Secular Communities, 1824–2000* (Westport, CT: Praeger, 2004), 3.

39. Owen, *Works*, 1:62.

40. Owen, *Works*, 1:61.

41. Owen, *Works*, 1:70–71.

42. George Bernard Shaw, *Back to Methuselah* (n.p.: BiblioBazaar, 2006): 55–56.

43. Bloch, *Principle of Hope*, 2:558.

44. Owen, *Works*, 1:51.

45. Owen, *Works*, 1:28.

46. Michael R. Katz and William G. Wagner, "Introduction: Chernyshevsky, *What Is to Be Done?*, and the Russian Intelligentsia," in Nikolai Chernyshevsky, *What Is to Be Done?*, trans. Michael R. Katz (Ithaca: Cornell University Press, 1989), 16.

47. Chernyshevsky, *What Is to Be Done?*, 117–18.

48. Chernyshevsky, *What Is to Be Done?*, 169.

49. Chernyshevsky, *What Is to Be Done?*, 190.

50. Karl Marx with Friedrich Engels, *The German Ideology* (Amherst, NY: Prometheus Books), 41, 42.

51. "Man will become immeasurably stronger, wiser and subtler; his body will become more harmonized, his movement more rhythmic, his voice more musical" (Trotsky quoted in Kumar, *Utopia and Anti-utopia*, 64). On the publication history of *The German Ideology*, see Terrell Carver, "*The German Ideology* Never Took Place," *History of Political Thought* 31.1 (2010): 107–27.

52. Something of the same holds true in Morris's *News from Nowhere*, where there seems little systematic effort to build character in an Owenite (let alone Bellamyan) fashion. The implication is rather that with old structures conducing to exploitation swept away, human beings will in a sense fall into the habit of being their best selves—cooperative, merry, and kind. The fundamental reason Morris's version of a socialist utopia doesn't need politics or power structures in the old sense is that a change in the conditions of production has transformed human character from the ground up.

53. Oscar Wilde, *Complete Works* (New York: Perennial Library, 1989), 1089. As noted in the introduction also, less often quoted is the completion of the point: "And when Humanity lands there, it looks out, and seeing a better country, sets sail. Progress is the realisation of Utopias."

54. Wilde, *Complete Works*, 1087–88. Wilde's rejection of punishment evokes not only the prisonless utopia of Morris's *News from Nowhere*—which had been published in *The Commonweal* from January to October 1890 and which, in the words of J. D. Thomas, "was almost certain to have been ready to the hand and thought of Oscar Wilde while he was preparing 'The Soul of Man under Socialism'" (86)—but also numerous scientific and literary challenges, issuing in the decades since Owen, to the idea that a sharp line may be drawn between criminal behavior and actions attributable to mental illness or mental variation. J. D. Thomas, "'The Soul of Man under Socialism': An Essay in Context," *Rice University Studies* 51.1 (1965).

55. Wilde, *Complete Works*, 1080, 1084.

56. Wilde, *Complete Works*, 1100.

57. Wilde, *Complete Works*, 1100–101.

58. Herbert Spencer, *First Principles* (New York: D. Appleton, 1898), 371.

59. B. F. Skinner, *Walden Two* (New York: Macmillan, 1976; first published 1948), v. Further citations will appear parenthetically in the text.

60. B. F. Skinner, *Beyond Freedom and Dignity* (Indianapolis, IN: Hackett, 1971), 184. Further citations will appear parenthetically in the text.

61. In *Utopias of One* (Princeton, NJ: Princeton University Press, 2018), Joshua Kotin remarks that "Pound's poetry . . . unites two utopian traditions. The first presumes that human nature is invariable and benign—and yet under constant threat from convention. . . . The second tradition presumes that consciousness does not govern human action. (Here, behavioral engineering is an important precursor—from behaviorism to urban planning.)" (119). Our tracing of the history of transformative utopias would suggest that Kotin's first tradition (descending from Rousseau most prominently) can in key ways be read as continuous with, rather than opposed to, his second (as manifested in Skinner).

62. Limning the literature of freedom, Skinner briefly mentions Mill, Leibniz, Voltaire, and Rousseau. In treating the literature of liberty, he names Joseph Wood Krutch and T. S. Eliot (32, 37, 37, 40, 66, 66).

63. George Kateb, *Utopia and Its Enemies* (New York: Free Press of Glencoe, 1963), 142. Further citations will be given parenthetically in the text.

64. Aldous Huxley, *Brave New World and Brave New World Revisited* (New York: HarperCollins, 2004), 36. Further citations will be given parenthetically in the text.

65. Kumar, *Utopia and Anti-utopia*, 354–55.

66. George Schuyler, *Black Empire* (Boston: Northeastern University Press, 1991), 47.

67. As Zamalin observes in *Black Utopia*, Belsidus's version of Black power "demands certainty, not ambivalence; closure, not openness; consolidation, not dissolution. This makes stillborn the possibility of popular rule" (74).

68. Jerome Meckier, *Aldous Huxley: From Poet to Mystic* (Zurich: Lit Verlag, 2011), 229.

69. Though in the introduction to a 2006 edition of *We*, Natasha Randall asserts that "Pavlov's experiments" are registered when in the novel "a young cipher is corrected with an electrical whip and yelps 'like a puppy'" (xvii).

70. Yevgeny Zamyatin, *We*, trans. Natasha Randall (New York: Modern Library, 2006), 12–13 (ellipsis Zamyatin's).

71. Zamyatin, *We*, 186, 188.

72. As Phillip E. Wegner, following Zamyatin's biographer Alex Shane, points out, Zamyatin's target was not the revolution itself; on the contrary, "Zamyatin remained until the end of his life committed to the utopian ideals he regarded to be embodied in the Bolshevik revolution." *Imaginary Communities: Utopia, the Nation, and the Spatial Histories of Modernity* (Berkeley: University of California Press, 2002), 149.

73. Hannah Arendt, *The Origins of Totalitarianism* (Orlando: Harvest, 1968), 438.

74. Arendt, *Origins*, 438, 457.

75. Hannah Arendt, *The Human Condition* (Chicago: University of Chicago Press, 1998), 45.

76. Arendt, *Human Condition*, 40.

77. Arendt, *Human Condition*, 322.

78. Arendt, *Human Condition*, 40.

79. Arendt, *Human Condition*, 45.

80. Arendt, *Human Condition*, 45.

81. Kateb observes that "Skinner promises to do, at small cost, what the elite of Aldous Huxley's Brave New World do at infinite cost: make all people *adequate* to their vocation and to all the demands imposed on them by their society" (214).

82. See particularly the ninth chapter of *The Open Society and Its Enemies* (first published in 1945), in which Popper remarks memorably that the "extreme radicalism" of Plato's and Marx's approach to social transfiguration seems "connected with its aestheticism, i.e. with the desire to build a world which is not only a little better and more rational than ours, but which is free from all its ugliness: not a crazy quilt, an old garment badly patched, but an entirely new gown, a really beautiful new world." Karl Popper, *The Open Society and Its Enemies* (Princeton, NJ: Princeton University Press, 2013), 154.

83. In his gripping, polemical study *Heidegger's Children* (Princeton, NJ: Princeton University Press, 2015; first published 2001), Richard Wolin traces Arendt's and Marcuse's rejections of "mass society" and difficulties in articulating "*a meaningful theoretical standpoint in the postwar world*" (8) to Heideggerian investments of which they couldn't or wouldn't divest themselves—including an investment in authenticity. Regarding *The Human Condition*, for example, Wolin remarks that for Arendt "it is not so much the *ends* of politics that matter" but rather that "speaking and acting in public is the means whereby political actors reveal their authenticity" (69).

Wolin meanwhile traces Marcuse's occupation with revolutionary praxis to the view that, as Marcuse himself put it in a 1928 commentary on Heidegger, "The fundamental question of all living philosophy is . . . : *What is authentic existence, and how is it generally possible?*" (144). For an extended and insightful consideration of Marcuse's "attempt to reconcile Marxism and utopia," see Ruth Levitas, *The Concept of Utopia* (Oxford: Peter Lang, 2010; first published 1990 by Philip Allan), 151–78.

84. Herbert Marcuse, *One-Dimensional Man* (Abingdon, UK: Routledge, 2002), 7.

85. In a 2013 interview, Kateb lauds Trilling as "a truly great teacher" whose classes he audited at Columbia (www.scielo.cl/pdf/revcipol/v34n3/art08.pdf). In an interview of two years later, Kateb names as models for his interpretive practice some literary critics he considers "masters . . . guides and inspirations . . . who . . . really know how to interpret ideas and texts, including Edmund Wilson, T. S. Eliot, R. P. Blackmur, and Lionel Trilling." George Kateb, *George Kateb: Dignity, Morality, Individuality* (Abingdon, UK: Routledge, 2015), 216.

86. Lionel Trilling, *Sincerity and Authenticity* (Cambridge: Harvard University Press, 1972), 11.

87. Trilling, *Sincerity and Authenticity*, 125, 132.

88. The one mention of utopia in *Sincerity and Authenticity* is, in this regard, instructive. Late in the book, Trilling explores what seems to him a contradiction within Marcuse's *Eros and Civilization*. On the one hand, Marcuse "foresees that the imperative and coercive nature of the superego . . . will become obsolete" (163), envisions a "destiny of peace, freedom, and pleasure which has been made feasible by the reduction of material necessity and the cultural constraints it entails" (164). Yet at one point in *Eros*, Marcuse's "argument diverges into a startling negation of itself. It suddenly is made plain that the relaxation of moral restrictions which is to be observed in the American culture of 1955" worries Marcuse rather than satisfies because what leads young people to develop valuably individual characters is precisely the struggle against repressive parents. Trilling explains that he hasn't been able to discover in *Eros and Civilization* the "dialectical ingenuity" that would "resolve the contradiction between Marcuse's predilection for the strongly defined character-structure that necessity entails and his polemical commitment to a Utopia which will do away with necessity. . . . The contradiction is allowed to stand, together with the baffling question of how the process of Utopian redemption is to be carried forward on the ground of such psychic changes as Marcuse observed in 1955, which issued in a character-structure and a culture which in his view are as deficient in grace as in authenticity" (167).

89. One such anxiety concerns machines—not only the fear that human beings could be dominated by actual machines but also the more permeating worry that human life and character could become subordinate to some superhuman system. As Trilling writes in *Sincerity and Authenticity*, "The anxiety about the machine is a commonplace in nineteenth-century moral and cultural thought. . . . The mechanical principle, quite as much as the acquisitive principle . . . was felt to be the enemy of being, the source of inauthenticity" (126–27).

90. E. M. Forster, *Selected Stories* (New York: Penguin, 2001), 94, 94, 116. Further citations will be given parenthetically in the text.

91. Robert Graves, *Seven Days in New Crete* (Oxford: Oxford University Press, 1983), 12, 18, 278, 279.

92. Graves, *Seven Days*, 12, 70, 200. Near the close, Venn-Thomas asks himself, "in order to lead what philosophers call 'the good life' without crime or poverty, must people be practically

half-witted?" His answering thought is, "Apparently" (235)—though he adds that he would choose the New Cretans over "American whole-wittedness" and "avoid stomach ulcers, ticker-tape and Sunday best" (236). A similar set of anxieties is articulated in the first part of Arthur C. Clarke's *Childhood's End* (New York: Random House, 2001; first published 1953). There, a group of aliens called Overlords who "have brought security, peace, and prosperity to the world" (11) are challenged by resistant groups such as the Freedom League, which demands "freedom to control our own lives" (11). Meanwhile the gifts of "steadily rising standards of living" and peace for the first time in history are "negative and unspectacular benefits, accepted and soon forgotten" by human beings (22). The novel may thus appear to begin in a familiarly antiutopian register. It soon becomes clear, however, that Clarke's sympathies are by no means with a drive for authenticity that would offhandedly reject the benefits of freedom from war and want.

93. Lois Lowry, *The Giver* (Boston: Houghton Mifflin, 1993), 119.

94. M. T. Anderson, *Feed* (Somerville, MA: Candlewick Press, 2012; first published 2002), 34–35.

95. Octavia Butler, *Parable of the Talents* (New York: Grand Central, 2000), 220.

96. Butler, *Parable of the Talents*, 345.

97. Walter Mosley, *Futureland* (New York: Warner Books, 2001), 34.

98. Mosley, *Futureland*, 319.

99. An undesired version of something approaching, if not quite, virtual experience is imposed by an invention in Marge Piercy's *Woman at the Edge of Time* (New York: Fawcett, 1977; first published 1976). There, inmates of a mental institution (including Connie Ramos, the novel's protagonist) are subjected to a machine that "can electrically trigger almost every mood and emotion—the fight-or-flight reaction, euphoria, calm, pleasure, pain, terror!" (196). This device contributes to the novel's larger effect of making the present we have feel far less authentic, in crucial senses, than the possible utopian future.

100. Quoted in Christopher Grau, "Bad Dreams, Evil Demons, and the Experience Machine: Philosophy and the Matrix," in *Philosophers Explore The Matrix*, ed. Christopher Grau (Oxford: Oxford University Press, 2005), 18.

101. Iakovos Vasiliou, "Reality, What Matters, and *The Matrix*," in Grau, *Philosophers Explore The Matrix*, 112. For the view that Cypher's choice is wrong, see, for instance, Christopher Grau's "Bad Dreams, Evil Demons, and the Experience Machine: Philosophy"; James Pryor's "What's So Bad about Living in the Matrix?"; and Hubert L. Dreyfus and Stephen D. Dreyfus's "Existential Phenomenology and the Brave New World of *The Matrix*"—all of these in *Philosophers Explore The Matrix*. See also Stephen Faller's *Beyond the Matrix: Revolutions and Revelations* (St. Louis, MO: Chalice, 2004); as well as Gerald J. Erion and Barry Smith's "Skepticism, Morality, and *The Matrix*"; Thomas S. Hibbs's "Notes from the Underground: Nihilism and *The Matrix*"; and Jennifer L. McMahon's "Popping a Biter Pill: Existential Authenticity in *The Matrix* and *Nausea*"—all in *The Matrix and Philosophy: Welcome to the Desert of the Real*, edited by William Irwin (Chicago: Open Court, 2002). For the opposing view, see, in addition to Vasiliou, Kevin Warwick's "*The Matrix*—Our Future" in the same volume. As some of these titles might suggest, philosophical debates in this area sometimes replay, in another key, critiques of utopia grounded in the value of authenticity.

102. Philosophical commentaries on *The Matrix* that cite Nozick include, in the Grau collection, Grau's "Bad Dreams," Pryor's "What's So Bad," Vasiliou's "Reality," and Warwick's "*The*

Matrix"; and in the Irwin collection, Erion and Smith's "Skepticism" as well as Theodore Schick Jr.'s "Fate, Freedom, and Foreknowledge."

103. Robert Nozick, *Anarchy, State, and Utopia* (New York: Basic Books, 1974), 42–43.

104. Nozick, *Anarchy*, 43–45.

105. The upper caste, as the Provost of Eton will later explain, originates from a germination ratio of "One egg, one adult" (148).

106. Nathaniel Hawthorne, *The Blithedale Romance* (New York: Penguin, 1986), 149–50.

107. Hawthorne, *Blithedale Romance*, 150.

108. Michael Walzer, *Spheres of Justice: A Defense of Pluralism and Equality* (New York: Basic Books, 1983), 261.

109. See, for example, *Persons, Identity, and Political Theory: A Defense of Rawlsian Political Identity* (Dordrecht, Netherlands: Springer, 2014), where Catherine Galko Campbell stresses that the "original position is a hypothetical decision procedure in which a person who is subject to certain unusual constraints is asked to select the principles she would like to govern her society" (11)—not an elaboration of a metaphysical theory of personhood but "merely a heuristic that makes vivid the sorts of reasons that can legitimately be used when arguing for political principles" (103). In his own defense ("Justice as Fairness: Political Not Metaphysical," 1985), Rawls stresses that the original position is a "device of representation: it describes the parties, each of whom are responsible for the essential interests of a free and equal person, as fairly situated and as reaching an agreement subject to appropriate restrictions on what are to count as good reasons. . . . Justice as fairness seeks to identify the kernel of an overlapping consensus, that is, the shared intuitive ideas which when worked up into a political conception of justice turn out to be sufficient to underwrite a just constitutional regime." Robert C. Solomon and Mark C. Murphy, eds., *What Is Justice? Classic and Contemporary Readings*, ed. (New York: Oxford University Press, 2000), 344.

110. Thomas Aquinas, "From *Summa Theologica*," in Solomon and Murphy, *What Is Justice?*, 51.

111. Aristotle, *Nicomachean Ethics*, trans. Robert C. Bartlett and Susan D. Collins (Chicago: University of Chicago Press, 2011), 164.

112. David Hume, *A Treatise of Human Nature* (London: J. M. Dent, 2003), 276–77 (italics Hume's).

113. John Rawls, *A Theory of Justice* (Cambridge: Harvard University Press, 1971), 126.

114. Michael Sandel, *Liberalism and the Limits of Justice*, 2nd. ed. (Cambridge: Cambridge University Press, 1998; first edition published 1982), 31–32.

115. It can certainly be said that Rawls did not do enough to foreground how the ideal of justice depends upon or derives from a condition of injustice. In a recent essay in the collection *Beyond Cosmopolitanism*, ed. Ananta Kumar Giri (Singapore: Palgrave, 2018), Hauke Brunkhorst introduces a point about human rights regimes with a straightforward dichotomy other commentators have also invoked: "The articulation of the *sense of injustice* (Barrington Moore) always precedes the *sense of justice* (Rawls)" (315). (Brunhkhorst here refers to Moore's 1978 book, *Injustice: The Social Bases of Obedience and Revolt*.)

In a contribution to the collection *Empire, Race and Global Justice*, ed. Duncan Bell (Cambridge: Cambridge University Press, 2019), Charles Mills highlights how the synchronic and abstract cast of the Rawlsian model raises impediments to the claims of rectificatory justice. He observes that bringing race to bear on justice thinking implies a "conceptual shift from distributive to corrective justice, from the distributive norms of a well-ordered society to the rectificatory norms appropriate for an ill-ordered society. . . . If we are directed by Rawls to think of society as 'a cooperative venture for mutual advantage,' whose rules are 'designed to advance the good of those taking part in it,' and never offered any complementary theorization of 'non-cooperative,' oppressive societies (aka, 'the world'), how can systemic structural injustice even be understood, let alone theorized and remedied?" (115).

116. Margaret Cavendish, Duchess of Newcastle, *The Description of a New World, Called the Blazing World* (Peterborough, Canada: Broadview, 2016), 126, 128.

117. A "person's good," Rawls writes in *Theory*, "is determined by what is for him the most rational long-term plan of life given reasonably favorable circumstances. A man is happy when he is more or less successfully in the way of carrying out this plan. To put it briefly, the good is the satisfaction of rational desire" (93). Later in the book, in a more extended discussion of life plans, Rawls makes clear the centrality of the plan to personhood itself: "I adapt Royce's thought that a person may be regarded as a human life lived according to a plan" (408).

118. Sandel, *Liberalism*, 29.

119. Marcel Wissenburg, *Imperfection and Impartiality* (London: UCL Press, 1999), 133.

120. Alexander Kaufman, introduction to *Capabilities Equality: Basic Issues and Problems*, ed. Alexander Kaufman (New York: Routledge, 2006), 2. Nussbaum's list of "Central Human Capabilities" has evolved over time. In 2006, as it appeared in the Kaufman volume, it had ten elements: life; bodily health; bodily integrity; senses, imagination, and thought; emotions; practical reason; affiliation; the ability to live meaningfully with other species; play; and control over one's environment. Martha Nussbaum, "Capabilities as Fundamental Entitlements: Sen and Social Justice," in Alexander Kaufman, ed., *Capabilities Equality: Basic Issues and Problems* (New York: Routledge, 2006), 52. Proponents of capabilities equality are usually understood to have taken their lead from Amartya Sen's influential 1980 article "What Is Equality?," but they may also be seen as falling into a larger tradition of associating justice with human possibility that includes the late nineteenth-century British idealists. For idealists such as T. H. Green and D. G. Ritchie, as David Boucher notes, "the aim of social justice is to remove as far as possible the impediments to" the attainment of "self-realisation," which is to say that "the role of the state is to maximise the conditions in which each citizen can develop or fulfil his or her potential capacities and talents." "British Idealism and the Just Society," in David Boucher and Paul Kelly, eds., *Social Justice: From Hume to Walzer* (London: Routledge, 1998), 84.

Chapter 3. Workers in Motion

1. Ernst Bloch, *The Principle of Hope* (Cambridge: MIT Press, 1995), 2:488.

2. Plato, *The Republic*, 2nd ed., trans. Desmond Lee (London: Penguin, 2007), 137–38.

3. Plato, *Republic*, 56–57, 88–89.

4. Plato, *Republic*, 92.

5. Jacques Rancière, *The Politics of Aesthetics: The Distribution of the Sensible*, trans. Gabriel Rockhill (London: Continuum, 2004), 12–13.

6. Rancière, *Politics*, 42–43, 13.

7. Jacques Rancière, *Dissensus: On Politics and Aesthetics* (London: Continuum, 2010), 36–37. (French: Jacques Rancière, *Aux bords du politique* [Paris: Gallimard, 1968], 240–41.)

8. Rancière, *Dissensus*, 37.

9. Rancière, *Dissensus*, 41.

10. Rancière, *Politics*, 40.

11. Jacques Rancière, *The Nights of Labor: The Workers' Dream in Nineteenth-Century France* (Philadelphia: Temple University Press, 1989), viii.

12. Rancière, *Nights*, viii.

13. Rancière, *Nights*, x.

14. Rancière, *Nights*, vii.

15. Rancière, *Nights*, 19. The pagination of the main text is the same in the later edition, *Proletarian Nights* (London: Verso, 2012).

16. Jonathan E. Hill, quoted in Jason Rudy, *Electric Meters: Victorian Physiological Poetics* (Athens: Ohio University Press, 2009), 69.

17. Thomas Hood, *Selected Poems* (Manchester: Carcanet, 1992), 103–5.

18. Karl Marx with Friedrich Engels, *The German Ideology* (Amherst, NY: Prometheus Books), 53.

19. In *The Postmodern Marx* (University Park: Pennsylvania State University Press, 1998), Carver observes that in Wataru Hiromatsu's edition of *The German Ideology*, part 1 (1974), "the whole passage" forming the first paragraph of the long quotation given above "is in Engels' hand, save for these few words inserted by Marx: 'or a critical critic'; 'criticise after dinner'; 'or critic.'" This suggests to Carver "that Marx, in reviewing and amending Engels' work, inserted these words and phrases humorously in order to send it up. . . . In Marx's view, . . . the hunter and fisherman were Utopian, naive, pre-industrial and an unconscious parody of Fourier by Engels. . . . Marx seems to have been telling Engels that this bucolic Utopia was just the sort of place where the 'critical critics' would be quite at home, because real production has become a folksy pastime and real intellectual effort has become after-dinner criticism. This is entirely consistent with the critical assessment that Marx made elsewhere of Fourier, praising his work for its attack on a class-divided society, but noting that it was Utopian precisely because Fourier did not, indeed could not, incorporate modern industry into his scheme" (106). Kathi Weeks calls attention to Carver's reading in "Utopian Therapy: Work, Nonwork, and the Political Imagination," her contribution to *An American Utopia: Dual Power and the Universal Army*, by Fredric Jameson, ed. Slavoj Žižek (London: Verso, 2016), a volume to which we'll return (259).

20. Thomas More, *Utopia*, trans. Ralph Robinson, in *Three Early Modern Utopias*, ed. Susan Bruce (Oxford: Oxford University Press, 1999), 22–23. Further citations will be given parenthetically in the text.

21. Richard Halpern, *The Poetics of Primitive Accumulation: English Renaissance Culture and the Genealogy of Capital* (Ithaca, NY: Cornell University Press, 1991), 1. In *Capital*, Marx writes that the most important revolutions in the history of primitive accumulation are "those moments when great masses of men are suddenly and forcibly torn from their means of subsistence, and hurled as free and 'unattached' proletarians on the labour market. The expropriation of the agricultural producer, of the peasant, from the soil, is the basis of the whole process. . . . In England alone . . . has [the history of this expropriation] its classic form." Karl Marx, *Capital*, trans. Ernest Untermann (New York: Modern Library, n.d.), 787. Scholars since Marx have offered much more detailed analyses of how capitalism emerged in England; see, for example, Robert Brenner's spotlighting of changes in agricultural leaseholding, which led to the "Brenner

debate" of the 1970s and 1980s and continues to have a presence in studies such as (the Brenne-rian) Spencer Dimmock's *The Origin of Capitalism in England, 1400–1600* (Leiden: Brill, 2014).

22. Halpern, *Poetics*, 155.

23. The second English edition of *Utopia* refers to six hours of work before noon, but Susan Bruce notes that this must be a misprint: the first edition mentions three hours, and the total number of hours worked must be six, since Hythlodaeus goes on to remark generally that the utopians "bestow but six hours in work" (59). Susan Bruce, explanatory notes to *Three Early Modern Utopias*, 222. The original Latin has "tres ante meridiem": Thomas More, *The Utopia of Thomas More* (London: Oxford University Press/Henry Frowde, 1895), 142.

24. "When their harvest day draweth near and is at hand, then the Philarchs, which be the head officers and bailiffs of husbandry, send word to the magistrates of the city what number of harvest men is needful to be sent to them out of the city. The which company of harvest men being ready at the day appointed, almost in one fair day dispatcheth all the harvest work" (52).

25. Latin: More, *Utopia of Thomas More*, 301–3.

26. For Hythlodaeus, according to Halpern, "the problem of excess knows of only one solution, and that is systemic: elimination of private ownership. . . . Utopia installs a rational and equitable distribution of goods, which supplies basic needs and yet avoids invidious accumulation of waste" (160–61). And yet, Halpern adds, the "supplemental logic" of excess emerges "in moments of textual 'excess'—the digression, the whimsical detail, the anecdote—when the rationality of Utopian description loosens its grip a bit" (*Poetics* 175).

27. On the excess of goods, More writes, "But these most wicked and vicious men, when they have by their unsatiable covetousness divided among themselves [*omnia inter se partiuerint*] all those things which would have sufficed all men, yet how far be they from the wealth and felicity of the Utopian commonwealth! . . . I dare be bold to say in the end of that penury [of famine years] so much corn or grain might have been found in the rich men's barns, if they had been searched, as, being divided among them [*quantum si fuisset inter eos distributum*] whom famine and pestilence then consumed, no man at all should have felt that plague and penury" (120–22).

28. J. K. Fuz, *Welfare Economics in English Utopias* (The Hague: Martinus Nijhoff, 1952), 96, 27, 28.

29. J. C. Davis, *Utopia and the Ideal Society* (Cambridge: Cambridge University Press, 1981), 316, 318.

30. Davis, *Utopia*, 202.

31. Robert Appelbaum, *Literature and Utopian Politics in Seventeenth-Century England* (Cambridge: Cambridge University Press, 2002), 166. (Appelbaum's phrasing.)

32. Davis, *Utopia*, 198–99. (Davis's phrasing.)

33. Quoted in Fuz, *Welfare Economics*, 66.

34. Davis, *Utopia*, 303.

35. Appelbaum writes that although *Macaria* "includes provisions for economic well-being, prosperity and full employment are not its main aims." Rather, "the main hope is that those responsible will take control over the administration of the nation, that nothing in this nation will be out of control, nothing left idle or out of order; nothing will be left a wilderness or a waste anymore. All will be of use, and everything of use will be of value" (*Literature and Utopian Politics* 124).

36. James Harrington, *Oceana*, in *Ideal Commonwealths*, rev. ed. (London: Colonial Press, 1901), 344.

37. It's worth noting here that the problem of waste in the sense of waste of productive land figured strongly in debates on enclosure. In *Making Waste: Leftovers and the Eighteenth-Century Imagination* (Princeton, NJ: Princeton University Press, 2010), Sophie Gee notes that pamphleteers in these debates changed "waste" from "a term that described a specific geography to a pejorative word that made commonly held land look valueless" (49). But this on both sides of the question: "even when major radical figures such as Gerard Winstanley opposed enclosure, they too made use of the term 'waste' to argue for improvement—in Winstanley's case, to claim the land on which the Diggers would establish their agrarian commune" (48).

38. Harrington, *Oceana*, 238, 393.

39. Quoted in Davis, *Utopia*, 205; see also Appelbaum, *Literature and Utopian Politics*, 186.

40. Davis, *Utopia*, 208–9.

41. "This will be a happy age for the human race," he writes, for example, in his *Esquisse du nouveau système politique*, published in his journal *L'Organisateur* in 1819, "when the functions of rulers will be reduced until they are no more than supervisors in colleges. . . . The scientists, artists, and artisans should direct the nation's work; the rulers should be concerned only with ensuring that the work is not hindered" (200).

42. Henri de Saint-Simon, *Selected Writings on Science, Industry, and Social Organization* (New York: Holmes and Meier 1975), 209.

43. Saint-Simon, *Selected Writings*, 209.

44. Saint-Simon, *Selected Writings*, 209.

45. Saint-Simon, *Selected Writings*, 214, 233.

46. In her introduction to *The Political Thought of Saint-Simon* (London: Oxford University Press, 1976), Ghita Ionescu summarizes some of the history of the question of whether "the basic division of labour between manual and non-manual work, or between what we now call blue-collar workers and white-collar workers, perpetuates itself in" Saint-Simon's "industrial society." In "socialist" interpretations of Saint-Simon, she notes, "the division of labour between the two orders is seen to melt in the process of the unification of all kinds of labour in the all-embracing category of producers, workers or industrialists," while in a countervailing "techno-cratic" interpretation, which tends to be "founded mainly on Saint-Simon's early works," this division of labor "constitutes the fundamental difference between those who rule by virtue of their position, and those who, also by virtue of their position, will always be ruled" (32).

47. Quoted in Jonathan Beecher and Richard Bienvenu, introduction to Charles Fourier, *The Utopian Vision of Charles Fourier: Selected Texts on Work, Love, and Passionate Attraction*, trans. Jonathan Beecher and Richard Bienvenu (Boston: Beacon, 1971), 47.

48. Charles Fourier, *Design for Utopia: Selected Writings*, trans. Julia Franklin (New York: Schocken, 1971), 134, 164. The same text finds Fourier marking the importance of full employment. One of the "evils of individual action in industry" is the "*intermission of industry*: lack of work, land, machinery, implements, workshops, and other gaps which constantly paralyse civilised industry"; but "these impediments are unknown in the associative *régime*" he has conceived, "which is always and abundantly provided with everything that is necessary for the perfection and the continuity of labour" (121–22).

49. Fourier, *Utopian Vision of Charles Fourier*, 253.

50. In the fourth essay in his *New View of Society* of 1813–16, Owen presses for legislation mandating the obtaining of "regular and accurate information relative to the value of and demand for labour over the United Kingdoms"; the act he imagines would mandate quarterly reports giving, for "each country or smaller district," the average price of manual labor; the number of those depending on daily work who, though "able to labour," are not employed; and the number of those who are partly employed and the extent of that employment. Robert Owen, *Selected Works* (London: William Pickering, 1993), 1:94.

51. The reality on the ground of Fourierist communities was perhaps never at the level of Fourier's intricacies, but happiness in work could be had nonetheless. In a historical treatment of the longest surviving Fourierist Association, the North American Phalanx (New Jersey, 1840s), Norma Lippincott Swan observes that there "seems to have been an atmosphere of joy among the workers at the Phalanx," notwithstanding one member's recollection that regarding the question of how authority was to be distributed, "It would scarcely be an exaggeration to say that our days were spent in labor and our nights in legislation for the first five years." The workers at the Phalanx were indeed "divided according to Fourier's plan into series with a chief at the head, and each series was divided into groups with a head for each group." There was an Agriculture Series, a Domestic Series, a Manufacturing Series, a Live Stock Series; and "the Festal Series had charge of music, dancing and dramatics" (259).

52. Edward Bellamy, *Looking Backward: 2000–1887* (New York: Signet, 1960), 96. Further citations will be given parenthetically in the text.

53. Bellamy's use of "men" is unfortunately apt as a designation for the generality in his utopia: women also serve in the industrial army but are under an "entirely different discipline" and "constitute rather an allied force than an integral part of the army of the men" (173). Even as Bellamy insists that women were "more than any other class the victims" of nineteenth-century civilization (174), his constructions remain paternalistic. Of the separate women's work force, Leete explains, "In your day there was no career for women except in an unnatural rivalry with men. We have given them a world of their own, with its emulations, ambitions, and careers, and I assure you they are very happy in it" (174). Moreover, the "higher positions in the feminine army of industry are entrusted only to women who have been both wives and mothers, as they alone fully represent their sex" (175).

54. William Morris, *News from Nowhere and Other Writings* (London: Penguin, 1993), 50–52.

55. Morris, *News from Nowhere*, 99–100.

56. H. G. Wells, *A Modern Utopia* (London: Penguin, 2005), 104–05. Further citations will be given parenthetically in the text.

57. Wells goes on to say that the "old fixity" taken for granted by More "was of necessity and not of choice. . . . Men may settle down in our modern Utopia for love and the family at last, but first and most abundantly they will see the world" (Wells, *Modern Utopia*, 39). For Wells, freedom of movement is the crowning glory of the modern Utopia—at least for "men." Wells leaves unclear whether his deployment of the term here encompasses both genders, though his associating of settling down with "love and the family" hints that it may not.

58. Charlotte Perkins Gilman, *Herland, The Yellow Wall-Paper, and Selected Writings* (New York: Penguin, 1999), 97.

59. As John Torpey notes in *The Invention of the Passport: Surveillance, Citizenship, and the State* (Cambridge: Cambridge University Press, 2000), "passport controls were reintroduced

across the continent" of Europe during the First World War, then for various reasons remained in place after war's end (111). As the "re" in Torpey's "reintroduced" indicates, however, the modern passport regime was by no means unprecedented. Prior to the nineteenth century, there were many places and situations in which travel required approval from some authority (thus the need for permission in More's Utopia), and the later nineteenth century, as Torpey notes, saw governments becoming "increasingly oriented to making distinctions between their own citizens/ subjects and others, a distinction that could be made only on the basis of documents" (93).

60. Richard Stites, "Fantasy and Revolution: Alexander Bogdanov and the Origins of Bolshevik Science Fiction," in *Red Star*, by Alexander Bogdanov, trans. Charles Rougle (Bloomington: Indiana University Press, 1984), 1.

61. Stites, "Fantasy and Revolution," 13.

62. Stites, "Fantasy and Revolution," 13.

63. Loren R. Graham and Richard Stites, preface to Bogdanov, *Red Star*, ix.

64. Phillip E. Wegner, *Imaginary Communities: Utopia, the Nation, and the Spatial Histories of Modernity* (Berkeley: University of California Press, 2002), 100–101.

65. Graham and Stites, *Red Star*, ix.

66. Mark B. Adams, "'Red Star': Another Look at Aleksandr Bogdanov" *Slavic Review* 48.1 (1989), 4. Stites adds that in 1897–98, at the time of the appearance of *The War of the Worlds*, Wells enjoyed "enormous popularity in Russia" and that Bogdanov may have drawn on Wells, Kurd Lasswitz, Percy Greg, and native Russian utopian science fiction. From about 1890 to 1917, "at least twenty Russian tales of utopian societies, fantastic voyages, and interstellar space travel" were published, some of them drawing on nineteenth-century utopian works by Vladimir Odoevsky, Chernyshevsky, and Vladimir Taneev. Moreover, a "whole series of European and American utopias appeared in Russian translation between 1890 and 1905: the works of August Bebel, Friedrich Engels, Karl Kautsky, Atlanticus, and Lili Braun, with their exaltation of electricity, communal apartment living, and the technologizing of everyday life, captured the imagination of Russian socialists who were looking for the ultimate purpose of revolution to inspire themselves and their followers" (4). In the 1920s, about two hundred works of "revolutionary science fiction," most dealing with "capitalist hells" and "communist heavens," saw print (14). Zamyatin's *We*, published in 1920, was "an emphatic repudiation of Bogdanov's utopia" (14).

67. Bogdanov (as Alexander Bogdanov), *Red Star*, 65. Further citations will be given parenthetically in the text.

68. Menni does hint, in passing, that native endowments may be a limiting factor in choice of occupation: "Assuming that an individual has the same or an approximately equal aptitude for two vocations, he can then choose the one with the greater shortage" (66). But the overall thrust is that liberty in choice of work is unencumbered.

69. Fredric Jameson, *Archaeologies of the Future: The Desire Called Utopia and Other Science Fictions* (London: Verso, 2005), 162. Further citations will be given parenthetically in the text.

70. Aleksandr Bogdanov (as A. Bogdanoff), *A Short Course of Economic Science*, 2nd ed. (London: Communist Party of Great Britain, 1927), 465.

71. Bogdanov, *Short Course*, 466.

72. Bogdanov, *Short Course*, 466.

73. Bogdanov, *Short Course*, 472.

74. Robert Service, introduction to V. I. Lenin, *The State and Revolution*, trans. Robert Service (London: Penguin, 1992), xli.

75. Nikolai Bukharin and Yevgeni Preobrazhensky (as N. Buharin and E. Preobrazhensky), *The ABC of Communism*, trans. Eden and Cedar Paul (n.p.: Communist Party of Great Britain, 1922), 74–75.

76. Lenin, *The State and Revolution*, 40.

77. Fredric Jameson, "An American Utopia," in *An American Utopia*, 15. Further citations will be given parenthetically in the text. Jameson ultimately withdraws the suggestion, however, on the grounds that "information technology now stands as an absolute historical break with whatever utopias might have been imagined on the basis of this uniquely relational system, . . . which Lenin, in *State and Revolution*, took as the Paris Commune's lesson for communism itself" (15).

78. Lenin, *State and Revolution*, 106.

79. Bukharin and Preobrazhensky, *ABC of Communism*, 71–72.

80. Friedrich Engels, *Anti-Dühring* (Moscow: Foreign Languages Publishing House, 1954), 389, 358.

81. Lenin, *State and Revolution*, 17, 86–87.

82. Lenin, *State and Revolution*, 74.

83. Lenin, *State and Revolution*, 80.

84. In a perceptive essay, Owen Holland observes that Wells's problem with human entanglements in *A Modern Utopia* recalls the uncomfortably adhesive web of connection in Hawthorne's Blithedale and the trammels of amorous relationship that persist in Morris's future England. Wells's description of the botanist as a "type" liable to "get into mighty tangles and troubles with women," Holland observes, "recalls the knotty complications of *The Blithedale Romance* as well as the love triangle formed by Dick, Clara, and an unnamed third man in [*News from*] *Nowhere*." "Spectatorship and Entanglement in Thoreau, Hawthorne, Morris, and Wells," *Utopian Studies* 27.1 (2016): 41–42.

85. Lenin, *Anti-Dühring*, 99.

86. Joel Nickels, *The Poetry of the Possible: Spontaneity, Modernism, and the Multitude* (Minneapolis: University of Minnesota Press, 2012), 157–58.

87. Nickels, *Poetry*, 159–60.

88. Seymour Melman, *After Capitalism: From Managerialism to Workplace Democracy* (New York: Knopf, 2001), 26.

89. Service, introduction to Lenin, *State and Revolution*, xxxix

90. Service, introduction to Lenin, *State and Revolution*, xxxix.

91. Anna Feldman Leibovich, *The Russian Concept of Work: Suffering, Drama, and Tradition in Pre- and Post-revolutionary Russia* (Westport, CT: Praeger, 1995), 87.

92. Leibovich, *Russian Concept of Work*, 90.

93. Richard Day, introduction to N. L. Bukharin, *Selected Writings on the State and the Transition to Socialism*, ed. Richard Day (Armonk, NY: M. E. Sharpe, 1982), xli. Susan Buck-Morss offers a fine overview of these matters in relation to the Soviet state's fashioning of internal ideological enemies in her *Dreamworld and Catastrophe: The Passing of Mass Utopia in East and West* (Cambridge, MA: MIT Press, 2000). "Truly dangerous to the legitimacy of Bolshevik Party sovereignty in the early years," she notes, "was resistance within the working class and revolutionary movements themselves" (5); the "degree to which the workers themselves could be relied upon by the party became a divisive issue" (26–27). In the 1920s, the rationale "for the extension of state institutions that would be answerable to the party at the top level" was that "since the party was political, the state did not have to be" (28).

94. Arvid Brodersen, *The Soviet Worker: Labor and Government in Soviet Society* (New York: Random House, 1966), 59, 39. *Engineer Menni*—a kind of prequel to *Red Star* that Bogdanov published in 1913—is prescient about tensions between the central administration and unions; it includes moments when Martian workers are "subdued by the military, their unions . . . disbanded, and their leaders . . . arrested" (Bogdanov, *Red Star*, 177) as well as episodes of falling wages, longer work days, mandated job transfer, and strikes (Bogdanov, *Red Star*, 179, 183). There's even a "Central Project Administration" that requires reform, under the hand of the novel's eponymous hero, so that it can once again become "simply a bureau for the collection and further dissemination of information" (193).

95. Brodersen, *Soviet Worker*, 74–75.

96. Donald Filtzer, *Soviet Workers and Late Stalinism: Labour and the Restoration of the Stalinist System after World War II* (Cambridge: Cambridge University Press, 2007), 160–61.

97. Filtzer, *Soviet Workers*, 161.

98. Filtzer, *Soviet Workers*, 8.

99. Filtzer, *Soviet Workers*, 9.

100. As has been much noted, one way to describe this result in the Bolshevik theoreticians' own terms would be to say that centralization here failed to resist the fall into bureaucracy. As Melman observes, the Communist Party, "notably upon Stalin's installation as its Secretary, became an organization predominantly of bureaucrats, a *Nomenklatura*" (26).

101. In *Red Star*, Wegner writes, "money, compulsory work, and artificial limits on personal consumption have been eliminated. Prefiguring the syndicalist PDC of Ursula K. Le Guin's *The Dispossessed*, Bogdanov pictures a centralized Institute of Statistics that maintains planetwide industrial production, guarding against any surplus or shortage of goods by monitoring output and directing the voluntary labor force to the areas where their skills are most urgently needed" (*Imaginary*, 104).

102. Ursula K. Le Guin, *The Dispossessed*, (New York: Perennial Classics, 2003), 267–68. Further citations will be given parenthetically in the text.

103. The future utopians in Marge Piercy's *Woman on the Edge of Time* (New York: Fawcett, 1977; first published 1976) describe a similar way of dealing with idleness. To the visitor Connie's question, "Suppose I just don't want to get up in the morning," the guide Luciente answers, "Then I must do your work on top my own if I'm in your base. . . . I'll come to mind that. Who wants to be resented? Such people are asked to leave and they may wander from village to village sourer and more self-pitying as they go. Sometimes a healer . . . can help" (93).

104. A similar, though more temporally bounded, subordination to work assignments prevails in the women's utopia of Joanna Russ's *The Female Man*, first published the year after *The Dispossessed*. "At seventeen," Whileawayans "are assimilated into the labor force. This is probably the worst time in a Whileawayan's life. Groups of friends are kept together if the members request it and if it is possible, but otherwise these adolescents go where they're needed, not where they wish." *The Female Man* (Boston: Beacon, 1986; first published 1975), 51.

105. Tony Burns thus well characterizes the "main theme" of *The Dispossessed* as "the moral dilemmas generated by the workings of the utopian impulse in politics" (129). *Political Theory, Science Fiction, and Utopian Literature: Ursula K. Le Guin and The Dispossessed* (Lanham, MD: Lexington Books, 2008).

106. Near the close of his discussion of Le Guin in *Imaginary Communities*, Wegner observes that "Zamyatin's and Le Guin's moments" witnessed "the transformation of the Bolshevik

revolution into a national-state bureaucratic project of modernization and the defeat of the radical political forces of the 1960s" (182). Wegner's point is surely to associate the Bolshevik transformation with Zamyatin and the 1960s defeat with Le Guin; the view presented here, again, is that the former historical event is enormously at play in *The Dispossessed* as well. On this point, it bears noting that Le Guin presents unflattering depictions of states resembling communist-authoritarian ones elsewhere in her fiction. In *The Left Hand of Darkness* (New York: Ace, 2000; first published 1969), for example, Orgoreyn—where all "are employees of the state" and the state must, at least theoretically, "find employment for all citizens" (118)—is highly administered and profoundly terrifying.

Urras itself, it must be added, is divided into several nations. In Peter Stillman's words, it "closely resembles our earth in 1974: a consumer capitalist society, A-Io, opposed to a state communist society, Thu, fighting ideological wars on Third World countries like Benbili." "The Dispossessed as Ecological Political Theory," in *The New Utopian Politics of Ursula K. Le Guin's The Dispossessed*, ed. Laurence Davis and Peter Stillman (Lanham, MD: Lexington Books, 2005), 67. See on this also, in the same collection, Chris Ferns, "Future Conditioned or Future Perfect? *The Dispossessed* and Permanent Revolution," 249. As many critics have noted, Le Guin's political allegories rarely settle into a one-to-one correspondence with those of twentieth-century Earth. Some aspects of Soviet history are registered in Thu, others in Anarres.

107. In *Archaeologies*, Jameson observes aptly that "anti-Utopian fears and anxieties will vary according to the forms of state power with which this or that historical society is confronted. . . . Bureaucracy is subject to much the same fluctuation in value: and the heroic moments of impersonal state service, the great literacy campaigns of *instituteurs*, the expansion of welfare programs and social workers let alone of committed revolutionary cadres, remind us that this stigmatized dimension of the state does not always have to be the object of generalized hostility" (195). Jameson makes a similar point in *An American Utopia* (316).

108. Bernard Williams nicely captures unfreedom's embedding in domination by others in *Shame and Necessity* (Berkeley: University of California Press, 2008; first published 1993): "[I]t is quite reasonable to say that the sailors acted freely in throwing the goods overboard, even though they were forced to do it by the weather, but it would be a great paradox to say that someone acted freely if forced to surrender his goods in a holdup. . . . To lack freedom is paradigmatically not simply to be short of choices, but to be subject to the will of another" (153–54). In "Shipwreck," the middle play of his *Coast of Utopia* trilogy (New York: Grove, 2007; first published 2002), Tom Stoppard's stage version of the agrarian socialist Alexander Herzen remarks, to the stage version of the historian Timothy Granovsky, "Where are we off to? Who's got the map? We study the ideal societies . . . power to the experts, to the workers, to the philosophers . . . property is a right, property is theft, the evil of competition, the evil of monopoly . . . central planning, no planning, free housing, free love . . . and each of them uniquely harmonious, just and efficient. But there's one question none of the maps explain: why should anyone obey anyone else?" (142–43, ellipses in original).

109. Russell Jacoby, *Picture Imperfect: Utopian Thought for an Anti-utopian Age* (New York: Columbia University Press, 2005), xiv.

110. Brian Z. Tamanaha, *On the Rule of Law: History, Politics, Theory* (Cambridge: Cambridge University Press, 2004), 122.

111. Harrington, *Oceana*, 183.

112. In *Valences of the Dialectic* (London: Verso, 2009), Jameson avers that "the last gasp of a properly Utopian vision . . . was a rather perverse one": "so-called free-market fundamentalism," which, "drawing on the unconscious operations of Adam Smith's invisible hand, . . . gambled everything on the unintentionality of its universal panacea" (412).

113. Surveys of uses of *neoliberalism* within literary scholarship routinely note this tension between the usefulness of the term and its pitfalls. See, for example, introductions to special issues of *Social Text* ("Genres of Neoliberalism," ed. Jane Elliott and Gillian Harkins: 31.2 [2013]); *Textual Practice* ("Neoliberalism and the Novel," ed. Emily Johansen and Alissa G. Karl: 29.2 [2014]); *Studies in 20th & 21st Century Literature* ("Neoliberalism and the Undoing of Time," ed. Necia Chronister and Lutz Koepnick: 40.2 [2016]); and *The Journal of Popular Culture* ("Neoliberalism and Popular Culture," ed. Michael J. Blouin: 51.2 [2018]). In a superb 2017 review of uses of *neoliberalism*, Leigh Claire La Berge and Quinn Slobodian note that invisible-hand thinking was not in any uncomplicated way foundational to the economic theories credited with grounding neoliberal positions. While F. A. Hayek was a great believer in the ultimate power of systems (as against individuals), his message and that of associated economists "was that, under the interconnected conditions of mass democracy, anti-imperial nationalism, and demands for social redistribution, the market would *not* take care of itself" (606). "Reading for Neoliberalism, Reading like Neoliberals," *American Literary History* 29.3 (2017).

114. Andrei Platonov (as Andrey Platonov), *The Foundation Pit*, trans. Mirra Ginsburg (Evanston, IL: Northwestern University Press, 1994), 3. Further citations will be given parenthetically in the text.

115. It's important to note here that the 1960s and 1970s are widely seen as, in Phillip Wegner's words, the moment of "a 're-birth' within science fiction of the utopian narrative form that had largely been in abeyance in the years following the publication of *Nineteen Eighty-Four*" (Philip Wegner, *Shockwaves of Possibility: Essays on Science Fiction, Globalization, and Utopia* [Bern: Peter Lang, 2014], 32). Where for Jameson the ecological and feminist utopias represent traditional utopias' last act, many other critics have regarded them as the dawn of something crucially new. In *Demand the Impossible: Science Fiction and the Utopian Imagination* (New York: Methuen, 1986), Tom Moylan sees Joanna Russ's *The Female Man* (1975) and Marge Piercy's *Woman on the Edge of Time* (1976), along with *The Dispossessed* and Samuel Delany's *Trouble on Triton* (1976), as opening up the genre of "critical utopias," which "negated the negation of utopia by the forces of twentieth century history" and, aware "of the limitations of the utopian tradition, . . . reject utopia as blueprint while preserving it as dream" (10; also reissue edition, xv). Or as Moylan would reframe the point for the 2014 reissue of *Demand* (Bern: Peter Lang, 2014), the critical utopia of the 1970s "is a formal/epistemological expression that *restores* the importance of the system utopia, but does so in a self-critical way" (xix). In the first part of *Scraps of the Untainted Sky: Science Fiction, Utopia, Dystopia* (Boulder, CO: Westview, 2000), Moylan offers a detailed history of how utopian science fiction has been read since the late 1960s and early 1970s, when "scholarly work in sf and utopian studies (along with utopian sf itself) developed in opposition to the reigning orthodoxies of academic literary studies" (9).

116. Robert Nozick, *Anarchy, State, and Utopia* (New York: Basic Books, 1974), 298. Further citations will be given parenthetically in the text.

117. The other is the abolition of taxes; instead of paying taxes, all citizens contribute labor (Jameson, *Archaeologies*, 220). It bears adding that emigration is politically crucial in Friedman's

utopian network not just because it enables one to choose one's community but also because it constitutes a kind of right of refusal of the political structure one leaves behind. A rule of Friedman's utopian communities is that they must be small enough and egalitarian enough to permit anyone's proposals for change to the structure to have a hearing. But either of two results may ensue for the proposer of an initiative: "Il y a, pour lui, deux seules éventualités: soit convaincre les autres et gagner leur consentement, soit émigrer, autrement dit quitter la groupe" (For him only two outcomes are possible: either convincing others and winning their consent, or emigrating, in other words, leaving the group). And thus "la migration sociale représente une sorte de grève á perpétuité, puisqu'un individu qui quitte un groupe en modifie la structure. . . . La migration représente une sorte de *grève civile*, défense de l'individu contre l'injustice sociale" (social migration represents a kind of endless strike, since an individual who leaves a group modifies its structure. . . . Migration represents a kind of *civil strike*, the individual's defense against social injustice). Yona Friedman, *Utopies Réalisables* (Les Coiffards: L'Éclat, 2000), 217–18.

118. Jameson notes that Friedman's second fundamental mechanism, the abolition of taxes in favor of contributed labor, "removes the medium whereby capital is accumulated" (220).

119. Northrop Frye, "Varieties of Literary Utopias," *Daedalus* 94.2 (1965): 326.

120. Doyne Dawson, *Cities of the Gods: Communist Utopias in Greek Thought* (Oxford: Oxford University Press, 1992), 23, 21.

121. Bloch, *Principle of Hope*, 2:491–93.

122. Robert Owen, *A New View of Society and Other Writings* (London: Penguin, 1991), 371–72.

123. Wegner, *Imaginary*, 112.

124. B. F. Skinner, *Walden Two* (New York: Macmillan, 1976; first published 1948), 214.

125. Patrick Hayden and Chamsy el-Ojeili, introduction to *Globalization and Utopia: Critical Essays*, ed. Patrick Hayden and Chamsy el-Ojeili (Houndmills: Palgrave, 2009), 6–8.

126. Samuel R. Delany, "On *Triton* and Other Matters: An Interview with Samuel R. Delany," *Science Fiction Studies* 17.3 (1990): 300–301.

127. Samuel R. Delany, *Trouble on Triton: An Ambiguous Heterotopia* (Middletown, CT: Wesleyan University Press, 1996), 104.

128. Delany, *Trouble on Triton*, 277.

129. This aspect of the novel would prove in a small way prophetic. Delany closes *Trouble on Triton* by recording the time and place of writing as "—*London, Nov '73/July '74.*" But he returned to New York City in summer 1975—just ahead of the city's fiscal crisis, one of the decade's major illuminations of the precarity that would become an increasingly visible feature of the US employment landscape in ensuing decades.

130. Chang-Rae Lee, *On Such a Full Sea* (New York: Riverhead, 2014), 2. Further citations will be given parenthetically in the text.

131. A version of such a service community is described, but not actually visited, in Butler's *Parable of the Sower*, and communities built to serve corporations or the rich are rife in the dystopian fiction of recent decades. See also, for example, Lauren Beukes's 2008 novel, *Moxyland*, and some passing notes in Walter Mosley's 2001 *Futureland* (New York: Warner Books, 2001): "By 2010 Vietnam was divided into twelve highly developed corporate micro-states that produced technical and biological hardware for various Euro-corps" (19); "Claw-Cybertech Angola has annexed Luxembourg, making that business-state the first Afro-European nation" (324).

132. In "The Real Ghosts in the Machine: Afrofuturism and the Haunting of Racial Space in *I, Robot* and *DETROPIA*," in *Afrofuturism 2.0: The Rise of Astro-Blackness,* ed. Reynaldo Anderson and Charles E. Jones (Lanham, MD: Lexington Books, 2016), Ricardo Guthrie notes that the 2012 documentary *DETROPIA* "examines the very real possibility that business and political leaders might resurrect the city [of Detroit] by purging it of black residents—under the guise of eliminating abandoned housing and combating crime" (54). B-mor is not entirely purged of Black residents, but it is nearly so, which is to say that it's an antiutopia for reasons in addition to its treatment of its Chinese-descended inhabitants.

133. Nalo Hopkinson, *Midnight Robber* (New York: Grand Central, 2000), 2. Jonkanoo Season on Toussaint, we learn a few pages later, is "the year-end time when all of Toussaint would celebrate the landing of the Marryshow Corporation nation ships that had brought their ancestors to this planet two centuries before. . . . Time to remember the way their forefathers had toiled and sweated together: Taino Carib and Arawak; African; Asian; Indian; even the Euro, though some wasn't too happy to acknowledge that-there bloodline" (18). Eric D. Smith compares Toussaint "to the international labor space known as the free zone. . . . The free zones (or 'EFZs') are spatially demarcated labor spaces, which the World Bank defines as 'fenced-in industrial estates specializing in manufacturing for exports that offer firms free trade conditions and a liberal regulatory environment'" (59).

134. Huw L. Williams and Carl Death, *Global Justice: The Basics* (London: Routledge, 2016), 4, 147.

135. Williams and Death draw on this article for their overview of "global justice," quoted above.

136. Gillian Brock, "Global Justice," *Stanford Encyclopedia of Philosophy* online, 2015, https://plato.stanford.edu/entries/justice-global/#WhaTheGloJus.

137. John Rawls, *A Theory of Justice* (Cambridge: Harvard University Press, 1971), 137. Further citations will be given parenthetically in the text.

138. Another key stimulus to discussion of the moral obligations of rich nations, though not one that built on Rawls, was Peter Singer's "Famine, Affluence, and Morality" (1972), which in their introduction to *Global Justice: Critical Perspectives* (New Delhi: Routledge, 2012), Sebastiano Maffetone and Aakash Singh Rathore call the inaugural paper of the global justice debate (2). Writing in the shadow of famine in East Bengal, Singer argued that "if it is in our power to prevent something bad from happening, without thereby sacrificing anything of comparable moral importance, we ought, morally, to do it" (17) and that this principle takes "no count of proximity and distance. It make no moral difference whether the person I can help is a neighbour's child ten yards from me or a Bengali whose name I shall never know, ten thousand miles away" (17). This implies further that the "traditional distinction between duty and charity cannot be drawn, or at least, not in the place we normally draw it" (20), and thus that private as well as governmental contributions to the developing world are morally required of affluent nations and their citizens.

139. Brian Barry, *The Liberal Theory of Justice: A Critical Examination of the Principal Doctrines in* A Theory of Justice *by John Rawls* (Oxford: Clarendon Press, 1973), 129.

140. Charles Beitz, *Political Theory and International Relations* (Princeton, NJ: Princeton University Press, 1979), 137, 140. Richard Vernon summarizes a widely shared view in writing, "When Charles Beitz published *Political Theory and International Relations* in 1979, it stood virtually alone as a normative account of our duties beyond our political borders. By now, however,

the literature is immense"; see Vernon, *Cosmopolitan Regard: Political Membership and Global Justice* (Cambridge: Cambridge University Press, 2010), 1. Beitz describes his project as an effort to "lay the groundwork" for a "normative theory of international relations" (6) by showing how a "suitable principle" of "international distributive justice" can be "justified by analogy with" Rawls's "justification . . . for the intrastate distributive principle" (8).

141. Beitz, *Political Theory*, 149–50.

142. Thomas Pogge, *Realizing Rawls* (Ithaca, NY: Cornell University Press, 1989), 11, 277.

143. Thomas Pogge, "Cosmopolitanism and Sovereignty," *Ethics* 103.1 (1992): 56.

144. Joseph Carens, "Aliens and Citizens: The Case for Open Borders," *The Review of Politics* 49.2 (1987): 252–56.

145. John Rawls, *The Law of Peoples* (Cambridge: Harvard University Press, 1999), 32. Further citations will be given parenthetically in the text.

146. Summarizing, in *The Rights of Others: Aliens, Residents, and Citizens* (Cambridge: Cambridge University Press, 2004), one form of the cosmopolitan case against *The Law of Peoples*, Seyla Benhabib writes: "As was the case for Kant, for Pogge and Beitz too it is *individuals* who are the units of moral and legal rights in a world society and not *peoples*. Peoples' interactions are continuous and not episodic; their lives and livelihood are radically, and not only intermittently, interdependent, as they were in the Rawlsian model of peoples" (97). Some theorists have sought to articulate a cosmopolitanism that would grant priority to communities over persons; see, for example, Joshua Anderson's *Justice, Community, and Globalization: Groundwork to a Communal-Cosmopolitanism* (New York: Routledge, 2019).

147. Liberalism's need to abide by its own commitment to tolerance is not the only reason why Rawls is willing to make peoples rather than individual persons the recipients of justice or fair treatment in *The Law of Peoples*. Another important rationale lies in his wish to propose not an impossible-to-realize ideal but what he calls a "realistic utopia." *The Law of Peoples*, he explains "hopes to say how a world Society of liberal and decent Peoples might be possible" (6); "political philosophy is realistically utopian when it extends what are ordinarily thought to be the limits of practicable political possibility and, in so doing, reconciles us to our political and social condition" (11).

148. As Stephen Macedo observes in a 2004 essay, the "problem with the diversity-based case for distinguishing justice within political societies and justice across political societies is that it is nonmoral" (1722). Macedo does go on to "offer a moral defense for Rawls's conditional accommodation of diversity among peoples" resting "not on the fact of global diversity but on the *moral significance of collective self-governance*" (1723). "What Self-Governing Peoples Owe to One Another: Universalism, Diversity, and the Law of Peoples," *Fordham Law Review* 72.5 (2004). Very much worth recalling in the context of these debates is Bruce Robbins's suggestion, in *Feeling Global* (New York: New York University Press, 1999), that something might "be gained if the arguments about universalism could be shifted from the terrain of culture to the terrain of power. . . . Thinking about universals in terms of unequal power, rather than solely in terms of cultural difference, makes visible the common or universalizing ground that we already occupy—whatever our necessary insistence on difference—from the moment that we protest against any injustice" (77).

149. Charles Beitz, "Cosmopolitanism and Global Justice," in *Current Debates in Global Justice*, ed. Gillian Brock and Darrel Moellendorf (Dordrecht, Netherlands: Springer, 2005), 21.

150. Thomas Pogge, *World Poverty and Human Rights*, 2nd ed. (Cambridge: Polity Press, 2008; first published 2002), 39, 111.

151. Nancy Fraser, *Scales of Justice: Reimagining Political Space in a Globalizing World* (New York: Columbia University Press, 2009), 2.

152. Gillian Brock, *Global Justice: A Cosmopolitan Account* (Oxford: Oxford University Press, 2009).

153. Ayelet Shachar, *The Birthright Lottery: Citizenship and Global Inequality* (Cambridge: Harvard University Press, 2009), 26.

154. Neera Chandhoke, "Who Owes Whom, Why and to What Effect?," in *Global Justice: Critical Perspectives*, ed. Sebastiano Maffetone and Aakash Singh Rathore (New Delhi: Routledge, 2012), 146.

155. Brooke Ackerly, *Just Responsibility: A Human Rights Theory of Global Justice* (Oxford: Oxford University Press, 2018), 192.

156. Margaret Kohn, "Globalizing Global Justice," in *Empire, Race and Global Justice*, 175. In *The Beneficiary* (Durham: Duke University Press, 2017), Robbins makes an eloquent case for maintaining attention to the moral implications of the wealth divide between inhabitants of affluent nations and inhabitants of poorer ones. There is, he reminds his readers, "ample empirical evidence that the geopolitical division between have and have-not countries not only persists but . . . outweighs the division between haves and have-nots within any given country. . . . To make a difference to global inequality, you will need beneficiaries to begin to see themselves as such, which means seeing themselves in global perspective and acting accordingly" (42–43). Robbins nonetheless joins other global justice theorists who have critiqued treatments of the wealth gap that tend to delink it from richer nations' hand in the creation of the divide: *The Beneficiary* focuses not on the disparity as such, "with its appeal to empathy and abstract fairness," but on the feeling "that your fate is *causally linked*, however obscurely, with the fates of distant and sometimes suffering others" (3). This means that citizens of richer nations must, among other things, address their *political* responsibility for global injustice—by, for example, working to elect officials whose policies are likely to diminish rather than exacerbate poverty and violence in other places.

157. On this see especially, in the Bell collection, Bell's introduction and essays by Katrina Forrester and Charles W. Mills. Earlier contributions in this broad area include Catherine Lu's chapter on "Colonialism as Structural Injustice," in Robert E. Goodin and James S. Fishkin's *Political Theory without Borders* (Chichester, UK: Wiley, 2016).

158. See on this, in the Bell collection, Bell's introduction again, along with contributions by Samuel Moyn, Sundhya Pahuja, Anne Phillips, Jeanne Morefield, Robert Nichols, and Catherine Lu. Earlier commentaries in this vein can be found in essays by Stephen P. Marks and Nicole Fritz in Christopher L. Eisgruber and András Sajó's *Global Justice and the Bulwarks of Localism* (Leiden: Martinus Nijhoff, 2005); and, in Ananta Kumar Giri's volume *Beyond Cosmopolitanism: Towards Planetary Transformations* (Singapore: Palgrave, 2018), Giri's introduction as well as contributions by Scott Shaffer, Anjana Raghavan and Jyotirmaya Tripathy, and Pnina Werbner. Defenses of aspects of cosmopolitan or global justice emphases on the rights of individuals may be found in, for example, Jürgen Habermas's "Remarks on Legitimation through Human Rights," *Philosophy and Social Criticism* 24.2–3 (1998): 157–71; Pogge's *World Poverty and Human Rights* (see 52); and Vernon's *Cosmopolitan Regard* (see 199–202).

159. Inés Valdez, "Association, Reciprocity, and Emancipation: A Transnational Account of the Politics of Global Justice," in Bell, *Empire, Race and Global Justice*, 124.

160. Anne Phillips, "Global Justice: Just Another Modernisation Theory?," in Bell, *Empire, Race and Global Justice*, 145.

161. Though Rawls does at times mention the good of choice of occupation or of fulfilling work. See *A Theory of Justice*, 290, 310, and 529; as well as Barry's discussion of same at Barry, *Liberal Theory*, 163–65.

162. Benhabib, *Rights*, 1–3.

163. Ariadna Estévez, *Human Rights, Migration, and Social Conflict* (New York: Palgrave 2012), 154.

164. Joseph Carens, *The Ethics of Immigration* (Oxford: Oxford University Press, 2013), 10. Further citations will be given parenthetically in the text.

165. Carens does notably include his own "cultural caveat" to his argument for open borders: "States have the right to restrict migration only if they can show, on the basis of evidence in an impartial (but internal) forum, that further migration would endanger the survival of the national language and culture, and they may exercise this right of restriction only so long as and to the extent that the danger persists" (286). To this, Benhabib might object that this concedes too much to dubious assumptions about the stability of cultures within national boundaries, excluding migrants' important contribution to cultures' ongoing shaping. For more on human rights and the claims of culture, see Robbins, *Feeling*, 139–45.

166. Similar arguments have been made by others in recent years, including a number of the contributors to Sarah Fine's and Lea Ypi's 2016 volume, *Migration in Political Theory: The Ethics of Movement and Membership*. In "Immigration as a Human Right," for example, Kieran Oberman argues—against the well-known contentions of theorists such as David Miller and Christopher Heath Wellman, who also appear in the collection—that "social costs" to the receiving nation "can only justify restrictions under two conditions: (1) the costs are particularly severe and (2) there is no acceptable alternative means to address them" (46). In her own contribution to the volume, Fine, observing that "racism and discrimination figure prominently in the history and politics of immigration controls" (139), argues (with an eye to problems in Wellman's arguments) that "if a defense of the state's right to exclude cannot diagnose ethnic and racial discrimination in immigration policy as a problem in a way that is consistent with that defense," its claims can hardly be persuasive (149).

For one of the many theorizations of justice around migration issues that pushes against Carens's open-border arguments, see *Immigration and the Constraints of Justice: Between Open Borders and Absolute Sovereignty* (Cambridge: Cambridge University Press, 2011), in which Ryan Pevnick introduces an "associative ownership view" as a new approach to "thinking about justice and immigration" (60). For Pevnick, "the citizenry constitutes an association extending through time that comes to have a claim over state institutions as the result of the efforts—from physical labor and tax payments to obeying the law—that make such institutions possible" (11). Pevnick avoids culture-based arguments like those of the communitarians (15), arguing, in a way that we could almost call the inverse of Shachar, from a consideration of entitlements evocative, in certain respects, of Nozick.

167. Brock, *Global Justice*, 194; Pevnick, *Immigration*, 85; Shachar, *Birthright Lottery*, 5.

168. Benhabib, *Rights*, 137, 85–86.

169. Oberman makes a similar point in the essay just cited. It may, he observes, be claimed that if the countries into which people are born offer "a decent choice of occupations, associations, religions, and so forth, . . . then the argument for a human right to immigrate collapses." Yet it "is relatively straightforward to see that people can have essential interests in accessing attachments that lie beyond an 'adequate' range. Consider for instance, the example of someone who believes in a religion that is not represented in her own state and wishes to go abroad in order to practice it. What is a proponent of the adequate range view to say to this person? 'It is sad that you cannot practice your religion here but there are other religions you could choose. Why not pick one of them instead?' For a religious believer, other religions are not genuine alternatives since they lack the primary quality the believer finds in her own religion: the quality of being the true religion" (38–40).

170. Shachar, *Birthright Lottery*, 138. For similar observations, see Benhabib, *Rights*, 20–21; Carens, *Ethics*, 226; and Kristen Hill Maher, "Who Has a Right to Rights? Citizenship's Exclusions in an Age of Migration," in *Globalization and Human Rights*, ed. Alison Brysk (Berkeley: University of California Press, 2002), 21.

171. We might even say that in cosmopolitan global justice theory, free migration and fair distribution are, in terms of efficacity, two versions of the same ideal. As Carens writes, "Those who would dismiss the importance of open borders because of its secondary importance for the task of reducing international inequalities miss two important points at the level of principle. First, the argument for open borders makes a crucial contribution to the critique of international inequality because it makes it harder for rich states to claim that they bear no responsibility for the persistence of inequality and the plight of the poor. Second, in a context of international inequality, freedom of movement is an important moral goal because of its contribution to equality of opportunity, quite apart from its effects on the overall level of inequality" (*Ethics*, 234).

172. In her dazzling Terra Ignota series of novels, Ada Palmer presents a utopia, or near-utopia, in which geographical birthplace has been eliminated as a determinant of life chances by a means other than open borders. In the future Earth that Palmer conjures, travel times have been dramatically reduced by readily available superfast transport, while war has long been forestalled by a system in which one chooses one's nation (or Hive, as each entity is known) on reaching maturity and enjoys membership without having to live in any particular location. In these novels' future—which maintains the goals of the utopian archipelago but discards its requirement that component communities be geographically fixed and bounded—a people is, in the words of one the new order's founders, "a group of human beings united by a common bond, not of blood or geography, but of friendship and trust," and a nation is "a government formed by a people to protect that common bond with common laws, so its members may enjoy life, liberty, happiness, justice, and all those rights we love." Ada Palmer, *Too Like the Lightning* (New York: Tor, 2016), 105.

173. See, for example, Sabine Dreher's brilliant *Neoliberalism and Migration: An Inquiry into the Politics of Globalization* (Hamburg: Lit Verlag, 2007), which shows, via examination of major policy documents and economic treatises since the 1970s, how immigration controls support neoliberal desiderata. Dreher notes that in addition to providing more vulnerable (and hence cheaper) workers (22–23), migration controls abet governments' prioritizing of the desideratum of inflation control, which benefits the affluent investor class, over the desideratum of full employment, which benefits the wider citizenry. See also Debdas Banerjee and Michael Goldfield,

"Neoliberal Globalization, Labour and the State," in *Labour, Globalization and the State: Workers, Women and Migrants Confront Neoliberalism*, ed. Debdas Banerjee and Michael Goldfield (London: Routledge, 2007), 9–10, and Larry Ray, "After 1989: Globalization, Normalization, and Utopia," in Hayden and el-Ojeili, *Globalization and Utopia*, 108.

174. Alison Brysk puts the point neatly in writing of international human rights: "A system that developed to defend and enhance the rights of citizens within states must now recognize that the greatest unmet need is *the rights of noncitizens*, whether women in the home, ethnic minorities or diasporas, refugees across borders, or workers in denationalized sweatshops." "Conclusion: From Rights to Realities," in Brysk, *Globalization and Human Rights*, 250.

175. Noting the absence of an "active collective of self-governing people making their own history" (119), Jodi Dean, in "Dual Power Redux," comments that to "solve an economic problem, Jameson's utopian proposal eliminates the political sphere" (132). Žižek, in "The Seeds of Imagination," observes that Jameson's "vision is not so much utopia as fantasy proper" in that it dreams of excising "the properly political process of making and enacting decisions that concern communal life" (297). Remarking the absence of "processes of collective decision-making and sites for the mediation of social antagonism," Kathi Weeks, in "Utopian Therapy: Work, Nonwork, and the Political Imagination," hazards that the "figure of the army . . . functions to deflect" questions about "internal structures and relational dynamics because it is equated with the very essence of order" (244). All in Jameson, *An American Utopia*.

176. In other words, the dream of the utopian archipelago appears to be discarded at precisely the same moment as the dream of work that would be fulfilling in itself. This said, it must be acknowledged that Jameson does signal a residue of the utopian archipelago within his utopian United States. At one point, he remarks that a key element of his American utopia would be "a decentralization scattered across its space like the distinctive city-states of Kim Stanley Robinson's Mars trilogy" (81); at another, he suggests that one of the virtues of the army is that "in our federal system, the army is virtually the only institution to transcend the jurisdiction of state laws and boundaries" (27). It may be, then, that Jameson assumes something like the utopian archipelago as foundational to his scheme, envisions a United States of relatively independent federalized units over which an army would extend not as a state but as one constituent of dual power (the other being the unit governments). This doesn't, however, alter the fact that the emphases of *An American Utopia* are quite different from those of the archipelago chapter of *Archaeologies*. In the more recent book, Jameson unquestionably puts freedom through geographical mobility in the background while heavily foregrounding freedom through control over leisure time. Nor does he indicate that different forms of leisure time (or labor) would prevail in the various decentralized units of the utopian America, or indeed that these units would differentiate themselves from each other in any particular way.

In 2009's *Valences of the Dialectic*, Jameson glances at the topic of migration through a commentary on Paolo Virno's *A Grammar of the Multitude*. Reflecting on the value of attempts "experimentally to declare positive things which are clearly negative in our own world, to affirm that dystopia is in reality Utopia if examined more closely," Jameson tries to descry the utopian in Wal-Mart and argues that Virno works a similar inversion of "what in Heidegger are clearly enough meant to be negative and highly critical features of modern society or modern actuality, staging each . . . as a promise of what he does not—but what we may—call an alternate Utopian future" (434). Among the Heideggerian assumptions Virno inverts is that of the existential anxiety of homelessness, Virno choosing instead to take, as "the multitude" on which the future pivots, the "population of . . . refugee camps as they supplant the promise of suburbs and the mobility of freeways which have become permanent traffic jams" (432). See also *Valences*, 578.

177. Delany, *Trouble on Triton*, 8.

178. Jameson here perhaps evokes not just Delany but also the anarchist notion of the Temporary Autonomous Zone disseminated by Hakim Bey in the 1991 book *T.A.Z.: The Temporary Autonomous Zone*. In an essay in Hayden and el-Ojeili's 2009 *Globalization and Utopia* collection, "(Con)Temporary Utopian Spaces," Giorel Curran puts forward a notion of "temporary utopian spaces" explicitly indebted to Bey's idea of TAZs—that is, in Curran's words, "zones, or spaces, that permit 'otherness', celebrate autonomy and challenge hierarchy" (203).

Coda

1. Robert Nozick, *Anarchy, State, and Utopia* (New York: Basic Books, 1974), 312.

2. Octavia Butler, *Bloodchild and Other Stories*, 2nd ed. (New York: Seven Stories, 2005), 214. Further citations will be given parenthetically in the text. "The Book of Martha" and "Amnesty" were both originally published in 2003.

3. Joshua Kotin, *Utopias of One* (Princeton, NJ: Princeton University Press, 2018), 2.

4. In an article on "Amnesty" and "The Book of Martha," Claire P. Curtis puts this kind of Butlerian moment—in which characters are confronted with the reality that resistance is futile, at least in terms of raw power dynamics—in an interesting light by casting Butler as "a gender egalitarian, modern-day Hobbes revisionist" who "uses the narrative devices of science fiction . . . to create scenarios analogous to Hobbes' state of nature." Butler, in Curtis's account, "notes that these scenarios properly produce fear; yet instead of recommending an authoritarian sovereign, she recognizes that individual responsibility and open communication about the conditions under which we live provide the most fruitful ground for moving forward." "Theorizing Fear: Octavia Butler and the Realist Utopia," *Utopian Studies* 19.3 (2008): 1. In a related book chapter on "Martha," Curtis provocatively reads the story as staging a version of Rawls's "original position." Tasked with making a drastic change in the parameters of human existence, Martha resembles the Rawlsian chooser, whose charge is to set up "the foundational principles that will guide the development and creation" of a political community. *Postapocalyptic Fiction and the Social Contract: "We'll Not Go Home Again"* (Lanham, MD: Lexington Books, 2010), 122.

5. The Chicago Homer online, *Theogony*, 223–24, 212.

INDEX

Ackerly, Brooke, 209, 246n67
Adams, John, 185
Adams, Mark B., 167
administration, 163–87; Arendt on, 120
Adorno, Theodor, 123
aesthetics, 43–44, 57, 99, 123, 144
Agamben, Giorgio, 52, 56, 245n62
Anderson, M. T., 129, 132
antipeponthos, 44
Appelbaum, Robert, 156, 261n35
Aquinas, Thomas, 40, 138
Aratus, 48
Arendt, Hannah, 118–20, 123, 125, 133, 183, 255n83
Aristophanes, 71
Aristotle, 53, 54, 248n85; on criminality, 97; on distribution of roles and rewards, 49, 52; on Hippodamus, 249n87; on justice, 40–41, 45, 46, 50–51, 56, 94, 138, 243n45, 244n48; on laws, 185; on money, 45, 243n45, 244n54; on *nomos*, 244n54; on rotation of rulers, 174
arrangement(s), 8–9, 29, 35, 37, 50, 58, 60–62, 65, 86, 140, 142, 144, 184–85, 215, 220; in Fourier, 93–94; in More, 48–49; Nozick on, 189–90; Rawls on, 46–47
Astraea. *See under* justice
Atwood, Margaret, 197, 199
Augustine, 43, 243n44, 244n48
authenticity, 8, 123–25, 127, 131, 133, 136, 220

Bacon, Francis, 60, 61, 92, 154, 192
Bakhtin, Mikhail, 191, 195
Barrell, John, 25
Barry, Brian, 204–5

Beaumont, Matthew, 237n3
Beukes, Lauren, 269n131
beauty, 43–44
Beauvoir, Simone de, 123
Beckett, Samuel, 3, 4
Beitz, Charles, 206, 207, 208–9, 270n140
behaviorism, 108–17, 119, 123, 254n61
Bellamy, Edward, 2, 6, 11, 29–31, 32, 39, 61, 73, 87, 101–3, 184, 193, 242nn20–21; industrial army of, 161, 217, 218; popularity and influence of, 237n3; women in, 263n53; work in, 160–61, 162, 163–64, 168
Bellers, John, 155
Benhabib, Seyla, 210, 212–13, 245n61, 271n146, 273n165
Benjamin, Walter, 144
Berger, Peter L., 52, 56, 245n62
Berking, Helmuth, 50–51
Berlant, Lauren, 243n46
Bey, Hakim, 276n178
birthright, 212–14
Blackness, 35–39, 64–65, 116, 226, 248n84, 255n67, 270n132
Bloch, Ernst, 4, 6, 17, 28, 50, 70–71, 72, 74, 103, 192, 245n62, 249n87, 250n103; on Aristotle and Plato, 40–41, 142, 156
blueprint utopias. *See* iconoclastic vs. blueprint utopias
Bogdanov, Aleksandr, 183, 184, 193, 202, 218; *Engineer Menni*, 266n94; Le Guin and, 180–82, 266n101; *Red Star*, 163, 167–70, 173–74, 178, 179–80, 187–88, 191; *A Short Course of Economic Science*, 170, 175; Wells and, 264n66.

Kohn, Margaret, 209
Kotin, Joshua, 227, 247n78, 254n61
Kremer, Gidon, 19
Krutch, Joseph Wood, 122
Kumar, Krishan, 10, 27, 114, 237n3, 238n15,
    251n8

La Berge, Leigh Claire, 268n113
labor. *See* workers
Laird, J. T., 237n4
Lane, Mary E. Bradley, 60, 62, 69
Laroche, Emmanuel, 51, 54
Larson, Jennifer, 54
Latta, Kimberly, 68
lawyers, 26, 47, 231
Lee, Chang-Rae, 198–201, 216
Le Guin, Ursula, 49, 73, 178–83, 188–89, 218,
    266nn105–6, 268n115; Delany and, 194–95
Leibovich, Anna Feldman, 177
Lenin, Vladimir, 170–71, 173–77, 265n77
Levitas, Ruth, 239
Lewis, Sinclair, 198
life plans, 140, 213, 215, 259n117
lifestyle choice, 5, 9, 194–95, 197, 211, 212, 219
Livy, 186
Lowry, Lois, 128–29, 132
Lummi People, 242n28

Macedo, Stephen, 271n148
Malkki, Liisa, 9
managerial vs. transformative utopias, 7–8,
    85–106, 117, 136, 140–41, 223, 255n82
Mannheim, Karl, 72, 242n24, 252n25
Manuel, Frank E. and Fritzie P., 253n35
Marcuse, Herbert, 8, 119, 123, 125, 255n83,
    256n88
Marshall, Ashley, 241n9
Marx, Karl (and Marxism), 147, 148–50, 151,
    167, 255n82; *Capital*, 260n21; *Critique of
    the Gotha Program*, 120, 172–73, 182; *The
    German Ideology* (with Engels), 105, 148,
    149, 150, 159, 162, 169, 172, 260n19
Matrix, The (film), 131–32, 133, 222, 223–24,
    227, 230
McCarthy, Cormac, 197

Melman, Seymour, 177, 266n100
metautopia, 9, 190–91, 211, 222–23, 228
migration, 9, 177, 190–91, 193, 197, 198, 200,
    202–3, 209–16, 219–21, 223, 230–31, 238n12,
    273nn165–66, 274n171; in Friedman, 268n115
Mills, Charles, 258n115
mobility. *See* workers; *see also* freedom of
    movement
More, Thomas, 3, 5, 6, 9, 11, 26, 27–29, 32, 35–36,
    37, 39, 55, 60–61, 66–68, 73, 99, 150–54,
    188, 192, 241n17, 249n90; on criminality,
    151–52; Hexter on, 88; influence of, 56,
    71, 249n86; Jameson on, 57, 60, 66, 89;
    justice in, 47–48, 56; love in, 244n48;
    managerial vs. transformative approaches
    in, 89–92, 94–97; workers in, 152–54, 166,
    261nn23–27
Morris, William, 2, 6, 31, 32, 49, 81, 127–28,
    149, 175, 265n84; character building in,
    254n52; Wilde and, 254n54; work in, 160,
    161–65, 234
Mosley, Walter, 130–31, 132, 224, 227, 269n131
Moten, Fred, 246n67
Moylan, Tom, 268n115
Mumford, Lewis, 249n86

Nancy, Jean-Luc, 52, 53, 56, 72, 247n78
nationalism, 15, 268n113
Native Americans, 36–38
nemesis, 8, 16, 50, 54–57, 63, 103, 137, 142, 185,
    202–3, 215, 247n78; in Butler, 226, 234,
    235; definitions and etymology of, 4–5,
    14, 50, 55–56; as deity, 54–55, 235; in
    Hawthorne, 82–84
Nersessian, Anahid, 247n78
neoliberalism, 14, 186–87, 203, 216, 268n113,
    274n173
Nickels, Joel, 176
Nightingale, Florence, 80
nomos, 7, 9, 50–53, 56, 59, 63, 65, 74, 84, 86, 113,
    137, 142, 154, 157, 185, 203, 214–15; Aristotle
    on, 244n54; counterindignation and, 72;
    definitions and usage of, 4–5, 50–51, 53,
    245nn61–62, 247n77; Harrington and,
    156; Rancière and, 144–46

A NOTE ON THE TYPE

This book has been composed in Arno, an Old-style serif typeface in the classic Venetian tradition, designed by Robert Slimbach at Adobe.

CPSIA information can be obtained
at www.ICGtesting.com
Printed in the USA
JSHW050720201020
8850JS00005B/12